Preparing the Way

Teaching ELs in the Pre-K-12 Classroom

fourth edition

Edited by Jane M. Govoni, PhD & Cindy Lovell, PhD

Kendall Hunt
publishing company

www.kendallhunt.com
Send all inquiries to:
4050 Westmark Drive
Dubuque, IA 52004-1840

Copyright © 2011, 2014, 2018, 2021 by Kendall Hunt Publishing Company

ISBN 978-1-7924-4083-0

Published in the United States of America

CONTENTS

About the Co-Editors and Contributing Authors   ix
Acknowledgments   xiii

**SECTION ONE   POLICIES, PRACTICES, AND PROFESSIONALISM:
                     ESOL FEDERAL AND STATE LEGISLATION   1**

Introduction...1
    Literacy Strategy: Talking Drawing 1
    Teacher Vignette: Ms. Miller, 3rd Grade, Florida 2
Resource Kit of Major Court Cases and Laws Related to English Learners 7
Acronyms in ESOL 12
Advocating for ELs 13
Florida Legislation..15

Chapter 1   ESOL Legislative Foundation: One State's Response 17
    Gloria M. Artecona-Pelaez

    Literacy Strategy: 60-Second Chat 17
EICM: ESOL Integration Curricular Model 20
Conclusion 22
Extended Thinking and Synthesis Questions 23
References..25
Website Resources...27
Activities..29

**SECTION TWO   CULTURAL PROFICIENCY:
                     EMBRACING DIVERSITY IN THE CLASSROOM   41**

Introduction...41
    Literacy Strategy: Exclusion Brainstorming 41
    Teacher Vignette: Ms. Gerrior, Kindergarten, Ohio 42
Personal Reflection: Analysis of Language and Culture.............................52
Conclusion 55
    Literacy Strategy: Double Entry Journal 56

Chapter 2   **Transforming Challenges into Opportunities:**
Becoming a Culturally Proficient Educator **57**
Samuel S. Perkins

Literacy Strategy: Probable Passage 58
Surface and Deep Elements of Culture. 59
Characteristics of Culture. 61
Culture and Learning Styles. 62
Literacy Strategy: Think-Pair-Share 69
Extended Thinking and Synthesis Questions 71
References. 73
Website Resources. 75
Activities. 77

Chapter 3   **Students With Limited or Interrupted Formal Education (SLIFE)** **91**
Andrea DeCapua

Literacy Strategy: Teach the Text Backwards. 91
Teacher Vignette: Mrs. Muñoz, Mrs. Mondicano, Mr. Ramesh,
9th Grade, Massachusetts 92
Literacy 97
Decontextualized Tasks Based on Academic Ways of Thinking. 99
The Dimensions of Collectivism and Individualism 103
Future Orientation. 104
What Can Teachers Do?. 105
The Mutually Adaptive Learning Paradigm (MALP®). 106
Extended Thinking and Synthesis Questions 111
References. 113
Website Resources 115
Activities. 117

SECTION THREE   APPLIED LINGUISTICS: LANGUAGE AND LITERACY   **129**

Introduction. 129
Teacher Vignette: Ms. Woodward, 5th Grade, New York. 130
Literacy Strategy: Dear Teacher Letter. 134

Chapter 4   **The Fundamentals of Applied Linguistics:**
Communication Through Language **135**
Elizabeth Platt

Literacy Strategy: Anticipation Guide 136
Phonology. 137
The Phonological System 137
English Consonants 138
Minimal Pairs: Listening and Speaking. 142
English Vowels. 143
Suprasegmentals 146

Morphology 148
   Classification of Morphemes 149
   Derivational Morphemes. 150
   Roots and Stems 151
   Inflectional Morphemes 152
   Developmental Errors. 154
   English Verb Morphology. 156
Syntax 157
   Theoretical Issues With Syntax 157
   Lexical and Functional Categories 157
   Universals in Word Ordering. 158
   Case-Marking. 159
   Order of Elements in Phrases. 160
   Prescriptive Grammar Rules 163
Semantics 164
   What It Means to Mean. 166
   Denotation and Connotation. 168
   Semantic Roles and Relations 168
   Concepts 170
   Metaphors. 170
   Semantic Relations: Meaning Beyond Word Level. 171
   Ambiguity 172
Pragmatics 174
   Dialects and Bilingualism 175
   Child Language Socialization 176
   Language Functions (Speech Acts) 177
   What's In a Name? 177
Extended Thinking and Synthesis Questions 181
References. 182
Website Resources 184
Activities 185

Chapter 5   **Analyzing Theories of Second Language Learning**. **197**
                    María Beatriz Mendoza, Elizabeth Platt, and Teresa Lucas

   Literacy Strategy: Previewing 197
   Teacher Vignette: Ms. Woodward (Continued). 198
Approaches to Language Development 199
SCT in the Language Classroom. 205
Ms. Woodward's Insights on SLA Theories 207
Learner Characteristics. 208
   Literacy Strategy: Story Mapping 214
Extended Thinking and Synthesis Questions 215
References. 216
Website Resource. 218
Activities 219

SECTION FOUR   ESOL METHODS, CURRICULUM, AND MATERIALS DEVELOPMENT: PLANNING AND IMPLEMENTATION   231

Introduction...231
    Literacy Strategy: Teach the Text Backwards...............................231
    Literacy Strategy: Wordsplash...232
    Teacher Vignette: Mr. Schroeder, Ms. Li, and Ms. Wu, Middle Grades, Minnesota ..233

Chapter 6   Bilingualism in the Classroom 239
    Oneyda Paneque and Teresa Lucas

Historical Perspective...240
Benefits of Bilingualism 241
Concepts for Teachers..243
Principles of Skill Transfer 244
Teaching for Transfer 245
Extended Thinking and Synthesis Questions 247
References...249
Website Resource..250
Activities 251

Chapter 7   Making the Connection to Literacy: ELs With Learning Disabilities   261
    Diane Rodriguez and Esmeralda Rodriguez

    Literacy Strategy: KWL 261
    Teacher Vignette: Teacher Reflection 263
Connecting With Instruction 265
Literacy and English Learners With Disabilities 267
    Case Study: Griselda...268
Strategies to Improve Reading Skills of English Learners With Learning Disabilities.....270
Assessment of English Learners With Learning Disabilities......................276
    Literacy Strategy: Character Frames.....................................277
Extended Thinking and Synthesis Questions 279
References...281
Website Resources...282
Activities 283

Chapter 8   Taking Off the Wrapper: Identifying and Serving Gifted English Learners 301
    Cindy Lovell

    Literacy Strategy: First Lines 301
    Teacher Vignette: Mrs. Allen, 4th Grade, Florida 303
'Gifted English Learner' Is Not an Oxymoron..................................304
Perceptions and Misconceptions About Gifted Students.........................305
Perceptions and Misconceptions About ELs 308

Underrepresentation of ELs in Gifted Programs. 310
   Identification Procedures 311
   Teacher Training. 311
   Family Advocacy. 312
Identifying Gifted ELs. 312
Serving Gifted ELs in the Mainstream Classroom 315
Extended Thinking and Synthesis Questions 321
References. 323
Website Resources. 325
Activities. 327

SECTION FIVE   **ESOL TESTING AND EVALUATION**   **339**

Introduction. 339
   Literacy Strategy: KWL 339
   Teacher Vignette: Ms. Whitecage, 3rd Grade, Ms. Jones, 7th Grade,
   and Mr. Blake, 7th–8th Grade, Colorado 340

Chapter 9   **Using Proficiency Testing to Improve Instruction:**
            WIDA ACCESS for ELLs. 343
            Florin M. Mihai

Proficiency Testing 344
Stages of Second Language Acquisition: A Foundation for the WIDA Standards. 346
The WIDA Standards and Language Proficiency Levels 348
Extended Thinking and Synthesis Questions 353
References. 354
Website Resources. 354
Activities. 355

Chapter 10   **ELs and Content Area Assessment:**
             Large-Scale and Classroom-Based Considerations 363
            Florin M. Mihai

Introduction. 363
   Teacher Vignette: Ms. Whitecage, Ms. Jones, and Mr. Blake (Continued) 364
WIDA Performance Definitions 366
Assessment Principles. 371
Types of Assessment 375
Test Accommodations for ELs: Definition and Examples. 375
Effectiveness of EL Accommodations. 376
ELs and Classroom-Based Assessments. 377
   Literacy Strategy: Sum It Up!. 379
Extended Thinking and Synthesis Questions 381
References. 383
Activities. 385

Index **393**

ABOUT THE EDITORS

© Jane Govoni

Jane Govoni received her MA in Spanish from Boston College and her PhD in Second Language Acquisition from the University of South Florida. Her background includes teaching Spanish at all levels, including elementary, middle, high school, and college. In addition, she teaches ESOL for Teacher Preparation Programs offering the ESOL endorsement. She held a tenured faculty position at Saint Leo University. Dr. Govoni is active on state and national educational boards, including the TESOL Professional Standards Committee, the Association of Teacher Educators (ATE), Executive Board for the Southeastern Regional Association of Teacher Educators (SRATE), and Sarasota Literacy Council (SLC). She has written several books related to teaching English learners in the Pre-K-12 mainstream classroom. She currently serves as the ESOL program coordinator in the College of Education at the University of South Florida. In addition to serving as co-editor of this textbook, Dr. Govoni created the teacher vignettes to offer practical and realistic classroom scenarios to support pre-service teacher candidates.

© Cindy Lovell

Cindy Lovell received her BA in Elementary Education and MA in Education from Stetson University. She earned her PhD in Education at The University of Iowa, specializing in ESOL and gifted education. She has held tenured faculty positions at Volusia County Schools, Stetson University, and Quincy University. Dr. Lovell served as executive director at the Mark Twain Boyhood Home & Museum in Missouri and the Mark Twain House & Museum in Connecticut. She has authored numerous publications, presented at various conferences, and is a consultant for the Florida DOE writing test items for the FTCE. Since 2017, Dr. Lovell has served as director of education at Epic Flight Academy where she works with hundreds of international students. She is also an adjunct professor at University of South Florida and Quincy University. In 2021, she received the USF College of Education Excellence in Undergraduate Education Award. In addition to serving as co-editor of this textbook, Dr. Lovell authored Chapter 8: Taking Off the Wrapper: Identifying and Serving Gifted English Learners.

ABOUT THE CONTRIBUTING AUTHORS

Andrea DeCapua earned her EdD from Teachers College Columbia University. She is an educator, researcher, and educational consultant. She has held academic appointments at various institutions, including New York University and the University of North Florida. Her research interests include developing intercultural awareness in a global society, culturally responsive teaching, second language acquisition, and struggling second language learners. Dr. DeCapua has published numerous articles in a variety of academic journals and authored/co-authored six books.

Teresa Lucas is an instructor in the School of Education and Human Development in the College of Arts, Sciences, and Education (CASE) at Florida International University in Miami. She holds a PhD in Multilingual/Multicultural Education from Florida State University, and an MA in TESOL from the University of Illinois. She teaches in the Modern Language Education/TESOL Master's program and is the ESOL coordinator for the undergraduate elementary, special education, and early childhood programs.

María B. Mendoza is the coordinator of the International Teaching Assistant (ITA) program at Florida State University in Tallahassee. She holds a BA in Modern Languages from Universidad Metropolitana in Caracas, Venezuela, and a PhD in Multicultural/Multilingual Education from Florida State University. She is in charge of oral proficiency assessment for ITAs and teaches English for Academic Purposes (EAP) to international graduate students. Dr. Mendoza's research interests include conversation and discourse analysis, instructional discourse and intelligibility, and best practices in ITA training.

Florin Mihai is a professor of TESOL and the director of the undergraduate TEFL Certificate in the Modern Languages and Literatures Department/College of Arts and Humanities at the University of Central Florida. In addition to articles published in *TESOL Journal, Journal of Adolescent & Adult Literacy, CATESOL Journal,* and *Middle School Journal,* he has published several books and book chapters with University of Michigan Press, Harvard Education Press, Routledge, and Pearson. He is also co-principal investigator in two federally funded grants through the U.S. Department of Education and Office of English Language Acquisition totaling more than US $5 million.

Oneyda Paneque is a professor at Miami Dade College School of Education in Miami, Florida. She holds an MA in Bilingual Education/Educational Psychology from the University of Illinois and an EdD in Exceptional Student Education from Florida International University. Her areas of interest include bilingualism, second language learning, and special education. She is a recipient of USDOE grants from the Office of English Language Acquisition and the Office of Special Education Programs and Rehabilitation Services.

Gloria Artecona-Pelaez was dean of the School of Arts and Education and Associate Provost for Institutional Effectiveness and Accreditation at St. Thomas University in Miami, Florida. She was born in Cuba and raised in Puerto Rico. She holds a Master's in TESOL from the University of Miami and an EdD in Curriculum and Instruction from Florida Atlantic University. Gloria taught ESOL in Miami-Dade County Public Schools before devoting her time to teacher preparation and curricular design at FAU, Barry University, Miami-Dade College, and the University of Miami.

Samuel Perkins has been an educator for more than 25 years engaging students from kindergarten to doctoral programs. He currently serves as director of the B.S./M.S. Program in Education at Barry University in addition to serving as the university's Certification Ombudsman. His teaching and research interests include culture, assessment, language development and usage, and student and teacher transformation.

Elizabeth Platt retired from the College of Education, Florida State University, in 2005, occasionally teaching in the second and foreign language education program thereafter. She has also worked as a State Department EFL consultant in Angola, Bangladesh, and Tanzania, and conducted teacher training in Nicaragua, the Dominican Republic, and Rwanda. As a volunteer, she recently enjoyed teaching communicative ESL to adult refugees from Syria and Congo and led a workshop for local teachers having refugee children in their classrooms.

Diane Rodriguez is a professor at Fordham University, Graduate School of Education where she earned a doctoral degree in Language, Learning, and Literacy. She has received numerous grants from the U.S. Office of Special Education and Rehabilitation Services and the Office of English Language Acquisition. She is the co-author of the book *The Bilingual Advantage: Promoting Academic Development Biliteray, and Native Language in the Classroom*. She is the Project Director of Every Girl is Important, a not-for-profit organization to educate and empower young girls.

Esmeralda Rodriguez is a bilingual teacher in New York City Public Schools. She earned her bachelor's degree from East Carolina University in North Carolina and her Master's with a specialization in Bilingual Education from Hunter College. Ms. Rodriguez joined Teach for America and embarked as an active member in the educational community. Over the years, she has advocated to empower Latino students to further their education.

ACKNOWLEDGMENTS

© Jane Govoni

With sincere gratitude and love, I acknowledge my father, **Raymond P. Gerrior.** He was an educator for 32 years in the East Boston public school system. My father taught me about resilience, diversity, passion, and persistence in striving for excellence. He inspired me to become an educator and it is in his memory that I dedicate this book. — J.M.G.

I gratefully acknowledge the support of my children, Angela and Adam, and dedicate this book to them. They cheerfully endured the challenges created by a working mother when I went back to school all those years ago. Between working and attending college full-time, I missed more than a few meals and events with them. Despite this, both supported me wholeheartedly to achieve my dream of becoming a teacher. Their love and encouragement made all the difference. — C.L.

Section One

Policies, Practices, and Professionalism: ESOL Federal and State Legislation

Introduction

 LITERACY STRATEGY: TALKING DRAWING

(1) In Part One, you will read about laws and policies governing Pre-K–12 education for English learners (ELs) across the nation.

(2) Before reading Chapter 1, draw a sketch of a classroom that you have observed in your teacher education program or from your childhood. Think back about how the layout of the room supported student interaction and participation. Include as many details as you can recall.

(3) After reading Chapter 1, refer back to your drawing and add to your design based on what you have learned about policies and practices for ELs.

(4) Share your sketch and briefly describe how you understand, at this point in your studies, how ESOL legislation affects the classroom environment.

Throughout this textbook, you will meet teachers from around the country working with ELs from around the world. As you read, notice the approaches used by various states. *Are they more alike than different? How do the teachers address cultures, methods, assessments, and technologies? Picture yourself teaching in these classrooms. What will you need to know to teach in your home state? Are there universalities that cross state lines?* The purpose of this textbook is to prepare you to effectively teach ELs in any state. You will begin by reading about Ms. Miller, a teacher in Florida.

TEACHER VIGNETTE: MS. MILLER, 3RD GRADE, FLORIDA

Ms. Miller earned her ESOL and reading endorsements during her studies in the elementary education program at a small college in west central Florida. During her first two years, she did not teach any **English learners (ELs).** This school year, her assistant principal distributes a 3rd grade list with the home languages and language proficiency levels of ELs in her class.

Name	Home Language	WIDA Proficiency Level
José	Spanish	Emerging
Ming	Chinese	Developing
Piedad	Spanish	Expanding
Bailey	French	Developing
Balendra	Hindi	Entering
Fakhir	Arabic	Emerging
Phoung	Vietnamese	Expanding

© India Picture/Shutterstock.com

She reviews the proficiency levels and acknowledges her undergraduate course work in **preparing the way** to meet the needs of all students; yet, she is hesitant about committing to knowledge on federal and state legislation. Ms. Miller seems anxious about feeling ill-prepared to teach this year. She is aware that Florida's English language learner population is ranked 3rd in the nation with more than 300 languages spoken across school districts. She realizes that she has to pursue a more comprehensive understanding in order to advocate for her students and parents as she plans for seven ELs, two gifted students, three ESE students, and ten other 3rd grade students.

Ms. Miller reviews **Every Student Succeeds Act (ESSA)**, which mandates that every state has a plan to ensure English proficiency and academic achievement. The former federal policy, **No Child Left Behind Act (NCLB)**, was replaced on December 10, 2015, when President Barack Obama signed into law ESSA, which allows states more authority in determining data on student achievement, timelines for progress, and graduation goals.

Ms. Miller thinks about her responsibilities for assessing English language proficiency and academic knowledge as she reads about ESSA's purposes for English learners.

SEC. 3102. PURPOSES.

The purposes of this part are—

(1) to help ensure that children who are limited English proficient, including immigrant children and youth, attain English proficiency, develop high levels of academic attainment in English, and meet the same challenging State academic content and student academic achievement standards as all children are expected to meet;

(2) to assist all limited English proficient children, including immigrant children and youth, to achieve at high levels in the core academic subjects so that those children can meet the same challenging State academic content and student academic achievement standards as all children are expected to meet, consistent with section 1111(b)(1);

(3) to develop high-quality language instruction educational programs designed to assist State educational agencies, local educational agencies, and schools in teaching limited English proficient children and serving immigrant children and youth;

(4) to assist State educational agencies and local educational agencies to develop and enhance their capacity to provide high-quality instructional programs designed to prepare limited English proficient children, including immigrant children and youth, to enter all-English instruction settings;

(5) to assist State educational agencies, local educational agencies, and schools to build their capacity to establish, implement, and sustain language instruction educational programs and programs of English language development for limited English proficient children;

(6) to promote parental and community participation in language instruction educational programs for the parents and communities of limited English proficient children;

(7) to streamline language instruction educational programs into a program carried out through formula grants to State educational agencies and local educational agencies to help limited English proficient children, including immigrant children and youth, develop proficiency in English, while meeting challenging State academic content and student academic achievement standards;

(8) to hold State educational agencies, local educational agencies, and schools accountable for increases in English proficiency and core academic content knowledge of limited English proficient children by requiring—

    (A) demonstrated improvements in the English proficiency of limited English proficient children each fiscal year; and

    (B) adequate yearly progress for limited English proficient children, including immigrant children and youth, as described in section 1111(b)(2)(B); and

(9) to provide State educational agencies and local educational agencies with the flexibility to implement language instruction educational programs, based on scientifically based research on teaching limited English proficient children, that the agencies believe to be the most effective for teaching English.

Source: https://www2.ed.gov/policy/elsec/leg/esea02/pg40.html

PAUSE AND REFLECT

Ms. Miller teaches in Florida, which has specific policies for teaching ELs.

1. Do you think other states have similar procedures?

2. Have you lived in another state and experienced this? Are they more stringent? Less stringent?

Go to Activity 1A

© xtock/Shutterstock.com

In 1965, the most comprehensive federal regulation passed into law was the **Elementary and Secondary Education Act (ESEA)** when President Lyndon Johnson sought to provide funding for states and access to an education for every student as part of the "War on Poverty." Over time, the growing concern about achievement gaps and minority students being "left behind" prompted an update to the legislation that focused on a system for testing and accountability in schools. This occurred in 2002 when President George W. Bush signed into law the **NCLB Act** with the understanding that *"every child can learn, we expect every child to learn, and you (teachers) must show us whether or not every child is learning."* However, the law led to an enormous amount of testing during class time and was often referred to as the *"cookie-cutter"* approach that did not seem to truly reflect high standards, accountability, and closing the achievement gap.

In 2015, **ESSA** was approved to promote more flexibility for states as to how and when tests are administered. With this Act, states have more input in determining types of intervention. In addition, English language proficiency (ELP) standards aligned to academic standards and an annual assessment with an entrance and exit process for identifying ELs and their English proficiency were established. In accordance with ESSA, states must set long-term goals and interim measures of progress for increases in the percentage of ELs achieving English proficiency (Norton & Petroshius, 2016).

The members of the **WIDA Consortium** meet the requirements of ESSA for monitoring and reporting the English language proficiency of ELs through **ACCESS for ELLs**. This assessment provides teachers with information to enhance strategies and make decisions about instructional planning and placement. **Wisconsin** and **Delaware** were the initial two states involved in the grant that provided funding for WIDA in 2002. **Arkansas** was at first involved, but withdrew early on. **Florida** joined the WIDA Consortium in 2015 and initially administered this assessment in 2016 in K–12 public schools. At this time, there are approximately 40 U.S. states, territories, and federal agencies involved in the Consortium.

The WIDA Consortium website provides information on standards, assessments, and links for every member state. Ms. Miller googles the WIDA Consortium and discovers the member resources for Florida. Her nervousness begins to diminish as she discovers more tools and resources to support both her teaching and her students' needs.

WIDA Consortium Map

https://wida.wisc.edu/memberships/consortium

Although Ms. Miller is feeling more confident in her understanding of current federal guidelines, she decides to review **landmark court rulings** regarding ELs to reflect on her teaching practices. Many of the laws and policies are the result of lawsuits over past decades. Research shows that teachers who investigate educational policies and practices about English learners have a stronger knowledge base on best practices to support all students.

PAUSE AND REFLECT

1. Go to the WIDA website at https://wida.wisc.edu/

2. Click on "TEACH" on the top of the page and choose any link to review.

3. Describe at least two ways to support your teaching based on what you discovered.

Ms. Miller recalls studying about federal policies for ELs that began in the late 1960s when Senator Yarborough from Texas proposed the **Bilingual Education Act** (BEA, 1968) to provide federal grants for schools. Yarborough stated:

> "*The problem is that many of our school-age children come from homes where the mother tongue is not English. As a result, these children enter school not speaking English and not able to understand the instructions that is [sic] all conducted in English. [There is] an urgent need for this legislation to provide equal educational opportunity for those children who do not come to school with English-speaking ability. We received almost unanimous enthusiasm and support for this legislation as being an effective remedial program.*" (U.S. Congress 1967:37037; in Bangura & Muao, 2001, p. 58; cited in DeJong, 2011, p.135)

BEA became a federal policy known as **Title VII of ESEA in 1968**. Stewner-Manzanares (1988) reported that "*it was the first federal recognition that limited English speaking ability students (LESA) have special educational needs and that in the interest of equal educational opportunity, bilingual programs that address those needs should be federally funded*" (p. 1) (https://ncela.ed.gov/files/rcd/BE021037/Fall88_6.pdf).

Ms. Miller thinks back to discussions in her undergraduate studies on the reauthorization of BEA and decides to create a resource kit on court cases related to ELs. In this way, she will be able to demonstrate a disposition of professionalism and leadership with her colleagues, administration, parents, staff, and local school community representatives.

RESOURCE KIT OF MAJOR COURT CASES AND LAWS RELATED TO ENGLISH LEARNERS

© xtock/Shutterstock.com

Q: *How should teachers begin to become informed of and understand policies and laws related to due process and equal protection for English learners?*

A: One suggestion is to review the **14th Amendment**, which focuses on due process and equal protection. Cases related to English learners are based on the due process and equal protection rights of the 14th Amendment. Section I of the 14th Amendment to the United States Constitution (1868) stipulates, "*All persons born or naturalized in the United States, and subject to the jurisdiction thereof, are citizens of the United States and of the state wherein they reside. No state shall make or enforce any law which shall abridge the privileges or immunities of citizens of the United States; nor shall any state deprive any person of life, liberty, or property, without due process of law; nor deny to any person within its jurisdiction the equal protection of the laws.*"

Q: *What U.S. Supreme Court case extends the protection of due process under the 14th Amendment for private language schooling for language minority students?*

A: *Meyer v. Nebraska (1923)*

This was a landmark case about a teacher who taught German to a 10-year-old boy at a time when teaching any language, other than English, was prohibited prior to the completion of eighth grade. It expanded on the concept of substantive due process and protection under the 14th Amendment (Source: Case Law).

Q: *What court case in Hawaii offers protection for after-school community language programs?*

A: *Farrington v. Tokushige (1927)*

This was an important case related to private language schools as the Hawaiian legislation approved the number of hours, textbooks, and curriculum of schools to be taught in the native languages of all students. The Court ruled against this regulation as being unreasonable for private schools and ruled that parents have the right to exercise control over how their children are educated.

⬦⬦⬦⬦⬦⬦⬦⬦⬦⬦⬦⬦⬦⬦⬦⬦⬦⬦⬦⬦⬦⬦⬦⬦⬦⬦⬦⬦⬦

Q: *What landmark Supreme Court case held that "separate but equal" educational facilities are inherently unequal and violate the protections of the 14th Amendment?*

A: *Brown v. Board of Education (1954)*

Oliver Brown claimed that his child was denied access to white schools and filed a case against the Topeka, Kansas school board. It was dismissed in federal court but Brown appealed to the Supreme Court, which held that "*segregation of public education based on race instilled a sense of inferiority that had a hugely detrimental effect on the education and personal growth of African American children.*" Chief Justice Earl Warren concluded that "*even if the tangible facilities were equal between the black and white schools, racial segregation in schools is 'inherently unequal' and is thus unconstitutional*" (Source: Justia U.S. Law Cases).

⬦⬦⬦⬦⬦⬦⬦⬦⬦⬦⬦⬦⬦⬦⬦⬦⬦⬦⬦⬦⬦⬦⬦⬦⬦⬦⬦⬦⬦

Q: *What legislation prohibits discrimination on the basis of race, color, or national origin for any program or activity receiving federal assistance?*

A: *Title VI Civil Rights Act (1964)*

This legislation sets a minimum standard for the education of any student regardless of race, color, or national origin, more specifically, prohibiting denial of equal access to education because of limited English proficiency.

⬦⬦⬦⬦⬦⬦⬦⬦⬦⬦⬦⬦⬦⬦⬦⬦⬦⬦⬦⬦⬦⬦⬦⬦⬦⬦⬦⬦⬦

Q: *What was the first official federal recognition for students whose first language is not English?*

A: It was the *Bilingual Education Act* (**BEA**) signed into law in 1968. It was reauthorized in 1974, 1978, 1984, 1988, 1994, and in 2001. The BEA, Title VII of the Elementary and Secondary Education Act, established federal policy for bilingual education for economically disadvantaged language minority students, allocated funds for innovative programs, and recognized the unique educational disadvantages faced by non-English speaking students.

⬦⬦⬦⬦⬦⬦⬦⬦⬦⬦⬦⬦⬦⬦⬦⬦⬦⬦⬦⬦⬦⬦⬦⬦⬦⬦⬦⬦⬦

Q: *What case centered on discrimination and equal education for Mexican American students?*

A: ***United States of America v. State of Texas, et al. (1971)***

This desegregation case focused on whether the San Felipe and Del Río school districts provided Mexican American students an equal educational opportunity. On August 6, 1971, Judge William Wayne Justice ordered the consolidation of the two districts. As a result of the lawsuit, the federal court ordered Civil Action 5281, which eliminates discrimination on grounds of race, color, or national origin in Texas public and charter schools.

Q: *What case in New Mexico addressed the linguistic needs of ELs?*

A: ***Serna v. Portales Municipal Schools (1972)***

This case focused on the specialized needs of "Spanish surnamed students" in New Mexico and ensured that schools focus on language and educational needs of ELs. It also raised the issue of bilingual education.

Q: *What case ruled that English learners could not be segregated from their English-speaking classmates?*

A: ***Keyes v. School District No. 1, Denver, Colorado (1973)***

The school desegregation case in Colorado was the first *de facto* segregation case heard in the U.S. The argument concerned a particular group of students (Latinos and Blacks) who were largely separated from their peers. The U.S. Supreme Court ruled that schools must desegregate their students. This ruling meant that English learners could not be segregated from their English fluent peers.

Q: *What is considered the most important court decision regarding the education of language-minority students?*

A: ***Lau v. Nichols (1974)***

This landmark case, brought by parents of Chinese American students in the San Francisco Unified School District, argued that the District was not providing an adequate education to their children. These students were placed in mainstream classrooms and left to "sink or swim." It ruled that there was "*no equality of treatment just by providing students the same facilities, textbooks, teachers, and curriculum.*" The case concluded that identical education does not constitute equal education under Title VI of the Civil Rights Act of 1964. School districts must take affirmative steps to overcome educational barriers faced by non-English speakers (http://caselaw.findlaw.com/us-supreme-court/414/563.html).

Q: *What Act affirms that no state shall deny educational opportunity based on race, color, sex, or national origin?*

A: ***Equal Educational Opportunities Act*** **(EEOA, 1974)**

Section 1703(f) of this act declares, *"No state shall deny educational opportunities to an individual on account of his or her race, color, sex, or national origin by (f) the failure of an educational agency to take appropriate action to overcome language barriers that impede equal participation by its students in its instructional programs"* (Source: Coloríncolorado).

⋄⋄

Q: *What court case made an effort to provide bilingual education in New York?*

A: ***Ríos v. Reed*** **(1975)**

Puerto Rican parents in the Eastern District of New York claimed that the transitional bilingual programs did not meet their students' needs. The federal court found the programs inadequate but issued no specific remedies; however, a strong case for offering appropriate bilingual education was presented.

⋄⋄

Q: *What landmark case identified three prongs required for educational programming of ELs?*

A: ***Castañeda v. Pickard*** **(1981)**

The Raymondville Independent School District in Texas argued that their local district was segregating students based on race and ethnicity and that the district failed to implement a successful bilingual education program for students to learn English. The United States Court of Appeals for the Fifth Circuit ruled that districts must establish a three-prong test for ensuring that the educational program for ELs is consistent with a student's right to an education. The three prongs provide programming that is scientifically known to be:

a.   based on sound educational theory;
b.   implemented with adequate commitment and resources; and
c.   evaluated and proven to be effective.

⋄⋄

Q: *What landmark case cited that students do not have to obtain a federal social security number to enroll in school?*

A: ***Plyler v. Doe*** **(1982)**

This case stipulated that "Free, equal and unhindered access to appropriate schooling is required for all immigrant students" in compliance with this U.S. Supreme Court ruling.

⋄⋄

Q: *What document defines Florida's policies and mandates for teaching ELs?*

A: **The Florida Consent Decree (1990) and the Stipulation Modifying Consent the Decree (2003)**

The **Florida Consent Decree** addresses the civil rights of ELs, foremost their rights to equal access to all educational programs; it provides a structure that ensures the delivery of comprehensible instruction, and the expectations for all teachers and personnel (Source: Florida Department of Education: English Language Learners).

Q: *What is the overarching goal of the Common Core State Standards?*

A: In 2009, the **Common Core State Standards (CCSS)** were initiated to serve as a national benchmark for what students need to know and be able to do at each grade level in many states. Approximately 40 states and territories have adopted the CCSS. Florida, for instance, developed its own standards called Florida Standards Assessment (FSA).

The CPALMS website is Florida's official source for information on standards with free resources for all teachers, including lesson plans aligned to state standards (Source: CPALMS).

Q: *What is the legislation passed in 2015 to provide more flexibility for states in addressing assessment for ELs?*

A: *Every Student Succeeds Act (ESSA)*

ESSA was signed into law by President Barack Obama on December 10, 2015. It replaces the No Child Left Behind (NCLB) Act enacted in 2002. The initial law was the Elementary and Secondary Education Act (ESSA), which sought equal opportunities for all students. Criteria of ESSA include equity, accountability, and assessment (Source: EdGov/ESSA).

NOTE

Links to court cases are available on the ESOL in Higher Ed website (https://www.esolinhighered.org/).

On this website, go to: *Policies, Practices, and Professionalism.*

PAUSE AND REFLECT

1. Click on any of the court cases listed on the ESOL in Higher Ed website.

2. Review two cases that you feel are relevant to your teaching practice.

3. Briefly explain each case and how it plays a role in your planning and assessment of ELs.

Ms. Miller's self-reflection and personal development in researching ESEA, NCLB, ESSA, and other prominent court cases refines her teaching practices as she designs lessons for her diverse group of 3rd graders. Because she teaches in Florida, she is also aware of her state's unique policies. She understands the rights of English learners and believes that she has reviewed sufficiently to begin to advocate for ELs and their families. However, she continues to flag sites and research articles in order to continue her examination later on. She also understands that local education agencies (LEAs), such as **charter schools**, must also follow state laws and regulations. This information is important because she is considering leaving her Title I school to teach at a local charter school. She has been contemplating this for quite some time and has read several articles on charter schools being a popular choice and the fastest-growing school option in many states. According to the National Center for Education Statistics (NCES, 2016), charter schools were first launched in **Minnesota** in 1991, and since then, legislation has been passed to approve these publicly funded schools in over 40 states. Ms. Miller will continue to research charter schools in her area while focusing on teaching her ELs this academic school year. She will be busy, but she can handle the task at hand. She is passionate, knowledgeable, and positive in focusing on her responsibilities as a teacher. She knows that the more she understands about state and federal policies, the more she can guide the parents of her ELs. **In addition, Ms. Miller is reading about legislative policies that guide Dual Language schools, because bilingual programs are becoming increasingly popular across the nation.**

ACRONYMS IN ESOL

Next, Ms. Miller decides to search for acronyms in identifying students whose first language is not English. She remembers from her college studies that being aware of acronyms, which are plentiful in the field of education, is important. She reasons that a review will be worthwhile since it has been a few years since she graduated. She first rereads the definition of an English learner by the Education Commission of the States.

Federal law defines a "limited English proficient" student as a student:

► who is aged 3 through 21;

► who is enrolled or preparing to enroll in an elementary school or secondary school;

► who was not born in the United States or whose native language is a language other than English;

► who is a Native American or Alaska Native, or a native resident of the outlying areas; and

► who comes from an environment where a language other than English has had a significant impact on the individual's level of English language proficiency; or

► who is migratory, whose native language is a language other than English, and who comes from an environment where a language other than English is dominant; and

► whose difficulties in speaking, reading, writing, or understanding the English language may be sufficient to deny the individual—

• the ability to meet the State's proficient level of achievement on State assessments;

• the ability to successfully achieve in classrooms where the language of instruction is English; or

• the opportunity to participate fully in society (www.ecs.org).

She remembers that these students are also referred to as **language-minority students, dual language, ESOL, English language learners (ELLs), English learners (ELs), bilingual students**, and **culturally diverse students**. She researches whether there is a consistent name to refer to these students in the public Pre-K–12 school setting and finds a website that lists how ELs are described state-by-state: The "50-State Comparison."

PAUSE AND REFLECT

1. Click on the "50-State Comparison" link from the ESOL in Higher Ed website.

2. Identify how ELs are defined by a state of your choice.

ADVOCATING FOR ELs

Research shows that there is an academic advantage for students who speak more than one language over monolingual students. There are approximately five million students whose first language is not English across the nation. Most are born in the United States and represent about 10% of the student population. **One in four students is not fluent in English.**

Legislation mandates: schools identify ELs; instruction is research-based and effective for all levels of English proficiency; and parents are informed of the reasons why children are identified as English learners, their children's level of English proficiency, how this was assessed, and what will be done to meet their needs. However, despite federal and state

ADVOCACY

regulations to advocate for these students and their families, there remains a gap in adequate teacher training across the nation. In **Florida,** the 1990 Consent Decree and the 2003 Stipulation Modifying the Consent Decree set the path for teacher training. Other states offer ESOL training or certification; however, for many states there is still little to no ESOL training for Pre-K–12 teachers.

It is compulsory under ESSA to track ELs' academic performance and to determine if their content knowledge is comparable to that of native English speakers. Ms. Miller understands that collaboration with her colleagues is essential if she is going to provide beneficial resources and effective lessons. She realizes that assessments in reading or language arts, math, and science are required for ELs. In addition, appropriate accommodations, including the option of assessments in native language of ELs, are essential in demonstrating both English proficiency and academic knowledge in content areas. **She aspires to lead with self-confidence and professional knowledge in preparing the way to meet the needs of ELs.** Ms. Miller will seek out the ESOL specialist at her school to learn more about the WIDA scores of her students. In this way, she will have a baseline of the English proficiency in reading, writing, listening, and speaking for each of her ELs. This will enable her to modify lessons according to the individual English proficiency of her students. She is excited to have this resource and keep these scores in her planning book.

PAUSE AND REFLECT

Explain at least three ways for teachers to advocate for ELs.

Even though Ms. Miller reminds herself of coursework in preparing to teach ELs from her undergraduate studies, she longs to know more. She considers Cecle-Murcia's claim that few teachers have an understanding of the history of teaching or the basis of teaching methods (2013). At first, she negates being a 'language' teacher; then, she pauses and notes that having ELs in her classroom means that she will, in fact, be teaching language skills. *After all, how do you present academic content without teaching vocabulary, expressions, and phrases?*

Ms. Miller is focused on developing interactive and creative lessons for her students at all levels of English proficiency. She knows that her peers will be valuable resources, as she remembers when her reading and ESOL professors planned and taught collaboratively throughout the semester. These were her favorite classes as she walked away with a much stronger understanding of strategies for ELs based on the concepts presented by both college professors. So now, Ms. Miller is even more determined to use that collaborative modeling strategy in her classroom.

She recalls studying about how Latin and Greek became popular after Johannes Gutenberg invented the printing press in the 1400s. And she notes reading about Latin grammar schools in the 1600s, modern language private academies flourishing in the 1700s, and when states passed laws prohibiting teaching of foreign languages in elementary schools during the Era of Isolationism (World War I—1920s). This historical perspective reminds her to reflect on ways to meet the needs of all students. She thinks back to her studies on **Comenius**, a teacher, writer, and philosopher from the Czech Republic who published about teaching techniques in the mid-1600s. His works included using imitation instead of rules to teach a language; having students repeat after the teacher; using limited vocabulary initially; helping students practice reading and speaking; and teaching language through pictures to make it more meaningful (Celce-Murcia, 1991). She considers these strategies and realizes that "former" teaching styles still have a place

Comenius

in today's classrooms. Comenius introduced an **inductive approach** to teaching language. Ms. Miller plans on increasing language proficiency of her ELs through observations, identification of language patterns, and practical strategies; thus, she will incorporate an inductive approach.

She is ready to rely on a teamwork approach for her 3rd grade class; but first, she decides to investigate other methods to be able to share with her colleagues. She reads about 20th century methods and strategies up to present day, such as total physical response and differentiated instruction. These methods and strategies are explained further in **Chapter 6**.

Ms. Miller is truly committed to being prepared to teaching ELs; that is, she not only researches laws and methods, but she further examines her own teaching practices. De Oliveira and Yough (2015) reported that teaching incorporates *"knowledge of teachers as learners of language, teacher practice and knowledge of self, knowledge and understanding of language learning and assessment, and procedural and declarative knowledge about language"* (p. 5). She begins to see that her own **interpersonal skills, cultural sensitivity, planning**, and **assessment strategies** play a pivotal role in her success and that of her students. An open mind toward her students' learning styles and abilities will certainly guide her in determining ways to make a difference.

Initially, when Ms. Miller was informed that she will have seven English learners in her class, her gut reaction was fearful astonishment. After all, these students bring six languages other than English into her classroom. After getting over that "deer in the headlights" feeling though, Ms. Miller's training kicks in. Instead of being reactionary, she becomes responsive. Her first instinct is to investigate legal requirements involved with teaching ELs, a prudent approach on her part. And in so doing, she not only understands the history and challenges of educating English learners in the United States, she encounters numerous research-based resources that she can use on Day One. She recalls reading Lucas's account that *"teachers need to be able to engage ELs in deep and sustained learning of academic content that will result in their mastery of rigorous language and literacy requirements of the Common Core Standards"* (de Oliviera & Yough, 2015, p. viii). She decides her next step is to focus on legislation and policies in her home state, Florida.

> **NOTE:** Here you will learn specifically about Florida legislation. Compare this to the laws for ELs in your home state.

FLORIDA LEGISLATION

Even though there is research that shows a lack of teacher training in instructing ELs across the nation, the mandate in **Florida** began in the early 1990s and set a path for district training and teacher preparation programs. The legal foundation for the requirements for teaching English learners in Florida is based on the *League of United Latin American Citizens (LULAC) et al. vs. The State Board of Education (SBE) et al. Consent Decree* (1990). The **Consent Decree** (also known as *META* or *ESOL Consent Decree*) is Florida's framework for compliance with federal and state laws and jurisprudence regarding the education of ELs. It addresses the civil rights of these students, with the primary right of equal access to comprehensible instruction.

© designer491/Shutterstock.com

The **Consent Decree** is the result of a class action suit filed by Multicultural Education, Training, and Advocacy, Inc. (META) on behalf of a coalition of eight minority rights advocacy groups in Florida, including LULAC, and a number of students. The **2003 Stipulation Modifying the Consent Decree** requires additional training in ESOL for school administrators, school psychologists, guidance counselors, as well as those seeking ESOL certification. The Consent Decree and the Stipulation Modifying the Decree may be read in full on the Florida Department of Education English Language Learners website.

Although in the back of her mind Ms. Miller is still thinking about teaching in a charter school, she sets aside time to read each section of the Decree and the 2003 Stipulation. She realizes being a professional educational leader means having a thorough understanding of school policies. Her anxiety is lessening as she becomes progressively more prepared to teach 22 3rd graders, 7 of whom are ELs speaking 6 different languages. She also respects that teacher education programs cannot provide enough graduates to fill the annual vacancies for all teaching positions. She knows that she is bound to meet other teachers in need of training and takes the initiative to be the lead teacher in advocating for ELs. She refers back to the research she flagged earlier and continues researching school, district, and governmental policies and legislation that impact the education of ELs.

 PAUSE AND REFLECT

Overall, the **1990 Florida Consent Decree** is the legislation that determines ESOL district policies and teaching certification requirements in Florida. Review the three major U.S. Supreme Court cases that impacted the Decree. Report on the following:

a. the significance of the ruling,
b. how the ruling impacts ELs in Florida, and
c. in which section of the Decree you would align the court case (Sections 1–6).

Lau v. Nichols (1974)	https://www.youtube.com/watch?v=1J8TXYZLdyM	(9.47 min)
Casteñeda v. Pickard (1981)	https://www.youtube.com/watch?v=UMvBwQCwRos	(4.26 min)
Plyler v. Doe (1982)	https://www.youtube.com/watch?v=qEk-UijyN2M	(7.21 min)

ESOL Legislative Foundation: One State's Response

Gloria M. Artecona-Pelaez

© donskarpo/Shutterstock.com

 LITERACY STRATEGY: 60-SECOND CHAT

(1) In 60 seconds, share your knowledge about policies and legislation for Florida teachers.

(2) Read Chapter 1.

(3) After reading the chapter, challenge yourself to explain the Consent Decree and Stipulation Modifying the Decree in 60 seconds to a friend, classmate, family member, or colleague.

Tips for Use with ELs: This is a simple and quick strategy to activate ELs' prior knowledge and cultural perspectives that supports academic language across content areas.

This chapter explores the impact of the 1990 **Florida Consent Decree** and state and federal laws that prescribe and protect the rights of English learners (ELs). The development of the author's **ESOL Integration Curricular Model** (EICM) explains how state-approved colleges and universities initiated the integration of ESOL standards and competencies into teacher education programs.

Educators, students, and administrators encounter ESOL-related issues almost daily in Pre-K-12 school communities as ELs are part of the mainstream across the United States. Classroom teachers are responsible for teaching and assessing students from diverse cultural backgrounds and at varying English proficiency levels. In 2012, Samson and Collins reported most states have a process to determine English proficiency, but instructional practices vary from state to state. Gándara and Santibañez (2016) emphasized teachers still have a long way to go to be highly qualified to teach ELs. In 2019, Mitchell reported mainstream teachers did not have the skills and knowledge to adequately teach ELs. Barone-Crowell (2020) showed a deficit in ESOL training for pre-service teachers in the mainstream classroom. She pointed out the potential effects of teachers' attitudes for ELs due to a lack of training. Although changes in legislative policies over the years have positively affected teacher training, there are still many states with teachers unprepared to teach ELs.

Protocol for identification, assessment, and teaching of ELs is well established in Florida. Teacher education programs provide ESOL-infused coursework and clinical field experiences. The Florida Consent Decree addresses the civil rights of ELs; foremost are their rights to equal access to all educational programs, and it provides a structure that ensures the delivery of comprehensible instruction and the expectations for all teachers and personnel. The 2003 **Stipulation Modifying the Consent Decree** stipulates additional training and requirements for educators.

The Consent Decree is Florida's framework for compliance with the following federal and state laws and jurisprudence regarding the education of ELs:

- 14th Amendment to the United States Constitution, 1868
- Title VI and VII Civil Rights Act, 1964
- Office of Civil Rights Memorandum (Standards for Title VI Compliance), 1970
- Section 504 of the Rehabilitation Act, 1973
- Requirements based on the Supreme Court decision in *Lau v. Nichols*, 1974
- Equal Education Opportunities Act, 1974
- Americans with Disabilities Act (PL 94-142), 1975
- Requirements of the Vocational Education Guidelines, 1979
- Requirements based on the Fifth Circuit court decision in *Castañeda v. Pickard*, 1981
- Requirements based on the Supreme Court decision in *Plyer v. Doe*, 1982
- Florida Education Equity Act, 1984

(Source: Florida Department of Education)

The LULAC et al. Consent Decree, also known as the **META Decree**, established specific requirements for services provided to ELs and training for educators. According to the Florida Department of Education's (FLDOE) Course Code Directory:

The ESOL Endorsement may be completed by either 300 master plan points (MPP) or 15 college semester hours in the following areas: Methods of Teaching ESOL, ESOL Curriculum and Material Development, Cross-Cultural Communication and Understanding, Applied Linguistics, and Testing and Evaluation in ESOL.

It is important to point out that the Consent Decree did not impose any direct requirements on institutions; however, students graduating from teacher education programs in Florida were affected by the consequences of the requirements imposed by the Decree. In essence, commencing with the 1990–1991 academic year, undergraduate students in Elementary, Exceptional Student Education, and English Education in Florida were required to obtain the equivalent of 15 credit hours or 300 hours of training in ESOL upon graduation. Questions were raised as to *whether curricula in teacher education programs were sufficient; if teacher education programs were effectively preparing future teachers to serve the needs of diverse student populations;* and *how teacher education programs could meet the mandate of the Decree.*

1992	Two prominent figures of the Florida Department of Education, R.E. LeMon and L. Clayton-Kandor, provided a challenge for teacher education programs by stating, "*[t]here are no undergraduate degrees in Florida's universities which produce graduates who are prepared to move directly into public school systems with a full endorsement in ESOL.*"
1993	A doctoral candidate at Florida Atlantic University developed an integrated program of studies for pre-service teachers and school districts. It was called the ESOL Integration Curricular Model (EICM) and it enabled pre-service teachers graduating with an Elementary Education degree to be eligible for certification in Elementary Education with an ESOL Endorsement.
1995	The Florida State Board of Education considered adopting rules to require teacher education programs "*to provide perspective teachers with the instruction necessary to enable them to teach students having limited proficiency in English.*" This became a requirement for teacher preparation programs under the Education Standards Commission in the 1997–1998 academic year.
1997	The TESOL international association released English as a Second Language (ESL) Standards for Pre-K through 12 to include best practices to meet the needs of English learners for teacher preparation programs.
1999	The Office of Multicultural Students Language Education (OMSLE), previously referred to as the Office of Academic Achievement through Language Acquisition (AALA), and currently called the Bureau of Student Achievement through Language Acquisition (SALA) of the Florida Department of Education (DOE), published a Language Arts through ESOL Guide as a resource for school districts on theories and strategies for ELs.
2001	The document, *Preparing Florida Teachers to Work with Limited English Proficient Students,* became a guide for teacher education preparation programs in integrating ESOL into existing curricula. It was updated in 2011 to meet the ESOL standards and is available on the Florida DOE website. It is called *Technical Assistance for Teacher Preparation: Meeting the Needs of English Language Learners (ELLs) in Florida.*
2003	The Stipulation Modifying the Consent Decree required further training in ESOL for administrators, guidance counselors, and school psychologists. In addition, educators passing the ESOL certification exam had to obtain 120 hours of ESOL training within a specified time period.
2004	All students graduating from state-approved Elementary, Exceptional Student Education, Pre-K/Primary, or English teacher education programs in Florida were required to complete ESOL training.

2010   The State Board of Education rule revised the ESOL competencies and skills for certification (12th Edition). A crosswalk between ESOL standards and ESOL competencies was developed.

The Bureau of Student Achievement through Language Acquisition (SALA), worked collaboratively with district teachers and other educators to develop the Florida Teacher Standards for ESOL Endorsement. These standards currently serve as the basis for ESOL training in Florida.

The Florida State Board of Education voluntarily adopted the Common Core State Standards (CCSS) along with more than 40 states across the country.

2011   The ESOL document to further support teacher preparation programs in infusing ESOL standards was made available on the Florida Department of Education website. It is called *Technical Assistance for Teacher Preparation: Meeting the Needs of English Language Learners (ELLs) in Florida*.

2013   Revisions of the English Language Proficiency Standards (2012) were proposed to reflect the Common Core State Standards for English Language Arts, and a draft of the K-1 English Language Development (ELD) standards was open for public comment on the Florida Department of Education website.

2014   The Florida Board of Education approved revisions to the Common Core State Standards that establish what students should know and be able to do in order to be prepared for college and the workforce. They are referred to as the Florida Standards.

2015   The WIDA Standards were adopted in Florida.
The WIDA Assessment was adopted in Florida for the 2015–2016 academic year.

2016   WIDA Access for ELLs was administered for the first time in K-12 public schools in Florida.

2017   The Florida Seal of Biliteracy Program was established to recognize a high school graduate who has attained a high level of competency in listening, speaking, reading, and writing in one or more foreign languages in addition to English.

2019   The TESOL international association updated the Standards for Initial TESOL Pre-K–12 Teacher Preparation Programs.

 Every state collects data through a **Home Language Survey** completed for every student newly enrolled in public Pre-K-12 schools. In this way, ELs are identified and assessed on their English language proficiency. What are the three primary questions on the Florida Home Language Survey? Hint: Go to the Florida Department of Education website.

c.   Does the student most frequently speak a language other than English?
b.   Did the student have a first language other than English?
a.   Is a language other than English used in the home?

EICM: ESOL INTEGRATION CURRICULAR MODEL

The EICM was purposefully aligned to the 1990 requirements of the Florida Department of Education (DOE) for pre-service teachers at Florida Atlantic University. The primary goal was to offer an accredited Elementary

Education/ESOL Endorsement program for undergraduate students earning a bachelor's degree and professional teaching certification in Florida. Other colleges and universities jumped on the bandwagon and began designing programs to meet the ESOL training needs for pre-service teachers. At first, many educators were hesitant about the EICM; yet, it served as the stepping-stone for ESOL training across the state. It was never designed for teachers to become ESOL specialists, but rather, for all teachers to be knowledgeable about ways to teach students from diverse cultures in their classrooms. **At a minimum, teachers were required to become more familiar with strategies and best practices in teaching ELs**.

One benefit in infusing ESOL and academic content is the inherent use of ELs' knowledge base in their native languages (Cummins, 2000; Krashen, 1992; Law & Eckes, 2000). Language is the tool that gives shape to our understanding of the world, of concepts and emotions, of knowledge of science, mathematics, and language itself. Vygotsky claimed that higher-order thinking, prior to going underground as an idea or internal speech, develops through the mediation of language (1986). The EICM sought to promote the acquisition of English skills and academic content for ELs to be successful in the mainstream classroom.

The model proved to foster equitable opportunities for all students. It was designed to be an eclectic mix of theories, strategies, and approaches that included constructivism, anchored instruction, situated cognition, and cognitive flexibility.

Constructivism posits that learning is an active, constructive process. It emphasizes knowledge that is gained through problem-solving situations within a particular context rather than through exposure to isolated facts. It promotes learning that is an active, constructive process. These problem-solving situations, or **anchored instruction**, are very similar to what Krashen (1992) called *enterprises*, which are 'problems that students genuinely want to solve, problems that naturally entail reading, writing, and discussion' in a second language. In other words, learning and teaching is designed around an *anchor* that is based on a contextualized case study or problem situation. **Situated cognition** is closely related in that it recognizes the importance of social factors in learning. It suggests that learning is *situated*, or takes place in a specific context, and provides for meaningful learning and the transfer of knowledge to real-life situations. **Cognitive flexibility** is the ability to respond to a situation by restructuring one's knowledge.

A classroom without a common language of instruction is demanding in itself. Cognitive flexibility enables teachers to restructure their delivery of instruction to reach students from diverse cultural and linguistic backgrounds. A central claim of the cognitive flexibility theory is that revisiting the same material, at various times, for different purposes, and from different points of view, is essential for knowledge acquisition to occur.

An in-depth analysis of the stipulations of the Florida Consent Decree reaffirmed the need for the EICM. Teachers were in need of ESOL training. In addition, undergraduates from teacher preparation programs were not prepared to meet the needs of diverse students. At the time, teacher education programs did not offer any ESOL training in Florida. This was desperately needed, and the model served as the initial step in teacher training across the State.

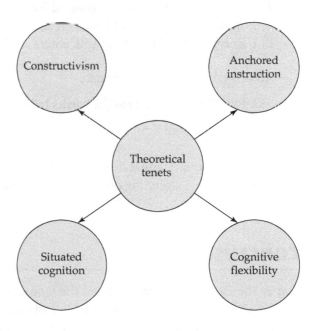

Design a visual representation to show how your ESOL training aligns to the theoretical tenets of the EICM.

School districts faced a mammoth task in complying with staff development mandates of the 1990 Consent Decree. Most did not have enough qualified personnel in ESOL. Superintendents spoke of the cost imposed by the mandates of the Decree, the required timeline, and the personnel necessary to comply with staff development. One of the main concerns was the continued burden these mandates imposed when hiring new teachers. So, the EICM set the foundation for teacher education programs. Ms. Miller, a former student of the program, most certainly demonstrates her knowledge and teaching techniques in fostering a positive and culturally diverse classroom environment.

By May 2004, state-approved teacher education programs were required to graduate teacher candidates with eligibility to obtain an ESOL Endorsement in Elementary, English Education, Exceptional Student Education, and Pre-K/Primary Education. Other education majors complied with the mandate through a three-hour ESOL course. The educational landscape was transformed to better serve all students from diverse backgrounds and at varying English proficiency levels. Research shows that successful models support the linguistic, academic, and social needs of ELs and the EICM was a way to train pre-service teachers.

The legal foundation was established in Florida to advocate for ELs and their families. As Ms. Miller, a former student of the program, will affirm, all educators must demonstrate knowledge of laws, policies, research, and best practices in second language and literacy instruction to support learning across all classrooms.

 Review the Florida coding for English learners and suggest two ways to enhance learning academic content and English for each classification.

In Florida, English language learners in grades Pre-K-12 are coded as follows:

LEA—Local Education Agency—Time in program—the amount of time an ELL has been in the ESOL program, from the date of entry until present date, or until date of exit
LY—an English Language Learner (ELL) currently in an ESOL program
LP—a potential ELL who is pending further assessment
LF—an exited (former) ELL in the two-year monitoring period
LZ—a former ELL whose two-year monitoring has concluded
ZZ—code for students who answered No on the Home Language Survey, or who answered Yes and were determined to be proficient based on assessment
ELL Entry Date—the date an ELL enters an ESOL program in Florida

All ELLs must have an entry date.

ELL Exit Date—the date an ELL exits from the ESOL program and becomes an LF

Immigrant student:
1) age 3–21,
2) was not born in any state (the 50 states, DC, and Puerto Rico), and
3) has not been attending one or more schools in any state for more than 3 full academic years.

(Source: Florida Department of Education)

CONCLUSION

Just as the Consent Decree changed the landscape for teacher preparation programs in Florida, so does the legislation of ESSA. Change is inevitable and often provides opportunities, such as Ms. Miller's next decision. She accepts a teaching position at a charter school opening in August. With her extensive research on laws and policies in supporting ELs and their families, she will be a rich resource for all teachers because ELs represent more than 50% of the school population. Ms. Miller will bring knowledge gained from her teacher preparation program, her resource kit on court cases and acronyms, and her experiences in teaching 7 ELs speaking 6 languages other than English. She is enthusiastic about advocating for ELs at the new charter school.

Extended Thinking and Synthesis Questions

1. Explain your understanding of how legal mandates and policies have impacted teaching in Pre-K-12 classrooms. Include the major U.S. Supreme Court cases to support your response (e.g., *Lau v. Nichols, Plyer v. Doe, Casteñeda v. Pickard*).

2. Summarize the implications for educators in Florida as mandated by the Consent Decree *and* the 2003 Stipulation Modifying the Consent Decree to show your understanding of requirements in determining district compliance with state and federal guidelines.

3. Explain how knowledge of the Consent Decree, the 2003 Stipulation Modifying the Consent Decree, the EICM, policies, research, and current practices in ESOL affect teaching and learning.

4. Reflect on how your ESOL training scaffolds knowledge, skills, and dispositions to impact the teaching and learning of ELs from culturally diverse backgrounds and at varying English proficiency levels.

5. Compare the theoretical underpinnings of the EICM with research and strategies associated with culturally responsive teaching. Refer to the ESOL in Higher Ed website for links and resources.

6. Go to the ESOL in Higher Ed website. Click on: *Policies, Practices, and Professionalism*. Scroll down and click on "*More Resources*" and review the **PowerPoint Presentation**—"*Understanding the Florida Consent Decree.*"

    a. Create a presentation to explain the impact of the Florida Consent Decree to colleagues, staff, and administrators at your school.

7. For pre-service teachers enrolled in teacher preparation programs *outside* of Florida:

   a. Are there required ESOL courses in your program? If so, briefly explain. If not, does your district or region offer ESOL training for K–12 teachers? If so, briefly describe.

   b. How can an awareness of the Florida ESOL policies and training guide your teaching of diverse students at varied levels of English proficiency?

8. In the current political climate in education, it is crucial for teachers, administrators, policy makers, and stakeholders to have a deeper understanding of the 14th Amendment of the United States Constitution adopted on July 9, 1868. This Amendment addresses three major provisions:

   a. The *citizenship clause* that grants citizenship to all persons born or naturalized in the U.S.

   b. The *due process clause,* which declares that states may not deny any person life, liberty, or the pursuit of happiness without due process of the law.

   c. The *equal protection clause* that declares that a state may not deny any person within its jurisdiction the equal protection of the law.

      ► Analyze the history of the 14th Amendment by taking a look at the *Dred Scott v. Sanford* decision from the U.S. Supreme Court in 1857.

      ► Locate and examine a current news story that relates to the rights guaranteed by the 14th Amendment.

      ► Develop a concise response to post on the class discussion board or to share in class.

9. Being an advocate for ELs requires an awareness of school, district, and governmental policies. Now that you have read about some ESOL legislation, reflect on ways to demonstrate your personal understanding of policies that impact the education of ELs by designing a PowerPoint, Prezi, or Google Doc presentation to share with teachers at your school to inform them of the policies, practices, and mandates for teachers regarding ESOL training and certification.

10. Refer back to the Talking Drawing activity at the beginning of the chapter. Complete steps 3 and 4.

REFERENCES

A day in the life of a multilingual high school (May 9, 2016). http://www.edweek.org/ew/section/multimedia/video-multilingual-high-school.html (2:47 min)

Barone-Crowell, H. (2020). Lack of preparation for mainstream teachers of English learners. Education and Human Development Master's Theses, Summer 2020. https://digitalcommons.brockport.edu/cgi/viewcontent.cgi?article=2307&context=ehd_theses

Bilingual Education Act. (2020). https://www.gpo.gov/fdsys/pkg/STATUTE-81/pdf/STATUTE-81-Pg783.pdf

Brown v. Board of Education of Topeka. (2020). https://supreme.justia.com/cases/federal/us/347/483/case.html

Celce-Murcia, M. (Ed.). (2013). *Teaching English as a second or foreign language* (4th ed.). Heinle & Heinle Publishers.

CPALMS—Resources for Florida teachers. (2020). http://www.cpalms.org

Cummins, J. (2000). *Language, power, and pedagogy: Bilingual children in the crossfire.* Multilingual Matters, LTD.

DeJong, E. (2011). *Foundations for multilingualism in education: From principles to practice.* Caslon, Inc.

de Oliveira, L. C., & Yough, M. (Eds.). (2015). *Preparing teachers to work with English language learners in mainstream classrooms.* Information Age Publishing, Inc., TESOL Press.

Dred Scott v. Sanford (1857). (2020). http://www.pbs.org/wnet/supremecourt/antebellum/landmark_dred.html

ELL Information Center. (2020). *Fact sheet series* (Migration Policy Institute). https://www.migrationpolicy.org/programs/ell-information-center

English-Language Learner Statistics. (2020). http://www.edweek.org/ew/section/multimedia/english-language-learner-statistics.html

ESSA Explained. (2020). *Education Week.* https://www.youtube.com/watch?v=zWQGmU-J80Q#action=share

Every Student Succeeds Act *(ESSA).* (2020). https://www.ed.gov/ESSA; https://www.gpo.gov/fdsys/pkg/BILLS-114s1177enr/pdf/BILLS-114s1177enr.pdf

Farrington v. Tokushige. (2020). https://law.justia.com/cases/federal/appellate-courts/F2/11/710/1543640/

Fifty-state comparison of how an English learner is defined. (2020). https://www.ecs.org/50-state-comparison-english-learner-policies/

Florida Consent Decree. (2020). http://www.fldoe.org/academics/eng-language-learners/consent-decree.stml

Florida Department of Education. (2020). www.fldoe.org

Florida Department of Education—English Language Learners. (2020). http://www.fldoe.org/academics/eng-language-learners

Fourteenth Amendment to the U.S. Constitution. (2020). https://www.law.cornell.edu/constitution/amendmentxiv

Gándara, P., & Santibañez, L. (2016). The teachers our English language learners need. *Educational Leadership, 5,* 73. http://www.ascd.org/publications/educational-leadership/feb16/vol73/num05/The-Teachers-Our-English-Language-Learners-Need.aspx

How educators can advocate for English language learners: All in! National Education Association. (2015). http://www.colorincolorado.org/sites/default/files/ELL_AdvocacyGuide2015.pdf

Keyes v. School District No. 1, Denver, Colorado. (2020). https://caselaw.findlaw.com/us-supreme-court/396/1215.html

Krashen, S. (1992). *Principles and practices in second language acquisition.* Pergamon.

Landmark court rulings regarding English language learners. (2020). http://www.colorincolorado.org/article/landmark-court-rulings-regarding-english-language-learners

Lau v. Nichols. (2020). http://caselaw.findlaw.com/us-supreme-court/414/563.html

Law, B., & Eckes, M. (2000). *The more-than-just-surviving handbook: ELL for every classroom* (3rd ed.). Portage and Main Press.

Legal Information Institute, 14th Amendment. Cornell University Law School. (2020). https://www.law.cornell.edu/constitution/amendmentxiv

Major provisions of ESSA related to the education of English learners CCSO. (2016). https://ccsso.org/resource-library/major-provisions-essa-related-education-english-learners

Meyer v. Nebraska. (2020). http://caselaw.findlaw.com/us-supreme-court/262/390.html; https://www.youtube.com/watch?v=CP77c-ZVjIE

Mitchell, C. (May 2019). Overlooked: How teacher training falls short for English learners and students with IEPs. *Education Week.* https://www.edweek.org/teaching-learning/overlooked-how-teacher-training-falls-short-for-english-learners-and-students-with-ieps/2019/05

National Alliance for Public Charter Schools. (2020). http://www.publiccharters.org/wp-content/uploads/2016/02/New-Closed-2016.pdf

National and State Level Graduation Rates for ELs. (2020). https://ncela.ed.gov/files/fast_facts/GraduationRatesFactSheet.pdf

National Center for Education Statistics (NCES) (2016). *English language learners in public schools.* https://nces.ed.gov/programs/coe/indicator_cgf.asp

National Clearinghouse for English Language Acquisition (NCELA), Office of English language acquisition (OELA). (2015). *Fast facts: English learners (ELs) and NAEP.* https://ncela.ed.gov/fact-sheets

Number and share of English language learners by state (Migration Policy Institute). (2020). http://www.migrationpolicy.org/programs/data-hub/charts/number-and-share-english-language-learners-state

Ríos v. Reed. (2020). https://nwlc.org/blog/reed-v-reed-40-landmark-decision/

Samson, J. F., & Collins, J. A. (2012). *Preparing all teachers to meet the needs of English learners: Applying research and practice to teacher effectiveness.* Center for American Progress. http://files.eric.ed.gov/fulltext/ED535608.pdf

Serna v. Portales Municipal Schools. (2020). http://www.leagle.com/decision/19721630351FSupp1279_11437/SERNA%20v.%20PORTALES%20MUNICIPAL%20SCHOOLS

Serving ELs: Laws, Policies, and Regulations. (2020). http://www.colorincolorado.org/sites/default/files/Policy_Guide_Final.pdf

Stewner-Manzanares, G. (1988). *The bilingual education act: Twenty years later.* https://eric.ed.gov/?id=ED337031

Title VI Civil Rights Act. (2020). https://www.eeoc.gov/workplace-laws-not-enforced-eeoc#titlevi

United States v. State of Texas. (1971). http://www.leagle.com/decision/1971366342FSupp24_1362/UNITED%20STATES%20v.%20STATE%20OF%20TEXAS

The U.S. Constitution, 14th Amendment. (2020). https://www.law.cornell.edu/constitution/amendmentxiv

The U.S. Constitution: 14th Amendment. (2020). https://www.archives.gov/founding-docs

U.S. Department of Justice & U.S. Department of Education. (2015). *Information for limited English proficient (LEP) parents and guardians and for the schools and school districts that communicate with them.* https://www2.ed.gov/about/offices/list/ocr/docs/dcl-factsheet-lep-parents-201501.pdf

Wallace, E. (2014). *Educating English language learners in the elementary classroom.* The College of Brockport, Education and Human Development Theses.

Webb, L.D., Metha, A., & Jordan, K.F. (2010). *Foundations of American education* (6th ed.). Pearson Education, Inc.

What does ESSA mean for ELs? (2020). https://www.colorincolorado.org/blog/what-does-essa-mean-ells

Wright, W. (2020). Every Student Succeeds Act (ESSA) and ELs. https://www.youtube.com/watch?v=p05nPGSBsSY

Wright, W. E. (2010). *Foundations for teaching English language learners: Research, theory, policy, and practice.* Caslon Pub. Inc.

WEBSITE RESOURCES

¡Colorín Colorado!
Link: https://www.colorincolorado.org/

ESOL in Higher Ed
Link: http://esolinhighered.org/

ESSA
Link: https://www.ed.gov/essa

Florida Department of Education: English Language Learners
Link: http://www.fldoe.org/academics/eng-language-learners/

NCELA
Link: https://ncela.ed.gov/

WIDA
Link: https://wida.wisc.edu/

1A
Activity!
TEACHING

You've "met" Ms. Miller in this chapter and gotten a sense of how she ensures that she will follow policies and guidelines. Review her approaches and positions and jot down key take-aways. Then, add any other topics you expect to address in your own classroom with regard to legislative policies and procedures.

You

Ms. Miller

1B
Activity!
LEGISLATION

Choose a state other than where you currently live. Do a quick online search regarding its laws and/or policies regarding ELs, and compare to your current state's laws/policies. Write a summary statement, and be prepared to discuss with classmates.

YOUR STATE: _____

OTHER STATE: _____

YOUR SUMMARY:

_____

_____

_____

1C

Activity!

LEGISLATION

Name: _____

The United States is a nation of immigrants, which has led to several landmark court decisions that impacted ELs' education. Choose one case. Describe it using cartoon panels and word bubbles. Can't draw? Stick figures are fine! The goal is to explain simply so anyone can understand!

CASE: _____

1D

Activity!

ADVOCACY

Name: _____

There are many ways to advocate for, or speak on behalf of, your English learners, such as signing a petition or speaking out to authority figures like the principal or school board members. Consider the suggestions below. Check each way you have advocated for someone or a specific group of people. Briefly jot down the details of these events.

1. Letter to the Editor
   ☐ Details:

2. Stopped someone from making derogatory remarks about a person or group in conversation
   ☐ Details:

3. Became a member of an advocacy organization   ☐ Details:

4. Taught or facilitated a workshop to educate a group   ☐ Details:

5. Sought assistance on behalf of someone in need   ☐ Details:

6. Advocated for someone via social media   ☐ Details:

7. Contacted a government official   ☐ Details:

8. Other?   ☐ Details:

1E

Activity!

50 STATES

In this chapter, you read the background of how Florida came to address the needs of its ELs after citizens filed a lawsuit. Since then, legislation and ongoing monitoring ensure compliance. What about other states? Choose any other state and research the history of how it determined to best serve its ELs.

STATE:

IN WHAT YEAR DID THIS STATE FIRST ACKNOWLEDGE THE NEED TO ADDRESS ENGLISH LEARNERS?

OVERALL, HAS THIS STATE DONE A BETTER OR WORSE JOB SERVING ITS ENGLISH LEARNERS COMPARED TO FLORIDA, OR ARE THEY COMPARABLE?

+ − =

KEY PEOPLE/POLICIES:

IMPACT ON STUDENTS/FAMILIES:

IMPACT ON SCHOOLS/EDUCATORS:

1F Activity!

NEEDS

Name: _____

In this introductory chapter, you learned the evolution of how Florida came to provide mandated training for pre-service teachers to be fully prepared to teach English learners. Think about other teacher requirements that will impact your ELs, such as classroom management, types of assessment, differentiated instruction, etc. Rate your confidence level in the areas below. Add other areas you feel you need to prepare for. Keep this chart, and revise it from time to time as your knowledge and confidence grow.

	I don't feel prepared yet.	I feel well prepared.
Classroom management	○	○
Able to differentiate instruction for students	○	○
Can recognize traits of gifted English learners	○	○
Can write content objectives that are specific and measurable	○	○
Aware of strategies for collaborating with parents of ELs	○	○
Able to support English acquisition while teaching other content areas (e.g., science)	○	○
Can create fun and engaging lessons that deliver solid academic content	○	○
Can prevent discipline problems through classroom management	○	○
Ability to use multiple forms of formative and summative assessments	○	○
Knowledgeable about teaching students with different cultural backgrounds	○	○
Able to recognize indicators of learning disabilities in ELs	○	○
Confident in my abilities to advocate for my ELs	○	○
Capable of teaching reading and language arts to ELs	○	○
Respectful and accepting of other cultures	○	○
Ethical and professional	○	○
Confident I can teach all subject areas/grade levels assigned to me	○	○
Other:	○	○
	○	○
	○	○
	○	○

Section Two

Cultural Proficiency: Embracing Diversity in the Classroom

Introduction

 LITERACY STRATEGY: EXCLUSION BRAINSTORMING

(1) Complete the following activity prior to reading Chapter 2.
(2) Circle the words that are associated with the term "culturally-relevant teaching."

Consent Decree	Nonverbal Communication
Self-transformation	Grammar Translation
Standards	Discrimination
Racism	Language Acquisition
Assessment	Assimilation
Conflict-resolution	Proficiency Test
Family Structure	CRT
Stereotypes	CASEL

(3) Read Chapter 2.
(4) Come back to your answers and determine if you would now circle more or fewer words.

Tips for Use with ELs: This activity allows teachers to make readings more applicable for all students by activating students' prior knowledge and making connections with words and their meanings.

PAUSE AND REFLECT

Share ways you have observed teachers or administrators fostering diversity. This might include decisions about the curriculum, lesson planning, teaching strategies, or even strategic planning to promote cultural diversity.

© realpeople/Shutterstock.com

TEACHER VIGNETTE: MS. GERRIOR, KINDERGARTEN, OHIO

Peyton was born in Dayton, Ohio and speaks several languages. Her grandmother speaks Spanish, her father and paternal grandfather speak Polish, and her mother speaks English. Upon Peyton's arrival into the world, she is consistently spoken and read to by her respective relatives. When Peyton begins kindergarten, she speaks at an age-appropriate developmental level. She is able to communicate with her peers without any noticeable differences in speech patterns or comprehension. However, her favorite language is Spanish, and at first, she attempts to use only this language. Her teacher, Ms. Gerrior, notices that Peyton follows along well in class. She socializes with others in a quiet but comfortable manner and seems to enjoy all aspects of school. Even though she is settling into kindergarten well, Ms. Gerrior decides to review Peyton's school file. She soon discovers that Peyton is trilingual at 5 years old. She also learns that there are several other students whose first language is not English.

© Diego Cervo/Shutterstock.com

Ms. Gerrior's class consists of seven ELs whose parents emigrated from South America, Korea, and China (both Cantonese and Mandarin languages); additionally, there are four special needs students and nine other kindergarteners. Some ELs were born in the United States and speak at least one other language. Peyton speaks two languages fluently at home. Based on the responses to the Home Language Survey, she and the other six ELs are assessed and found to qualify for the ESOL program at school. Ms. Gerrior soon appreciates that she will have quite a diverse group of students this academic year, and she will need to connect students' languages and cultural backgrounds to lessons and activities.

© spass/Shutterstock.com

She considers possible gaps, such as **school-readiness, academic achievement**, and **cultural and linguistic differences**. Each of these factors plays a significant role in teaching and learning. She reads the research by the U.S. Department of Education (2015) that reports many students enter kindergarten already behind their peers in academic and social-emotional skills, and that Latino students, the fastest-growing group in Dayton, Ohio and in the U.S., have the lowest rate of participation in preschool. She reflects on whether the three ELs in her class from South America were previously enrolled in school. She has not noticed a difference in their social skills in class as of yet. But, she knows **the more informed teachers are about students' prior schooling experiences, the more success teachers have in meeting students' needs**.

In addition, Ms. Gerrior reviews the identifying factors that contribute to achievement gaps. The National Education Association (NEA) identifies factors **within the schools' control,** such as teachers' experience, resources, and schools' involvement with families. They also identify factors **outside the schools' control,** such as students' access to health and social services, family income, and bias (e.g., racial, ethic, class) (NEA, 2020). Her school is one of the lowest in socioeconomic status (SES) in the district, and all students are on the National School Breakfast Program (NSBP) and the National School Lunch Program (NSLP). The school's data reveal its Pre-K–5th population as White, Black, Chinese, Korean, Hispanic, Latino, Asian, and 2% as other. All teachers and administrators have attended training in **Culturally Responsive Teaching** (CRT), sometimes referred to as **Culturally Relevant Teaching**. Snyder and Staehr-Fenner (2021) define five guiding principles for culturally relevant teaching. One approach is an assets-based perspective where students' cultures, home languages, and families are valued. You can read more about an assets-based perspective at https://getsupported.net/elassets/.

Research, reflection, and working collaboratively with colleagues are essential steps in fostering a positive and multicultural environment where students are encouraged to be critical thinkers and active learners based on their individual beliefs and values. Thus, Ms. Gerrior starts her journey by reflecting on Ladson-Billings instructional method from the early '90s. According to Escudero (2019), her framework "informs every aspect of a teacher's practice and rests on three fundamental pillars: academic achievement, cultural competence, and sociopolitical consciousness. These three pillars work in tandem with one another. In other words, a culturally relevant teacher cannot focus on one pillar without also inherently focusing on the others" (see: https://www.teachforamerica.org/stories/how-to-engage-culturally-relevant-pedagogy).

 Describe a culturally relevant teacher in your own words. What does this teacher look like? How does this teacher talk? How does this teacher act? What does this teacher do in the classroom? In planning lessons? In assessing students?

Ms. Gerrior takes the time to include sensory, graphic, and interactive supports designed to promote student engagement and interaction (see: https://wida.wisc.edu). For example, she groups her ELs with native English speakers and provides visuals that match the alphabet sounds. In addition, she incorporates videos, magazines, and realia into her daily lessons. At the beginning of the school year, she teaches a science lesson on the differences between day and night in which she asks students to share what they did over a long weekend. She has visuals of the sun and moon, along with photos of her family barbecuing in the afternoon and sitting around the fire pit in the evening. The students share their own activities, such as getting up early to do chores, helping to prepare a traditional family meal, playing soccer with friends, celebrating birthdays, attending bilingual classes at the local university, walking to their neighbor's home with a family dish, going grocery shopping, reading quietly, attending church, and more. From this activity, individual cultural identities are evident in the responses differentiating day and night.

Ms. Gerrior also connects stories and events to cultural traditions. She contacts parents to read stories related to students' cultures; for example, she asks parents to volunteer to read cultural books, such as *Mooncakes* by L. Seto (about the Chinese moon festival), *My Name is Yoon* by Helen Recorvits (about a Korean girl learning to write in English), and *I Love Saturdays and Domingos* by Alma Flor Ada (about visiting two culturally different sets of grandparents). Peyton's grandmother is in the classroom on a weekly basis and reads stories about the Hispanic, Latino, and Spanish cultures. She brings in songs and activities to showcase traditions. On the Colorín Colorado! website, Freeman and Freeman provide a rubric on the cultural relevance of a book. Students relate the events, characters, places, and other details in the reading to their families and personal experiences by answering the questions on the rubric. The rubric is available at: https://www.colorincolorado. org/article/choosing-childrens-books-cultural-relevance-rubric.

The kindergarteners are exposed to varied cultures of their classmates in practical and relevant ways. Ms. Gerrior is certainly modeling the traits of a culturally responsive teacher. She strives to promote family engagement among the parents of her ELs. She sets high expectations for her students and provides lots of opportunities to practice listening, speaking, reading, and writing in English.

Ms. Gerrior continuously focuses on her ELs' home languages, schooling, cultural backgrounds, and diverse needs. She endeavors to build trust among her students, and she remains active in the school community with parents, staff, administration, and local vendors to support her class activities. Her goal is for all students and their parents to have a positive school experience early on. However, along with focusing on her students' needs, she takes a step back to reflect on her own personal experiences. Her primary consideration is on **cultural gaps** as she is part of **the majority of elementary teachers in the U.S., a white, middle-class, monolingual female**. She earned her ESOL endorsement and wants to be sure to build a positive linguistic and cultural environment that fosters an academically rich setting. She reaches out to families to introduce them to the school's policies and present ways to get involved in their child's education. She seeks to gather support from her colleagues, to advocate for all students, and to communicate with families about the culture of the school community. DeCapua (2016) stated:

> *"To establish an effective learning environment, teachers and learners need to establish and maintain a relationship by developing an understanding of each other and their classroom roles and expectations through two-way communication, rather than assuming these roles and expectations are 'obvious'."* (p. 33)

Ms. Gerrior thinks back to her experiences in elementary school. She recalls not eating lunch in the school cafeteria with her friends because she had a disagreement with them and ended up sitting by herself. A feeling of loneliness, isolation, and a gut-wrenching sadness came over her as she remembered that particular day. She had wanted to cry but stayed stoic. She ate very little of her sandwich and carefully watched for others to finish and head to the library. She knew she could join in then. This feeling of awkwardness, silence, and not belonging is what ELs often endure when there is a language or cultural barrier that is not addressed in the classroom. **ELs tend to feel left out of school activities as early as kindergarten**. They are often timid and attempt to avoid calling attention to themselves. The lunchroom experience constantly reminds Ms. Gerrior that **it is the responsibility of teachers, staff, and administrators to assist all students in acclimating to the U.S. school system and in feeling a sense of belonging**.

Establishing classroom rules and routines enables all students to understand class expectations and be treated equitably, regardless of cultural and linguistic background. Ms. Gerrior considers creating a library for students to be able to check out books from her class. In this way, she will be more confident in knowing that all students have readily available reading materials and that they will be able to reinforce skills practiced in class in their homes, regardless of the language spoken at home. She will search for bilingual books and provide glossaries to support English proficiency. She will also translate memos into the languages of her ELs and send home weekly updates regarding curriculum expectations. Thinking back to a situation that occurred during her first year of teaching, she remembers when her colleague sent a letter home to parents that was translated through a software program but never edited by a member of the school community. The teacher wrote about an Open House for families to get to know each other and explained the curriculum. However, in translation, the memo stated that *parents* should hold an Open House for the teacher to get to know them. This caused much chaos and embarrassment.

Ms. Gerrior remembers reading:

> *"Because ELs have such varied backgrounds and experiences, it is essential that candidates and teachers of ELs be able to reflect on students' prior knowledge and experiences in order to make connections to new concepts as well as look for background information that students might need to make connections to new content."* (Fisher, Frey, & Lapp, 2012, p. 177)

She is well aware of the challenges teachers face with the diverse language backgrounds of students, yet promises herself that she will meet each one in a positive way. As she seeks lessons aligned to the kindergarten curriculum and to the needs of all students, she considers both their academic and social–emotional needs.

The **Collaborative for Academic, Social, and Emotional Learning** (CASEL) organization identified five social-emotional-learning competencies: self-awareness, self-management, social awareness, relationship skills, and responsible decision-making. In looking at ways to foster these learning dimensions, Ms. Gerrior makes sure to comment in her planning book and keeps a visual chart on her desk. In this way, she frequently checks to assure herself that she is addressing each competency. She consistently focuses on building students' social skills and is gratified to observe her 5-year-olds becoming cognizant of their strength in working together, making good decisions, and managing their time well.

Mitchell (2017) reported:

> "*While most ELs are born in the U.S., the researchers argue that educators need a deeper understanding of how to address the social-emotional needs of those who are foreign-born, including refugees with interrupted formal education, migrant children, unaccompanied minors, and undocumented children.*" (p. 12)

PAUSE AND REFLECT

Thus far, you have read about several strategies that Ms. Gerrior has implemented in her classroom. Choose two of these strategies and describe how you will adapt them to fit the needs of your ELs.

Ms. Gerrior is aware that two of her ELs were born outside the U.S. and that one is possibly an undocumented student. She recalls from the **Plyler v. Doe** (1982) case that she cannot ask for information regarding the legal status of this student. And no matter if her ELs are born in or outside the U.S., they still need guidance to develop their English and academic proficiency. She is motivated to further research the impact of culture to support her instructional and assessment practices.

Ms. Gerrior reads Grognet's (2014) depiction of **culture** from the 1900s when it was viewed as a map, an abstract representation of an area in which words, actions, and artifacts of a human group could be understood. American anthropologists, such as *Ruth Fulton Benedict (1887–1948)* and her student *Margaret Mead (1901–1978),* along with *Edward Sapir (1884–1939)* and *Clyde Kluckhohn (1905–1960),* witnessed every group developing its own culture, generally in isolation, to solve basic problems such as food, clothing, shelter, family, and social organizations. Kluckhohn was born in Lemars, Iowa and spent time studying the Navaho culture. His mother died at birth and his father remarried when he was three years old. Soon after, he went to live with his mother's brother who eventually adopted him at 7 years old. Due to an illness at 17 years old, he became captivated with the Navaho culture, which led to his research on the interplay between an individual and patterns of culture. American anthropologist Melville J. Herskovits (1964) explained the significance of Kluckhohn's work, writing:

© AlexisP/Shutterstock.com

"*He never lost sight of the fact that human beings function within the institutional setting of human societies. At the same time, he fully recognized the importance of the reciprocal of this fact, that the institutions of any society being studied must be taken as resulting from and reflecting the patterned system of values of the human beings who live their lives in terms of the framework of traditional sanctions they provide.*" (p. 129)

Culture is a universal fact of human life; it is learned. Cultural patterns change over time. Kluckhohn and Kelly (1945) explained, "*By culture we mean all those historically created designs for living, explicit and implicit, rational, irrational, and non-rational, which exist at any given time as potential guides for the behavior of men*" (p. 78). The Center for Advanced Research for Language Acquisition (CARLA) defined **culture** as "*the shared patterns of behaviors and interactions, cognitive constructs, and affective understanding that are learned through a process of socialization. These shared patterns identify the members of a culture group while also distinguishing those of another group*" (CARLA, 2017). Merriam-Webster dictionary defines culture as:

1a. the customary beliefs, social forms, and material traits of a racial, religious, or social group;

  b. the set of shared attitudes, values, goals, and practices that characterizes an institution or organization;

  c. the set of values, conventions, or social practices associated with a particular field, activity, or societal characteristic;

  d. the integrated pattern of human knowledge, belief, and behavior that depends upon the capacity for learning and transmitting knowledge to succeeding generations (https://www.merriam-webster.com/dictionary/culture).

PAUSE AND REFLECT

Review the definitions of culture presented in this chapter and describe culture in your own words. Provide one example to support your definition.

Language and culture are closely related. Culture is transmitted through language, and language reflects cultural patterns. What the exact interrelationship is between language and culture remains a question for linguists, anthropologists, and other specialists. **Linguists** view language as a communication system. They seek to map out the meaningful sounds of a language, the significant units of meaning, the rules or grammar for combining these units, and the meanings attached to them. **Anthropologists,** on the other hand, look at language to examine lexical items and their width and depth of differentiation as critical. They ask whether there are more separate terms or synonyms, and more fine distinctions made in reference to the culture with which the speaker is most concerned. For example, they investigate why some languages have different terms for *potato* and some have no word for *snow*. Several decades ago, Keesing (1973) described anthropologists as examining questions such as: *How have cultures developed? How are cultures learned? How different and unique are cultures?*

The viewpoints of anthropologists and linguists still guide teachers in understanding what other cultures are like. Being able to study how other cultures communicate with each other, whether through their language or their cultural norms, fosters ways for students to feel more comfortable communicating in the classroom. **Having an understanding of cultural backgrounds allows teachers the opportunity to create lessons in which students do not feel out of place or offended based on their cultural norms.**

 Google *"Linguistics and Anthropology YouTube"* and describe two examples of each viewpoint.

It should be clear that linguistics and anthropologists examine language and culture from unique perspectives, and understanding both fosters effective communication. That is, teachers must look for ways to understand the cultural values and beliefs of their students, as well as ways to communicate. **Verbal language is just one means of communication; nonverbal is another**. Many aspects of communication are expressed nonverbally. In class, Peyton and her classmates typically display many **nonverbal expressions**. She often shrugs her shoulders, crosses her arms, opens her mouth wide, and throws her arms in the air during language arts or science lessons to show her amazement or boredom. Others distance themselves when sitting on the carpet during language arts instruction. The ELs whose families are from China typically avoid eye contact with their peers in collaborative activities.

Nonverbal communication (e.g., facial expressions, body movement, spatial distance) is just as powerful as verbal. **Communication is based on what you are taught and is influenced by cultural and societal experiences**. Therefore, communication is affected by attitudes, assumptions, and judgments toward or about others. Every culture demonstrates unique non-verbal behaviors that can easily be misunderstood or misinterpreted in the classroom. For Peyton and her peers, it might seem naïve to claim that 5-year-olds can possess such dispositions and judgments; however, it is not only possible, it is likely. **Cultural backgrounds define nonverbal**

© Maksym Bondarchuk/Shutterstock.com

communication and are learned behaviors. Therefore, it is important for teachers to continuously promote and foster effective verbal and nonverbal communication. Teachers can easily offend students and their families due to a lack of knowledge about cultural differences.

Google nonverbal cultural differences, such as eye contact, gestures, nodding of the head, silence, humor, and others. Describe at least three differences within a given culture.

Language reflects cultural behavior. Knowledge of students' cultural backgrounds fosters more meaningful experiences. **Culture** is the blueprint that determines how one thinks, feels, and behaves (Gollnick & Chinn, 2017). **Culture makes our surroundings understandable and predictable.** Misunderstandings arise when an individual comes into contact with another very different culture; for example, in the U.S., a child who loses his tooth typically will place it under his pillow for the tooth fairy to leave him money. Yet, in the Greek culture, a child tosses his tooth on the roof. **Culture** is a set of common beliefs and values shared by a particular group. **Culture** is a way of perceiving, a way of thinking, a way of communicating, a way of behaving, and a way of evaluating. **Culture plays a strong role in the classroom**.

PAUSE AND REFLECT

Describe ways to promote cultural competence (i.e., ways cultural identities affect academic proficiency for ELs), home/school connections (i.e., ways to build partnerships with families of ELs), and the inter-relationship between language and culture.

Ethnocentrism is when one's culture, race, and ways of life are considered superior to all others. It is the superimposition of one group over another. Koppelman (2020) shared sociologist Robin Williams' 1954 example of ethnocentrism when the English colonists called a bird a robin because it looked like an English robin even though these two types of birds were not related. The colonists judged the bird by their own type of bird and superimposed the name onto another culture. Gollnick and Chinn (2017) emphasized the primary outlook of school curriculum as following the dominant culture; however, they explain how communities foster ethnocentrism when students' ethnic cultures are the core of a curriculum. Examples of this curriculum are evening classes for a specific cultural group or private schools centered on the values of an ethnic group.

Along with federal and state mandates regarding the education of ELs, every school must promote a cultural understanding and sensitivity toward all students. The laws set the foundation, **but the school environment sets the everyday experiences for students, teachers, staff, and administration.** Thus, teachers who understand the cultural backgrounds of their students are more able to connect to what students need to know to be academically successful across all content areas. DeCapua (2016) affirmed:

> "The culture in which individuals are raised is the most important determinant of how they view
> and interpret the world. Members of different cultural groups see and interpret events differently;

through the enculturation process, they develop attitudes, beliefs, and values that affect the meanings they assign to the world around them. Culture bestows a set of lenses for seeing the world, lenses that influence the way members of groups choose, decipher, process, and utilize information." (p. 16)

Stereotypes stem from incomplete, distorted information and limited personal experiences. They are natural, but they are often unfair and interfere with communication. Koppelman (2020) defined stereotypes as a positive or negative trait toward a group. They are reinforced by textbooks, media, technologies, and classroom ancillaries. School curricula reflect the viewpoints and expertise of a group and most certainly impact the classroom. Teachers who strive to be effective in the classroom build relationships with their students and align cultural backgrounds with appropriate lessons. This requires that teachers know who they are as a person, teacher, and professional leader. Teachers who leave their biases, attitudes, and "baggage" outside the school walls are more adept at making an impact in the classroom. Banks (2016) explained that *"the major goal of multicultural education is to help students develop the knowledge, attitudes, and skills needed to participate effectively in their cultural communities, within the civic culture of the nation-state and in the global community"* (p. xx). This begins in kindergarten and continues with the mission and goals of each school community.

PAUSE AND REFLECT

List three adjectives that come to mind when you hear or read about the following groups: Floridians, New Englanders, Westerners, Latinos, Blacks, students with disabilities, English learners, and gifted students. Share your list. Are your descriptions similar or different? Positive or negative? Why?

Deep culture consists of values and beliefs beneath the surface of everyday social customs; however, values assume different meanings in different cultures. For example, most cultures value 'family'; yet, for farmworkers, the importance of family may mean keeping their children home from school to spend time together on rainy days when fieldwork is suspended. For others, the importance of family means fulfilling one's obligation by attending school no matter what other events may be going on. Similarly, others express the importance of family by expecting adult children to work in close proximity to the extended family. In other families, the importance of 'family' is expressed by the expectation of economic success—adult children may be expected to live far from their extended family to take advantage of education and employment opportunities. These examples illustrate how groups with the same value (e.g., importance of family) express those values in very different ways. It is often hard to see that there are many ways to express the same value when we grow up with a subconsciously strict view of what is right (Burns & Agresta, 2015).

PERSONAL REFLECTION: ANALYSIS OF LANGUAGE AND CULTURE

It is essential to provide varied learning opportunities to increase students' academic knowledge, social interactions, and self-esteem. In order to do this, **teachers must know who their students are, they must know about students' linguistic and cultural upbringing, and they must acknowledge their own subconscious expectations of others.** Reflecting on deep-rooted assumptions, biases, and beliefs is a positive step, along with identifying your perceptions of how language shapes cultural norms. One effective approach is to maintain a **professional journal**. For example, Ms. Miller journaled about an incident when Peyton's mother approached her to share a story about a student in the class. Peyton spoke about a classmate named Gigi and described her as always squinting when she looked at her. When Peyton's mother dropped her off at school, Gigi was outside, and Peyton shouted her name. Her mother quickly realized that her classmate was an Asian student. At first, the mother thought that maybe the kindergartner might need glasses and was waiting for the right moment to share Peyton's observations with the teacher. When she realized the cultural observation of her daughter, she quickly sought out books to read at bedtime about diverse cultures.

Following are **three journal topics** to provide a good starting place. You will likely think of other topics to include as you reflect on your own cultural experiences.

© Yeamake/Shutterstock.com

Part I: Self-Analysis

Teachers juggle many social factors in the classroom, such as when ELs' cultures do not match the classroom philosophy. When teachers do not take time to notice students' cultural backgrounds, confusion often arises. Staehr-Fenner (2014) reported that *"students and teachers bring their culture with them into the classroom, but that culture may be largely invisible"* (TESOL.org). Therefore, getting to know yourself, and what you are made of, will set the foundation for building ways to get to know your students.

Think about your childhood and teen years to reveal the beliefs and customs that you grew up with—that is, beliefs that are likely to be reinterpreted and reevaluated in diverse classrooms. Here are some suggested questions to help you write about the language and culture themes in your life:

- ▶ Did you know people who spoke more than one language when you were growing up? What was your family's general attitude toward immigration and people of different nationalities? Did you enjoy the ease of having only one language used throughout your home and school experience? How far back does your family history have to go to find speakers of languages other than English?

- ▶ How was illness or weakness addressed in your family? Did your parents characterize other people (your friends, other family members, neighbors, celebrities, etc.) in negative terms? Looking back, what do you think motivated those feelings?

- ▶ What kinds of conversations took place in your home? Were there topics or specific words that were never to be discussed or used (i.e., taboo topics and taboo language)? Who made the rules about how your family conversations were conducted? How did you participate in family 'talk'? Did everyone take turns? Did the loudest one win? Were children to be seen and not heard?

 # Part II: Other Analysis

One way to learn about your students is through **interviews**, which is a process that is invaluable for every educator to acquire more insight into the cultural backgrounds of students and erase any stereotypical attitudes previously held.

Interview an EL in your community with the goal of learning about a culture different from your own and a perspective on learning another language. Take note as to whether you have met others from this culture. It is well known that people tend to socialize with others who are similar; yet, as a teacher, you will need to build relationships outside your typical social group. This interview process is an opportunity to discover or deepen a relationship with an EL whose background is different from your own. Nieto (2012) reported that interviews to learn more about an individual improves student behaviors and academic performance.

Ask your interviewee, your EL, if he (she) would like you to use his (her) name in your report or if he (she) would rather remain anonymous. If the latter is the case, use a pseudonym in your report. Plan your interview ahead of time. Asking questions about culture may be sensitive. Reflect on what you learned about yourself. From there, ask your EL to reflect on how his (her) experiences and beliefs were shaped. To gain a greater understanding of the experience of learning a new language, ask your EL about his (her) experiences.

For example, ask about:

▶ the different kinds of language learning that took place in school, at home, in the neighborhood, with friends, and others;

▶ helpful materials used for different aspects of language learning at different ages;

▶ personal difficulties experienced in learning English;

▶ most helpful techniques or activities experienced in learning English;

▶ and recommendations for you, as a teacher.

Reflect on Peyton. She experiences several cultural traditions and languages by the time she is five years old. She is exposed to a typical American lifestyle by her mother and celebrates Polish and Spanish holidays throughout the year. For example, her grandparents typically prepare Polish meals, such as pierogies, borscht, and babka. Her family celebrates American holidays in addition to Epiphany on January 6th and Polish Flag Day on May 2nd. Her maternal grandmother used to read fairy tales from various cultures, such as Cinderella, or *La Cenicienta* in Spanish, to teach her about cultural interpretations. Peyton is learning at a young age how to respect and value other cultures and languages. Being exposed to culturally diverse books, technologies, and materials in the classroom and at home will benefit Peyton and all students in better understanding each other's linguistic, cognitive, and sociocultural characteristics. Teachers can learn even more about their students through informal conversations, attending school and community events that students are involved in, and conducting home visits (Staehr-Fenner, 2014). It takes extra time, effort, and a passion for teaching all students.

Part III: Reflection on Preparing the Way to Teach ELs

For the third step in this activity, reflect on what you have learned thus far about your own life journey in preparation for teaching ELs from different cultural backgrounds and at varying levels of English proficiency. You may want to consider the following questions:

▶ How can you develop a positive relationship with ELs who speak in ways that you may not like or that make you uncomfortable?

▶ How can you develop respect for parents if you see that their children have many unmet needs?

▶ How will culture play a role in your classroom?

▶ In what ways will you include ELs in promoting cultural diversity? Parents? Administration? Your colleagues? Staff members? School community?

▶ How do sociopolitical factors and legislation impact ELs?
(Activity adapted from Burns & Agresta, 2015.)

CONCLUSION

Learning is more meaningful when ELs are able to make connections to what is going on in the classroom to their own lives. They come from diverse ethnic, cultural, linguistic, educational, and socioeconomic backgrounds; yet, they typically want to be actively engaged in class activities. All teachers, like Ms. Gerrior and Ms. Miller, face academic and language challenges, but their commitment to getting to know the sociocultural backgrounds of all students makes a positive difference.

The cultural differences of Ms. Gerrior's 20 students, and the 22 diverse 3rd graders in Ms. Miller's classroom, define the foundation for instructional and assessment practices. **Scaffolding, providing reading materials ahead of time, working directly with families, listing academic content vocabulary, promoting home languages,** and other **meaningful strategies** are possible suggestions. A plausible next step is to establish a **Parent Leadership Council** (PLC) to encourage parental involvement and discuss tips to guide and facilitate students' practice and learning at home. Include cultural factors, WIDA's language proficiency levels, and WIDA's Can Do Descriptors, which can be found at https://wida.wisc.edu. These actions will promote more collaboration and interaction with parents and a deeper understanding of your students' needs.

Peyton often shares words in Polish and Spanish with her classmates. When her grandparents serve a Polish meal, Peyton typically brings in some for lunch the next day. Her classmates always want to know more about her foods. She is a bright and articulate young girl, but she still needs support and guidance from her teacher. Peyton's cultural and language upbringing is all she knows. She will learn more in school as she continues to actively participate in activities with her classmates, teachers, and members of her school community. Right now, Peyton only knows what her family has taught her. Peyton's cultural and linguistic background will expand as she is extended other experiences within the school community. She, and the other six ELs, have much to offer others just as others have much to offer ELs. It is the role of every teacher to foster this rich and meaningful experience across all content areas and grade levels. Scarino and Liddicoat (2009) reported that culture is a framework for individuals to live their lives and communicate shared meanings with others.

LITERACY STRATEGY: DOUBLE ENTRY JOURNAL

Refer back to the beginning of this chapter and copy three or four interesting statements that you believe are pertinent for educators to understand in the left-hand column. Write down the page number where the statements are found. In the right-hand column, share your thoughts, reactions, and impressions about each statement. Exchange papers with a classmate. If you agree with your classmate's comments, add them to your list.

Statements/Page   **Comments/Reflections**

1. _____   _____

2. _____   _____

3. _____   _____

4. _____   _____

5. _____   _____

Tips for Use with ELs: A Double Entry Journal is a reading log in which the page is divided into two columns. Quotes or notes from the reading are recorded in the left hand column. In the right-hand column, a reflection about the quote is shared. Reflections may include referencing it to your own life, how it made you react, or some other personal connection. It is an appropriate strategy for ELs, as after reading the chapter or text the teacher may use the quotes to highlight key points. ELs may also work with a partner to find the key points in the chapter. In this way, ELs focus on particular points or paragraphs from the reading.

Adapted from Tompkins, G. 1998. *50 literacy strategies step-by-step*. Upper Saddle River, NJ: Merrill.

Transforming Challenges into Opportunities: Becoming a Culturally Proficient Educator

Samuel S. Perkins

© Olivier Le Moal/Shutterstock.com

LITERACY STRATEGY: PROBABLE PASSAGE

(1) Fill in the culture matrix below before reading the chapter.
(2) Share your responses with a classmate.
(3) Read Chapter 2.
(4) Refer back to your matrix and check your work.

CULTURE MATRIX

Define each of the following terms as you understand them at this point in your ESOL training.

Cultural Characteristics	Cultural Pluralism	Multicultural Education	Cultural Proficiency

Adapted from Wood, K.D. 1984. "Probable passages: A writing strategy." *The Reading Teacher* 37(5): 496-499.

Tips for Use with ELs: This pre-reading strategy assists students in better understanding the chapter or text by providing vocabulary presented in the upcoming reading. It is typically used for story structures to support the development of setting, characters, and plot. It is a useful technique to support reading comprehension.

Educators like Ms. Gerrior and her colleagues often consider interactions with and instruction of ELs from diverse cultural backgrounds challenging; however, these are opportunities to learn and develop as a professional. It is important to take the time to reflect on the definitions of culture, along with elements and characteristics of surface and deep culture; the relationship between culture, learning, and teaching; cultural pluralism; multicultural education; and cultural proficiency.

A focus on change of self is the first step. To understand, accept, respect, and value other cultures, it is essential to understand your own culture and biases. Ms. Gerrior conscientiously reflects on her prejudices and assumptions in striving to plan effective lessons. She understands that *her* identity influences the school community; that is, students, parents, and teachers are affected by her biases, attitudes, and teaching style. She believes it is every educator's responsibility to engage in a self-examination of one's prejudices to inform instruction.

Educators engaging in processes of developing such self-awareness promote role models for students to develop empowering and enlightening self-awareness. **Transformation** in education ultimately leads to a culturally-proficient community with empowered teachers. Ms. Gerrior and Ms. Miller affirm the effects of teaching styles within a school community. That is, teachers, administrators, staff, and school personnel must be knowledgeable about the cultural and linguistic backgrounds of ELs, legislation affecting ELs, and the overall arching social context and dynamics of the classroom. The impact is clearly observable through student engagement, parent communications, and ultimately performance data. Characteristics about ELs, from schooling, cultural values, literacy, learning styles, motivation, and interests, play a major role in schools. Teachers must be able to respond to students' diversity in fostering educational equity.

Gorski (2016) reflects on accepting, respecting, and valuing other cultures as follows:

> *"Regardless of how we might define it, we probably can agree culture is important in the sense that it is one aspect of students' identities. If we think of culture in everyday terms, outside the context of the dozens of theoretical conceptions of culture that continue to befuddle the scholars studying it, it is difficult to imagine a sensible argument for striking the concept from the list of equity concerns. Certainly, as educators we position ourselves to be more effective, more equitable, when we understand and are responsive to the individual cultures of our students and their families."* (p. 223)

 Describe ways to empower teachers, staff, and administrators to examine their own biases and assumptions in promoting a positive classroom environment.

The Interstate New Teacher Assessment and Support Consortium **(InTASC)** Model Core Teaching Standards encourage a transformation in education through self-reflection and self-examination of teaching practices. In particular, **Standard #9: Professional Learning and Ethical Practice** articulates that teachers engage in ongoing professional learning and use evidence to continually evaluate their practices, particularly the effects of choices and actions on others (learners, families, professionals, and communities), and adapt practices to meet the needs of each learner (InTASC, 2013). Gollnick and Chinn (2017) affirmed that knowledge about students' cultures allows for more meaningful teaching by relating to students' experiences and building on their prior knowledge; however, they pointed out that educators are challenged in truly reflecting on students' cultures, as they are at a disadvantage in not living in the communities of their students. Thus, in order to build relationships and create effective multicultural learning environments, self-reflection and examination by all educators is an essential process.

SURFACE AND DEEP ELEMENTS OF CULTURE

With regard to surface and deep elements of culture, the names illuminate their definitions. **Surface**, or explicit, elements of culture are those that can be perceived by one or more of the five senses (hearing, seeing, smelling, tasting, and touching). These elements include arts, costumes, dress, famous personalities, food, holidays, and history of a cultural group. Identifying, describing, discussing, and examining surface elements of culture are beneficial steps in fostering a supportive learning environment. Surface elements are easier for classroom teachers like Ms. Gerrior to implement because they are tangible.

As you probably discovered in writing in your professional journal, **deep**, or implicit, elements of culture are those beneath the surface. In other words, such elements cannot be perceived by the use of the five senses. Identifying, describing, discussing, and examining these elements requires going beyond the artifacts and behaviors of members of a cultural group to discern and understand why they value these artifacts and exhibit certain behaviors. **Table 2.1** provides a listing of deep elements of culture. It may be more difficult for

Mrs. Gerrior to implement elements of deep culture because they can be more nuanced.

Attire and grooming	Folk myths	Religion
Ceremonies	Gender behaviors and roles	Rewards
Communication modes	Health and hygiene	Roles
Courtship and marriage	Life cycle	Substinence
Duties and privileges	Ownership	Taboos
Education	Precedence	Time concepts
Esthetics	Proxemics	Work and play
Ethics	Relationships	

Table 2.1.   Deep Elements of Culture.

Deep elements of culture can be discerned by asking questions beginning with *why*; for example, *Why do members of the _____ culture practice the behavior of _____* ? Being aware of ELs' cultures and cultural experiences supports curriculum development and classroom instruction. In addition, they feel more respected and accepted, which helps lead to academic success. Overall, consideration of both surface and deep elements of oneself and students' cultures are required for effective interaction and instruction. Using the metaphor of a cultural iceberg, concepts **above** the surface are visible and typically addressed; however, concepts **below** the surface are unseen and therefore require a plan and specific strategies to ensure educators and students become culturally aware of accepting and respecting diversity. **See Figure 2.1.** In other words, the metaphor of a **cultural iceberg** demonstrates how *on the surface* one witnesses explicit, taught, tangible behaviors, but *below the surface* are cultural values, habits, and judgments.

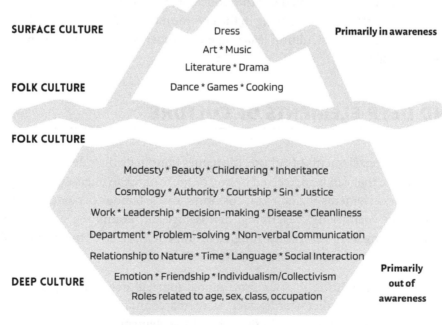

Adapted from Gary Weaver, in R.M. Paige, ed., *Cross-Cultural Orientation: New Conceptualizations and Applications.* (Rowman & Littlefield, 1986).

Figure 2.1   Cultural Iceberg.

Provide an example to show how your own culture and your ELs' cultures positively impact academic achievement.

PAUSE AND REFLECT

1. Refer back to your definition of culture. Based on what you have read thus far, has that definition changed? If so, explain.

2. As an additional opportunity for reflection, going beneath the surface, identify one surface element of a cultural group to which you belong. Examine the philosophy/ies underlying this surface element for you, your family, and your neighborhood. Complete the following prompt: I am a(an) _____.

Did you conclude that the prompt to which culture do you belong is misleading? Keep in mind, everyone belongs to multiple cultures at any point in time.

CHARACTERISTICS OF CULTURE

There are numerous characteristics of culture, and in the classroom, these include:

Culture is learned. Cultural attitudes, behaviors, beliefs, and values are learned through experiences, communication, media, the Internet and in the classroom. Cultural connections between students, parents, and teachers, and both teaching and learning styles are interrelated and intertwined.

Culture is shared. Members of a cultural group share patterns of artifacts, attitudes, behaviors, beliefs, and values. In the classroom, shared values and beliefs are essential in establishing rules and effective communication.

Culture is used to predict people's behaviors. It is natural to categorize people, as members of a cultural group share similar patterns (i.e., artifacts, behaviors, values). For teachers and students to achieve success, an understanding of the cultural value of an education is essential.

CULTURE AND LEARNING STYLES

Based on the premise that teaching does not occur unless there is learning, there must be a relationship between culture and teaching. Students' cultural experiences and backgrounds impact their learning styles. **Building on students' prior knowledge, which is built on their (cultural) backgrounds and experiences, provides a foundation for effective and efficient learning and teaching**. It is every educator's charge to be aware of teaching styles and modify as needed to meet the diverse learning needs and styles of all students. It is a prerequisite for the goals that are addressed next, that is cultural pluralism, multi-cultural education, and cultural proficiency.

© Kolett/Shutterstock.com

Cultural Pluralism

Cultural pluralism refers to a process of compromise and communication characterized by mutual appreciation and respect between members of two or more cultural groups. When cultural pluralism is practiced, members of diverse cultural groups are permitted to retain many of their cultural artifacts, attitudes, behaviors, beliefs, and values as long as these conform to the practices deemed necessary for social harmony and the survival of society as a whole. The essence of cultural pluralism conflicts with the common practice of cultural assimilation. The difference lies in the fact that when **cultural assimilation** is practiced, members of a cultural group surrender some or all of their cultural artifacts, attitudes, behaviors, beliefs, and values as they are absorbed into the majority culture of a society. In this context, the majority, or minority, does not necessarily refer to numbers. It refers to the degree to which members of a cultural group can (majority) or cannot (minority) exert power in society.

The often admired and frequently practiced analogy of a melting pot has been used to justify practices of cultural assimilation. The analogies of mosaic, quilt, stained-glass window, tapestry, and tossed salad have also been used to describe practices of cultural pluralism. In each of these analogies, each component of the finished product provides its own unique and necessary contribution. This holds true with a learning environment composed of students who are members of diverse cultures, as **without each student's contribution to the classroom, learning opportunities are lost**.

©Tatiana Grozetskaya/Shutterstock.com

Ms. Gerrior sets the tone for establishing the climate of a learning environment through personal attitudes, behaviors, beliefs, and values represented in her teaching style and interactions with students, parents, and colleagues. She is a role model for determining whether the learning environment is one that is, or is not, built on acceptance of and respect for diversity.

How can educators promote cultural pluralism and model acceptance of, and respect for, cultural diversity?

Educators often teach as they were taught. Ms. Gerrior attended a small elementary school north of Boston where the school community encouraged students to take responsibility for their own learning. The process included interactive activities and independent learning, such as the use of board games, providing matching activities, word walls, recorded readings, the daily newspaper, and manipulatives. Lab experiments and group work were readily observed across all content areas. In Ms. Gerrior's classroom, there are cooperative activities, whiteboards, learning spaces, computer centers, and visuals to match her learning style. Part of the development of an awareness of a teaching style is an attentiveness to biases and prejudices underlying the style. Sometimes educators forget that they are first and foremost human beings, meaning that teachers have biases and prejudices too. This is part of being human. Negativity arises when educators are not aware of their biases and prejudices that adversely impact their interactions with students, parents, and school personnel.

 Describe ways to build a positive, respectful, and equitable learning environment.

Multicultural Education

Multicultural education is composed of learning and teaching in which the primary goal is to promote the development of all students in reaching their potentials and realizing that success and brilliance are present among all cultural groups. Every teacher has a responsibility to and for all students. **Multicultural education involves the practice of cultural pluralism, which means that in multicultural learning environments, there is a mutual appreciation of and respect for all diverse cultural groups.** The winning implementation of multicultural education into learning environments is dependent upon the knowledge, skills, and dispositions of teachers and whether their interactions and instruction accomplish the goals discussed in this chapter.

Becoming a multicultural educator is a process of action, not passivity. And it is a process every educator should model. Ms. Gerrior shows acceptance of and respect for diversity to meet the learning needs of her students. She promotes positive multicultural interactions to support her students in becoming increasingly multicultural. For example, when Ms. Gerrior connects stories and events to cultural traditions, she purposefully attempts to compare story structures, plots, characters, and moral dilemmas to show cultural similarities and differences.

© michaeljung/Shutterstock.com

Identifying differences and modifying instruction accordingly promotes equity. If students understand how they learn, this creates the foundation for a teaching-learning partnership in which students are active participants in structuring and executing their learning. This is an integral component to becoming lifelong, independent, and successful learners.

Equally significant is the informal **hidden curriculum** and its impact on ELs. The components of this curriculum are often not written and include philosophies, procedures, and processes unknown to students. Likewise, the **null curriculum** impacts ELs by what is left out of the curriculum, the knowledge and skills left out of instruction. This can include routines and procedures that are not taught; for example, if students are not taught study skills, they may be at a loss as to how to prepare for a test. If they are not taught to think critically or question disparaging language in books and materials, they are actually learning these things are presumably not important.

Another goal of multicultural education is the continued fostering of democratic values. These include equity and the inalienable human rights of life, liberty, and the pursuit of happiness. Multicultural education encourages a search for truth; freedom to express thoughts; and fair-minded critical thinkers, decision-makers, and problem-solvers.

PAUSE AND REFLECT

Provide specific examples that you have observed in your own classes, either as a student or during field experience, that promotes multicultural education.

Ms. Gerrior promotes a classroom environment that is equitable and accepting for her kindergartners through guided interactions with parents, student-centered strategies, and the use of technologies. She strives to think critically about resources for her teaching and students' learning. For example, she asks questions such as:

- *Which cultures are represented in the texts and technologies?*
- *Are these cultures accurately and justly represented?*
- *Which cultures are not included?*
- *Are there prevalent biases in the resources and technologies?*
- *Do the resources represent all students' cultures in the classroom?*
- *Are assessment questions free of bias?*

Banks (2006, 2012, 2016) developed a typology of four approaches for the curriculum development of multicultural education. These are the *contributions, additive, transformation,* and *social-action/decision-making approaches*. The **contributions approach** focuses on cultural heroes and heroines, holidays, isolated events, and other surface elements of cultures. It depicts the least amount of involvement in a multicultural approach. Examples of implementing this approach in the classroom include activities to celebrate holidays, such as Martin Luther King Day, Cinco de Mayo, or Thanksgiving.

With the implementation of the **additive approach**, cultural concepts, content, perspectives, and themes are integrated into existing curricula. These additions are usually marginal in nature; however, it is a step forward in making multicultural education a reality. An example of this approach is to introduce the story of Thanksgiving from the perspective of the Indians.

With the **transformation approach** to curricular development in multicultural education, the structure of existing curricula is fundamentally changed to enable students to view concepts, content, and events from diverse cultural perspectives. The focus is on teaching students to think critically and to justify their own interpretations of situations. An example of this approach is to design a thematic unit on Thanksgiving in which students analyze cultural perceptions, themes, and diversity.

An extension of the transformation approach is the **social-action/decision-making approach**, which enables students to make decisions on important social issues and take developmentally-appropriate actions to resolve them. An example is for students to write letters to legislators regarding a current issue discussed in class to express their own viewpoints. Other examples are projects and activities related to content that facilitates student development with a sense of personal and civic responsibility.

PAUSE AND REFLECT

1. Define multicultural education in your own words. Go to the ESOL in Higher Ed website for resources.

2. Describe how Banks' curricular approaches and goals support diversity in the classroom.

3. Predict what would happen if the concept of multicultural education disappeared from the curriculum.

Cultural Proficiency

Cultural proficiency builds upon the aspects of multicultural and culturally-relevant teaching. Diversity is perceived as an opportunity, a benefit, and having the knowledge, skills, and dispositions of culturally-relevant teaching. A culturally-proficient educator honors the differences between and among cultures leading to informed and respectful interactions with and instruction of ELs.

PAUSE AND REFLECT

Describe how changes in society occur through multicultural education characterized by cultural pluralism and culturally-proficient education.

A core concept of multicultural education, culturally-relevant teaching, and cultural proficiency is helping students reach their potentials. **Imagine the societal impact of self-actualized students developing into self-actualized citizens.** These self-actualized students are empowered with social awareness, creativity, critical thinking, decision-making, and problem-solving skills. They are armed with knowledge, skills, and dispositions to be change agents and effective leaders in an increasingly diverse and interdependent world. *"The kind of knowledge that teachers examine and master will have a powerful influence on the teaching methods they create, on their interpretations of school knowledge, and how they use student cultural knowledge"* (Banks, 2016, p. 4).

 What opportunities have you observed in teaching ELs from diverse backgrounds?

Race and Ethnicity

Race and ethnicity overlap with culture. Therefore, to understand culture and its role in fostering an accepting classroom environment, teachers must understand the constructs of race and ethnicity. Merriam-Webster defines **race** (https://www.merriam-webster.com/dictionary/race) as "any one of the groups that humans are often divided into based on physical traits regarded as common among people of shared ancestry" and **ethnicity** (https://www.merriam-webster.com/dictionary/ethnic) as "of or relating to large groups of people classed according to common racial, national, tribal, religious, linguistic, or cultural origin or background." The term 'race' was originally used to refer to speakers of a common language and later to denote national affiliations. However, the term began to refer to physical traits by the 17th century. The term 'ethnic' was first used in 1920. These terms continue to evolve linguistically, and terminology to describe various groups has evolved over the years. 'Caucasian', for instance, also refers to 'White'.

An example of race is White, whereas an example of ethnicity is Hispanic. Those who identify their origin as Hispanic, Latino, or Spanish may be of any race. For instance, some forms list the category of White/Non-Hispanic and Black/Non-Hispanic. All of these nuances can be confusing. The U.S. Census collects and reports the country's population every 10 years based on race and ethnicity, and schools also categorize students in this way, although they use different criteria.

For example, the **2020 U.S. Census** defined the following categorizations:

- **White**—A person having origins in any of the original peoples of Europe, the Middle East, or North Africa.
- **Black or African American**—A person having origins in any of the Black racial groups of Africa.
- **American Indian or Alaska Native**—A person having origins in any of the original peoples of North and South America (including Central America) and who maintains tribal affiliation or community attachment.
- **Asian**—A person having origins in any of the original peoples of the Far East, Southeast Asia, or the Indian subcontinent including, for example, Cambodia, China, India, Japan, Korea, Malaysia, Pakistan, the Philippine Islands, Thailand, and Vietnam.
- **Native Hawaiian or Other Pacific Islander**—A person having origins in any of the original peoples of Hawaii, Guam, Samoa, or other Pacific Islands.

Note the U.S. Census provides no specific category to address the ethnicity of Hispanics. However, the **National Center for Education Statistics** categorizes students this way:

- White
- Black
- Hispanic
- Asian
- Pacific Islander
- American Indian/Alaska Native
- Two or more races

PAUSE AND REFLECT

Although the U.S. Census categorizes and collects population data one way, schools categorize it somewhat differently. Why do you think this is done? Are there advantages to one or the other? Why or why not? How are these data used? How are they helpful? President Obama called on the U.S. Census to broaden its categories when collecting census data; however, this was not done. What changes would you consider making?

On your school district's website, locate population data. How are groups labeled or defined? What is the percentage of each group? How can this information help you as a teacher?

Sex, Gender, and Sexual Identity/Orientation

Certainly, members of a group share cultures while also belonging to other cultures. We would be remiss if we failed to address the role sex plays in the context of cultural diversity. After all, students do not leave this aspect of their identity at home when they come to school, and teachers must take this into account to establish a welcoming and accepting classroom environment. Understanding basic definitions is a good place to begin. **Sex**, as defined by Merriam-Webster (https://www.merriam-webster.com/dictionary/sex), is "either of the two major forms of individuals that occur in many species and that are distinguished respectively as female or male especially on the basis of their reproductive organs and structures." In other words, 'sex' is assigned at birth as either female or male based solely on physical traits. **Gender** (https://www.merriam-webster.com/dictionary/gender) is often incorrectly substituted for 'sex' in modern usage. Merriam-Webster defines gender as "the behavioral, cultural, or psychological traits typically associated with one sex." Teachers should not presume gender roles for students.

As a side note, gender, like many words, has multiple meanings. Those who have studied Spanish, French, or certain other languages have learned about gender roles in language. English, on the other hand, does not rely on this partly arbitrary construct to determine agreement. This is another meaning of 'gender' entirely.

Human development includes the development of sexual identity and orientation. Merriam-Webster defines **sexual orientation** as "a person's sexual identity or self-identification as bisexual, heterosexual, homosexual, pansexual, etc.: the state of being bisexual, heterosexual, homosexual, pansexual, etc." Teachers must be cognizant of ever-changing terminology, such as LGBTQ+, Latinx, etc. and consider implications within the classroom to ensure respect and acceptance. When planning parent-teacher conferences, you should expect at times to meet with same-sex couples to discuss their child. 'Culture' encompasses all of these aspects and more.

 PAUSE AND REFLECT

Think about the grade level you plan to teach. How will elements of culture determine your approach to teaching?

Other Cultural Elements

Culture extends into other areas of life. Many children have or have had an incarcerated parent. That is a unique culture, but it is shared by many children. Politics, health, illness, and even intellectual abilities and disabilities are aspects of culture. **Too often, educators limit their thinking about culture to heritage, race, ethnicity, and language.** This fails to take into consideration other powerful elements that comprise a child's world and create that child's worldview. Poverty and homelessness are elements of culture. If you and your family live in a gated community, your personal culture varies tremendously from someone who lives with their family in a car. Being able to appreciate and respect students and colleagues who are culturally diverse should be the aspiration of every educator. This requires honest self-reflection. How will you make this happen for both ELs and non-ELs?

 LITERACY STRATEGY: THINK-PAIR-SHARE

(1) Think back to when you were in elementary, middle, or high school. Write three adjectives to describe yourself, (e.g., quiet, adventurous, and skinny). Add three more adjectives to describe your family and neighborhood, (e.g., small, friendly, social). Next, identify your favorite teacher and describe your rationale for selecting this individual.

(2) Pair up with a classmate and share your responses.

(3) As a class, explain how cultural values, beliefs, attitudes, and learning styles influenced your decision in identifying your favorite teacher.

Extended Thinking and Synthesis Questions

1. Describe an artifact that presents a different message to other cultural groups, such as a work of literature, movie, novel, sitcom, children's story, or current event.

    a. Explain the cultural aspects/issues of the main people and/or characters, and the actions/morals of the main people/characters.

    b. Connect the cultural aspects/issues represented in the artifact with classroom learning to demonstrate respect for students' cultural, linguistic, and family backgrounds.

    c. Identify ways to convey high expectations for all students and connect the cultural aspects/issues of the artifact with teacher planning and parental involvement.

2. Provide links and resources and describe each resource (texts, URLs, software, videos, etc.) to show how it supports an equitable and effective school environment.

3. Define the following terms: *cultural characteristics, cultural pluralism, multicultural education, culturally-relevant teaching, cultural proficiency, racism, stereotyping,* and *discrimination.* Explain how these terms affect teaching and learning for ELs from diverse backgrounds and at varying English proficiency levels. Refer back to your definitions in the Probable Passage activity to support your answer.

4. The *hidden curriculum* is defined as a set of rules that teachers think students know, but never truly take the time to teach. One example is expecting students to be quiet when the teacher is talking or waiting to ask the teacher a question if the teacher is attending to a student. Share the *hidden curriculum* observed in your practicum or field experience. How does it affect ELs' acquisition of English and learning of the academic content?

5. The *null curriculum,* or what teachers leave out, can make important ideas conspicuous by their absence. Think back to important knowledge you learned later that you think should have been explicitly taught. Have you witnessed the null curriculum in your observations? (Of course, if teachers are leaving it out, you might not recognize it.) What might be left out that could significantly impact ELs in negative or positive ways?

6. Go back to the beginning of Section 2 and complete Step 4 of the Literacy Strategy: Exclusion Brainstorming activity.

REFERENCES

Banks, J. (2016). *Cultural diversity and education: Foundations, curriculum, and teaching* (6th ed.). Routledge Publishers, Taylor and Francis.

Banks, J. A. (2006). *Cultural diversity and education: Foundations, curriculum, and teaching* (5th ed.). Pearson Education, Inc.

Banks, J. A., & McGee, C. A. (1989). *Multicultural education*. Allyn & Bacon.

Blad, E. (2017). *Teacher-prep slow to embrace social-emotional learning*. Education Week. www.edweek.org

Burns, R., & Agresta, L. (2015). TSL Syllabi, USFSM.

Center for Advanced Research on Language Acquisition (CARLA). (2020). *What is culture?* (2020). http://carla.umn.edu/culture/definitions.html

Center for Education Statistics (2020). *Racial/Ethnic Enrollment in Public Schools*. (2020). https://nces.ed.gov/programs/coe/indicator_cge.asp

Chartock, R. K. (2001). *Strategies and lessons for culturally responsive teaching: A primer for K–12 teachers*. Pearson Education, Inc.

Collier, V. P., & Thomas, W. P. (2009). *Educating English learners for a transformed world*. Fuente Press.

Cultural Relevance Rubric. (2020). https://www.colorincolorado.org/article/choosing-childrens-books-cultural-relevance-rubric

DeCapua, A., & Wintergerst, A. C. (2016). *Crossing cultures in the language classroom* (2nd ed). University of Michigan Press.

Echevarría, J., Frey, N. E., & Fisher, D. (2016). *How to reach the hard to teach: Excellent instruction for those who need it most*. ASCD.

Echevarría, J., Vogt, M. E., & Short, D. (2004). *Making content comprehensible for English language learners: The SIOP model* (2nd ed.). Allyn & Bacon.

Escudero, B. (2019). How to practice culturally relevant pedagogy. https://www.teachforamerica.org/stories/how-to-engage-culturally-relevant-pedagogy

Fisher, D., Frey, N., & Lapp, D. (2012). *Text complexity: Raising rigor in reading*. International Reading Association, Inc.

Gay, G. (2010c). *Culturally responsive teaching: Theory, research, and practice* (2nd ed.). Teachers College Press.

Goldin-Meadow, S., & Singer, M.A. (2003). From children's hands to adults' ears: Gesture's role in teaching and learning. *Developmental Psychology, 39*(3), 509–520.

Gollnick, D. M., & Chinn, P. C. (2017). *Multicultural education in a pluralistic society*. Pearson Education.

Gonzalez, N., Moll, L. C., Floyd-Tenery, M., Rivera, A., Rendon, P., & Gonzales, R. (1993). *Teacher research on funds of knowledge; Learning from households* (Educational Practice Rep. No. 6). National Center for Research on Cultural Diversity and Second Language Learning.

Gonzalez-Mena, J. (2005). *Foundations of early childhood education. Teaching children in a diverse* society (3rd ed.). McGraw-Hill.

Gonzalez-Mena, J. (2010). *50 strategies for communicating and working with diverse families* (2nd ed.). Pearson Education, Inc.

Gorski, P. (2016). Rethinking the role of "Culture" in educational equity: From cultural competence to equity literacy. *Multicultural perspectives*, 18(4), 221–226. National Association for Multicultural Education. http://www.edchange. org/publications/Rethinking-Culture.pdf

Gorski, P. C. (2005). *Multicultural education and the Internet: Intersections and integrations* (2nd ed.). McGraw-Hill.

Govoni, J. M. (Ed.). (2008). *Perspectives on teaching K–12 English language learners* (2nd ed.). Pearson Custom Publishing.

Grognet, A. (2014). Embracing cultural diversity: Implications for the classroom. In Govoni, J. (Ed.) *Preparing the way: Teaching English learners in the pre-k–12 classroom*. Kendall Hunt Publishing.

Hammond, Z. (2015). *Culturally responsive teaching and the brain promoting authentic engagement and rigor among culturally and linguistically diverse students*. Corwin Press.

Herskovits, M. J. (1964). *Clyde Kay Maben Kluckhohn 1905–1960: A bibliographical memoir*. National Academy of Sciences, Washington DC. http://www.nasonline.org/publications/biographical-memoirs/memoir-pdfs/kluckhohn-clyde.pdf

Kaplan, R. B. (1966). Cultural thought patterns in intercultural education. *Language learning*. 16: 1–20.

Keesing, R. M. (1973). *Theories of culture*. Annual review of anthropology. Annual Reviews Inc. https://www. annualreviews.org/doi/abs/10.1146/annurev.an.03.100174.000445

Kluckhohn, C., & Kelly, W. H. (1945). The concept of culture. In R. Linton (Ed.). *The Science of Man in the World Culture* (pp. 78–105).

Koppelman, K. L. (2014). *Understanding human differences: Multicultural education for a diverse America* (4th ed.). Pearson Education, Inc.

Koppelman, K. L. (2020). *Understanding human differences: Multicultural education for a diverse America* (6th ed.). Pearson Education, Inc.

Ladson-Billings, G. (1994). *The dreamkeepers*. Jossey-Bass Publishing Co.

Lindsey, R. B., Robins, K. N., & Terrell, R. D. (2003). *Cultural proficiency: A manual for school leaders*. Corwin Press, Inc.

London, C. B. (1992). Curriculum as transformation: A case for the inclusion of multiculturality. In C. Hedley, D. Feldman, & P. Antonacci (Eds.). *Literacy across the curriculum* (pp. 211–231). Ablex Publishing Corporation.

Mitchell, C. (2017, March 8). *Schools are falling short for many ELLs: Well-prepared teachers in short supply, report finds*. Education Week, 36, 24 (p. 12).

National Center for Education Statistics (2020). Racial/Ethnic Enrollment in Public Schools. https://nces.ed.gov/ programs/coe/indicator_cge.asp

National Education Association. (2020). https://www.nea.org

Nieto, S. (2012). *Affirming diversity: The sociopolitical context of multicultural education*. Longman.

Reeves, J. (2006). Secondary teacher attitudes toward including English-language learners in mainstream classrooms. *Journal of Educational Research*, 99(3), 131–142.

Robles de Melendez, W., & Beck, V. (2007). *Teaching young children in multicultural classrooms: Issues, concepts, and strategies* (2nd ed.). Thomson Delmar Learning.

Robles de Mendez, W., & Osterlag, V. (1997). *Teaching young children in multicultural classrooms*. Delmar Publishers.

Romero, S., & Elder, J. (2003, Aug. 6). Hispanics in the US report optimism. *The New York Times*.

Saifer, S., Edwards, K., Ellis, D., Ko, L., & Stuczynski, A. (2011). *Culturally responsive standards-based teaching: Classroom to community and back* (2nd ed.). Sage Publishing.

Scarino, A., & Liddicoat, A. J. (2009). *Teaching and learning languages: A guide.* Australian Government, Department of Education, Employment and Workplace Relations.

Snyder, S., & Staehr-Fenner, D. (2021). *Culturally responsive teaching for multilingual learners in a virtual or hybrid setting: Where do we go from here?* Corwin Press.

Staehr-Fenner, D. (2014). *Advocating for English learners: A guide for educators.* Corwin Press.

Taylor, L. S., & Whittaker, C. R. (2003). *Bridging multiple worlds: Case studies of diverse educational communities.* Pearson Education Group, Inc.

The Interstate New Teacher Assessment and Support Consortium (InTASC). (2020). https://ccsso.org/resource-library/intasc-model-core-teaching-standards-and-learning-progressions-teachers-10

Tiedt, P. L., & Tiedt, I. M. (2010). *Multicultural teaching: A handbook of activities, information, and resources.* Pearson Education, Inc.

Tompkins, G. (1998). *50 Literacy strategies step by step.* Merrill.

Tompkins, G. E. (2002). *Language arts: Content and teaching strategies* (5th ed.). Pearson Education, Inc.

Tompkins, G. E. (2010). *Literacy in the middle grades: teaching reading and writing to fourth through eighth graders* (2nd ed.). Pearson Education, Inc.

Wood, K. D. (1984). "Probable passages: A writing strategy." *The Reading Teacher 37*(5): 496–499.

Wood, K. D. (2001). *Literacy strategies across the subject areas.* Allyn and Bacon.

U.S. Census (2020). About. https://www.census.gov/topics/population/race/about.html

U.S. Department of Education. (April 2015). *A matter of equity: Preschool in America.* https://www2.ed.gov/documents/early-learning/matter-equity-preschool-america.pdf

WEBSITE RESOURCES

¡Colorín Colorado!
Link: https://www.colorincolorado.org/

ESOL in Higher Ed
Link: http://esolinhighered.org/

National Association of Bilingual Education (NABE)
Link: https://nabe.org

Teaching Tolerance
Link: https://www.tolerance.org/

TESOL
Link: https://www.tesol.org/

WIDA
Link: https://wida.wisc.edu/

2A

Activity!

CULTURE

Select a children's book appropriate for the grade level you plan to teach. It should focus on a culture different than your own. Jot down 1) title & author, 2) grade level, 3) year published, 4) paragraph description including the culture, and 5) how you can use it in your classroom.

_____

_____

_____

_____

_____

_____

_____

_____

_____

_____

_____

2B

Activity!

CULTURE

X marks the spot! Where have you lived? Which countries have you visited? Draw an X on the map where you have already been. Then, draw circles where you hope to visit someday. List/name these places below.

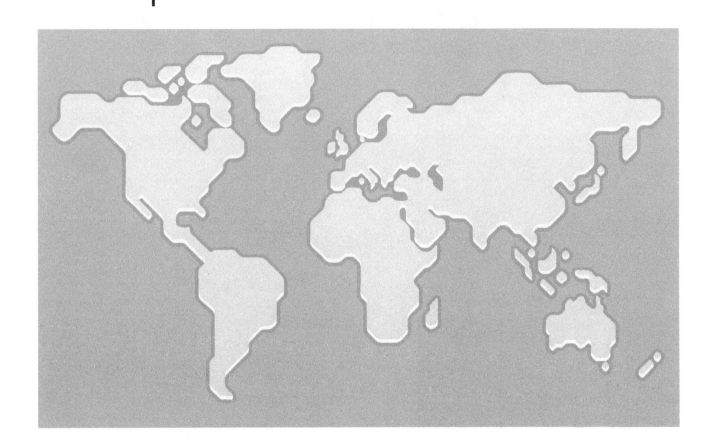

WHERE I'VE BEEN:

WHERE I'M GOING:

2C

Activity!

BODY LANGUAGE

Name: _____

Body language is a form of nonverbal communication. *Psychology Today* has created a "Body Language I.Q. Test" published here: https://www.psychologytoday.com/us/blog/cutting-edge-leadership/201410/test-your-body-language-iq

Take the test, and complete the activity here.

What was your score? _____

Jot down any concepts you missed:

Now, jot down examples of body language that you believe may be directly tied to one's culture. Discuss.

2D Activity!

HIDDEN–NULL

Both the hidden curriculum and the null curriculum can have immediate and long-lasting negative impacts on students. Consider your own school experience and classrooms you have observed. Create two lists of crucial information and knowledge that could potentially be placed on either of these lists. Compare your list with others and discuss the types of consequences that can result from the hidden and/or null curriculum.

Hidden	**Null**
◯ ————————	◯ ————————
◯ ————————	◯ ————————
◯ ————————	◯ ————————
◯ ————————	◯ ————————
◯ ————————	◯ ————————
◯ ————————	◯ ————————

2E
Activity!
MULTICULTURAL

Name: _____

James Banks's work on multicultural education is widely respected. Most educators agree that if teachers are not careful, simply using the contributions approach and additive approach may reinforce stereotypes since they are dealing with culture primarily at the surface level. Most agree that integrating the transformation approach and social action/decision-making approach is far more effective, although it requires greater thought and more effort. Choose a topic you are likely to teach in your classroom. Them, write an activity for this topic at each of Banks's levels. Which do you think will have the greatest impact?

Topic: _____

CONTRIBUTIONS	ADDITIVE
TRANSFORMATION	**SOCIAL ACTION/DECISION-MAKING**

2F

Activity!

CULTURE

In this chapter, you learned about cultural pluralism, multicultural education, and cultural proficiency. Explore these three concepts by completing each of the related activities below. Share with a classmate, and discuss each other's interpretations.

Cultural Pluralism

Describe a scenario to illustrate an example of cultural pluralism as it exists *outside* the classroom.

Multicultural Education

Describe a scenario in which a classroom teacher plans instruction using the "transformation approach."

Cultural Proficiency

Write a note to a teacher from the perspective of the school principal who observed a culturally proficient lesson. Describe what the principal witnessed that compelled her to congratulate the teacher.

2G
Activity!
IDENTITY

Who are you? How does the rest of the world see you? What do they want or need to know about you? Below are excerpts of questions from actual forms that people fill out on a regular basis. Reflect on these questions as they pertain to you, and then reflect on the types of questions we are asked about our identities. See more on the next page.

1. Bank of America Credit Card Application:

Are you a U.S. citizen? ❓

( ) Yes   ( ) No

Do you have a dual citizenship? ❓

( ) Yes   ( ) No

2. Florida DHSMV Car Title Application (respond to circled areas):

FLORIDA DEPARTMENT OF HIGHWAY SAFETY AND MOTOR VEHICLES
APPLICATION FOR CERTIFICATE OF TITLE WITH/WITHOUT REGISTRATION
SUBMIT THIS FORM TO YOUR LOCAL TAX COLLECTOR OFFICE
www.flhsmv.gov/offices/

CHECK APPLICATION TYPE: ⭘ ORIGINAL ⭘ TRANSFER VEHICLE TYPE: ⭘ MOTOR VEHICLE ⭘ MOBILE HOME ⭘ VESSEL OFF-HIGHWAY VEHICLE: ⭘ ATV ⭘ ROV ⭘ MC

1		OWNER / APPLICANT INFORMATION				
Customer Number	Check this box if you are requesting the certificate of title to be printed. ☐	Are you a Florida resident? ⭘yes ⭘no Are you an alien? ⭘yes ⭘no	Owner ⭘yes ⭘no ⭘yes ⭘no	Co-Owner	Unit Number	Fleet Number

⭘ OR ⭘ AND NOTE: When joint ownership, please indicate if "or" or "and" is to be shown on title when issued. If neither box is checked, the title will be issued with "and."
If applicable: ☐ Life Estate/Remainder Person ☐ Tenancy By the Entirety ☐ With Rights of Survivorship ☐ Owner's County of Residence:

Owner's Name As It Appears on Driver License (First, Full Middle/Maiden, & Last Name)	Owner's Email Address	Date of Birth	Sex	FL Driver License or FEID/Suffix #
Co-Owner/Lessee's Name As It Appears on Driver License (First, Full Middle/Maiden, & Last Name)	Co-Owner's/Lessee's Email Address	Date of Birth	Sex	FL Driver License or FEID/Suffix #

3. Urgent Specialists New Patient Form (respond to circled areas):

NEW PATIENT APPOINTMENT				
First Name		MI	Last	
Address			Apt/Unit # City:	State Zip code
DOB	SSN		Gender ☐ Male ☐ Female	Preferred Language
Phone (H)	(C)		PREFERRED METHOD OF CONTACT: ☐ Phone (Voice) ☐ Text ☐ Email	
Get connected to the patient portal! Have access to visit notes, receipts with ease!			Email For Patient Portal:	
Employer		Employer Phone	Occupation	

RACE		ETHNICITY	MARITAL STATUS
☐ White ☐ American Indian ☐ Asian ☐ Native Hawaiian ☐ Hispanic	☐ Black or African American ☐ Other ☐ Alaskan Native ☐ Other Pacific Islander ☐ Declined	☐ Hispanic/Latino ☐ Not Hispanic/Latino ☐ Declined	☐ Single ☐ Married ☐ Widowed ☐ Divorced ☐ Declined

Activity 2G—Filling out forms (continued)

4. From the U.S. 2020 Census Questionnaire:

What is Person 1's sex?

Mark ONE box: male or female

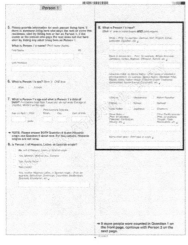

What is Person 1's race?

Mark one or more boxes and print origins: White, Black or African American; American Indian or Alaska Native; Chinese; Filipino; Asian Indian, Vietnamese; Korean; Japanese; other Asian; Native Hawaiian; Samoan; Chamorro; other Pacific Islander; some other race.

Is Person 1 of Hispanic, Latino, or Spanish origin?

NOTE: Please answer both Question 8 about Hispanic origin and Question 9 about race. For this census, Hispanic origins are not races. Hispanic origin can be viewed as the heritage, nationality, lineage, or country of birth of the person or the person's parents or ancestors before arriving in the United States. People who identify as Hispanic, Latino, or Spanish may be any race.

Students With Limited or Interrupted Formal Education (SLIFE)

Andrea DeCapua

© donskarpo/Shutterstock.com

 LITERACY STRATEGY: TEACH THE TEXT BACKWARDS

(1) Skim through Chapter 3.
(2) Review the **bold-faced** words, *italicized* words, and Figure 3.2.
(3) Preview the questions at the end of the chapter.
(4) Read Chapter 3.

TEACHER VIGNETTE: MRS. MUÑOZ, MRS. MONDICANO, MR. RAMESH, 9TH GRADE, MASSACHUSETTS

In Chapter 1, Ms. Miller presents ways to enhance her current professional knowledge of federal and state guidelines and historical court cases regarding the education of ELs beyond her undergraduate studies. She is driven to design innovative and appropriate lessons for all of her students, especially the seven ELs who speak six different languages other than English. She becomes more aware of ways to collaborate with her colleagues and truly realizes the challenges educators face in teaching and assessing ELs.

In the previous chapter, Ms. Gerrior recognizes that knowledge of students' backgrounds is essential for social and academic learning to be meaningful. Her critical analysis and personal reflection guide her in planning lessons to meet state standards and curriculum guidelines. In observing Peyton and six other ELs, Ms. Gerrior furthers her understanding of ways to incorporate their cultures and languages into lessons and activities. She strives to promote a culturally responsive classroom. Take a moment to visualize your classroom. How diverse will it be? How will you accommodate all learning styles and linguistic diversity?

In this chapter, observations of three 9th grade teachers and profiles of seven ELs are described to further strengthen an understanding of the role of students' diverse literacy backgrounds, prior learning experiences, types of cognitive thinking, and the cultural dimensions of collectivism and individualism. We present the components of mutually adaptive learning as an instructional approach to assist students in transitioning to the classroom in a culturally responsive way. The classroom teachers are Mrs. Muñoz, Mrs. Mondicano, and Mr. Ramesh. They teach in a high school north of Boston, Massachusetts. According to the Massachusetts Department of Education, RETELL (Rethinking Equity in the Teaching of English Language Learners) addresses the gap in academic proficiency by ELLs. (Note: English learners are referred to as ELLs in this state.) There are specific training and licensure requirements for core academic teachers and others who supervise or evaluate ELLs. There are varied instructional programs available, from Sheltered English Immersion (SEI), Dual Language (DL), and Students with Limited or Interrupted Formal Education (SLIFE). Visit the **Massachusetts Department of Elementary and Secondary Education—English Language Learners** website at https://www.doe.mass.edu/ele/ for more information.

In Mrs. Muñoz' 9th grade high school math class, there are 23 students, of whom 15 are native speakers of English and 8 are ELs. Mrs. Muñoz is trained in inclusion for ELs in the mainstream classroom and is well aware of scaffolding and differentiating practices. Four ELs are following along with other native-speaking students using Google Translate, a variety of resources, and worksheets that she prepared in their first languages. The other four ELs are sitting in the far back looking at the same resource sheets but doing nothing. As students form groups and work on different practice problems, these same four ELs continue to sit and look at the papers on their desks. Mrs. Muñoz approaches and asks why they, once again, are not doing their work. She points to the resources and worksheets, reminds them that the explanations and word problems are written in their home languages, and that the whole class just did similar types of problems earlier in the week. **The four students smile, look at their papers, but continue to do nothing. Why?**

Later, in joining Mrs. Mondicano's 9th grade English Language Arts (ELA) class, where they are reading *To Kill a Mockingbird,* there are 25 students, of whom 18 are native speakers of English and 7 are ELs. Like Mrs. Muñoz, Mrs. Mondicano is trained in inclusion for ELs in the mainstream classroom and aware of scaffolding and differentiating practices. For example, she has made the book available in the native languages of the ELs, provided bilingual glossaries of key English vocabulary, and shared an outline of important cultural elements from the novel in the students' first languages. During the observation, they work on their first drafts of essays on a topic that they chose from a list Mrs. Mondicano provided. Earlier, the students had worked in small groups to discuss various questions related to the essay topics. **One EL carefully copied sentences from another student's draft. Three other ELs had very little written on their papers.**

There are 18 students in Mr. Ramesh's beginning level ESL class. They come from seven different countries and speak four different languages; most, however, speak Spanish. All the students are learners of English and have been studying the differences between the simple present and present progressive tenses. The lesson begins with a review activity that is a modified version of charades. Students take turns walking to the front of the class, choosing a slip of paper, and performing the action written on it. The rest of the class states in a complete sentence what each student is miming: *Daniel is brushing his teeth.* Once the class repeats the sentence together, each student turns to a partner to practice forming a sentence using the present tense of the same action: *Daniel brushes his teeth every day.* After a while, Mr. Ramesh shares that they are going to read a short story that uses both present and present progressive tenses. He then asks them to turn to page 10 in their books and follow along as he reads the story aloud. When he finishes, he tells them to look at the questions that follow the story and answer them on a separate sheet of paper. They may work alone or with a partner. He also reminds them to look at the black and white drawings that illustrate the story to help answer the questions. **As Mr. Ramesh circulates to check their work, he finds that four of the students are not doing the assignment**.

The three different class observations show that not all ELs participated despite teachers scaffolding the material for learning, providing native languages resources, and, in the case of Mr. Ramesh, employing solid ESL pedagogy. *What are the feelings of these teachers? What are their observations?*

Mrs. Muñoz:

These four ELs are not your typical ninth graders, because they're 16 and 17 years old. I realize that they don't have the same math skills that the rest of the students have, including the other ELs. But this particular group of ELs doesn't seem to take advantage of any of the resources I provide the way the other ELs do. They just ignore what I give to them. I've even tried giving them basic math worksheets from lower grade levels, but these don't seem to help them either.

Mrs. Mondicano:

I have to teach what the curriculum requires. They don't have the English proficiency to read *To Kill a Mockingbird*—but I've provided them with versions in their respective first language. It's very frustrating that they still don't read the book, never mind do the assignments or participate in class. And then there are one or two students who make it a habit to just copy from someone else, no matter how many times I tell them not to.

Mr. Ramesh:

I've taught ESL for years and have been successful in helping my ELs progress in their English language proficiency, but some of these are just so unlike others I've taught. They have so many difficulties with the basics, like even knowing what to do with the book, and most tried-and-true ESL best practices don't work with them. I try to give them as much help as I can, but there's so much they don't know, and I don't know where to begin.

Let's begin by learning a little more about the ELs to whom these three teachers are referring:

Khadijah: 16 years old, from Iraq, native speaker of Arabic. Attended school in her home country for six years but was forced to interrupt her schooling when armed conflicts broke out and it became too dangerous for her to continue.

Muhamed: 16 years old, Somalian, grew up in a refugee camp in Kenya. He speaks Oromo, Arabic, and Kiswahili. He attended Qur'anic school for approximately four years.

Oliver: 15 years old, from a rural area in Guatemala, native speaker of an indigenous Mayan language, K'iche. Speaks some Spanish, had schooling through 3rd grade when he left to work and help the family. Came as an undocumented minor to escape violence and gangs.

Rosalina: 17 years old, Oliver's sister and also a native speaker of K'iche. Her Spanish is stronger than Oliver's because she worked as a domestic for a family in a small city in Guatemala before coming with Oliver as an undocumented minor to the U.S. She also completed through 3rd grade.

Kasongo: 16 years old, from the Democratic Republic of the Congo (formerly Zaire), native speaker of Tshiluba. Kasongo lived most of his life in a refugee camp. He attended school in the camp until he left for the U.S. Class sizes were large, with up to 70 students in a class with few school supplies. Most teachers were not trained and many "teachers" were simply volunteers or young adults in the camp.

Juan: 16 years old, from Mexico, native speaker of Spanish. He is from a rural area, attended school until 6th grade, and worked on the family farm until he arrived in the United States.

Jimena: 14 years old, from a rural area of Honduras, native speaker of Spanish. She never attended school prior to coming to the U.S., but instead worked in the home and on the farm. She can recognize and write her name.

PAUSE AND REFLECT

1. What struck you in reading the brief profiles of these ELs?

2. What did you notice about their prior schooling?

3. How do their schooling experiences compare to that of their peers, whether ELs or other students?

4. How would their schooling experiences impact a teacher's ability to effectively plan instruction?

These seven students represent a specific subpopulation of ELs, **students with limited or interrupted formal education,** or **SLIFE**. These ELs are frequently overlooked and underserved for various reasons. For example, only a few states (e.g., Massachusetts, Minnesota, and New York) require identification of these students as opposed to aggregating them together with other ELs. Even when SLIFE are identified, there are local and state inconsistencies in how they are identified and tracked (Browder, 2014), further complicated by the fact that various labels and acronyms are used. New York state, for instance, refers to these students as SIFE (students with interrupted formal education) while WIDA refers to them as SLIFE. Some researchers and educators refer to these students as "emergent literate" or "low-literate" ELs, terms that can be misleading; however, these terms are also used with young English native speaking children encountering literacy for the first time. While not ideal, the acronym SLIFE does convey the idea of who this subpopulation of ELs is. Identifying SLIFE is critical in order to provide appropriate services. As you will discover, **conventional ESL pedagogy and best practices in differentiation and scaffolding strategies will not best serve the needs of most of SLIFE because they have considerably different needs than other ELs.**

 ## WAYS OF LEARNING CONTINUUM ACTIVITY

The far left of this continuum represents those who have never had any education and no literacy; the far right represents those who have literacy and formal education appropriate to their age.

← ─── →

No education   Age-appropriate education
No literacy   Literacy

(1) Re-read the profiles of the seven SLIFE: Khadijah, Muhamed, Oliver, Rosalina, Kasongo, Juan, and Jimena.
(2) With a partner, discuss where you might place them along this continuum.
  • What factors influenced your decision?
(3) As a class, compare and discuss your answers.
  • Did your classmates' decisions change yours? If yes, how and why?

(Adapted from DeCapua & Marshall, 2011; Marshall & DeCapua, 2015)

More than likely, it was easy to decide where to place Jimena who never attended school prior to enrolling in a U.S. school. For the other students, there were probably questions about how and where to place them, given the little information about their schooling that was provided. The number of years they attended school possibly played an important role. However, while this is a key factor, the quality and type of school is also important, reflected in the 'L' of the acronym, SLIFE, that is, 'limited'.

Limited formal education refers to the fact that not all schooling is the same. Consider the brief description of the type of schooling Kasongo experienced in the refugee camp in which the depth and breadth of subject-area content knowledge students were exposed to was limited by class size, available resources, and teacher background. Classes were very large, there were few supplies of any sort, and many teachers were not trained educators. Most learning in such conditions is based on recitation and memorization; only the teachers may have access to textbooks from which they read and write down what students need to copy and learn.

Oliver, Rosalina, and Juan had some schooling experiences that took place in rural areas of their countries, areas prone to high levels of poverty. Such schools have only limited means and resources, with irregular instruction when teachers and students are absent for economic, family, or weather-related reasons. These schools also emphasize rote learning and memorization (Flaitz, 2016), and students in such schools rarely receive schooling on par with their peers in more economically strong communities. In addition, these schools may focus more on domestic or community skills rather than on academic content knowledge.

Muhamed is a different example of limited formal education. In his case, he attended a Qur'anic school, the purpose of which is for students to memorize and recite the Quran. Such schooling is different from our concept of, and beliefs about, what formal education is.

Another significant factor in identifying SLIFE is the gap between when ELs last attended school in their home country and their age in again starting school after arriving in the U.S. These students represent the 'I' in the acronym; that is, ELs whose schooling was *interrupted* by a minimum of two years, but usually quite a bit more. The reasons for these interruptions vary. Khadijah's schooling was interrupted, for instance, by armed conflict, whereas Oliver, Rosalina, and Juan left school for economic reasons.

PAUSE AND REFLECT

In addition to armed conflict or economic reasons, what are other reasons a SLIFE might experience interrupted schooling?

Because of the long interruption in schooling, you can probably surmise that Rosalina and Juan will have only basic literacy skills. While Khadijah will have greater literacy skills, it is also clear that she will need to learn a new alphabet. For all seven students, it is conclusive that they will not have the subject-area content knowledge of their peers with age-appropriate formal education. **They, like all SLIFE, vary in their placement along the ways of learning continuum based on how much they participated in formal education and the quality of that education.**

As seen in the brief profiles and the continuum activity, SLIFE are unlike other ELs. **In addition to the need to develop English language proficiency, SLIFE must also develop age-appropriate literacy skills, develop**

foundational content knowledge, and acquire an identity as a learner, that is, understand how to behave in school and how to learn (DeCapua, Smathers, & Tang, 2009). Moreover, because their participation in formal education was incomplete or even non-existent, they need to develop the ability to think in cognitively different ways than they have been accustomed to (DeCapua, 2016; DeCapua & Marshall, 2015; 2011). The following is an examination of the implications of the needs of SLIFE with respect to what occurred in the classrooms of Mrs. Muñoz, Mrs. Mondavico, and Mr. Ramesh.

LITERACY

Formal education is predicated on literacy. From the first days of school (and increasingly preschool), teachers focus on developing students' literacy skills. In primary grades, students are instructed on the alphabet, phonics, sight words, basic decoding, comprehension skills, and writing skills. As they progress through the grades, students read and write increasingly complex text. Once they reach secondary school, students no longer explicitly receive literacy instruction unless it is *remedial*. The expectation is that by secondary school students are able to access and transmit information and meaning through the written word.

PAUSE AND REFLECT

1. Make a list of all the ways you have used reading and writing in the last two days, whether personally, in school, or at work. As you prepare your list, remember to include less obvious literacy activities, such as reading the aisle signs in a supermarket, reading road signs, reading a restaurant menu, deciphering a public transportation timetable, or in using an ATM or gas pump.

2. Compare your list with your classmates' lists. Discuss what this activity illustrates about the role of literacy in your lives.

3. Reflect on a time when you visited a foreign country where you were not proficient in the written form of the native language. How did this affect you when trying to find your way somewhere? Needing basic information? Feeling safe, comfortable, or confident?

Few secondary school teachers are prepared to address the literacy needs of SLIFE because they are content specialists. And while they may have been trained on accommodations and differentiation strategies for ELs, like Mrs. Muñoz and Mrs. Mondicano, these strategies are premised on literacy. By the same token, ESL teachers like Mr. Ramesh were trained in conventional best ESL pedagogy. Texts and materials for ELs beyond the first years of schooling presuppose age-appropriate literacy (Montero, Newmaster, & Ledger, 2014; Woods, 2009). SLIFE, however, come with diverse literacy backgrounds as outlined here (DeCapua, Smathers, & Tang, 2009; Haverson & Haynes, 1982).

Pre-Literate

Students have never been exposed to literacy. This may be due to various factors including the possibility that the home language is only an oral language; in other words, the language does not exist in written form. Or, the home language may have only recently received a written form, and/or there may be few materials available written in the home language.

Non-Literate

Students' home language is written, has a relatively long tradition of the written word, but students themselves have not developed literacy.

Semi-Literate, Roman, or Very Similar Alphabet

Students have learned basic decoding skills only.

Semi-Literate, Non-Alphabet Literate

Students have very basic literacy skills and must now develop literacy skills in a new language and writing system.

Although these categories are helpful, not all SLIFE fit neatly into one or the other. For example, Oliver and Rosalina from Guatemala have some literacy in Spanish, the dominant language of their country and a language with a long, rich tradition of the written word. Their home language, however, is K'iche, an indigenous Mayan language. K'iche, a very different language than Spanish, has a long history of its own, but is generally not the language of school. Thus, the basic literacy skills Oliver and Rosalina do have are not in their home language and not in a language in which they are proficient.

In addition to reading and writing skills, literacy teaches people to interact with the world differently. With the development of literacy, representational forms take on meaning that do not exist in the three-dimensional, concrete world of everyday life. A popular teaching strategy is to use pictures to help students learn vocabulary, illustrate text meaning, and support information in text. **Yet, for those with no or low literacy, such pictures, particularly if they are drawings or diagrams, may be of little or no help because it is literacy that develops people's ability to interpret images**. In their extensive review of research on literacy and adult SLIFE, Bigelow and Schwarz (2010) observed that when people are not literate or have very low literacy, they have difficulty processing two-dimensional forms, such as diagrams, line drawings, and even photos, particularly black and white ones. These are representations of actual, tangible items that they have not necessarily learned to "read." Therefore, any drawings, diagrams, or other abstract two-dimensional representations that Mrs. Muñoz, Mrs. Mondicano, or Mr. Ramesh incorporate into their lessons most likely would not be scaffolds for the SLIFE in their classrooms. Instead, these drawings or abstracts would be additional obstacles given the students' low or nonexistent literacy skills.

The resources and scaffolds provided by Mrs. Muñoz and Mrs. Mondicano demand literacy. Whether information is provided in the home language or not is irrelevant if students are unable to use print to access and transmit information. And, in Mrs. Muñoz' case, using worksheets from elementary school is not an effective strategy. Elementary school worksheets typically have pictures, stories, and vocabulary appropriate for younger children, not high school adolescents. Also, worksheets are a decontextualized task based on underlying academic ways of thinking.

With respect to Mr. Ramesh, he is a language teacher, not a literacy teacher. His focus is on developing English reading and comprehension skills of ELs using ESL best practices. While these are effective with ELs, they are not effective with SLIFE who do not have the same age-appropriate literacy skills. Some SLIFE, like Kasango and some of the others profiled here, will have decoding and copying skills, but they will not be accustomed to drawing meaning from text (e.g., locating information in a story to answer questions). They will also find it difficult to construct sentences without additional scaffolds, such as sentence frames. Other SLIFE, such as Jimena, who has no literacy, will initially find any sentence or paragraph overwhelming until they have learned the very basics of reading and writing.

DECONTEXTUALIZED TASKS BASED ON ACADEMIC WAYS OF THINKING

At all grade levels, including adult education, students are expected to engage in decontextualized school tasks. The purpose of such tasks is to allow students to build knowledge and demonstrate mastery of knowledge (DeCapua & Marshall, 2011; Marshall & DeCapua, 2013). **However, like the seven students profiled, SLIFE do not have the educational background of their peers, ELs or otherwise**. Because these tasks are based on academic ways of thinking, how to do them will be largely unfamiliar to SLIFE.

Before beginning a discussion on decontextualized tasks based on academic ways of thinking, complete the next activity.

 EXAMINING DECONTEXTUALIZED TASKS ACTIVITY

(1) Look at the list of common classroom tasks.

(2) Check all the ones familiar to you.

_____ completing KWL charts (What I Know, What I Want to Know, What I Have Learned)
_____ completing graphic organizers, such as a Venn Diagram or a T-Chart
_____ interpreting graphs
_____ matching or sorting information
_____ reading maps
_____ labeling items
_____ looking up words in dictionaries or glossaries
_____ answering true/false questions
_____ answering multiple-choice questions

(3) Share with a partner what kind(s) of thinking you believe underlie each classroom task.

This activity lists many common classroom tasks, all of which presuppose literacy and academic ways of thinking. One way to understand academic ways of thinking is to consider **Bloom's Taxonomy**, proposed by Bloom in 1956 and later revised by associates (Anderson et al., 2001). This is a framework of ways of thinking intended to assist educators in seeing the different types of thinking in order to move students from initial levels of thinking to increasingly complex ones. What is not immediately evident is that this taxonomy, like others of this nature, is based on specific and abstract ways of understanding and interpreting the world developed through participation in formal education. **Formal education** is characterized by the centrality of print, abstract modes of organizing information and knowledge, the separation of knowledge into subject areas, and teaching students how to learn (Flynn, 2007; Robinson, 2011).

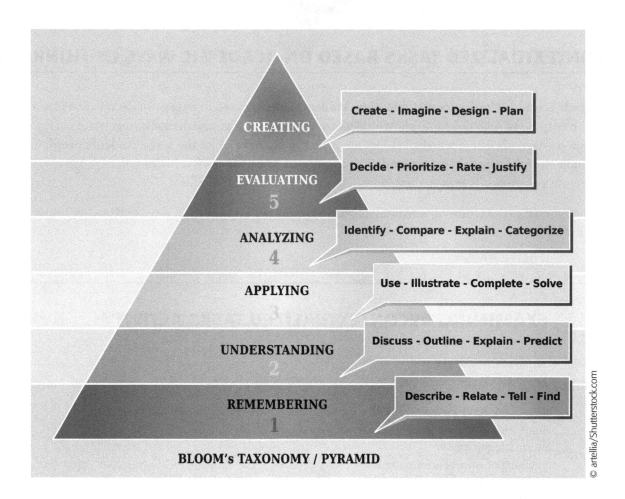

Determining the underlying way of thinking of decontextualized tasks is easier in some cases than in others. A **Venn Diagram**, for example, is a graphic organizer made up of two overlapping circles (**Figure 3.1**). From the design of the graphic, it is apparent that the academic way of thinking is to compare and contrast (assuming that you know how to read this type of diagram). Students add information from one source into one circle and add different, contrasting information into the opposite circle. They write shared information into the middle where the two circles overlap.

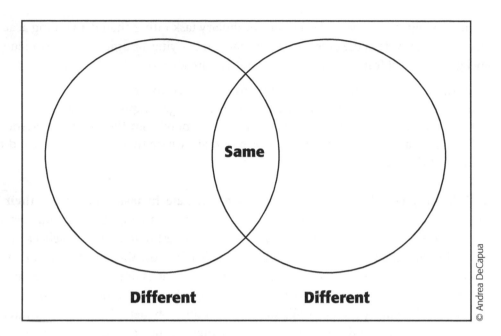

Figure 3.1   Venn Diagram.

Another common classroom task is **labeling.** In elementary schools, for instance, students develop map skills by labeling the continents and geographical features, such as bodies of water, rivers, and mountain ranges. Think about what is taking place in Mr. Ramesh's beginning ESL class in the following activity.

PAUSE AND REFLECT

Mr. Ramesh is working with his ELs on "geography vocabulary" in the context of where the students come from. They have seen photos of each other's countries and important geographical features in their regions, such as major volcanoes in Central America, major lakes in sub-Saharan Africa, mountain ranges in Asia, and rivers in the Middle East. The students are now supposed to complete a worksheet with a colorful drawing of a stylized landscape and labeling on the various geographical features they have studied (e.g., river, mountain, desert).

In the class, there are four of the SLIFE mentioned earlier: Jimena, Rosalina, Oliver, and Kasango. Because he knows that this is Jimena's first time in school, Mr. Ramesh prepared labels for her to stick in place rather than trying to write the words.

- Jimena pushes the labels around on her desk without sticking them to the worksheet.
- Rosalina and Oliver turn to each other and chat about the mountain where their village is.
- Kasango draws a picture of a water barrel from which his family used to get their water while living in the refugee camp.

Aside from low language proficiency and low literacy skills, what other reasons can you suggest why these SLIFE are not participating in this labeling task?

On the surface, map labeling may seem like a basic vocabulary task rather than demanding academic ways of thinking. However, the opposite is the case. There are many underlying assumptions for students to be able to successfully label geographical features, namely that students are able to:

- interpret drawings and pictures as representations of the real world.
- separate physical entities into groups or classes, in this case, geographical features.
- extrapolate knowledge and information (i.e., move and apply from their own experience to the more abstract and wide-ranging, such as the river or mountain where they lived to rivers and mountains as geographical entities elsewhere).

All learners feel disengaged when they are asked to participate in tasks that, from their perspective, are difficult, pointless, and incomprehensible. Yet, teachers cannot assume that the four depicted here are disengaged. Instead, take the perspective that they are trying their best to follow the teacher's instructions. For Jimena, who has no literacy, the labels are a meaningless jumble of words. She may or may not know the letters of the alphabet since she can recognize and write her name, but this does not mean that she can decode words and assign meaning to words, especially in a new language, English. Before Jimena can do a labeling task, she first needs to develop rudimentary literacy skills starting with the alphabet, phonological awareness, phonics, common sight word recognition, and the features of basic sentences such as capitalization and periods.

Rosalina and Oliver may or may not have personal familiarity with volcanoes, but since volcanoes are generally a type of mountain, they have made a valid association to something familiar to them (e.g., the mountain where their village is located). This does not mean that Rosalina and Oliver are ready to generalize from "their" mountain to all mountains to a visual drawing of mountains, no matter how colorful. For them, the drawing on the handout lacks context. The geographical features on a two-dimensional landscape are not real to them. Being able to infer meaning from visual representational and decontextualized text is an inherent part of becoming literate and developing academic ways of thinking (Ardila et al., 2010).

Literacy and formal education create specific pathways in the brain, different from those evident in people who do not have age-appropriate literacy and formal education (Cole, 2005). **Because SLIFE have had vastly different prior learning experiences, they have developed different cognitive pathways (i.e., different ways of thinking than those expected in students who have received formal education)**. It is critical to understand what academic ways of thinking entail. When teachers understand this, they can understand how assuming SLIFE share these ways of thinking sets them up for failure. Teachers must not expect them to know how to engage in decontextualized tasks premised on ways of thinking unfamiliar to them. Only by explicitly introducing and practicing these new, academic ways of thinking and the new, decontextualized tasks will SLIFE develop new ways of thinking, behaving, and understanding the world—ways that are typical and expected in a classroom setting.

In addition to literacy and decontextualized school tasks based on academic ways of thinking, the U.S. formal educational system encompasses a vastly different world than what SLIFE are used to. Think back to what Mrs. Mondicano said, ". . . *there are one or two students who make it a habit to just copy from someone else, no matter how many times I tell them not to.*" A significant reason this may be occurring is the students' prior learning experiences. SLIFE have had most, and, in some cases like Jimena, all their learning experiences take place outside formal educational

settings. Such learning is referred to as **informal ways of learning.** This is learning that is situated in the community and family and learning that is based on sociocultural practices and needs; learning occurs when appropriate and necessary, regardless of age (Paradise & Rogoff, 2009; Rogoff, 2003). Such learning is concrete, pragmatic, and immediately relevant. Individuals learn what they need when they need it (Mercer & Howe, 2012). It is also learning in which learners and mentors work closely together: learners observe, imitate, receive (generally nonverbal) feedback from more experienced persons, and practice repeatedly until they achieve mastery (Mejia-Arauz, Rogoff, Daxter, & Majafi, 2007). For SLIFE coming from such learning experiences, copying from a more knowledgeable student would be acceptable and appropriate.

Formal education, in contrast to informal ways of learning, refers to learning that occurs within a formal educational setting located in specially designed buildings with classrooms composed of age cohorts led by highly trained teachers. Teaching and learning are guided by set curricula in which knowledge is separated into discrete subject areas (Robinson, 2011). Individual effort, responsibility, and assessment are regarded as vital to learning. Students are held individually accountable for their work and expected to work on their own much of the time. Even when cooperative learning and group learning are encouraged, ultimately, each student is assessed on his or her own work (Morrison, 2009). Thus, from Mrs. Mondicano's perspective, copying from another student is unacceptable.

THE DIMENSIONS OF COLLECTIVISM AND INDIVIDUALISM

There are significant differences among cultures in how members view themselves with respect to others, referred to as **collectivism** and **individualism**. These two concepts are not two opposite constructs, but rather describe cultural dimensions that place cultures along a continuum of how much they reflect principal values of collectivism or individualism (DeCapua, 2016; DeCapua & Marshall, 2011).

Cultures in which members see themselves primarily as highly interconnected, interdependent parts of a whole are termed collectivistic or "we" cultures. The "whole" refers to the perceived group to which one belongs. This group may be the extended family, ethnic, social, or other group. One's relationship within and to one's group is the focus of a person's identity and greatly influences responsibilities, behaviors, and decisions (Li, 2012). In collectivistic cultures, members value interdependence and share a strong sense of mutual obligation to the other members of their group.

Those cultures in which the emphasis is on individuals and independence are regarded as individualistic, or "me" cultures. In these cultures, people have strong relationships with others, but the emphasis is on individual wants, desires, and responsibilities (Hofstede, 1986). Members of more individualistic cultures value personal independence, autonomy, and self-reliance.

The U.S. is a highly individualistic culture, although there are subcultural differences. The individualistic orientation of the U.S. is evident in the educational system with the emphasis on individual participation, achievement, and accountability. A common buzzword in education is **scaffolding**, which conveys the idea that students are provided necessary supports until they are able to learn or do the work on their own.

Since most cultures globally range more to the collectivistic end of the continuum than to the individualistic end (Triandis, 1995), the majority of SLIFE come from collectivistic cultures (United States Government, Department of Homeland Security, 2012). Keeping this in mind, revisit Mrs. Mondicano's comment, "... *there are one or two students who make it a habit to just copy from someone else, no matter how many times I tell them not to.*" In addition to evaluating this behavior on the part of Mrs. Mondicano's SLIFE as reflective of their prior experiences in the context of informal ways of learning, you can also see it as an aspect of collectivistic behavior. **In collectivistic cultures, sharing, mutual cooperation, and assistance are the norm. Copying—and letting someone copy from you—is seen as providing support for learning.** In the individualistic culture of the U.S., student individual effort and performance are the standard, and teachers rarely regard copying from others as part of the learning process. Likewise, a common tendency for SLIFE to move around a classroom to seek aid from others, even after the teacher has instructed students to work on their own, is not, from their collectivistic perspective, disobedience or disregard for the teacher, but a normal practice to help them accomplish the assigned work.

 THE CHOPSTICKS ACTIVITY

Nicole and Jared Truong had a loud, angry argument over something trivial. After much shouting at each other, they stormed off to their rooms, convinced that they couldn't possibly be brother and sister and that they hated each other. Their father, Bao, a Vietnamese immigrant, went to their rooms and insisted that they follow him to the kitchen table. He put chopsticks in front of them, told them to choose one, and see if they could break it. Nicole and Jared easily broke their chosen chopstick in half. Bao proceeded to tie four other chopsticks together, stating that each chopstick represented one of the members of their family—himself, Nicole, Jared, and their mother. Bao handed the bundled chopsticks to Jared and dared him to break them. No matter how hard he tried, Jared couldn't break them. When he gave up, Bao explained to Nicole and Jared that one chopstick was easy to break, but together they were not; just like they, together as a family, could withstand everything.

- Discuss how this story illustrates the concept of collectivism.

(Adapted from DeCapua & Marshall, 2011, p.12)

FUTURE ORIENTATION

Another central aspect of formal education is the emphasis on the future. Students are expected to learn in preparation for an upcoming test, in order to move to the next level, class, or grade, and to prepare them for life after school. **SLIFE**, on the other hand, **are not used to thinking of the future in the way students are trained to do in formal education**. At the beginning of this chapter, Mr. Ramesh stated most tried-and-true ESL best practices were not successful with his SLIFE. A chapter in his ESL textbook focused on the present tense in the context of different careers (e.g., doctor, teacher, policeman, pilot, nurse). The non-SLIFE ELs had no difficulty with the question, "What do you want to do?" The SLIFE, on the other hand, did. They either said that they wanted to be a doctor or didn't respond at all. Aside from any linguistic or literacy issues, there is a conceptual matter here. For SLIFE, their lives have been primarily, if not exclusively, rooted in the concrete here and now of the immediate relevance of informal ways of learning and survival needs.

SLIFE may not be able to respond to the question of what they want to do, because it is not the kind of forward thinking previously fostered in their lives. When SLIFE do respond to such a question, they typically answer with something along the lines of "doctor" because they may be familiar with a particular profession, they may feel in awe of or have great respect for it, or other such reasons without knowing or understanding the long trajectory that pursuing such a career entails.

In summary, this chapter has explored some key differences between the learning paradigm of SLIFE and those of formal education:

- a preference for oral transmission versus the centrality of literacy
- pragmatic tasks ground in socio-cultural experiences versus decontextualized tasks based on academic ways of thinking
- collectivism versus individualism
- immediate relevance versus future orientation

At this juncture, the focus will be on what educators can do to make formal education accessible and comprehensible to SLIFE, a subpopulation of ELs, that is frequently ignored, shunted aside, and underserved.

WHAT CAN TEACHERS DO?

When SLIFE enter the world of formal education, they enter a profoundly different culture, school culture, and experience cultural dissonance, the sense that school culture is confusing, challenging, incomprehensible, and alienating (Masinde, Jacquet, & Moore, 2014). At the same time, when educators like Mrs. Muñoz, Mrs. Mondicano, and Mr. Ramesh first encounter SLIFE, they, too, experience this cultural dissonance, since their training has not adequately prepared them for such significantly different students. The conventional approach in teaching SLIFE is to use pedagogical practices familiar to educators, continually modifying them in the hopes of addressing the needs of this population. In general, a deficit view tends to prevail (i.e., a focus on what SLIFE *can't* do or "still" haven't learned) (Roy & Roxas, 2011). Viewed through the lens of formal education, SLIFE are certainly "lacking." However, SLIFE have extensive experiences, knowledge, and skills (or "funds of knowledge") (González, Moll, & Amanti, 2005) foreign to most educators, because these are not part of, nor valued in, formal education and school culture.

SLIFE come with considerably different backgrounds than other ELs and, unlike these students, must learn and develop literacy skills, content knowledge, and academic ways of thinking. As you will recall, SLIFE do vary in their exposure to and participation in formal education and in their literacy skills. Jimena, for instance, never attended school and has no literacy skills or familiarity with formal education. Khadijah, on the other hand, did have six years of education, has literacy skills in her home language, and has familiarity with formal education. Nevertheless, all SLIFE need a different pedagogical approach than conventional ones developed for ELs with age-appropriate formal education. SLIFE, unlike other ELs, must make a major shift in their accustomed learning paradigm when they enter U.S. classrooms. To facilitate this radical change, educators must employ different pedagogy for SLIFE to help them successfully navigate the demands and expectations of formal education.

Given the considerable needs of SLIFE, this population is best served in a newcomer program or newcomer school with teachers who are qualified in early literacy development and aware of and able to implement pedagogical approaches for this population. Well-designed and structured newcomer programs and classes for SLIFE provide these students essential foundational training to help reduce cultural dissonance, foster academic success, and close the achievement gap. Newcomer programs are defined as "programs designed for recent immigrants at the secondary school level who have little or no English proficiency, and limited or no formal education in their native countries" (Colorín Colorado, 2020). Their goals are to help children prepare to enter general education classes by developing linguistic survival skills as they adapt to a new culture.

In addition, it is critical that educators have an instructional approach to help them in designing appropriate pedagogy for SLIFE. One such instructional approach is the Mutually Adaptive Learning Paradigm® (MALP®), initially developed in the 1990s for working with Hmong refugees in Green Bay, Wisconsin. It has since been widely embraced by educators.

THE MUTUALLY ADAPTIVE LEARNING PARADIGM (MALP®)

The **Mutually Adaptive Learning Paradigm (MALP®)** is an instructional approach designed specifically for this population (DeCapua, Marshall, & Tang, 2020; DeCapua & Marshall, 2015, 2011; Marshall & DeCapua, 2013). MALP® provides educators with a means for understanding what works best with SLIFE, what doesn't, and why. MALP® is premised on the belief that educators must transition SLIFE to the demands and expectations through a culturally responsive, mutually adaptive approach whereby *both* educators and SLIFE adapt. As noted in the previous chapter, **culturally responsive teaching** requires that educators understand deep, underlying cultural factors that affect teaching and learning in order to develop effective strategies and a conducive learning environment (Gay, 2000; 2010). Mutually adapting requires that there are **certain crucial elements from the SLIFE learning paradigm that educators:**

- *accept* and incorporate into their classroom.
- *combine* with crucial elements from the paradigm of formal education.
- *focus* on critical, new elements in the paradigm of formal education.

To understand this better, we examine MALP® in greater detail (see DeCapua & Marshall, 2011; 2015 and Marshall & DeCapua, 2013 for in-depth discussion). As you continue reading, think about Mrs. Muñoz, Mrs. Mondavico, Mrs. Ramesh, and the seven SLIFE (Khadijah, Muhamed, Kasongo, Oliver, Juan, Rosalina, and Jimena).

In the MALP® approach, learning is conceptualized as consisting of three major components. These three components work together so that the entire approach, as its name indicates, is mutually adaptive. Both SLIFE and educators adapt to assist SLIFE in transitioning to the expectations and demands of formal education.

1. Accept Conditions for Learning

The first component is *accept conditions for learning*. Conditions refer to what needs to be in place in the classroom to support learning. SLIFE come from traditions of informal ways of learning whereby they immediately implement what they are learning. Whether they are engaged in cooking, farming, crafts, or other activities, they learn the techniques, steps, and skills as they are doing them. Learning is *immediately relevant*. Jimena learned her household skills in the context of working as a domestic; Juan learned his agricultural skills by working on the family farm. They did not participate in formal education first. In formal education, much, if not most, of what students learn has no relevance to later jobs or careers but is centered on learning how to learn (Bruner, 1966).

SLIFE are generally members of collectivistic cultures characterized by close, mutually dependent relationships. As noted in the discussion of collectivism and individualism, they are not used to or comfortable with learning solo. In informal ways of learning, their learning experiences occurred within their community, family, and/ or group. In classrooms, they need to become *interconnected with one another,* that is, develop a sense of community and close ties with members of their learning environment.

PAUSE AND REFLECT

What examples of immediate relevance and interconnectedness from this chapter or in your experience with SLIFE come to mind?

Teachers accept the SLIFE conditions of *immediate relevancy* and *interconnectedness* by ensuring that something in every lesson in every class is immediately relevant to the lives and needs of SLIFE. This immediate relevance does not refer to the curriculum or subject matter, but to students' personal experiences and funds of knowledge. Teachers also strive to foster interconnectedness and a sense of community among the students as well as with them. For example, in Mr. Ramesh's geography vocabulary lesson, he might have begun with students identifying and talking about geographical features important in their lives, such as the mountain on which Rosalina and Oliver's village was located. Since the topic is related to something in their lives that they share with others, it is immediately relevant and builds interconnectedness when the other students share their own landscapes.

2. Combine Processes for Learning

The second component is *combine the processes for learning* from the learning paradigm of SLIFE and from that of formal education. Processes in the MALP® approach refer to how people prefer to learn and share information. For SLIFE, oral transmission is the norm; in formal education, literacy is paramount. To transition SLIFE to literacy, teachers diligently integrate (i.e., *combine oral and written modes*) with one another using basic literacy techniques commonly used in child literacy development but generally unfamiliar to ESL and content-area teachers. These early literacy strategies vary significantly from such conventional techniques where students discuss, then write or read, and then discuss again. Instead, basic literacy techniques, such as sound-letter correspondence, choral reading, and word pointing and reading aloud are employed. Teachers should not, however, use materials developed for young readers; this would be inappropriate for adolescents or adults.

The other element in this second component is that teachers combine group responsibility with individual accountability. You are likely already familiar with the concept of **cooperative learning**, which is much more than simply putting students into groups. One of the five essential elements found in cooperative learning is structuring for positive interdependence, a strategy that could prove useful when working with SLIFE, especially those whose values were formed in a "we" culture. SLIFE are accustomed to working with others because of their prior experience in informal ways of learning with its emphasis on mentoring and their (generally) collectivistic backgrounds. They are not comfortable with the demand to learn or demonstrate mastery on their own in the classroom and on assessments. To transition SLIFE to individual accountability, teachers must provide opportunities in class where SLIFE can work together but where they must also complete something by themselves. This combining of *group responsibility* and *shared responsibility* prepares SLIFE for situations when they cannot work with someone else, such as during testing.

 Combining the oral and written modes is different than thinking in terms of the four skill areas: speaking, listening, reading, and writing.

(1) Research early literacy strategies for adolescents and/or adults.

(2) Share with the class one strategy you believe would be useful and effective.

3. *Focus on New Activities for Learning*

The third component is *focus on new activities for learning*. Earlier we explored how students are expected to engage in decontextualized school-based tasks based on academic ways of thinking, such as defining, categorizing, and analyzing. For SLIFE to develop these new ways of thinking, teachers must explicitly instruct them in how to engage in decontextualized school-based tasks that reflect academic ways of thinking. Initially, when the task itself is unfamiliar, teachers scaffold the task by using familiar language and familiar content. Once SLIFE have learned how to engage in a specific task and employ an academic way of thinking, teachers introduce new language and content.

For example, in Mrs. Muñoz' 9th grade high school math class, students are expected to solve word problems focusing on mean, median, and mode, a common task requiring an academic way of thinking. Because word problems are already a challenge for her ELs, and especially SLIFE, Mrs. Muñoz makes the task appear familiar simply by using familiar content. She writes several numbers on the board, telling the students they are the number of students in each homeroom class. As she writes the names of the teachers next to each number, students murmur, "That's my homeroom!" while they wonder what their teacher is doing. Next, she reviews the concepts of mean, median, and mode, asking students to help with calculations. By the time they finish, they have created an original word problem, albeit orally (a condition for learning for many SLIFE), and students feel engaged and successful. Together, they create another word problem based on how many students are wearing certain colors, and finally students come up with their own word problems in small cooperative learning groups. By scaffolding knowledge familiar to students (i.e., number of students in their homerooms), Mrs. Muñoz engages students with the more abstract concepts of mean, median, mode, and word problems. In one lesson, she effortlessly decontextualizes several school-based tasks.

 1. Choose a decontextualized task for students from a content-area textbook or website.

2. Outline what familiar language and content you would use to scaffold the task and underlying way of thinking before your SLIFE would do the actual task.

To summarize, the Mutually Adaptive Learning Paradigm, or MALP® is outlined in **Figure 3.2**.

All three components of MALP® need to be present in a lesson for the instruction to be fully aligned with the model and for SLIFE to benefit from this culturally responsive, mutually adaptive approach. To help in implementing MALP®, teachers can use the MALP® Teacher Planning Checklist (**Figure 3.3**), designed as a planning and reflection tool to assist in the full implementation of MALP®. It can also be used by coaches and others as an observation tool.

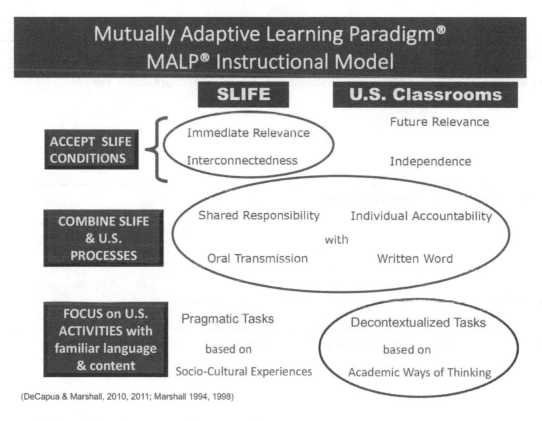

(DeCapua & Marshall, 2010, 2011; Marshall 1994, 1998)

Figure 3.2 Schematic of the Mutually Adaptive Learning Paradigm (MALP®).

Mutually Adaptive Learning Paradigm®
MALP® Teacher Planning Checklist

A. Accept Conditions for Learning
A1. I am making this lesson/project immediately relevant to my students' lives. How?
A2. I am helping students develop and maintain interconnectedness with each other. How?
B. Combine Processes for Learning
B1. I am incorporating both shared responsibility and individual accountability. How?
B2. I am scaffolding the written word through oral interaction. How?
C. Focus on New Activities for Learning
C1. I am focusing on decontextualized tasks requiring academic ways of thinking. How?
C2. I am making these new tasks accessible with familiar language and content. How?

Figure 3.3   MALP® Teacher Planning Checklist.

Extended Thinking and Synthesis Questions

1. Using any textbook, make a list of the decontextualized tasks that students are asked to do. Analyze each one to determine the underlying academic way(s) of thinking. For example, students may be asked to sort words into groups (e.g., historical person, famous document, historical events):

Abraham Lincoln	Declaration of Independence	Slavery
Thomas Jefferson	Emancipation Declaration	Freedom from England

The task is sorting; the underlying academic way of thinking is categorization. In addition, this is a literacy activity. Not only must students be able to read the words, but by paying attention to punctuation, they have an important clue to help them in this task.

2. Read the following scenario.

The SLIFE in Mrs. Cranshaw's class are engaged in creating text through the learning experience approach (LEA) (VanAllen & VanAllen, 1967). The LEA approach essentially consists of four steps: (1) share an experience; (2) create text based on the experiences; (3) read and revise this text; (4) read and re-read the text. Read the next scenario about the LEA in Mrs. Cranshaw's class:

The class planted three different kinds of seeds one month ago in small containers. Some of these containers were placed on a window shelf. Others were put on Mrs. Cranshaw's desk, which is over in one corner of the room, not too far from the windows. The remaining containers were located on a bookshelf in an area with little natural light. They have been watching the seeds sprout and recording their observations on a simple table. Now they are talking about what they have observed over the last month. Yasmineh says that in her family's home, they only plant vegetables where there is a lot of light because they don't grow otherwise. Pedro adds that where he comes from, light isn't as important as the water because there is "no much." As the students discuss what they have been seeing in the class, the relationship between light and growth, and some of their personal experiences, Mrs. Cranshaw writes what they say on a sheet of chart paper. Once they have produced a paragraph, she stops, and the students practice reading the text. First, they read the text chorally as Mrs. Cranshaw points to the words. They then take turns reading the sentences as another student points to the words. The last activity of the day is for students to copy at least two sentences into their own notebooks. Planting and watching seeds grow under different environmental conditions is a learning experience many elementary school teachers will be familiar with. What is significant in Mrs. Cranshaw's class is that she is implementing this with high school SLIFE and intentionally incorporating the elements of MALP®.

a. Refer to **Figure 3.3**: The Mutually Adaptive Learning Paradigm (MALP®). Under *Accept Conditions*, we see the word "interconnectedness." Under *Combine Processes*, we see the phrase "group responsibility." Remember that these two terms are different. ***Interconnectedness*** refers to developing and maintaining a web of relationships within the class. ***Group responsibility*** refers to working together and sharing learning.

Reread the scenario from Mrs. Cranshaw's class, and identify what you see as promoting either interconnectedness or group responsibility.

b. Refer again to **Figure 3.3**: The Mutually Adaptive Learning Paradigm (MALP®). For *Combine Processes*, how do you see Mrs. Cranshaw combining the oral mode with the written mode? Group responsibility with individual accountability?

c. Earlier in this chapter, we looked at Venn Diagrams. Discuss how Mrs. Cranshaw could incorporate a Venn Diagram into a later lesson and what extensions she might make to develop academic ways of thinking. Remember to begin with familiar language and content and then, when the task and academic way of thinking are familiar, expand to academic language and content knowledge.

3. Shadow one SLIFE for at least two days.

▶ Describe the student, why s/he is SLIFE and what this student is experiencing in the classroom.

▶ Explain how s/he is accessing (or not) language, content, and school tasks based on academic ways of thinking.

▶ Discuss what the teacher (or teachers) is doing to support the SLIFE.

4. Observe SLIFE classes for at least two days.

▶ Describe the students, why they are SLIFE, what struggles they are having, what works well with them, and evaluate what you observe based on what you learned from this chapter.

▶ Offer suggestions for change and explain why.

5. Use the MALP® Teaching Planning Checklist to evaluate a lesson you have planned or observed.

▶ Consider what changes and modifications you would make based on what you learned in this chapter.

REFERENCES

ABC English. (2020). http://www.teachabcenglish.com/

Anderson, L. W., Krathwohl, Airasian, P. W., Cruikshank, K. A., Mayer, R. E., Pintrich, P. R. Raths, & J. Wittrock, M. C. (2001). *A taxonomy for learning, teaching, and assessing: A revision of Bloom's taxonomy of educational objectives, abridged edition.* Pearson Education.

Ardila, A., Bertolucci, P., Braga, L., Castro-Caldes, A., Judd, T., Kosmidis, M., Matute, E., Nitrini, R., Ostrosky-Solis, F., & Rosselli, M. (2010). Illiteracy: The neuropsychology of cognition without reading. *Archives of Clinical Neuropsychology, 25,* 689–712.

Bigelow, M., & Schwarz, R. (2010). Adult English language learners with limited literacy. Paper commissioned by the National Institute for Literacy.

Bridges to Academic Success. (2020). http://bridges-sifeproject.com/

Browder, C. (2014). English learners with limited or interrupted formal education: Risk and resilience in educational outcomes. (Unpublished doctoral dissertation). University of Maryland.

Bruner, J. (1966). *Toward a theory of instruction.* Harvard University Press.

Cole, M. (2005). Cross-cultural and historical perspectives on the developmental consequences of education. *Human Development, 48,* 195–216.

¡Colorín Colorado! (2020). http://www.colorincolorado.org/faq/what-are-newcomer-programs-what-are-their-pros-and-cons

DeCapua, A. (2019). *SLIFE what every teacher needs to know.* University of Michigan Press.

DeCapua, A. (2016). Reaching students with limited or interrupted formal education: A culturally responsive approach. *Language and Linguistics Compass, 10,* 225–237.

DeCapua A., & Marshall, H. W. (2011). *Breaking new ground: Teaching students with limited or interrupted formal education in U.S. secondary schools.* University of Michigan Press.

DeCapua, A., & Marshall, H. W. (2015). Reframing the conversation about students with limited or interrupted formal education: From achievement gap to cultural dissonance. *NASSP Bulletin, 99,* 356–370.

DeCapua, A., Marshall, H. W., & Tang, L. (2020). *Meeting the needs of SLIFE: A guide for educators* (2nd ed.). University of Michigan Press.

DeCapua, Smathers, W., & Tang, F. (2009). *Meeting the needs of students with limited or interrupted schooling.* University of Michigan Press.

Emergent Readers. (2020). http://www.emergentreaders.org/

English Language Learner University (E-LLU): Literacy Information and Communication System (LINCS). (2020). https://lincs.ed.gov

ESL Literacy Network. (2020). https://centre.bowvalleycollege.ca/networks/esl-literacy-network

Flaitz, J. (2016) *Understanding your refugee and immigrant students: An educational, cultural and linguistic guide.* University of Michigan Press.

Flynn. J. (2007). *What is intelligence?* Cambridge University Press.

Gay, G. (2000). *Culturally responsive teaching: Theory, research and practice.* Teachers College Press.

Gay, G. (2010). *Culturally responsive teaching: Theory, research and practice* (2nd ed.). Teachers College Press.

González, N., Moll, L., & Amanti, C. (2005). (Eds.). *Funds of knowledge: Theorizing practices in households, communities, and classrooms* (pp. 167–181). Lawrence Erlbaum.

Haverson, W., & Haynes, J. (1982). ESL/Literacy for adult learners. In S. Behrens (Ed.), *Language in education: Theory and practice* (Number 49). Center for Applied Linguistics.

Hofstede, G. (1986). Cultural differences in teaching and learning. *International Journal of Intercultural Relations, 10,* 301–320.

Li, J. (2012). *Cultural foundations of learning: East and West.* Cambridge.

Marshall, H. W., & DeCapua, A. (2013). *Making the transition to classroom success: Culturally responsive teaching for struggling language learners.* University of Michigan Press.

Marshall, H. W., DeCapua, A., & Antolini, C. (2010). Engaging English language learners with limited or interrupted formal education. *Educator's Voice, 3,* 56–65.

Masinde, M., Jacquet, M., & Moore, D. (2014). An integrated framework for immigrant children and youth's school integration: A focus on African Francophone in British Columbia-Canada. *International Journal of Education, 6,* 90–107.

Massachusetts Department of Education for ELLs. (2020). https://www.doe.mass.edu/ele/

Mejia-Arauz, R., Rogoff, B., Daxter, A., & Najafi, B. (2007). Cultural variation in children's social organization. *Child Development, 78,* 1001–1014.

Mercer, N., & Howe, C. (2012). Explaining the dialogic processes of teaching and learning: The value and potential of sociocultural theory. *Learning, Culture and Social Interaction, 1,* 12–21.

Montero, K., Newmaster, S., & Ledger, S. (2014). Exploring early reading instructional strategies to advance the print literacy development of adolescent SLIFE. *Journal of Adolescent & Adult Literacy, 58(1),* 59–69.

Morrison, G. (2009). *Teaching in America* (5th ed.). Pearson.

Multilingual Minnesota. (2020). http://www.multilingualminnesota.org/glossary.php

Mutually Adaptive Learning Paradigm® Instructional Approach (MALP®). (2020). http://malpeducation.com/what-is-malp/

Paradise, R., & Rogoff, B. (2009). Side by side: Learning by observing and pitching in. *Ethos, 37,* 102–138.

Robinson, K. (2011). *Out of our minds: Learning to be creative.* John Wiley and Sons.

Rogoff, B. (2003). *The cultural nature of human development.* Oxford University Press.

Roy, L., & Roxas, K. (2011). Exploring counter-stories of Somali Bantu refugees: Experiences in "doing school." *Harvard Educational Review, 81,* 521–542.

Triandis, H. (1995). *Individualism and collectivism.* Westview Press.

United States Government, Department of Homeland Security. (2012). *Yearbook of Immigration Statistics 2012.* Retrieved from https://www.dhs.gov/immigration-statistics/yearbook/2015

Van Allen, R., & Van Allen, C. (1967). *Language experience activities.* Houghton Mifflin.

Woods, A. (2009). Learning to be literate: Issues of pedagogy for recently arrived refugee youth in Australia. *Critical Inquiry in Language Studies, 6* (1/2), 81–101.

WEBSITE RESOURCES

¡Colorín Colorado!
Link: https://www.colorincolorado.org/

ESOL in Higher Ed
Link: https://www.esolinhighered.org

MALP
Link: http://malpeducation.com/what-is-malp/

3A

Activity!

SLIFE

Perspective is everything. Teachers must put themselves in someone else's shoes every day to be empathetic and to support their students. You are in college, so you have an education. But imagine if you were to move to another country next month where you could not speak the language, were unfamiliar with the culture, and enrolled in graduate classes.

Country and language:

What challenges do you expect to have in class?

What challenges do you expect to have outside of class?

What can your instructors do to help?

3B

Activity!

SLIFE

Name: _____

A continuum is like a spectrum. Items can be placed along it from one degree to the next, with two items rarely occupying the same spot. Teachers must assess ELs and other students from many perspectives in order to effectively differentiate instruction. Practice using a continuum here.

Identify 6 family members, including yourself. Place them along the continuum based on height. If you needed something from the highest shelf, who would you ask for help?

shorter   **taller**

⟵————————————————————————————————⟶

Using the same 6 family members, including yourself, place them along the continuum based on who has the most expansive vocabulary. Think about how this might affect what they choose to read.

smaller vocabulary   **larger vocabulary**

⟵————————————————————————————————⟶

Summarize in one sentence how this can be useful to you as a teacher:

3C
Activity!
LITERATE

A secondary teacher knows you have studied ESL pedagogy. Her principal told her she will soon be teaching 4 refugee students who are somewhat older than the rest of her students. She asks your advice. What do you tell her for each of these literacy needs?

ABCDE
FGHIJK
LMNOP
QRSTUV
WXYZ

Pre-Literate

Non-Literate

Semi-Literate, Roman, or Very Similar Alphabet

Semi-Literate, Non-Alphabet Literate

3D Activity!

SLIFE

Have you heard of **The Hobart Shakespeareans**? For approximately 40 years, Rafe Esquith taught 5th graders at Hobart Elementary in Los Angeles. All of his students spoke English as a second language, and many were SLIFE. All were impoverished. Rafe taught them how to play music and create a budget. They read great literature. And they performed entire plays by Shakespeare. They achieved acclaim and success unlike any classroom anywhere. View a short video on YouTube about them and respond to the questions below. Title: "Hobart Shakespeareans Fox Special" URL: https://www.youtube.com/watch?v=5acffzecCcs

What surprised you the most in this video?

How do you think these 5th grade ELs were able to learn how to play music, read complete novels like *To Kill a Mockingbird* and *Adventures of Huckleberry Finn,* and perform Shakespeare?

Is it realistic for all 5th grade teachers to reach this level of success with ELs? Why or why not?

3E

Activity!

REFUGEES

Refugee children commonly experience interrupted schooling. View a YouTube video titled "No School for Thousands of Syrian Refugees" at https://www.youtube.com/watch?v=nZVPuSzTu7Y and respond to the questions below.

List each challenge you observed for Syrian refugee children:

Syria

The mother of a boy says, "His only weapon is education." What does she mean by that?

What if one of these Syrian refugee children enrolled in your class? How would you rise to the occasion?

3F

Activity!

MALP®

Name: _____

In this activity you'll modify a lesson with MALP® in mind. Go to the Scholastic website at: https://www. scholastic.com/teachers/lessons-and-ideas/ Select a lesson plan, and analyze it for the characteristics shown below. Pay close attention to Lesson Extension and Home Connections.

LESSON TITLE & GRADE LEVEL:

ACCEPT CONDITIONS FOR LEARNING

COMBINE PROCESSES FOR LEARNING

FOCUS ON NEW ACTIVITIES FOR LEARNING

Section Three

Applied Linguistics: Language and Literacy

Introduction

© donskarpo/Shutterstock.com

TEACHER VIGNETTE: MS. WOODWARD, 5TH GRADE, NEW YORK

In the previous chapter, three 9th grade teachers, Mrs. Muñoz, Mrs. Mondicano, and Mr. Ramesh, presented ways to promote a meaningful understanding of the role of students' diverse literacy backgrounds, prior learning experiences, types of cognitive thinking, and the cultural dimensions of collectivism and individualism. The author, Andrea DeCapua, presented the components of mutually adaptive learning as an instructional approach to assist students in transitioning to the classroom in a culturally responsive way. In Chapter 4, you will be learning about the fundamentals of applied linguistics through an analysis of speech sounds (**phonology**), an investigation of forms and functions of words (**morphology**), an exploration of word order and arrangement (**syntax**), a treatment of meanings (**semantics**), and insights into how language is used in communication (**pragmatics**). The author, Elizabeth Platt, explores this topic through the eyes of Ms. Woodward and her

students, in particular Vinn and his sister, Marta. In Chapter 5, Ms. Woodward reviews her knowledge and understanding of second language acquisition (SLA) theories. She continuously strives to integrate language and academic content in her daily lessons.

Vinn was born in the Dominican Republic and came to the U.S. a few days prior to his eighth birthday. He speaks Spanish at home with his three older brothers, younger sister, and parents. He is very social and enjoys playing games on his iPad and listening to Caribbean music. He has been enrolled in the New York City public school system since 3rd grade where he has been participating in the **Dual Language** (DL) program. Instruction for Vinn is provided in two languages: 50% in English and 50% in Spanish. There are English language learners (ELLs) and non-ELLs in his class. *(Reminder: Students whose first language is not English are referred to differently by state; in New York, they are called ELLs.)* His parents chose this program to support his skills in both languages. They aspire to have their children biliterate as they truly understand the benefits of speaking more than one language.

His older brothers participated in the **Transitional Bilingual Education** (TBE) program in which the primary language of instruction was in Spanish; English was gradually added as students' proficiency improved. This model worked well for his brothers who did not speak English fluently when they arrived to the U.S. Early-exit programs, or TBE, are designed to assist students in moving into English-only mainstream classrooms. It is a common program model for ELLs in the elementary grades as their first language is typically phased out over an extended period of time.

Vinn's sister, Marta, is enrolled in the **English as a New Language** (ENL) program where she primarily focuses on her English proficiency. Her teachers provide specific second language acquisition techniques aligned to her English proficiency across all content areas. The curriculum for the ENL program, sometimes referred to as English as Second Language (**ESL**), is designed in collaboration with mainstream teachers to guide ELLs in developing appropriate English language skills while mastering the academic content. Unlike Vinn, Marta needs more connections between her home language and the culture of U.S. schools. Her daily instruction focuses on the structure of the English language, meaningful ways to comprehend the academic vocabulary, and a classroom that promotes an environment where she, along with other ELLs, can take risks in speaking

English while improving their reading and writing skills. Marta and other ELLs are exposed to activities that focus on word meanings, grammar structures, and conversational phrases.

© Asia Images Group/Shutterstock.com

To be eligible to exit services, ELLs must pass the NYSESLAT (New York State English as a Second Language Achievement Test). Vinn's brothers remained in the TBE program for several years. However, Vinn's 5th grade teacher, Ms. Woodward, thinks he will certainly pass the test this academic year as his English proficiency in reading, writing, speaking, and listening is exemplary. His academic grades are outstanding, and he seems motivated to learn. Since New York is not a member state of the WIDA Consortium, Vinn needs to attain a level of "Commanding" to demonstrate proficiency and to exit ESL services. NYSESLAT is the state's compliance with ESSA in assessing and monitoring ELLs' language proficiency in K–12. The levels of proficiency are: Entering, Emerging, Transitioning, Expanding, and Commanding (NY State Ed.Gov).

Ms. Woodward and her colleagues are in agreement that Vinn is one of the top students in the class. He is a gregarious and an easy-going young boy who demonstrates self-confidence. He enjoys math and science. Typically, these classes lend themselves to lots of engaging and cooperative learning activities. At first, Ms. Woodward presumes that Vinn speaks fluently in English but is lackadaisical about turning in assignments. She sees that he works well in class, but truly believes that he is just a "typical" young boy who could work harder. He follows along in class and is always one of the first students to raise his hand and answer questions. He speaks both Spanish and English with little difference in fluency in either language. He is not afraid to answer a question or even ask a question. He typically listens attentively and is engaged in math centers, language arts stations, science labs, social studies activities, and PE and music lessons in late afternoon. He sits close to his teacher and frequently volunteers to be the group leader in projects or class activities. After school, he plays soccer with his classmates and is well-known for being a leader on the field.

Within six to eight weeks of the school year, Vinn becomes mischievous is often called out by Ms. Woodward. He yells out answers, moves around in his chair during science labs, faces his classmates to ask questions unrelated to the lessons, and acts out inappropriately throughout the day. He is definitely disruptive. His writing assignments become increasingly more illegible and his academic grades are slipping fast. Yet, his PE teacher reports that Vinn is positive and very skillful. Vinn's art teacher describes him as being on task and enjoying creating sculptures. Both teachers praise him for his work, attention, and focus on class activities.

Ms. Woodward runs out of options by early December and decides to recommend Vinn for testing through special education services as she strongly feels he could have ADHD (Attention Deficit Hyperactive Disorder) due to his inattentiveness, impulsivity, and hyperactivity in class. Her colleagues are also in agreement as his demeanor has changed dramatically in a short period of time. Vinn's behaviors are not typical of his character, and there appears to be no other possible explanation for this other than a behavioral disorder. She checks on his home life, and there seems to be no indication that there are any dramatic changes. Her team also inquires about his past performance from 3rd grade to present, and there is never an indication that he is a discipline problem. Therefore, Vinn is tested.

Weeks later, Ms. Woodward is informed that Vinn will remain in the 5th grade classroom with no special education services or accommodations. Although surprised by the results, she is also relieved that Vinn does not need behavioral support as he will be graduating in a few months, and she is aware that these services might be cumbersome for such a social student advancing to middle school next year.

Shortly afterward, Ms. Woodward determines that Vinn is acting out in order to get help with understanding words and phrases in language arts and social studies, which are the two academic areas where he is most disruptive. He is at a complete loss and does not know how to ask for help. In the past, he was given a list of academic words in both languages aligned to class readings. Often, he had graphic organizers, lists of phrases, or an opportunity to work with a buddy. In addition, he has access to a bilingual glossary but is not taking advantage of this resource anymore. He was always on top of his schoolwork, and Ms. Woodward now realizes that this was because he had been given the support to understand the academic language and vocabulary of the textbooks and lesson activities. It was an ah-ha moment for Ms. Woodward who specifically knows that strategies and modifications are an essential part of ELs' learning processes.

Due to Vinn's outstanding grades and class participation, Ms. Woodward conscientiously stopped providing extra assistance or support in English. In witnessing his misbehavior, she learned a valuable lesson. Kinsella (2017) noted, *"Vocabulary plays a crucial role in all aspects of academic competence in schooling"* (p. 1). Ms. Woodward's lack of awareness of his **academic language**, or the language used in textbooks, assignments, assessments, and class instruction, may have contributed to his disruptions. Common Core defines **academic vocabulary** as "words that are traditionally used in academic dialogue and text . . . words that are not necessarily common or frequently encountered in informal conversation" (Learning A-Z Learning: https://.learninga-z. com/site/what-we-do/standards/common-core/academic-vocabulary).

Gottlieb and Ernst-Slavit (2014) explained, *"Because academic language conveys the kind of abstract and complex ideas and phenomena of the disciplines, it allows users to think and act, for example, as scientists, historians, and mathematicians. Thus, academic language promotes and affords a kind of thinking different from everyday language"* (pp. 4–5). Ms. Woodward discovers that as the linguistic complexity of the materials and the resources in the 5th grade curriculum become more demanding, Vinn needs more experiences in English to demonstrate his competency. It is a lesson for everyone as Ms. Woodward and her team will affirm. They all noted a change in Vinn's behavior; yet, no one ever even considered that the academic language of the 5th grade curriculum was snowballing on him. The pressure was challenging, even as he attempted to hide it, and his teachers were slow to become aware of his struggles.

However, Vinn scored well on his written tests, and his academic language increased with learning expectations. Gottlieb and Ernst-Slavit (2014) defined **academic language** as *"the language of the school related to acquiring new and deeper understandings of content related to curriculum, communicating those understandings to others, and participating in the classroom environment"* (p. 188). The authors reiterate that every student must acquire the academic language in the classroom as an "additional" language and conclude:

"Therefore, all teachers must have the academic language and linguistic knowledge of their discipline to identify and address the language demands required of instruction. Culturally and linguistically responsive teaching, by being sensitive to individual student characteristics, facilitates student attainment of academic language within and across disciplines." (p. 159)

Ms. Woodward interprets her role as a teacher in not only preparing students to be successful in her classroom, but also in becoming productive citizens in the workforce. She envisions teachers as *"wearing many hats"* to demonstrate effective teaching strategies, knowledge of subject matter, appropriate disciplinary techniques, usage of technology, and an understanding of students' cultures and language proficiency levels. She and the other teachers pull out their former college textbooks. They remember reading *Why TESOL?* in which the authors succinctly describe ways for schools to meet the needs of ELs. They skim through the text and modify the authors' list to meet the needs of ELs as follows:

© alex74/Shutterstock.com

Teachers must …

- have high expectations for the academic success of all students.
- promote and attain high levels of parental involvement.
- value ELs' home languages and cultures.
- provide outreach and communication in the home languages of ELs.
- be involved in making placement decisions on the basis of adequate assessment and consultation.
- provide dual language or bilingual programs whenever possible.
- ensure academic programs to meet the needs of ELs.

Ms. Woodward and her colleagues collaborate regularly to foster ways to address the needs of all students. In looking at their class rosters, along with Vinn, there are forty-eight 5th grade students whose first language is not English. Vinn is one of seven ELs from the Dominican Republic. Other families come from China, Yemen, Mexico, Bangladesh, Uzbekistan, and Haiti. Along with English, the languages spoken in their four classes are Chinese, Arabic, Bengali, Russian, Haitian-Creole, and French. With this list in hand, the teachers are aware that scaffolding lessons for ELs is a challenge but one that must be mastered for everyone's success. She and her colleagues appreciate that **schools are extensions of society where students interact and learn from each other and from their teachers**. They agree that **motivating students, making learning meaningful, fostering academic growth, acknowledging cultural and language differences, and managing social behaviors** are responsibilities of each and every teacher. But, they are still apprehensive about meeting the academic needs of every student as well as nurturing English proficiency for ELs.

Ms. Woodward and her colleagues appreciate that **language and cultural diversity continuously change school demographics**. A repertoire of ways to address the needs of all students is a must from day one and every day after that. An understanding of language as an integrative and communicative system is essential. Thus, she decides to focus on language structures, and second language acquisition. In this way, Ms. Woodward will be able to support Vinn's needs as well as all her other students. Her colleagues also agree to focus on the role of language for their own personal knowledge, professional growth, and their students' needs. Their plan is to study *"what it means to know a language."* Denton (2013) explained:

"Skillful language teaching is language that supports students in three broad ways: gaining skills and knowledge, developing self-control, and building their sense of community. Across all of these areas, language is a tool that helps teachers articulate a vision, convey faith that students can attain it, give feedback that names students' strengths, and offer guidance that extends students' strengths." (p. 7)

Ms. Woodward reviews the definition of "language." Take a few minutes to complete the "Dear Teacher Letter" activity below.

 ## LITERACY STRATEGY: DEAR TEACHER LETTER

(1) Define "language" in 10 words or less.
(2) Review the statements below.
(3) Choose three statements that you believe support teachers of ELs at varied levels of proficiency.

> Language is a tool for thought and a medium of self-expression.
> Language is a system of communication.
> Language is culturally transmitted.
> Language is arbitrary; it is a set of symbols that convey conventions of meaning that are derived and used in a speech community.
> Language is systematic; the order and rules of words are rule governed.
> Language is creative.
> Language has duality or double articulation; it is organized into layers of sound units, or phonemes and combining these phonemes allows for meaningful communication (i.e., /n I t/ = knit).
> Language has displacement; messages can be created that are not tied to the present.
> Language is discrete; there are differences between sound units and meaning (i.e., /b/ vs. /p/).
> Language is interchangeable as an individual may speak and listen at the same time.
> Language is acquired by people in much the same way; language and learning have universal characteristics.
> Languages are diverse but share universal properties; they are complex.

(4) Read Chapter 4, then refer back to this section to complete questions 5–6.
(5) Refer back to your statements and add to them based on your new knowledge of "language as a system" (phonology, morphology, syntax, semantics, and pragmatics).
(6) Compose a letter to a teacher or an administrator describing how an understanding of "language as a system" is essential for all teachers.

Tips for Use with ELs: This strategy is a way for ELs to summarize learning in a quick and practical way. Composing a letter can be done through drawings, referring to a list of academic vocabulary, creating sentence strips, or working with a partner. Based on ELs' proficiency levels, teachers may direct them in creative ways to summarize their knowledge.

The Fundamentals of Applied Linguistics: Communication Through Language

Elizabeth Platt

© donskarpo/Shutterstock.com

LITERACY STRATEGY: ANTICIPATION GUIDE

Complete prior to reading Chapter 4

1. Read each statement.
2. Decide whether you agree or disagree by placing a check in the correct box under the **Before Reading** column.
3. Read Chapter 4. Come back to the Anticipation Guide, and respond to each statement by placing a check in the correct box under **After Reading**.

Before Reading Agree-Disagree	Statements	After Reading Agree-Disagree
_____	1. Linguistics is the systematic study of languages.	_____
_____	2. Second language learners are more likely to produce developmental errors than errors based on the sounds of their first language.	_____
_____	3. Minimal pairs differ in meaning and by one similar phoneme in the same position in the two words.	_____
_____	4. The vowel system of English has a greater variety of sounds than that of Spanish.	_____
_____	5. The patterns of stress and pitch in a language are called inflections.	_____
_____	6. Bound morphemes are attached to nouns and verbs in nearly all languages.	_____
_____	7. The predominant word order pattern in world languages is SVO (subject, verb, object).	_____
_____	8. Case marking in English is found in its system of pronouns.	_____
_____	9. Meaning inheres in words.	_____
_____	10. Semantic relations include deixis, contradiction, entailment, and others.	_____
_____	11. A key concept in understanding pragmatics is the importance of context.	_____
_____	12. Speakers of most of the world's languages utilize the same speech functions.	_____
_____	13. Second language learning/acquisition entails many factors and processes, but a few simple theories capture them all.	_____
_____	14. The more time spent in the context of a language, the quicker a child learns the language.	_____
_____	15. All children learn a second language in the same way.	_____

4. Discuss responses with classmates.

Tips for Use with ELs: This strategy activates students' prior knowledge before reading about a given topic or text. It requires students to agree or disagree with a set of statements related to a topic and check their responses.

Source: Tompkins, G. 1998. *50 literacy strategies step by step.* Upper Saddle River, NJ: Merrill.

PHONOLOGY

When Vinn walked into his 5th grade classroom, Ms. Woodward introduced him as Vicente. He was rather confused at hearing this name, but he did not know what to do or say. After a few days, it eventually became shortened to Vinn, and because he liked his teacher so much, Vinn accepted the name and never challenged or corrected her.

When he and some of his other Spanish L1 classmates pronounced this name, they were likely to say something like 'bean'. As you read this section, you will be able to explain why it was pronounced /b/ instead of /v/ and the 'long e' represented as /i/ in the vowel system of English, instead of the 'short i', /I/ as in 'bin'.

The study of the sound system of languages, called **phonology**, helps teachers understand many challenges English learners (ELs) face, both in hearing and producing the sounds of a new language. This knowledge also assists teachers in diagnosing errors second language (L2) readers typically make when reading aloud and in predicting how this affects comprehension, accuracy, and fluency.

This section begins with a description of the basic concepts of phonology. The next is about two types of sounds, **consonants** and **vowels**. Following that is a brief section about pronunciation and a description of the processes involved in learning a new language. Throughout this chapter, there are useful figures and activities to apply knowledge of phonology to understand how to help ELs overcome challenges and difficulties.

The Phonological System

The **phonological system** of languages is **rule governed**. That is, languages operate under certain rules. Language is a way of communicating. It is **systematic** and made up of sounds that occur in predictable patterns. The smallest segment of sound that can distinguish two words is called a **phoneme**. For example, **pit** and **bit**. They differ in their initial sound /p/ and /b/ respectively. A set of symbols that linguists use to describe the sounds of languages is the **International Phonetic Alphabet**. Check out the sounds at: https://www.ipachart.com/.

The sound of /p/ in English actually has three different variants, the *aspirated* [p] in 'pit', the unaspirated in 'shopping' and the unreleased in 'stop'. Even though English has these variants, called **allophones**, of [p], they are still the same **phoneme**. That is, the same symbol is used to represent all the variants of /p/ for English. **Aspiration** of a sound involves the accompaniment of a *puff of air* on the sound's onset. You can detect this by putting your finger in front of your lips when starting to say 'pit'. If you say the word 'pit' twice, once with aspirated /p/ and once with unaspirated /p/, the meaning of the word does not change. However, in **Hindi** and **Arabic** there are two /p/ phonemes because speakers produce both aspirated and unaspirated sounds in the same environment, and they cannot be used interchangeably. Other languages, such as **Korean**, do not make a distinction between /p/ and /f/, so there is only one sound that represents these two phonemes. A specific instance of phonemic difference is in **Spanish**, which has two /r/ phonemes, one written as 'r', and the other as 'rr', as in 'pero', meaning 'but', and 'perro', meaning 'dog'. So, a phonemic (sound) difference can indicate a difference in word meaning too.

/θ/	Voiceless 'th' sound as in: thick, thank, wealthy, tenth, path
/ð/	Voiced 'th' sound as in: the, that, weather, teethe, bathe

In the previous chapter, DeCapua defines the "we" and "me" cultures of collectivism and individualism based on ways members view themselves with respect to others. In this section, you will find an example of how this principle applies to learning a language, such as when non-native English speakers cannot hear or produce the "th" or /θ/ sound as in 'three', and instead produce 'tree' or 'free', we may wonder why they do not say 'three', which is so simple. The fact is that /θ/ is uncommon across languages, as well as late-acquired by children. When Vinn read aloud a story he had written about his family, including his 'tree older brudders', Ms. Woodward did not overtly correct his pronunciation. Instead, she praised his storytelling abilities while modeling the correct pronunciation, exclaiming, "*What a wonderful story. You and your three brothers have had some fascinating adventures!*"

Later on, Ms. Woodward helped Vinn by pointing to the diagram of where sounds are made in the mouth. She then directed Vinn to imitate her gesture, then try to pronounce the sound himself as she did it. She continued saying other words (this, them, there, other, brother, mother) having the voiced /ð/ sound and asking him to practice with her.

English Consonants

English consonants are formed by the passage of air through the vocal tract. The chart in **Table 4.1** provides information on the following: the *place of articulation* for each sound from front to back in the mouth, the pairing of sounds via their *voicing* properties, and whether air passing through the vocal tract *stops* or *continues*.

In studying the chart, note that most consonant phonemes are represented by letters of the alphabet, while other symbols represent sounds that are written with two letters. For the system to be useful and clear, a symbol must uniquely represent only one phoneme. A key word below each non-alphabetic symbol on the chart helps to identify the sound it represents.

English Consonants

Manner Place →	Bilabial	Labio-dental	Inter-dental	Alveolar	Palatal	Velar	Glottal
Stop *Voiceless* *Voiced*	/p/ - *top* /b/ - *bee*			/t/ - *two* /d/ - *do*		/k/ - *car* /g/ - *go*	
Nasal Voiced only	/m/ - me			/n/- no		/ŋ/- ring	
Fricative *Voiceless* *Voiced*		/f/ - *fun* /v/ - *vote*	/θ/ – *thick* /ð/ – the	/s/ - so /z/ - zoo	/ʃ/ –shoe /ʒ/vision		/h/ have
Affricate *Voiceless* *Voiced*				/tʃ/-watch /dʒ/ – joy			
Glide Voiced only	/w/ *way*				/j/-yes	/w/	
Liquid Voiced only				/l/ love /r/ rot			

Table 4.1 The Consonant System of the English Language.

PAUSE AND REFLECT

1. With a partner, produce each sound in **Table 4.1** to become more familiar with the overall system.

2. English sounds are produced using three *articulators*: the lips, teeth, and tongue. Consult the chart to identify which articulators are used to produce each phoneme.

3. The *place of articulation* from front to back in the vocal tract is where an articulator touches a location in the mouth. As you pronounce each sound again, try to describe its point of articulation. For example, /p/ is made using the lips.

4. Compare the labels of the place of articulation on the chart in **Table 4.1** with the positions in the vocal tract shown in **Figure 4.1**.

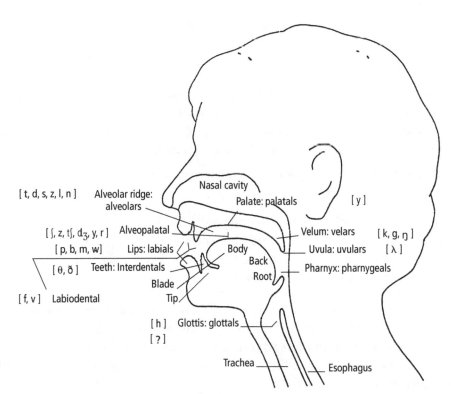

Figure 4.1   Organs of Speech Production.

From *Why TESOL? Theories & Issues in Teaching English to Speakers of Other Languages in K-12 Classrooms* by Ariza et al. Copyright © 2010 by Kendall Hunt Publishing Company. Reprinted by permission.

It is important to note that all English phonemes, except for /h/, are made in the area from the lips to the *velum*. But each language has a different system of phonemes, some more, some less than those of English. For example, **Arabic** speakers produce *uvular, pharyngeal, laryngeal,* and *glottal* sounds. So, you can imagine how difficult it is for English learners of Arabic to master some sounds.

1. Look at the *voiced* and *voiceless* pairs on the chart in **Table 4.2** below. Produce each voiced sound in the pair first, placing your index finger across your 'voice box' and trying to feel the vocal cords vibrate.

2. Now produce the voiceless member of each pair and note that there is no vibration.

	Word-Initial	**Word-Medial**	**Word-Final**
Voiced	<u>z</u>ap	pha<u>s</u>ing	bu<u>zz</u>
Voiceless	<u>s</u>ap	fa<u>c</u>ing	bu<u>s</u>

Table 4.2   Voiced/Voiceless Pairs.

Tables 4.1 and **4.2**, along with **Figure 4.1**, illustrate that voicing is an extremely important feature of pronunciation. The occurrence of so many voiced/voiceless pairs in English, resulting in differences at the level of meaning, attests to the importance of noticing and producing the sounds in each pair carefully.

Although many languages have voicing pairs word-initially, several, such as **Spanish** and **German**, *devoice* consonants word-finally. Thus, Spanish- and German-speaking ELs tend to pronounce 'pig' as 'pick', 'cab' as 'cap', and 'fuzz' as 'fuss'. The process of devoicing in L2 learning is one kind of *transfer* or *interference* from a first language (L1).

1. Referring to **Table 4.1**, locate the pairs /p, b/, /t, d/, and /k, g/. Think back to the term "aspiration" or the accompaniment of a "puff of air" on a sound's onset. Which sounds are aspirated? Insert a piece of paper in front of your mouth to help you make this decision. Does the paper move? If so, the sound is aspirated. If not, it is an unaspirated sound.

2. Now look at the fricatives in the chart. Which ones do you think are aspirated?

Speakers of some languages have difficulty hearing and producing the difference between the /b/ in 'cab' and the /v/ in 'calve'. Although Spanish has both /b/ and /v/ phonemes, they may both be pronounced the same, where the sound is produced with air passing between the lips instead of stopping. The words 'very' and 'berry' are often pronounced almost identically by **Spanish** speakers.

Speakers of some languages spoken in Ethiopia, as well as **Korean**, have difficulty with the /p, f/ distinction. A Ethiopian colleague reported that his student from a rural area told him, *"Flease, Sir, I am foor. I have no any money."* Another example is **French** speakers who tend to pronounce the /ð/ in 'this' as /zis/ for 'this', or the voiceless /θ/ in 'thing' as 'sing'. ELs will tend to produce sounds from their own collection of phonemes that are closest to the English sounds.

PAUSE AND REFLECT

1. One pair of sounds, /dʒ/- /tʃ/ (as in 'jerry' and 'cherry') are stop/continuants (called *affricates*); /dʒ/ starts with /d/ and ends with /ʒ/; /tʃ/ starts with /t/ and ends with /ʃ/.

    Look at the nasals and explain why they are placed where they are. Can you speculate why there are no nasals in the fricative columns?

2. Consulting **Table 4.1**, where and how in the mouth are the semi-vowels (glides) produced?

The two affricate sounds, /tʃ/ and /dʒ/, can be challenging for ELs, for example, 'batch' and 'badge'. Also, the distinction between the affricate, /tʃ/ and the fricative, /ʃ/, as in 'cherry' and 'sherry' can be difficult to pronounce for **Spanish** speakers. An example is seen when Ms. Woodward rotates jobs in her classroom, including putting chairs on top of desks at the end of the day. When it is Vinn's turn to do this job, he is proud to help. As Marta waits for him to finish so they can walk home together, she offers to help her brother with the 'shairs' so he can finish earlier.

Another difficulty Spanish speakers tend to have is in producing /m/ finally, either omitting it, such as in "My nay is . . . ." or substituting with /n/ or /ŋ/, as in 'Hong Depot'. This is because **nasals** are produced with the impeding of air through the nasal passage. When that passage is blocked, as with a cold or a pinched nose, the voiced stop is produced, "by dose is all plugged up."

*Note. The IPA chart (ipachart.com) is an extremely helpful resource for helping teachers locate sounds of any of the world's languages. At this site you can hear, as well as see, a representation of all the sounds.

It might seem quite odd to see /l/ placed in the /dz/tʃ/ column in **Table 4.1**, until you experiment a bit and find that it is formed by touching the tip of the tongue at the alveolar ridge. (Try it!) Speakers from Taiwan may produce /l/ for /ð/ as in 'raler' for 'rather'.

It might also seem strange to see /w/ in the bilabial column. But when /w/ is formed, as in 'wonder', the lips are round, thus, producing a bilabial sound. On the other hand, 'y' as in /j/ is formed in the palatal area and has vowel-like properties like /w/. The two sounds are vowel-like because the airflow is not impeded in their production as with stops and fricatives. In Ms. Woodward's classroom, she realizes that ELs may pronounce the sounds in English based on the phonemes of their native languages. **Transfer or interference from their L1 may occur when their language lacks the phonemic contrasts that English has.** So, she provides lots of listening activities and technological opportunities to hear the English language and the academic vocabulary of each lesson. The task is sometimes daunting, but the results are always positive and upbeat. She finds that as her ELs become more proficient in English, their pronunciation approximates more closely to the native English speakers in the classroom. **She always keeps a copy of the WIDA ACCESS for ELLs report near her lesson plans to remind herself to focus on the language proficiency of each of her students.**

Minimal Pairs: Listening and Speaking

When an EL has difficulty producing an English sound, Ms. Woodward analyzes the error in comparison to what others in the classroom produce and asks the class as a whole to listen to the two pronunciations and identify the difference. For example, a student may say "I want a baby 'pick'" instead of 'pig' because, in the L1, voicing of consonants does not occur word-finally. The words 'pig and pick' constitute a **minimal pair**, which consists of two words having *two minimally contrastive sounds in the same position in a word.*

PAUSE AND REFLECT

1. Study the pairs of words in the chart below. Say them aloud, and underline pairs that are minimally contrastive. *Remember, only one contrast in the same position in both words constitutes a minimal pair.* Don't be fooled by spelling. For example, the words in the first pair do not use the same spelling pattern, but they do constitute a minimal pair.

buy/pie	fan/vat	catch/glitch	Sue/zoo
rush/rouge	bank/bag	lip/lib	than/thin
tan/Dan	fuss/fuzz	cheap/jeep	red/rent
half/halve	gum/come	veal/feel	puck/pug

1. To listen to speakers of many different languages reading the same passage in English, go to the speech accent archive (http://accent.gmu.edu/). Click on browse; click on any language, then find the list of speakers reading the same short paragraph.

2. In pairs or small groups, identify errors you heard and create minimal pairs to help the speaker(s) hear the difference between the two sounds. Consider consulting the consonant chart or your personal experiences in listening to ELs to complete this activity.

There are typically two ways to assist ELs with new sounds—through listening activities and visual presentations. For example, Ms. Woodward begins by introducing minimal pairs to help students hear the difference between two sounds as in 'pick' and 'pig'. She presents *two minimally contrastive words* orally so that students can hear the difference. For Marta, her teacher was aware of her inconsistencies in pronouncing the /s/ and /z/ consonant sounds and designed flash cards of the /s-z/ sounds in medial and final positions, such as fussy/fuzzy, lacy/lazy, prices/prizes, bus/buzz, piece/peas, and ice/eyes. In this way, Marta can practice these sounds at home on her computer.

Once students can hear the differences, they are ready to say the words. You can use your hands, videos, or drawings of the vocal tract to demonstrate. There are numerous websites with lists of minimal pairs for teaching the sounds. Visit the ESOL in Higher Ed website for suggestions.

English Vowels

Vowels are produced with no airflow obstruction, but always involve the tongue and vocal folds in their production. The simplest vowel system is found in some dialects of **Arabic**, with only three vowels.

Table 4.3 shows the English vowel system as either tense or lax. **Tense** vowels are long and **lax** vowels are often called short vowels.

Tongue Position	Front			Central		Back		
Tongue Height								Tongue Height
	Tense	Lax				Lax	Tense	
High	/i/ 'neat'	/ɪ/ 'knit'/				/ʊ/ 'nook'	/u/ 'newt'	High
Mid	/ey/ 'Nate'	/e/ 'net		/ʌ/ 'nut' /ə/ 'about'		/ɔ/ 'naught'	/ow/ 'note'	Mid
		/ɛ/ 'gnat'						
Low				/a/ 'not'				Low

Table 4.3   The Vowel System of English.

PAUSE AND REFLECT

1. Now pronounce the vowel pair /i/ and /I/, first independently, then in the words 'neat' and 'knit', noting the difference in tenseness or laxity of your tongue. If you exaggerate the difference, you might be able to feel the difference more easily.

2. If your first language does not make the tense/lax distinction, work with a native English-speaking partner to work on the difference.

3. Now do the same with the other English vowel pairs.

For ELs who speak languages with few vowels, such as **Spanish** with five vowels, there is a transfer from LI that is often carried into L2 development, even **fossilized** (permanently fixed) in late learners. However, for speakers of languages having many different vowel sounds, such as **Vietnamese**, English vowels present fewer problems. Those speakers are already attuned to distinguishing subtle differences across their own vowel systems.

Ms. Woodward is vigilant regarding English vowels and her students' needs. She provides scaffolding, oral activities, and lots of encouragement for her ELs.

PAUSE AND REFLECT

1. Study the vowel system of English with its tense and lax vowel pairs, simple vowels, and diphthongs in **Table 4.4**.

2. As you do so, note the key words in each position; say each word and listen to the very subtle difference between the two phonemes in each tense/lax pair.

3. Holding one hand, palm up, and pretending that it is your tongue, relax it, then tense it a few times. Pronounce the two words in each tense and lax pair as you relax and tense your hand. This kinesthetic activity is an effective way in helping ELs *feel* the difference between the two sounds.

Phonemes	Words with the Sound	Other Examples
/i/ (tense)	neat	feel, teach, meat, cede, people, receive, believe
/I/ (lax)	knit	sit, mix, pick, film, rid, build
/ey/ (tense)	Nate	bait, rate, plain, may, weigh, favor bait, rate, plain, may
/e/	net	weigh, favor, bet, said, rent, fence, bread
/ɛ/	gnat	tack, sap, fan, magic
/a/	not	mop, father, calm, sock, Tom, jolly
/u/ (tense)	newt	luke, tune, fruit, room, blue, fool, tour, move, do, two, blew
/ʊ/	nook	look, put, foot
/ow/ (tense)	note	vote, poll, coat, broke, holy, so, sew, Roman, sold, though, low, beau
/ɔ/ (lax)	naught	caught, song, crawl, fought, ball, paw
/^/	nut	sun, luck, mother, enough, rung
/ɔi/	noise	toy, moist, Freud, foyle
/aw/	noun	round, house, cow, now
/ai/	night	fight, kind, mine, type, sign, fry, buy
/ar/	narc	farm, park, sorry, heart
/^r/	nerd	clerk, bird, learn, worry, first, hurt
/or/	norm	storm, for, tore, born, boar

Table 4.4   The Pronunciation and Spelling of English Vowels and Diphthongs.

PAUSE AND REFLECT

1. The chart in **Table 4.4** illustrates the system, the key words associated with each phoneme, and other words having the same vowel phonemes as each key word, in many cases not sharing the same spelling as the key words. Members of tense/lax pairs are positioned adjacent to each other. Pronounce each of the words again and note the additional diphthongs and the words influenced by /r/. As you produce the dipthongs, you should notice the movement of the tongue from one position to another as you produce each diphthong.

2. Discuss with a partner or in a small group the reading, listening, and speaking difficulties you might expect ELs to face given both the subtle tense/lax differences and the spelling variations.

3. Devise ways to help ELs confront the realities of learning English pronunciation of vowels, using your knowledge of the specific difficulties experienced by L1 speakers of languages you know.

Suprasegmentals

Suprasegmental is a feature of speech that can include *length, stress, pitch, intonation,* and *tone.* Besides phonemes, these properties of pronunciation affect accent and communication. **Length** can be a natural occurrence, demonstrated by the words 'hat' and 'had'. If you say these two words a few times, you will notice that the vowel sound is slightly longer in 'had'. The same occurs with 'cab/cap, fuss/fuzz, bag/back'. However, in some languages vowel lengthening does not just occur when the final consonant is voiced. For example, in **Swahili,** there is a phonemic difference between the words 'choo' (toilet), and 'cho' (a locative particle within a verb). Thus, vowel length produces a difference in meaning, though the vowel is produced in the same place in the mouth in both words. As for Ms. Woodward, she often explains to her students that short and long vowels refer to differences in *sound,* not actual vowel length. **Teachers should be aware that vowel lengthening is not the same as the actual pronunciation difference represented by the terms 'short' and 'long' vowels.**

Stress, or the intensity or loudness of the airstream, occurs at the syllable level. In the following three-syllable English words, the stress occurs on different syllables in each: Canada (1st), aroma (2nd), disappear (3rd). The underlying rules of syllable stress are complex and can be difficult to master. Many languages of the world have more regular stress patterns, such as **Spanish** where stress on most words is on the next-to-the-last syllable. Other languages, such as **Japanese,** have minimal syllable stress. Ms. Woodward is aware that recognizing where to stress the correct syllable in English is challenging and models appropriate pronunciation and stress throughout the day.

Pitch is the frequency of vibration of the vocal cords. More frequent vibrations produce a higher pitch. Patterns of frequencies are called **intonation**. In English, falling intonation is often associated with statements, and rising intonation with yes/no questions. Saying the same phrase such as "we don't" using several different intonation patterns results in subtle meaning differences. Try it! The rising and falling intonation patterns of English statements and questions are not universal. It is important to teach ELs about acceptable intonation patterns in English. **Tonal languages** are those where a difference in pitch of a vowel in a syllable represents a different phoneme. Chinese, Vietnamese, Thai, Lao, and some African and Scandinavian languages are tonal languages. **Vietnamese,** a mono-syllabic tone language, has a high tone, a low tone, a falling tone, and a contour (rising/falling) tone. Changing the tone of a syllable produces a difference in meaning. In **Mandarin Chinese,** the word '*ma*' means *scold* when pronounced with a falling tone, and 'hemp' when pronounced with a rising tone. ('Ma' has several other meanings, such as 'horse' and 'mother'.) Speakers of tonal languages may be able to transfer their sensitivity to tones to learning English intonation patterns. The point is that teachers should be aware of intonation patterns, just like Ms. Woodward when she likens language to the melodies and rhythm of music.

In concluding this section on phonology, keep in mind that children are not really taught language; they 'pick it up' from the linguistic environment of their homes. Some cultures believe language is actually taught. If children grow up in a bilingual or trilingual environment, they acquire all the sounds of the languages they hear and begin to speak. If children are in the environment of a new language in school, for example, they may experience **interference** or **transfer** from the home language at first. But because the brains of children are quite flexible before puberty, they generally lose their *accents* early in the language learning process. Research has shown that if a person learns a new language after the age of puberty, it is likely that first language effects will occur in speaking the new language. For example, **Spanish speakers learning English may have difficulty producing the difference between the /i/ in 'beet' and the /I/ in 'bit', or between the initial sounds in 'cherry' and 'sherry'.** They will almost always have an accent from their L1, although over time the accent may move closer to that of a native speaker of the target language. Ms. Woodward understands that children are not born with the sounds of their parents, but rather with the 'capacity' to acquire these sounds. **She defines 'acquire' as subconscious; whereas, learning is a conscious process.** You will read more about subconscious versus conscious learning in the next chapter when you review Krashen's Hypotheses. For now, Ms. Woodward knows that she will not be able to immediately perfect the native English sounds of her ELs, but she strives to use varied strategies to meet proficiency levels of all her students.

PAUSE AND REFLECT

1. Review page 137 about one of Vinn's early experiences with pronunciation, that of how his name 'Vinn' is pronounced in English. How did he and some of his Spanish L1 classmates pronounce it? Using your understanding of the English consonant and vowel systems after working with this section, explain their pronunciation and hypothesize about the processes underlying it.

2. Consider some relatively common names that might have more than one pronunciation, such as Mia, Eva, Yvonne, Caroline, Madeline, and Noel. Say them aloud, and discuss the different ways they could sound. How would a teacher determine the "correct" pronunciation?

3. As you think about the four basic language skills in English (listening, speaking, reading, and writing), how would a lack of ability to hear, pronounce, and write English words create problems for students in the classroom?

4. What is the value of minimal pair drills and learning how to create them? Based on your experience with non-native English speakers, create a minimal pair drill for a learner who is having difficulty with two minimally contrasting words such as 'parking' and 'barking', (a difficulty speakers of Arabic experience), or 'right' and 'light', problematic for speakers of Japanese and several languages of East Africa.

5. Your EL has difficulty with the beginning sound of 'think'. What symbol is used to write it? Working in pairs, explain either with you hands or with a drawing how you could help the student produce the sound.

6. In a small group, discuss whether or not an understanding of the English consonant and vowel systems would enable you to more effectively teach English language learners in your classroom.

MORPHOLOGY

Vinn's sister, Marta, is in a classroom where her teacher uses strategies to increase English proficiency. Marta and her classmates are expected to be proficient in English and content areas. In the ENL program, Marta and her classmates demonstrate their understanding of the academic content while acquiring English through connections between their L1 and L2 (e.g., Spanish and English). The teachers in the pod meet often to discuss students' learning needs and to actively engage parents in the learning process.

In this section, you will be reading about how Ms. Woodward and Marta's teacher focus on the study of words and word forms and the processes by which words are created and modified. This is the study of **morphology**. *"The development of morphological awareness by ELs may be even more crucial than for L1 (first language) English-speaking students because of the importance of English learners' ongoing acquisition of oral English vocabulary alongside their literacy development"* (Hickey & Lewis, 2013, p. 70). Words and word parts are stored and accessed from the *lexicon,* where they are associated with meaning, which is studied in the field of semantics. To support the listening, speaking, reading, and writing skills of her ELs, Ms. Woodward shares her understanding of how ELs use their previous knowledge in analyzing words to understand new words in English.

Figure 4.2 illustrates the concepts associated with different kinds of morphemes. Words are *free morphemes;* prefixes and suffixes attached to free morphemes are called *bound* morphemes, of which there are two types depending on their function. Examples of *inflectional morphemes* are '-s', indicating plural; '-ed', indicating past tense or the participial form of a verb; and '-est', indicating what is called the superlative form of an adjective. **Inflectional morphemes do not change the meaning of the lexical morpheme**. There are a small number of inflectional morphemes in English, but a great many in other languages, such as Spanish or Swahili.

On the other hand, English has a great many *derivational* morphemes; these alter the meaning of the lexical morpheme in various ways and are added either to the beginning or end of the lexical item as *prefixes* or *suffixes*. In addition to prefixes and suffixes, infixes may occur in other languages, although they occur minimally in English, such as *cupsful* (-s) and *spoonsful* (-s).

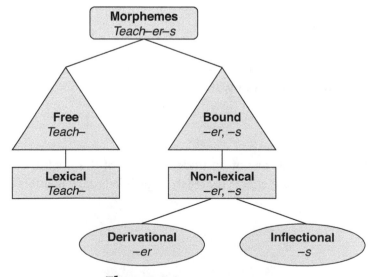

Figure 4.2 Morphology.

Classification of Morphemes

Morphemes are the smallest units of meaning in a language. Note the etymology of the word *morphemic*: *morph* (form) and *-emic* pertaining to language specific phenomena. This is parallel to the term *phonemic*, pertaining to a language-specific sound. A classification of English morphemes is shown in **Table 4.5** with examples.

Lexical items, also called content words, include nouns, verbs, and adjectives, the traditional *parts of speech*. Although for most languages the characteristics of meaning are similar, the formal characteristics are widely varied. Some languages, such as **Vietnamese**, are monosyllabic, so information about number, tense, and the like occurs as separate morphemes. Thus, identifying and distinguishing among parts of speech is difficult for ELs without morphological marking in their L1s. Yet, form and meaning characteristics of the lexical categories for English are *fairly* well-defined, as shown in **Table 4.6** (Hudson, 2000).

		Morphemes		
Free (a morpheme [word element] that can stand on its own, i.e., run, the, book)			**Bound** (morphemes that cannot stand alone to form a word, i.e., a compound word)	
Lexical (content words)	**Non-lexical** (grammatical or functional words)	**Lexical** Stems/roots	**Non-lexical** Derivational	**Non-lexical** Inflectional
book, family, pleasantness	and, only, of, now, our	-vis- (invisible) -volv-, volu- (revolution)	-ish (bookish) -ness (bookishness)	-s (books) -ed (booked)

Table 4.5   Classification of English Morphemes.

Parts of Speech	Formal Characteristics	Meaning Characteristics
Nouns: puppy, house, imagination, believer, birthday, Tallahassee	plural: -s puppies possessive: -s puppy's	names of animate beings, labels of events, places, concrete objects, or abstract concepts
Verbs: cook, take, identify, become, is/are, reside	cook<u>s</u>, cook<u>ed</u>, cook<u>ing</u>, have cook<u>ed</u> bak<u>er</u>, pian<u>ist</u>	express actions, being, states of being
Adjectives: tall, round, hungry, beautiful, interesting Note: Nouns can sometimes be used as adjectives, as in 'dog house'	Comparative: -(i)er Superlative: -(i)est	modifies nouns or noun phrases

Table 4.6   Lexical Morphemes (Parts of Speech).

1. You have probably noted that meaning characteristics described above suggest that there are exceptions to the 'rules'. Provide examples of some modifiers and some actions that can be used as nouns, and some nouns that can be used as adjectives or verbs.

2. Can you add any formal characteristics to any of the lexical categories?

3. Another characteristic of the three lexical categories (also called *open class* words) is that new words are added to lexicon all the time, and some words drop out over time. Go to the Internet and search for obsolete words, as well as new words in the English language.

Not all words are lexical. **Non-lexical** or *functional* morphemes in English include prepositions (of, to), determiners (the, a), temporal adverbs (now, soon), conjunctions (but, and), pronouns (we, them), auxiliaries (be, have), modals (can should), and quantifiers (some, both). Although many prepositions do have lexical content and they pattern like nouns, verbs, and adjectives at the phrasal level, they are often placed in the *non-lexical* category because they behave like other closed class words in lacking formal characteristics and not changing over time or increasing in number.

Derivational Morphemes

Derivation is a process involving the addition of a bound morpheme, called an *affix,* to the beginning or ending of an existing word. Derivational affixes are both *prefixes* and *suffixes* in English (although some languages also have *infixes*).* Examples of prefixes and suffixes are found in **Tables 4.7** and **4.8** respectively. Note that **Table 4.7** shows that a prefix retains the grammatical category of the root word, but changes its *meaning*.

Table 4.8 shows that a suffix changes the *grammatical category* (form) of a word, but retains its meaning. This distinction holds for most cases.

Learning derivational morphemes is difficult for ELs, especially for those whose languages lack prefixes and suffixes. However, these morphemes are taught to native speakers as part of the language arts curriculum, so elementary, language arts, and English teachers should already have effective ways of teaching them. Ms. Woodward uses foldables, matching activities, read alouds, and apps to support ELs in her classroom. She also tries to provide technological resources for her colleagues.

Prefix	Change of meaning	Examples
ex-	former	ex-wife, ex-boyfriend
de-	not, or opposite	deactivate, deconstruct
dis-	opposite	disappear, dislike
mis-	wrong	misunderstand, misrepresent
re-	again	reconsider, redo
un-	reverse action, or not	uncover, unreliable
-in/-im	not	inconvenient, impossible
-con	with	convene, conduct
-sub	under	submarine, subterranean

Table 4.7   Prefixes, Change of Meaning, and Examples.

Suffix	Change of Grammatical Category	Examples
-able	Adjective from Verb	movable, readable
-ing	Adjective or Noun from Verb	reading (class), moving (target)
-ive	Adjective from Verb	impressive, subjective, adaptive
-al	Noun form Verb	refusal, arrival
-ant	Noun from Verb	defendant, informant
-dom	Noun from Noun or Adjective	kingdom, freedom
-ful	Adjective from Noun	fearful, blissful
-ous	Adjective from Noun	poisonous, ruinous
-ize	Verb from Noun or Adjective	capitalize, hospitalize
-en	Verb from Adjective	blacken, harden
-ly	Adverb from Adjective	slowly, lightly
-ity	Noun from Adjective	superiority, ability

Table 4.8   Suffixes, Change of Grammatical Category, and Examples.

* Tagalog, a language spoken in the Philippines, uses infixes. For example -*um* is the infix to form the infinitive of a verb; sulat (write)—sumulat (to write)

Roots and Stems

Not all bound morphemes are affixes. Some originate in **Latin** or **Greek** languages, from which a very great number of English words have been borrowed, often through French or Middle English. These *stems* or *roots* are bound lexical morphemes and they form the primary meaning of a word. Although some are words in their own right, others are not, as shown in **Table 4.9**.

Stems/Roots (language of origin, meaning)	Examples
-port- (from L. portare, carry)	transport, export, portable
-duc- or -duct- (from L. ducere, lead)	conduct, deduct, inductive
-vis- (from L. videre, see)	visage, invisible, revise
-volve-, -volu- (from L. volvere, roll)	involve, revolution, voluble
-cred- (from L. credere, believe)	incredible, credulous, credential
-fin- (from L. finir, end, conclusion)	finish, infinite, refined
acro- (from G. akros, topmost, extreme)	acrophobia, acrobat, acronym
logo/o (from G. word, doctrine, discourse)	logic, anthology, dialogue

Table 4.9   Latin- (L) and Greek- (G) Based Stems/Roots.

Inflectional Morphemes

Some languages have a great many inflectional affixes. Romance languages, such as **Spanish**, **Italian**, and **French**, use suffixes to indicate gender (masculine/feminine) and number (singular/plural) on nouns; determiners and adjectives must *agree* with their corresponding nouns by adding the same suffix, as shown in the following sentences in **Table 4.10a**. These languages also indicate number, person, and tense on verbs using suffixes, as shown in **Table 4.10b**.

El	libro	está	en	la	mesa.
Determiner (masculine, singular)	noun (masculine, singular)	verb	preposition	determiner (feminine, singular)	noun (feminine, singular)
The	*book*	*is located*	*on*	*the*	*table*
Los	**libros**	**están**	**en**	**las**	**mesas**
Determiner (masculine, plural)	noun (masculine, plural)	verb	preposition	determiner (feminine, plural)	noun (feminine, plural)
The	*books*	*are located*	*on*	*the*	*tables.*

Table 4.10a   Spanish Nouns: Number and Gender Agreement.

Present tense	*hablo(1ps)*	*hablas(2ps)*	*habla(3ps)*	*hablam-os(1pp)*	*ha-bláis(2pp)*	*hablan(3pp)*
Preterite tense (past)	*hablé*	*hablaste*	*habló*	*hablamos*	*hablasteis*	*hablaron*
(Note: ps=person singular; pp=person plural) (http://www.studyspanish.com/lessons)						

Table 4.10b   Spanish Verb (Hablar, to Speak), Person, Number and Tense Marking.

PAUSE AND REFLECT

1. **Elementary teachers:** With a partner or in a small group, address the issues in this scenario: You have a class with ELs, some of whom speak Romance languages, but several of whom do not. How would you organize instruction of a unit on derivational morphology that would be fair for speakers from both backgrounds? What learning aids or activities would you assign to help ELs learn these morphemes independently?
2. **Language arts teachers:** You have strategies and resources for teaching root words and affixes. Suggest ways you might augment your teaching of these affixes for ELs.
3. **Secondary teachers:** All academic areas utilize affixes as well as root words. List several examples in your academic content and suggest ways you might help ELs to learn them.
4. Working in pairs or small groups, add six of each type to the lists of derivational morphemes in each of the tables, 4.7, 4.8, and 4.9.

Swahili and other Bantu languages spoken across much of Africa make use of even more affixes on nouns and verbs, as demonstrated in this example: *Tulimwendeshia Dar es Salaam garini letu* in **Table 4.11**. *We drove him to Dar es Salaam in our car.* Prefixes and infixes precede the verb stem (go), while suffixes augment the verb's meaning. Modifiers of nouns must agree with their noun *classes,* or *genders,* of which there are several in Bantu languages, most having singular and plural forms.

Tu-	-li-	-m(w)-	end(a)-	-eshia	Dar es Salaam	gari-	-ni	I-	-etu
1ps We	past	3ps him/her	go	cause to		car	in	Agr, li/ ma class sing	1pp our

Table 4.11   Explication of Swahili Sentence.

Should learning the English system be easy because of its few inflectional morphemes? Unfortunately, it turns out that inflectional morphemes are quite problematic for ELs, so teachers must be aware that inflectional morphemes need to be given a lot of attention. The chart in **Table 4.12** lists these morphemes. For example, notice that '-s' may be added to a verb as well as a noun, and that '-ed' may indicate either past tense or perfective aspect of a verb.

Part of Speech	Morphemes	Examples
Nouns	Plural -*s* Possessive -*s*	cars Mary's car
Verbs	3rd Person Singular -*s* Present Participle -*ing* Past –*ed* Past Participle -*ed/-en*	Mary likes you. Mary is reading. Mary liked the book. Mary has cooked. The eggs were broken.
Adjectives	Comparative -*er* big – Superlative -*est* big –	bigger biggest
Adverbs	-*ly*	slowly, quickly

Table 4.12   Inflectional Morphemes of English.

Developmental Errors

Ms. Woodward realizes that morphemes are often challenging and ELs, like native-speakers of English, produce developmental errors when they encounter difficulties in English. Research conducted with **Spanish** and **Italian** children learning their first language showed that they acquire the functions and forms of tense, person, gender, and number marking earlier than English speaking children learn their inflectional system with far fewer morphemes. This is because of the *regularity* and *salience* in the inflectional systems of Spanish and Italian. The **learnability** of the Spanish and Italian systems is less complex than that of English.

The learnability rule is a two-part explanation of why Spanish and Italian inflectional systems are easier to learn than those of English. Part A: ***One form to one meaning is learned earlier than one form to many meanings.*** With reference to **Table 4.12**, the inflectional morpheme '-ing' has one function; the present participle(ing) indicates the progressive tense. On the other hand, when spoken, the morpheme '-s' can indicate three different functions: a plural (cars), a possessive (Mary's car), and a third person singular verb (likes). The plural form is generally learned early and the other two are learned late. Similarly, the morpheme '-ed' has two functions: to mark the regular past tense and to indicate the regular past participle, which can be used with both the auxiliary 'have' and 'be' forms (have cooked, were cooked).

Most native English-speaking children learn these forms later, especially the past participle form. It is often surprising to hear English-speaking children produce common irregular verbs before the regular forms. This is because the '-ed' form, as in 'worked' or 'finished' is not as *perceptually salient* as an irregular form, as in 'broke' or 'took'. Speakers of many languages, such as **Vietnamese**, whose words end either in a vowel, a nasal, or unreleased stop, lack words ending in cons + s such as 'takes' /teyks/, or ending in cons + cons + s such as 'nests' /nEsts/ or seemingly impossible words such as 'lengths', which ends with a nasal + k + th + s.

The fact that two stop consonants (p, b, t, d, k, g) occur together at the end of the word is very difficult for many non-native speakers whose languages do not allow such clusters; the /t/ ending, as in /workt/, is not salient (i.e., it is not noticeable). As for verbs like 'need' and 'plant' (those that end in /t/ or /d/), adding -ed creates an extra syllable, making the ending salient. When learning to read English aloud, many learners overgeneralize the /Id/ form, producing '/laikId/' (lik-ed) or /muvId/ (mov-ed), assuming these verbs are similar to /nidId/ (needed). Although the '-ed' form is usually not salient, the irregular forms are, so these are often produced earlier in the L2 learning sequence.

 PAUSE AND REFLECT

1. To understand the concept of perceptual salience, pronounce the words 'like' and 'liked' to yourself. Note that both have only one syllable and that the /t/ follows /k/, forming a cluster of two voiceless stops.

2. Explain the learnability rule (parts A and B) in your own words and provide your own examples, if possible.

Learners might produce *"I broke it"* or *"I ate it"* before they produce *"I pushed it"* or *"I cooked it."* Later, when they begin to understand the function of '-ed', they overgeneralize with irregular verbs, producing such utterances as "I breaked it," "I broked it," or "I eated it." **Language learners create rules to apply to new situations.** Ms. Woodward models appropriate grammatical rules in her classroom to guide her ELs in understanding spoken English. For example, ELs tend to say 'go-ed' when sharing about what they did over the weekend. She immediately models the word 'went' and realizes that when ELs create a rule they are overgeneralizing or extending a rule.

Part B of the learnability rule is that *one meaning to one form is learned earlier than one meaning to many forms.* A good example is the pronunciation of the past tense '-ed' endings of regular verbs. **Table 4.13** lists examples of the '-ed' sound - /t/, /d/, or /Id/.

liked	fixed	missed	impeded	picked
buzzed	weighed	inferred	jailed	rated
planted	banned	dropped	laughed	moved
begged	finished	judged	freed	formed
watched	lobbed	needed	hanged	blanketed

Table 4.13   Regular Past Tense Verb Forms.

 PAUSE AND REFLECT

1. With a partner or in a small group, pronounce the regular past tense forms in **Table 4.13** and note whether you produce /t/ or /d/ for the regular '-ed' ending. Do not distort the pronunciation but produce it as you would in normal conversation.

2. Put the verbs into either a /t/ list or a /d/ list; then, explain your reasoning. Hint: Note the *voicing* of /t/ and /d/.

3. Do you think native English-speaking children have to learn how to pronounce these verb endings correctly? Or does this come 'naturally' to them?

Ms. Woodward often reminds her colleagues that learning three different sounds for the 'ed' ending (/t/ as in liked, /d/ as in loved, and /Id/ as in needed) is difficult, especially for adolescents and adult English learners.

She also knows that English-speaking children pick up this pronunciation easily—they do not have to be taught. It will take some practice for ELs to hear, then produce these endings.

Now note that the plural -s morpheme also has three forms: /s/ as in 'pipes', /z/ as in 'cars', and /Iz/ as in 'churches'. The following minimal pairs can be used to help ELs hear, then produce the voiced/voiceless distinction: pigs/picks, buzzes/buses, mates/maids, calfs/calves, mobs/mops, britches/bridges. Can you identify the sound preceding each of the plural morphemes for each word in each pair? Then can you make a generalization about the morphemes for each pair of words?

English Verb Morphology

In teaching an ESL class of Vietnamese, Cambodian, Spanish, and Arabic speakers, everyone made the same errors in the past tense, even though some of their native languages have past tense endings. For Ms. Woodward, she is aware of first language interference, probable grammar errors, and the need to set realistic expectations for ELs in acquiring the English language.

Table 4.14 portrays seven main sentence types using the 3rd person verb 'buy' in the present tense. Note how the verb is altered across the sentence types.

Affirmative	Negative	Yes/No question	Wh- question	Emphasis	Tag question	Passive
Ari <u>buys</u> groceries in Tampa.	Ari <u>doesn't buy</u> groceries in Tampa.	<u>Does</u> Ari <u>buy</u> groceries in Tampa?	Where <u>does</u> Ari <u>buy</u> groceries?	Ari <u>does buy</u> groceries in Tampa.	Ari <u>buys</u> groceries in Tampa, <u>doesn't</u> he?	A lot of groceries <u>are bought</u> in Tampa.

Table 4.14   Sentence Types.

PAUSE AND REFLECT

1. From your own experience, list some typical examples of English verb morphology errors produced by English learners.

SYNTAX

In 1959, Noam Chomsky, a well-known linguist of the 20th century, challenged the claims of B. F. Skinner, a noted behaviorist, that language learning can be explained as a series of stimulus/response events. Chomsky presented an alternative idea, namely that language is *innate*, and that language learning, or acquisition, is possible because a child is already *predisposed* to activate his/her language *organ*. Over the years, Chomsky and his followers, developed and revised a theory to explain an innate disposition for language, referred to as the **language acquisition device (LAD)**. These linguists used the term **acquire**, as opposed to **learn**, to refer to subconscious processes that occur during the early years of life. Chomsky's major work focuses on the structural level of language called **syntax**, which goes beyond word level—phrases and sentences.

Noam Chomsky

© deepspace/Shutterstock.com

Theoretical Issues With Syntax

So far you have read about phonology, the sound system, and morphology, word forms and functions. In this section, you will read about **syntax**, or structural components of language that are systematic and rule governed.

In any language, a sequence of words may represent a sentence. But a sentence in a language cannot simply be just any sequence of words; it must conform to the *rules* underlying it. For example, the rules of English syntax do not *generate*, or describe, the sequence 'girl book see'. The elements are out of order; the verb does not indicate tense or number and articles are missing. Native speakers are able to recognize word combinations that violate these rules as **ungrammatical**, thus incorrect. This is not necessarily based on a speaker's familiarity with *prescriptive* language rules, but comes from knowledge often outside of awareness, acquired as you age. Moreover, the grammaticality of a sentence is not necessarily linked to meaning. Chomsky's (1957) famous sentence *colorless green ideas sleep furiously* doesn't make sense, but it conforms to the correct ordering of English and illustrates the separation of grammaticality and meaning. Think back to Ms. Woodward's class when Vinn struggled with the 5th grade curriculum; as a second-language learner, he did not always grasp such sequences of words in English as "and come to think of it," "speaking of which," or "having said this." Therefore, when asked to put in order or categorize readings, he did not have sufficient familiarity with the structure of the English language. Ms. Woodward quickly realized that it was her responsibility to make learning meaningful and provide ways for Vinn to connect strings of words.

Lexical and Functional Categories

To analyze the structure of phrases and sentences, it is essential to review word level categories. Languages have two major groups of words: *lexical* and *functional*. These categories are listed in **Table 4.15** (or refer back to **Table 4.6**). Linguists assume that all languages have the same categories. Functional categories are listed in **Table 4.16**.

Lexical categories	Examples
Noun	book, city, girl, idea
Verb	write, sing, become, be
Adjective	lazy, slow, interesting, young
Preposition	on, under, of, at
Adverb (Adv) – a lexical category that does not conform to the same phrase structure rules as the other categories; Single word adverbs, as well as some prepositional phrases, function adverbially in sentences; for example, single-word adverbs and their functions: *always, never* (frequency) *slowly, angrily* (manner) *yesterday, tomorrow* (temporal).	

Table 4.15   Lexical Categories.

Functional category	Examples
Determiners (Det)	
Article	a, the
Possessive	her, our
Demonstrative	this, those
Auxiliaries (Aux)	
Modal	will, can, may, might, must, could, etc.
Non-modal	be, have, do
Conjunctions (Con)	and, or, but
Degree word (Deg)	too, quite, only, etc.

Table 4.16   Functional Categories.

Universals in Word Ordering

What is important about these categories of words is that in any given language, they are *ordered* in specific ways. This is a *universal* aspect of all languages. The ordering rules of English are quite strict, and the order subject/verb/ (object) (SVO) is the **canonical**, or typical, order. (The object category is parenthesized because not all sentences have objects.) However, SVO is not the only possible word order, though it is widespread throughout the world, especially in languages of Western Europe. Languages of Korea, Japan, North Africa, and the Indo-Iranian family are predominantly subject/(object)/verb (SOV). Verb-first orders are less common (though they include Arabic and several Celtic languages); object-first languages are rarer still, with American Sign Language (ASL) being among the very few of the OVS type, and Klingon (the language of a certain tribe of aliens encountered by the fictional *Star Trek* crew) being the <u>only</u> OSV language.

PAUSE AND REFLECT

1. Create some sequences of words that do not constitute a sentence, and any other sequences that 'obey the rules' of English, but do not make sense.

2. Because ELs come from a variety of L2 backgrounds, not all of whom share the English word order in sentences, they benefit from tasks that require putting words in the correct order. You can cut up sentences and mix the words from each sentence so that students can reassemble the sentences. Or you can provide specific apps to support ELs' learning about word order by going to the ESOL in Higher Ed website for suggestions.

Case-Marking

In examining **Japanese** and **Korean**, we find that the word order may be a bit looser than it is in English. That is because in these languages nouns are assigned *case* according to their functions in the sentence, such as subject, object, possessive, instrumental, and so on. In each situation, a ***case marker*** indicates the function of the noun. For example, a grammatical sentence in Japanese might be expressed as 'boy' (subject marker) 'horse' (object marker) 'kick'. Or it might read as 'horse (object marker) boy (subject marker) kick'. Both sentences have the same meaning because the case, not the word order, indicates who is doing what to whom. Because Japanese is a head-final word order language, however, the verb must come last, no matter what the order of words in noun phrases is. The **verb phrase** is the core of sentence structure and, as noted previously, there are two options for the ordering of the constituents within the verb phrase in the majority of world languages: verb first (English) and verb last (Japanese).

Although many of the world's languages have no case-marking at all, others have ten or more. The most common case is nominative (subject); accusative (direct object) is also common. In addition to Japanese and Korean, other **case-marked languages** are Latin, Slavic (Russian, Ukarainian, Polish, Czech, Bulgarian, Serbo-Croation, etc.), Baltic (Lithuanian and Latvian), and Finno-Urgaic, (Finnish, Hungarian, Estonian). Lithuanian has the same seven main cases as Latin, as well as three additional locative cases, and gender and plural marking.

Old and Middle English had case-marking on nouns, but Modern English retains case only on pronouns. Each person and number has subject, object, and possessive forms. For example, the first person singular forms are 'I', 'me', and 'my' respectively; the third person plural forms are 'they', 'them', and 'their' respectively. The distinction among these forms is usually learned late in first language acquisition (me want kitty), and may also pose difficulties for ELs.

You might imagine that English speakers learning case-marked languages would find this aspect quite difficult, and this is probably true. However, for speakers of these languages learning English, the lack of case marking poses problems in ways that affect the ordering of phrases within an English sentence. Speakers of case-marked languages have the freedom to *order elements to provide focus* where they want it and *do not necessarily follow a strict word order.*

The following examples from a narrative about a naughty baby owlet told by a bilingual native speaker of **Russian** and **Czech**, both case-marked languages, demonstrate this difficulty. Note that the speaker, Natasha, places focused information at the end of the sentence in ways different from the way the information would be placed by English speakers.

1. And then first egg, broked and was born Frankie. And afterward second, from second egg was born Marushka. And after another while was born, Bedjik.
2. When she wanted to show her husband their new babies, it was in the bed only Frankie and Marushka.
3. After summer start school.
4. After this movie Bedjik played with Marushka and Frankie that he is bandit and he wants to shoot them.
5. Marushka and Frankie saw . . . that came, and spoke with Bedjik this big animal, red animal Lishka (fox).
6. And Lishka saw that he is so non-educated and he doesn't know who she is and then she wants to play with him game.

1. After carefully examining the ways in which Natasha orders her sentences, imagine that she is a student in your classroom. With a partner or in a small group, discuss ways to help Natasha with word order problems. (Ignore for the moment some other problems such as omission of articles.)

2. Can you explain why Natasha might have begun her phrase about who was in the bed with 'It was in the bed only Frankie and Marushka'?

Order of Elements in Phrases

A very interesting aspect of languages is that by and large the noun, verb, adjective, and prepositional phrases usually follow the same pattern. For example, in the English verb phrase 'kicked the horse', the verb precedes its object, while in the **Korean** phrase 'horse (object marker) kicked', the verb follows the object. Examining other phrase types in English or Korean, they all follow the same order as the verb displays. See **Table 4.17.**

Phrase Types	Specifier	Head	Complement
Noun Phrase (NP)	The A	boy pig	wearing a tie
Verb Phrase (VP)		operates goes	a machine
Adverb Phrase (AP)	very	clean hard	 as a rock
Prepositional Phrase (PP)	just	under around	the trees the corner

Table 4.17   English Phrase Structure.

PAUSE AND REFLECT

1. Using a reference, or based on your own experiences, construct a chart of phrases from another language similar to those in **Table 4.17**. If possible, select a language that follows the SOV order.

Word order structures may vary by language structures, such as the complex noun phrase in **Table 4.18**. Examine the string of words in the table and place them in their grammatical order.

Cereal	Those	Yellow	Bowls	Large	Three

Table 4.18   Complex Noun Phrase (NP).

This string is not a sentence, but a noun phrase with several adjectives. **Native English speakers almost always agree on the order, but often cannot explain the 'rule' that describes it.** When given this string of words to put in order, ELs may experience difficulties because of its complexity, and also because their own languages may not permit such strings. For Ms. Woodward, she is aware of the challenges her ELs face daily in the classroom and strives to provide activities to support their English skills.

PAUSE AND REFLECT

1. Try to discern the ordering rules for similar noun phrases by substituting other words. For example, substitute 'his' for 'those'. Can other kinds of words fit into the same slot?

2. When you recognize what kinds of adjectives occur in which position, create a chart like **Table 4.17** and label each column to show the order of the various types of modifiers. Use this as a teaching device for your own classroom

3. Now that you have seen how English orders phrases, translate each of the words in the phrase above into Spanish or another language you may know.

4. Arrange them in their correct grammatical order. Is the order the same as that for English noun phrases? Do you have to add any words to make a good translation?

1. Construct similar examples based on the same pattern.

2. When you recognize what kinds of adjectives occur in which position, create a chart like **Table 4.17** and label each column to show the order of the various types of modifiers.

Ms. Woodward tries to teach word order to Vinn and the other students as she knows that ELs don't always get the 'feel' for the correct order. She guides ELs by providing examples of word order patterns that they can recognize and later follow the rules to create well-ordered phrases. She provides activities for students to practice putting words in order to form sentences in English. She uses Brain Pop to support learning as well as word strips and word walls.

Prescriptive Grammar Rules

Knowledge of English word order is typically not taught in school because native speakers tend to acquire it as young children. Frequently, the *grammatical rules* taught in upper elementary language arts and secondary English courses in schools are **prescriptive**, rather than *descriptive* rules, those that portray how the language actually works. Many so-called 'rules' are actually quite old and were proposed by English grammarians based on a study of Latin. For example, the 'rule' *do not end a sentence with a preposition* works for Latin, but not for English. We accept *"who are you going with?"* even though the question ends with a preposition. Another incorrect rule is *use a singular verb with a plural subject and a plural verb with a singular subject*. In examining the sentences in **Table 4.19**, you can see that the rule is not correct. Neither 'I' nor 'you', both singular, requires the verb to be marked with '-s'.

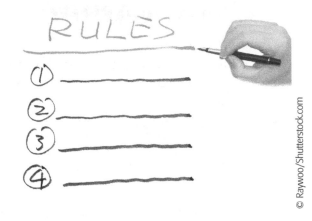

Person, Number, Singular	Subject	Verb	Person, Number, Plural	Subject	Verb
1st	I	read	1st	we	read
2nd	you	read	2nd	you	read
3rd	he, she, it	reads	3rd	they	read

Table 4.19   The Third Person Singular Rule.

In fact, only one person, 3rd person singular, takes a so-called 'plural', e.g., she likes. But, as noted in the morphology section, the '-s' does not represent a plural, but simply denotes the 3rd person singular form of the present tense verb. In older versions of English, verbs were marked for person and number, just as in Spanish and other European languages. Only the 3rd person singular form has remained in English. In some dialects of English it, too, is not used, and may someday disappear from English all together. The point is for all students to understand how a language really works in spoken and written discourse.

In reviewing her former notes about Chomsky, Ms. Woodward recalls that he claimed that language is an organ, just as the heart and lungs are organs, providing an innate linguistic capacity that allows young children to acquire language. Because language is an organ, Chomsky argues, we are born with the capacity to use the organ already partially pre-programmed, such as with the knowledge that language obeys certain ordering rules, with all phrase types (noun, verb, etc.).

Ms. Woodward recalls that the work of Chomsky was challenged by other linguistics who raised questions about the notion of a programmed language template. Yet, she realizes that second language acquisition (SLA) theories set the foundation for teachers to plan effectively and create activities and assessments to support ELs' listening, speaking, reading, and writing skills.

PAUSE AND REFLECT

1. Explain Noam Chomsky's basic belief about first language learning. Do you believe it better reflects the reality of child first language learning than a behaviorist view? Discuss with a partner or in a small group.

2. Ms. Woodward attempted to ask her students to use "May I ...?" instead of "Can I ...?" She was not successful in eliminating students from saying "Can I ...?" What other prescriptive rules of English might be questioned when you look at how the language actually works in real situations?

3. In a small group or in a class activity, debate the utility as opposed to the uselessness of some prescriptive rules. (Remember that language is always changing, whether we like it or not.)

SEMANTICS

You have read about phonology (system of sounds), morphology (word forms and formation processes), and syntax (how words join to form larger units), which are the three levels of language considered to be innate. The next two levels are semantics and pragmatics, both seen as *learned* aspects of language, according to the Chomskian perspective. The branch of linguistics that studies changes in meaning and the principles that govern the relationship between words and their meanings is the field of **semantics**. In this section, you will read about lexicon, teaching vocabulary meaning, denotation and connotation, semantic relations at word and sentence level, and ambiguity. There are suggestions for discussion and ways to assist Vinn, his sister, and other English learners.

Experimental research has revealed that words are organized and stored in many different ways in the mind. For example, if you can't remember a word, you may remember its beginning sound, form a mental representation of the word (such as 'dog'), or locate the word according to its category. **Table 4.20** provides a list of categories of word knowledge (Nation, 1990), which help to illustrate how words are stored in the *mental lexicon*.

Types of Word Knowledge	Examples – deep
Spoken form of a word	/dip/
Written form of a word	d-e-e-p
Co-occurrence with bound morphemes	deep (adjective); also depth (noun), deepen (verb), deep -er, -er -est (comparative, superlative forms) deeply (adverb)
Grammatical behavior of a word	The pool is deep (predicate adjective). He's going into deep water (adjective before noun). It's too deep for wading (adjective with specifier & complement).
Collocational behavior of a word	(as) deep (as the ocean), often used with words pertaining to bodies of water or places below ground
Frequency of a word	how often it occurs in speech or writing
Stylistic register constraints; when a word is inappropriate to use	It would be inappropriate to use slang or swear words when speaking with a person who is interviewing you for a job. Referring to a potential supervisor as 'really deep' would be such an inappropriate thing to say.
Conceptual meaning of a word	Representation of a small figure at the bottom of a large tank of water
Associations with related words	Deep: shallow (antonym), profound (synonym), far down in water or underground place (paraphrase)

Table 4.20   Types of Word Knowledge.

Table 4.21 provides some suggested strategies for learning academic vocabulary (EduKatie and Reading Rockets).

Suggestions by EduKatie:

1. Review the academic vocabulary from readings and introduce to ELs prior to lesson.
2. Build vocabulary based on ELs' prior knowledge.
3. Teach synonyms and antonyms and add words based on preexisting knowledge of vocabulary.
4. Reinforce vocabulary through pre-reading, during reading, and post-reading activities.
5. Teach academic vocabulary systematically and comprehensively.
6. Promote motivating and interesting activities to learn new words.

Suggestions by Reading Rockets:

1. Establish routines to introduce new words.
2. Provide activities that promote in-depth processing of word meanings.
3. Foster participation and student accountability in learning academic vocabulary.

Table 4.21   Principles for Enhancing Academic Vocabulary.

Ms. Woodward and other teachers in Vinn's school understand that there are numerous strategies to teach academic vocabulary. They display charts like **Table 4.21** in their classrooms and refer to them often during writing activities.

What It Means to Mean

Early in the nineteenth century in Central Europe, **semantics** emerged as a separate subfield of linguistics to study *meaning*. According to the Western Rationalist position, meanings are not *contained* in words (or larger units), but are *assigned* to these units by speakers and hearers over time in public discourse. However, if meanings were contained in language, they would not change over time. Since there are so many meanings assigned to some words in the lexicon, a single conceptualization can be difficult to pin down. For example, the meaning of *run* in 'run a race' is not the same as *run* in 'run a business'.

The core meaning of *run* is 'to move quickly on foot' because speakers of English understand it that way. Yet, we might instead have started using the word 'bleb' (a non-word), or 'correr' (the word in Spanish) instead of 'run'. Specific words are simply *arbitrary* combinations of sounds that are assigned meanings by speakers. Whenever a new concept emerges, somebody names it, the name spreads, and soon it becomes a part of the lexicon, or the language of the speakers. When a new edition of a dictionary appears, it contains these new words in the communal language.

Adults are able to distinguish between a word and its *referent*. A referent is a person, thing, or idea that a word stands for (Nordquist, 2020). Yet, developmental studies show that young children do not always conceptually separate words from their referents. Research shows that bilingual children have an advantage over monolinguals. For example, when shown a picture of the moon, told it is a 'bleb', and asked if the picture is still of a moon, some monolingual English-speaking children said "no." But because Spanish/English bilingual children of the same age had already learned that the moon can be called both *luna* and *moon*, they were more likely to say that the picture still depicted the moon, despite its being called 'bleb'. They knew that two different words can have the same referent. See **Table 4.22**.

Definition and Part of Speech: credible (adjective), believable	**Translation:** Spanish creíble
Use in a sentence: His story about the accident was not <u>credible</u>. I think he was lying.	*Words with same root*: incredible, credit, credulous, creditor (from Latin, credere), accreditation

Table 4.22   Illustration of a Flashcard Students Can Make to Help Them Deeply Learn a Word.

PAUSE AND REFLECT

1. Recall from the morphology section that all words, or *lexical* and *non-lexical items*, are *free morphemes* and that word parts are *bound*. Explain whether you think bound morphemes are also stored in the mental lexicon with their meanings/uses, or whether they are stored with individual free morphemes.

2. For information about language and the brain, visit: https://www.linguisticsociety.org/resource/language-and-brain or Google for other resources.

3. With a partner or in a small group discuss ways you have observed vocabulary learning in the classroom.

4. How would you encourage ELs to identify and use their individual preferences for learning new words?

Denotation and Connotation

Two terms important to address at this point are denotation and connotation, each of which is an aspect of meaning. **Denotation** is presented in dictionary descriptions; for example, the word 'rat' is defined in Merriam-Webster's Online Dictionary as, "any of numerous rodents (rattus and related genera) differing from the related mice especially by considerably larger size." This is its denotative meaning; however, this does not constitute the variety of associations this word can evoke. **Connotation** is the emotional or imaginative association surrounding a word. Ms. Woodward tries to provide the literal definition of the academic vocabulary she introduces in her lessons; but, she also is aware of cultural differences in word meanings. For example, 'blue' might simply denote the color for some students, but for others, it might trigger an emotion of sadness, feeling blue. For many people, a rat calls to mind feelings of disgust, fear, or even plague. In the Chinese culture, however, the rat is the first sign of the zodiac and has several positive associations; "…. attributes of an animal with spirit, wit, alertness, delicacy, flexibility and vitality." The word rat *connotes* a variety of associations in one's mind; these are both culturally and individually influenced, or they may be personal or restricted to small groups of people, such as a family or a sub-culture.

PAUSE AND REFLECT

1. Check dictionary definitions for five common words, for example, 'marriage'. Write the denotation and connotations for each (refer to the 'rat' example).

2. Find examples from different cultural backgrounds. In mainstream American culture, a couple usually makes the major decisions regarding their future life together; but, elsewhere marriages may be arranged by parents. What do you think 'marriage' connotes for a prospective bride who is only twelve or thirteen years old?

Semantic Roles and Relations

Words can play several different *semantic* roles in sentences. These roles are different from the syntactic roles, *subject* and *predicate,* which are not so useful when it comes to meaning, and will not help ELs when they struggle with sentence meanings. Noun phrases in English fulfill various kinds of semantic roles. Four are listed in **Table 4.23**, along with definitions and examples (Hudson, 2000). Recognizing the semantic role of noun phrases can help readers, including ELs, better understand the connections among various parts of a sentence.

Agent	doer, actor	<u>The</u> <u>woman</u> came here.
Patient	entity affected by what agent or causal agent does	The police punished <u>the teenagers</u>.
Recipient	receiver of deed of agent	I bought the gift for <u>my mother</u>.
Experiencer	preceiver of a stimulus	Rain pleased <u>the farmers</u>.

Table 4.23   Semantic Roles.

Semantic roles are not an aspect of word meaning; words attain role status only when they are used in sentences. For example, the word 'dog' plays different roles in each of the following sentences:

1. Agent: The dog is chewing on a bone.
2. Patient: We chased the dog out of the house.
3. Experiencer: Several fleas were annoying the dog.

Recognizing the semantic roles of noun phrases can help second language readers better understand connections among various parts of a sentence, as will be shown in the section on ambiguity. Several kinds of semantic relations exist among words, as shown in **Table 4.24**. Categorizing words in these ways assists learners to extend their vocabularies; flashcards and a variety of games enable students to learn words independently or in small groups. Later is this section you will learn about semantic relations occurring within larger units (clauses, sentences) and across sentences.

Although concepts might be fuzzy within a language, they become even more problematic across languages. For example, the word 'aunt' in English may represent any of five relationships: mother's sister, father's sister, mother's brother's wife, father's brother's wife, or close family female friend of the parents' generation. However, no such generic word as 'aunt' exists in **Vietnamese**, for there are different words for various people in familial relationships according to the following criteria: the side of the family (mother's or father's), birth status in the parents' respective families (older or younger sibling of the parent), and relationships by marriage. Although it may seem strange to be required to learn all of these possible relationships, it is essential for the young child to do so, for every person she/he meets is addressed, not by using a word for 'you', but by the label of one of these relationships (Good morning, *mom's younger sister word*, Thuy; or, Greetings, *father's elder brother word*, Tam). The point to be made here is that **semantics, including word meaning, creates the bridge between language and culture,** for it is at this intersection where meaning is ascribed to events, objects, roles, and relationships among members of a culture. **Meanings are culture-bound in immeasurable and often surprising ways.**

Semantic Relation	Examples
Synonomy, same meaning	big/large, fat/thin, wrong/mistaken
Polysemy, refers to words having multiple meanings	bank, chair, foot
Homophony, same sound	bear/bare, hear/here, two/too
Antonymy	Opposites: wide/narrow; gradable: long stick/long car; complementary: single/ married; relational: fold/ unfold
Hyponomy, meaning of one word included in meaning of another; pertains to subordinate & superordinate categories	dog/animal, carrot/vegetable, rose/flower

Table 4.24   Semantic Relations at the Word Level (From Yule, 2010).

1. With a partner or in a small group, make a short list of necessary and sufficient conditions for two or three of the following: dog, cup, table, bachelor, cushion, coat, friend.

2. Identify counter-examples for your conceptual descriptions. What 'fuzzy areas' did you encounter? Were some of the examples 'fuzzier' than others?

3. Make a Venn diagram to represent the relationship between the concepts 'language' and 'communication'. Are they two separate concepts? Or does one concept include the other? Or do they overlap or mean the same thing?

Concepts

Word meaning is closely related to how **concepts** are represented in the mind. An earlier way of thinking about concepts is that *necessary and sufficient conditions* exist for an object to be called a certain thing. For example, the defining conditions of 'bird' are generally thought to be something like [animal, small, able to fly]; although, we would have to admit that ostriches are birds though they are neither small, nor do they fly. A more recent view is that concepts lack clear-cut boundaries; there are 'fuzzy' boundaries around them. Thus, if you try to state the necessary and sufficient conditions for something to be a chair or a game or a bird, you will find some chairs, games, or birds that don't fit the core definition. Certain fossil forms demonstrate a biological link between ancient reptiles and birds. So, are they birds? Are 'Ring around the Rosy' or 'London Bridges' games in the same way that Monopoly and football are games? Is a beanbag a chair even though it doesn't have legs?

1. Among the overriding concepts that define Americans are the related ideas of *individualism* and *independence*. What do you think may be the origins of these concepts? If your own background, or that of some of your students, highlights the value of different concepts (e.g., loyalty, respect, family), how do these influence behavior and performance in the classroom?

2. In Ms. Woodward's class and the other 5th grade classes, there are ELs from the Dominican Republic, China, Yemen, Mexico, Bangladesh, Uzbekistan, and Haiti. English, as well as Chinese, Arabic, Bengali, Russian, Haitian-Creole, and French are spoken in these classrooms. Identify two concepts that exist in any of these cultures, or regions of the country in the United States. Bear in mind that it may be that these other cultural backgrounds influence culture in the U.S. in ways that have become "mainstream," such as having piñatas at birthday parties.

Metaphors

Another important aspect of word meaning is **metaphor**, not simply a literary device used by writers, but a pervasive feature of all languages. Examples in English include, the *commodity metaphor* for talking about time (we waste, save, spend, and lose time), the *conduit metaphor* for 'packaging' mental activities (we get points across, put our thoughts into words, and get through to each other), and the *gun metaphor* (shooting for next week, no silver bullet, parting shot, targeting). When we learn an interesting new metaphor in another language, such as 'the clock is sleeping' or 'the idea escaped from me', we don't always recognize that our own language makes such wide use of metaphors. Thus, for second language learners, our many metaphors are often difficult to understand. "Let's cross that bridge when we come to it." In previewing reading materials, Ms. Woodward identifies metaphors and prepares a list to teach prior to a reading lesson so that her learners can 'cross the bridge' as they read the new text.

PAUSE AND REFLECT

1. Make a list of metaphors using the names of body parts in English (the head of the bed, the leg of a chair, the long arm of justice).

2. After composing a list, make generalizations about some of them. Do you know of other languages that use body part words metaphorically?

Semantic Relations: Meaning Beyond Word Level

Semantic relations also exist among sentences as shown in **Table 4.25**. When a person 'knows' a language well, these various relationships within and among sentences are usually quite obvious, but they are not so obvious for ELs. For example, 'My brother lost consciousness on the operating table' is a statement that *entails* several possibilities such as 'He didn't know what we were talking about' or 'He couldn't get up and walk around'. But the entailment is not always stated in the text. A good follow-up question the teacher could ask would be, "So would the brother be able to have a conversation with the doctor?'

As another example, indirect speech acts can be difficult for learners. If you say "It's really hot in here" and the person does not respond by offering to open the window, he may not have understood your **indirect request**. Non-native speakers may also appear rude when they say something in a direct manner that native speakers express indirectly, such as "I want you to give me x" rather than "I could certainly use x." In addition, other direct requests most Americans consider inappropriate are: "How much money do you make?" and "How old are you?"

Semantic relations	Definition	Examples
Paraphrase	one statement with a meaning similar to another statement	The cat chased the mouse. The mouse was chased by the cat.
Entailment	one statement entailing the consequence of the second	The hunter killed the bear. The bear is dead.
Contradiction	two contrary statements	Charles is a bachelor. Charles is married.
Presupposition	a statement assuming a pre-existing truth	When did you stop beating your wife?
Deixis	elements in a statement implying the location of the speaker	A bear is going into the tent. A bear is coming into the tent!
Speech Acts	associations with the utterance of a statement	'I can't reach the salt' is an indirect way of telling someone to pass it. 'I pronounce you man and wife' is an act that produces a concrete result.

Table 4.25   Semantic Relations Within/Across Sentences.

1. With a partner or in a small group, write five indirect statements by English speakers.
2. Check with people from other cultural backgrounds, or use the Internet, to search for examples of indirectness.

Ambiguity

Sentences or phrases in a language can be **ambiguous**; that is, they may be understood in more than one way. For example, the simple phrase 'a large hat box' may refer to a box for large hats or a large box for hats (of any size). This is a **structurally ambiguous** phrase because we don't know whether the referent of 'large' is a hat or a box. Ambiguity may also be lexical. For example, in the phrase 'put the money in the bank' the word 'bank' might refer to a place where people go to exchange money, or it could refer to the area beside a river. *Plays on words, such as puns,* are a wonderful source of humor, but can also challenge ELs. Lucas (2004) studied how adult learners in an intensive English language program disambiguated puns; for example, the ambiguity in these two statements are plays on words:

1. "One morning I shot an elephant in my pajamas. How he got into my pajamas I'll never know."
2. Groucho Marx: Let's talk about rights and lefts. You're right, so I left.

Ambiguity is found in phrases where words are left out, as in newspaper headlines. The ambiguity could be caused by omission of words or by modifiers in the wrong place. For example, in the phrase 'miners refuse to work after death'; it would be helpful to resolve the ambiguity if it had said 'another miner's death'. **Table 4.26** provides a list of several humorous headlines. As you can well imagine, many of these pose considerable difficulties for ELs.

1. Panda Mating Fails; Veterinarian Takes Over
2. Juvenile Court to Try Shooting Defendant
3. Miners Refuse to Work after Death
4. British Left Waffles on Falkland Island
5. Typhoon Rips Through Cemetery; Hundreds Dead
6. Man Struck by Lightning Faces Battery Charge
7. Include Your Children When Baking Cookies
8. Something Went Wrong in Jet Crash, Expert Says
9. Police Begin Campaign to Run Down Jaywalkers, Safety Experts Say
10. School Bus Passengers Should be Belted
11. Drunk Gets Nine Months in Violin Case

Table 4.26 Ambiguous Phrases.

1. Identify the source of the ambiguity in at least three of the ambiguous headlines listed in **Table 4.26**. Apply what you have learned about semantic roles to disambiguate each headline.

2. Item 4 can have two meanings. The two words 'left' and 'waffles' in item 4 can each be one of two parts of speech. Write two alternative sentences using the two words, and provide an alternative sentence for each one using a different meaning.

3. **Semantics** is the study of the meaning of words, phrases, and sentences. Word meanings are stored in the **lexicon**, which is located both in the head and among members of a speech community, in the form of an abstract list of words organized in a number of different ways. However, meaning is not in the word. Meanings are assigned to words, concepts, and events by speakers of a language within a particular culture milieu; they are <u>not</u> *contained* in words or sentences. Semantic relations hold between words; synonyms, antonyms, and homonyms are examples. Semantic relations also hold at the sentence level. Examples are deixis, entailment, and presuppositions. It is possible to create ambiguity in statements; ambiguity makes it possible for speakers to say one thing and mean another.

PAUSE AND REFLECT

1. We have learned in the previous three sections that phonology, morphology, and syntax appear to be rule-governed, systematic, and possibly closer to innate aspects of the mind. How would you characterize semantics?

2. One of Ms. Woodward's goals is to prepare all students to be "productive citizens in the workforce." To do so, a proficient understanding of the characteristics of the language spoken in the community is essential (e.g., English). Semantics, as you have read, is the study of meaning and word/phrase relationships. How does knowledge of semantics support teaching and learning in preparing all students? What are specific ways for teachers to present vocabulary, word phrases, and relationships between words and their meanings?

3. How do you think an understanding of semantic roles in a sentence will help Vinn and his sister, Marta, better understand the meaning of the sentence?

4. Interview a student or a friend who comes from a different cultural background than your own and ask him/her which people in the family would be referred to as brothers and sisters, as cousins. Ask him/her for some popular metaphors in the home language.

PRAGMATICS

So far in this chapter, you have proceeded from learning about the more structural aspects of language, those claimed to be innate and universal, to those more closely associated with communication and culture. You have learned that the focus on meaning is semantics. **Pragmatics** is the branch of linguistics that studies how people use language by looking beyond the literal meaning of an utterance and considering language as an instrument of interaction.

Pragmatics, or 'speaker meaning' is often called *invisible meaning* (Yule, 2010) because comprehension of an utterance may involve not just the spoken words but also the *context* in which two people interact. For example, in a restaurant a customer asks: *"Can I have a hamburger?"* Is it that the customer would like to order a burger or ask for approval to eat a burger? The context of pragmatics can include setting, roles, and relationships of people, and shared history and assumptions. When speakers do not share the same assumptions, communication problems arise, as is often the case between a teacher and an EL, and/or a student who does not know the *norms of participation* in the situation. These norms are often unspoken and native English speakers may be aware of them only when they are not followed. Thus, in studying about pragmatics, we need to consider the notion of *shared context*.

When something is "lost in translation," it is frequently lost in pragmatics. Consider humor. In the case of humor, such as with jokes, literal meanings are not always funny. A broader understanding of context is necessary for humor to be obvious.

 PAUSE AND REFLECT

Scan the comics and find examples of humor that rely on pragmatics. Share in class and discuss implications for ELs trying to find the humor.

Dialects and Bilingualism

An interesting dilemma with Chomsky's theory of a single language in a speaker's head, sometimes called a **language template**, is the fact that many people in the world speak at least two languages or two dialects of the same language. This means that people can have two or more *grammars* in their heads at the same time. When speakers of **Jamaican English** understand and speak several dialects of the same language, it is difficult to know what *grammar rules* are in their heads because the different dialects operate according to different

rules. Bilingualism and bidialectalism pose a problem for a Chomskian-only approach to language. Speakers use the available linguistic resources in the many contexts where they interact with others or express themselves in writing. For example, many bilinguals freely switch, often mid-sentence, between their two languages, thus mixing rules as well.

Although Ms. Woodward provides Vinn and the other ELs with grammar and vocabulary instruction in English, her teaching is incomplete without also helping them to function in communicative settings. Those who have grown up speaking the English language from childhood participate in a wider *speech community* of English and control the various dialects of their ethnic and geographical backgrounds. They also reflect the *social register(s)* shaped by their home upbringing and in their occupational or educational endeavors, and they can shift the way they speak depending on whether the speaker is a three-year-old, an old high school friend, or a bureaucrat in an office. ELs, like Vinn and his sister, often code switch, or shift from English to their native Spanish dialect, to be accepted or receive approval from Ms. Woodward and classmates.

PAUSE AND REFLECT

1. Go to the ESOL in Higher Ed website or search the Internet to find descriptions of language varieties and dialects of American English or other languages.

2. With a partner or in a small group, explore the wider speech community of your neighborhood, and listen for dialect differences. Use voice memo, Voice Thread, or other technologies to record speech.

3. Note similarities and differences across your data, summarize your findings about each dialect, their approximate age, and their educational and socioeconomic level.

4. Share the results of your research with your classmates and discuss general findings.

5. Take an online quiz (based on the Harvard Dialect Survey) to gain insight into your own American English. Print your map and bring to class to discuss. URL: https://www.nytimes.com/interactive/2014/upshot/dialect-quiz-map.html

Child Language Socialization

Cross-cultural studies of child language development have shown that even with a wide range of *inputs*, young children grow up speaking the language spoken around them. Although child-rearing practices concerning language vary greatly across cultures, similar types of language phenomena are probably found across child L1 learners (one-word stage, two-word stage, etc.). Even deaf children who grow up in homes with hearing parents create their own 'home sign', an individual language having structural properties similar to those of spoken languages. But children also learn to participate in the **communicative practices** of their homes and neighborhoods, and these vary quite widely.

Child language socialization is a process of helping children participate in various discourses of home and neighborhood. It is not to be confused with talking to children about values or how to behave in various situations. Language socialization practices are part of the often-hidden aspects of culture; parents teach children these practices by engaging in them and by rewarding them when they 'perform' those ways of speaking well. Some families engage in joke-telling or teasing, others in chastising, others in arguing, and others in praising. Their children learn those practices by example. In Ms. Woodward's classroom, she seeks to better understand ways to support her ELs' academic and cultural needs by consciously guiding her students in the secondary language socialization practices of the school. If teachers are familiar with the communication practices of the students' homes, it is more likely that they can make the appropriate connections. When they are not aware, however, and do not understand the cultural underpinnings of those practices, they may view students' interactional styles in unfavorable ways.

Nuanced (indirect) and direct communications carry various meanings. This is a function of pragmatics. Consider the act of complaining. You might take a more passive approach when asked how your meal is and subtly hint, "The soup isn't very hot." Or, you might be more direct with, "Could you please reheat my lukewarm soup?" Culture and language are equally important to effective communication, especially with regard to pragmatics.

1. A very common practice in middle American class homes is reading books to or with very young children. Reflect on how you read books with very young children. Do you ask children questions about the pictures as you go along? What kinds of questions?

2. Now compare this activity with a Japanese mother who reads a story with her child (Kato-Otani, 2004). She would not ask information questions, or even try to teach vocabulary, but instead demonstrate language that evokes in the child empathy with the characters.

3. What do you think might be the implications for children in each scenario when an American child enters a Japanese school, or a Japanese child enters an American school?

Language Functions (Speech Acts)

The field of pragmatics includes attention to the **functions** of language, such as greeting, promising, requesting, negotiating, asking and answering questions, talking back, teasing, and lying, to name a very small subset of those used in a North American context. It is interesting to realize that each cultural group highlights certain functions more than others, or lacks functions found in another community altogether. For example, in the U.S., people in some speech communities value and engage in the practice of relating information and explaining something, while people in other communities find such talk boring, preferring to tell each other stories. The previous group gives TED talks; the others might become comedians like Jimmy Kimmel and Dave Chappelle, or storytellers like Ellen DeGeneres and Garrison Keillor.

In the Caribbean, telling a good story is highly valued, but the truth value of the story may be less important than its stylistic or emotional impact. Bragging is very important in some communities, while it is looked down upon as immodest and arrogant in others. Gossiping, or **chisme**, is a very important aspect of life among women in the Dominican Republic. When Ms. Woodward studied applied linguistics in her education program, her professor from Santo Domingo created a scenario in which "chisme" was skillfully and humorously presented. Everyone in the class became masters of "chisme" in a short period of time. In her classroom now, she brings in humor and chismes whenever the opportunity arises.

What's In a Name?

At the beginning of the phonology section, you read about Vinn and the way his name was changed by Ms. Woodward. Recall that Vinn was somewhat confused because she called him Vicente or Vincent; but, he never corrected her. Although Ms. Woodward was trained in ways to effectively instruct ELs, she overlooked this simple, but important, speech act. In thinking back, Ms. Woodward recalls a lecture by a professor in the education program and of one teacher-candidate who profusely disagreed with the professor's point. The candidate asked, *"What if a student wants to be known by a new name? Shouldn't that be respected in the same way?"* The professor conceded her point, realizing that some children, teenagers, or adults may want the right to claim a particular new name. But in the beginning, she still would err on the side of trying to pronounce new students' names as closely as possible to the way they are named by the parents or other speakers of their language.

Here is a counter-example. When the author of this chapter first started teaching children from Vietnam, she worked at pronouncing their names as well as she could, struggling with the various tones. A few of them chided her for mispronouncing their names, claiming that Americans couldn't get the tones right. So, tune in to the way your students speak to each other, talk about naming preferences, and let your ELs be the experts. **It is important for all educators, teachers, administrators, and school staff to remember that one's name is very precious, a personal attribute of one's own.**

PAUSE AND REFLECT

1. Select one of the speech acts keeping in mind how it functions in the society, and in what contexts it is used.

2. Describe ways for Ms. Woodward to teach her ELs how to perform the function in English.

3. Plan a role play to present the speech act in class, or one that you could later assign your students.

4. If you have worked with speakers of other languages, what situations arose among the group that pertained to naming?

The concept of language development, a term somewhat interchangeable with acquisition and learning, has been presented in this chapter. You have read that, according to the Chomskian view, phonology, morphology, and syntax are acquired by young children without having to be taught. Chomsky and other linguistics believe that basic language structures are universal and innate. But the contents of semantics and pragmatics are learned within the cultural contexts of one's upbringing. Pragmatic knowledge is an important aspect of language learning, but pragmatic competence may be of greater importance than correct forms. For example, in some communities an explainer may command less attention than one who has a *way with words*. Ms. Woodward shares with her colleagues that oftentimes individuals are unaware of the pragmatic rules of one's own language unless they are broken by someone who does not know those unspoken rules. **She emphasizes that it is impossible for educators to know how pragmatics works in all language communities represented in a school; but, by listening, looking, and learning, every educator can make language 'rules' come to light**.

PAUSE AND REFLECT

1. With a partner or in a small group, select a topic that you teach at your grade level or in your content area.

2. Imagine a scenario in which an EL enters your classroom with very limited English. Create an assessment task that will allow you to properly accommodate the EL with respect to this topic.

3. With your classmates role-play the scenario.

Extended Thinking and Synthesis Questions

1. What languages are spoken by ELs in your school district? Go to the ESOL in Higher Ed website to explore websites and resources on data of ELs across the nation, in your state, and in your community.

2. In the section on lexicon, several ideas were presented for helping students develop vocabulary knowledge. Select some that would be appropriate for your ELs and suggest others that have been successful in your classroom.

3. Select or write several sentences containing words an EL tends to mispronounce because of L1 interference.
   A. Describe how you would help this student produce the words correctly.
   B. Identify sentences from EL's writing that contain errors in morphology or syntax. Explain how you would help the student to understand the nature of the errors and to learn to correct them him/herself.
   C. Provide sentences containing words that have multiple meanings and suggest ways in which ELs can identify the correct one.

4. Refer back to the "Dear Teacher Letter" that you wrote at the beginning of this chapter. Reflect on your responses and add to them based on your knowledge of "language as a system" (phonology, morphology, syntax, semantics, and pragmatics). Compose a letter to a teacher or an administrator describing how an understanding of "language as a system" is essential for all teachers.

5. Refer back to the *Anticipation Guide* at the beginning of this chapter, and complete the column on the right. Share your responses with a classmate.

6. Write a letter to a leader in your school community (e.g., teacher, administrator, school board member, superintendent) explaining how knowledge of language as a system is important for educators in supporting ELs in acquiring proficiency in English and academic literacy across all grade levels and content areas.

REFERENCES

Abrahams, R. D. (1972). The training of the Man of Words in talking sweet. *Language in Society, 1,* 15–29.

Adger, C. T., Snow, C. E., & Christian, D. (Eds.). (2002). *What teachers need to know about language.* ERIC Clearinghouse on languages and linguistics: The Center for Applied Linguistics.

Ariza, E. N., Morales-Jones, C. A., Yahya, N., & Zainuddin, H. (2010). *Why TESOL? Theories and issues in teaching English to speakers of other languages in K–12 classrooms.* Kendall Hunt Publishing.

Bear, D. R., Helman, L., Templeton, S., Invernizzi, M., & Johnston, F. (2007). *Words their way with English language learners: Word study for phonics, vocabulary, and spelling instruction.* Pearson Education, Inc.

Carrell, P. L., & Grabe, W. (2002). Reading. In N. Schmitt (Ed.), *An introduction to applied linguistics.* (pp. 233–250). Edward Arnold.

Cazden, C. B. (1988). *Classroom discourse: The language of teaching and learning.* Heinemann.

Chomsky, C. (1957). *Syntactic structures.* The Hague. Mouton.

Chomsky, C. (1965). *Aspects of the theory of syntax.* MIT Press.

Chomsky, N. (1959). A review of B. F. Skinner's *Verbal Behavior. Language, 35*(1), 26–58.

Cook, G. (2000). *Language Play, Language Learning.* Oxford University Press.

Curtain, H., & Dahlberg, C. A. (2010). *Languages and children: Making the match: New languages for young learners, grades K–8* (4th ed.). Pearson Education.

Davis, S. (1991). *Pragmatics: A reader.* Oxford University Press.

deOliveira, L. C., & Yough, M. (2015). *Preparing teachers to work with English language learners in mainstream classrooms.* TESOL Press.

Denton, P. (2013). *The power of our words: Teacher language that helps children learn* (2nd ed.). Center for Responsive Schools, Inc.

Figueroa, R. (1990). Assessment of linguistic minority group children. In C. Reynolds & R. Kamphaus (Eds.), *Handbook of psychological and educational assessment of children: Intelligence and achievement* (pp. 671–696). The Guilford Press.

Fisher, D., Rothenberg, C., & Frey, N. (2007). *Language learners in the English classroom.* Illinois: National Council of Teachers of English

Gottlieb, M., & Ernst-Slavit, G. (2014). *Academic language in diverse classrooms: Definitions and contexts.* Corwin Publishing.

Govoni, J. M. (Ed.). (2008). *Perspectives on teaching K–12 English language learners* (2nd ed.). Pearson Custom Publishing.

Hall, J. K. (1993). The role of oral practices in the accomplishment of our everyday lives. *Applied Linguistics, 14,* 145–166.

Hall, J. K. (1998). Researching classroom discourse and foreign language learning. *Pragmatics and Language Learning,* vol. 9. 293–311.

Halliday, M. (1975). Some aspects of sociolinguistics. In E. Jacobsen (Ed.) *Interactions between linguistics and mathematical education.* UNESCO.

Heath, S. B. (1983). *Ways with words: Language, life and work in communities and classrooms.* Cambridge University Press.

Hickey, P.J. & Lewis, T. (2013). The Common Core, English Learners, and Morphology 101:Unpacking LS.4 for ELLs. *The Language and Literacy Spectrum, 23,* 69–84.

Hudson R. (2000). I amn't. *Language, 76*(2), 297–323.

Hulit, L. M., Howard, M. R., & Fahey, K. R. (2011). *Born to talk: An introduction to speech and language development* (5th ed.). Pearson Education.

Inhelder, B., & Piaget, J. (trans. A. Parsons and S. Milgram). (1958). *The growth of logical thinking from childhood to adolescence: An essay on the construction of formal operational structures*. Routledge and Kegan Paul.

International Phonetic ALphabet (IPA). (2020). https://www.ipachart.com/

Kachru, B. B. (1990). *The alchemy of English: The spread, functions, and models of non-English Englishes*. Pergamon Press.

Kachru, B. B., Kachru, Y., & Nelson, C. L. (2006). *The handbook of world Englishes*. Wiley-Blackwell.

Kato-Otani, E. (2001). *Joint book reading between Japanese mothers and their children*. Harvard Graduate School of Education Publishing.

Kieffer, M. J., & Lesaux, N. K. (2008). The role of derivational morphology in the reading comprehension of Spanish-speaking English language learners. *Reading and Writing: An Interdisciplinary Journal, 21*(8), 783–804.

Kieffer, M. J., & Lesaux, N. K. (2012). Effects of academic language instruction on relational and syntactic aspects of morphological awareness for sixth graders from linguistically diverse backgrounds. *The Elementary School Journal, 112*(3), 519–545.

Kinsella, K. (2017, March). *Helping academic English learners develop productive word knowledge. Language Magazine.*

Learning A-Z. (2020). Common Core. (2020). https://.learninga-z.com/site/what-we-do/standards/common-core/academic-vocabulary#AcademicVocab

Lightbown, P., & Spada, N. (2006). *How Languages are Learned* (3rd ed.). Oxford University Press.

Lucas, T. (2004). *Deciphering the meaning of puns in learning English as a second language: A study of triadic interaction*. Ph.D. dissertation, Florida State University, Tallahassee, FL.

Mendoza, M. B. (2004). *Collaborative construction of word knowledge in vocabulary-related group activities in the ESL classroom*. Ph.D. dissertation, Florida State University, Tallahassee, FL.

Nation, I. S. P. (1990). *Teaching and learning vocabulary*. Cambridge University Press.

Nation, I. S. P. (2001). *Learning vocabulary in another language*. Cambridge University Press.

Nation, P., & Meara, P. (2002). Vocabulary. In N. Schmitt (Ed.), *An Introduction to Applied Linguistics* (pp. 35–54). Edward Arnold.

NYC Dept. of Education. English Language Learners. (2020). https://.schools.nyc.gov/learning/multilingual-learners/english-language-learners

O'Grady, W., Archibald, J., Aronoff, M., & Rees-Miller, J. (2005). Semantics: The analysis of meaning (5th ed.). *Contemporary Linguistics: An Introduction* (pp. 201–244). Bedford/St. Martins Press.

Omaggio-Hadley, A. (2001). *Teaching language in context* (3rd ed.). Heinle and Heinle.

Oxford Academic. Applied Linguistics. (2020). https://academic.oup.com/applij/pages/about

Parkay, F. W., & Stanford, B. H. (2010). *Becoming a teacher* (8th ed.). Merrill-Pearson Education.

Platt, E., Harper, C., & Mendoza, M. B. (2003). Dueling philosophies: Inclusion or separation for Florida's English language learners? *TESOL Quarterly, 37*(1), 105, 133.

Platt, E. J. (2004). "Uh uh no hapana": Intersubjectivity, meaning, and the self. In J. K. Hall, L. Marchenkova, & G. Vitanova (Eds), *Dialogue with Bakhtin and second language learning*. Lawrence Erlbaum Associates.

Rivera, C., & Stansfield, C. (2004). The effects of linguistic simplification of science test items on the performance of limited English proficient and monolingual English speaking students. *Educational Assessment, 9*(3–4), 79–105.

Shuy, R. D. (1970). *Teaching Standard English in the Inner City*. Center for Applied Linguistics.

Slobin, D. I. (2000). Verbalized events: A dynamic approach to linguistic relativity and determinism. In S. Nieimeier and R. Dirven (Eds.), *Evidence for linguistic relativity* (pp. 107–138). John Benjamins.

Stanford Encyclopedia of Philosophy. (2020). Pragmatics. https://plato.stanford.edu/entries/pragmatics/

Tompkins, G. (1998). *50 Literacy strategies step by step*. Merrill.

Whelan-Ariza, E. N., Morales-Jones, C. A., Yahya, N., & Zainuddin, H. (2006). *Why TESOL? Theories and issues in teaching English to speakers of other languages in K–12 classrooms*. Kendall Hunt Publishing.

Yule, G. (2010). *The study of language* (4th ed.). Cambridge University Press.

Zainuddin, H., Yahya, N., Morales-Jones, C. A., & Whelan-Ariza, E. N. (2007). *Fundamentals of teaching English to speakers of other languages in K–12 mainstream classrooms* (2nd ed.). Kendall Hunt Publishing.

Zimmerman, C. B. (2009). *Word knowledge: A vocabulary teacher's handbook*. Oxford University Press.

WEBSITE RESOURCES

IPA Chart
Link: https://www.ipachart.com

Speech Accent Archive
Link: http://accent.gmu.edu/

WIDA
Link: https://wida.wisc.edu

4A
Activity!
LINGUISTICS

Name: _____

In your own words... The concepts of applied linguistics are the building blocks for language acquisition. Write your own definition for each of these important concepts. Include an example, and be prepared to discuss with your classmates.

PHONOLOGY:

MORPHOLOGY:

SYNTAX:

SEMANTICS:

PRAGMATICS:

4B

Activity!

LINGUISTICS

Morphological Magic—Teachers frequently make up games to teach or reinforce important concepts. Go ahead and fill out each space with either a prefix, root word, or suffix. Next, define each whimsical word.

Prefix	Root	Suffix	Definition
re	sleep	ify	*Going back to sleep twice in one morning*

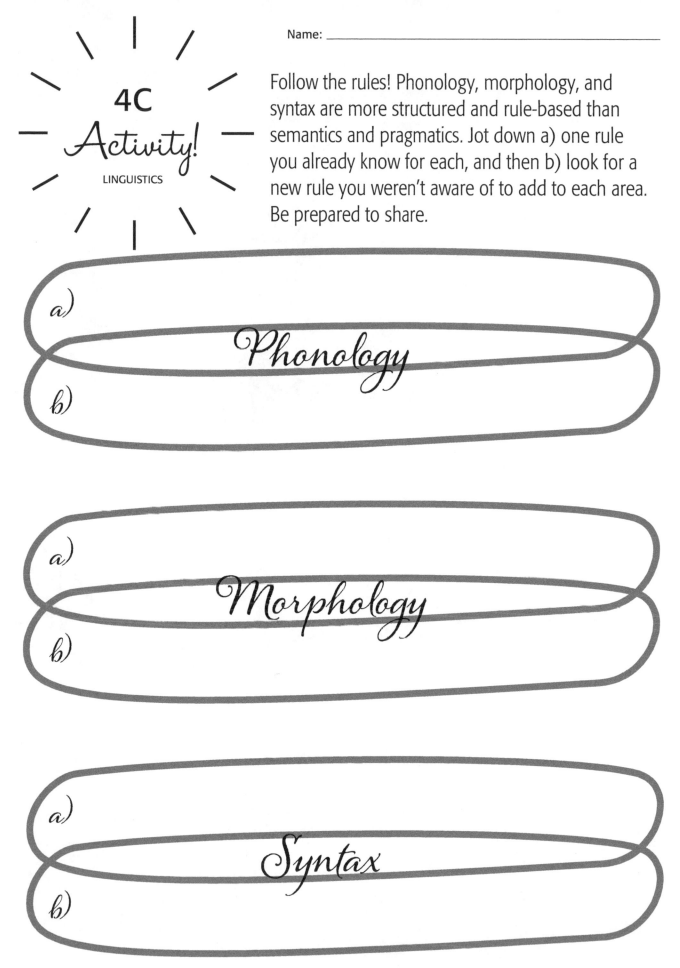

4C
Activity!
LINGUISTICS

Name: _____

Follow the rules! Phonology, morphology, and syntax are more structured and rule-based than semantics and pragmatics. Jot down a) one rule you already know for each, and then b) look for a new rule you weren't aware of to add to each area. Be prepared to share.

a)

Phonology

b)

a)

Morphology

b)

a)

Syntax

b)

4D
Activity!
LINGUISTICS

Idioms can be confusing for ELs. Look at the images below, and write the corresponding idiom for each. Discuss with a classmate what each idiom really means. Just in case you get stumped, the answers are below (upside-down).

Raining cats and dogs; a dime a dozen; don't judge a book by its cover; don't let the cat out of the bag; a piece of cake; heard it through the grapevine.

4E
Activity!
LINGUISTICS

This cube includes the 5 areas of applied linguistics and one blank space for you to write a topic of your choice. Cut it out, glue or tape it together, and use it like a die to create word games focusing on whatever side shows.

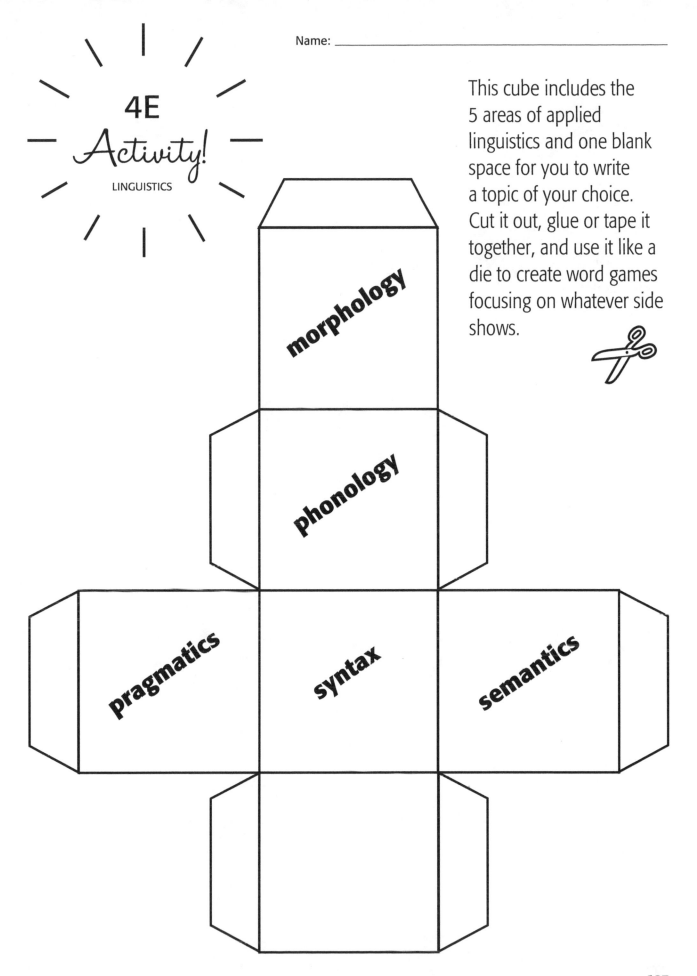

morphology

phonology

pragmatics

syntax

semantics

4F
Activity!
LINGUISTICS

This cube is intentionally left blank. Write directions on each side for students to complete (e.g., 'Pronounce these words in all ways possible: wind, tear, close, sewer'.). Create a new linguistics game.

Analyzing Theories of Second Language Learning

María Beatriz Mendoza,
Elizabeth Platt, and
Teresa Lucas

© donskarpo/Shutterstock.com

LITERACY STRATEGY: PREVIEWING

(1) Review the **bold-faced** and *italicized* words throughout the chapter.
(2) Share how you believe the reading connects to theories and research in second language acquisition.

Tips for Use with ELs: In this strategy the teacher draws attention to items such as the title, table of contents, glossary, introduction, summaries, headings, and any graphics in a text with the goal of supporting students in navigating through the reading.

Adapted from Vacca, J.L. & Vacca, R.T. 1996. *Content reading area.* 5th ed. NY: Harper Collins.

TEACHER VIGNETTE: MS. WOODWARD (CONTINUED)

Ms. Woodward is still uncertain about ways to promote ELs' language and content learning. Quite often she googles suggestions to support ELs or gathers ideas and resources from Pinterest to develop her lessons. She even visits TeachersPayTeachers.com for ideas. However, she has recently decided to explore second language acquisition (SLA) theories and developmental stages of language to expand her expectations for Vinn and other ELs in her classroom. Ms. Woodward wants to better understand how learning a second language differs from learning a first. She reconsiders how individuals learn languages and begins to realize that a much deeper understanding of SLA theories will guide her teaching practices. Her college professor used to say, *"Just as a slab sets the foundation in construction, theories provide the foundation for designing, rationalizing, and implementing specific and relevant strategies. Without a solid foundation, structures may collapse; without an alignment to SLA theories, lesson planning and teaching strategies for ELs may break down."* In this chapter, we present an overview of SLA theories and Ms. Woodward's insights, along with her colleagues' input.

PAUSE AND REFLECT

1. How do people learn languages? Is there a difference between children and adults?

2. How do ELs learn English in the mainstream classroom?

3. Can you think of how learning a second language differs from acquiring your first language?

4. What are effective ways to support learning of a second language?

APPROACHES TO LANGUAGE DEVELOPMENT

Early ideas about language learning followed the concepts of the psychological theory of **behaviorism,** developed in part by **B. F. Skinner** during the early 20th century. He was a professor of psychology at Harvard University from 1958 until his retirement in 1974. He is credited with introducing a scientific approach to the study of human behavior. Skinner suggested that children learn language through listening to their caretakers' speech, repeating what they hear, and receiving positive reinforcement in order to continue speaking.

PAUSE AND REFLECT

1. How do children learn how to write?

2. Is writing the same across cultures? Why/why not?

Following the **behaviorist** model, **Charles Fries** looked at second language learning as a matter of listening and repeating to form foreign language habits. He and **Robert Lado** proposed comparing first and second languages by concentrating on their differences and selecting practice drills based on their findings. The process of comparing languages is called **contrastive analysis.** Here, second language learning is dependent upon transfer from the first language. A positive transfer occurs if the languages share similar structural components, order, and meaning; however, if the structural components, order, and meaning do not transfer appropriately, then there is a negative transfer or interference. An example of negative transfer for Spanish speakers is when they say *"Is happy"* for *"She is happy."* The subject (she), is not needed in Spanish like it is in English. When ELs transfer structures that are not the same in both languages this is called **negative transfer.**

Robert Lado, Tampa, Florida (1915–1995)
First Dean, Georgetown University School of Languages and Linguistics

The premise is that teachers should be able to predict the elements of negative transfer and drill these items to form the "correct" language habit. The language teaching method based on repetition and practice is called the **audiolingual approach.** The teacher directs and controls all class activities. The emphasis is on memorization using scripted dialogues and

Charles Fries (1887–1967)
American linguist, founder of the English Language Institute, University of Michigan

sentence patterns, for example. The belief is that repetition leads to habit formation (i.e., language learning). The **grammar-translation method** is the traditional way of analyzing and studying the grammatical rules of a language. For example, teaching vocabulary through translations, elaborating on grammar rules, and focusing on definitions in readings. It is a teacher-centered approach. The audiolingual approach shifted the attention from the study of written language, prevalent in the grammar-translation method, to the study of oral language.

In the 1950s, **Noam Chomsky**, who is considered by some to be "*the father of modern linguistics*," pointed out that children do not just repeat what they hear, but create novel utterances. He posited that we have an innate *language acquisition device (LAD)* that allows us to infer the rules of language from the language we hear, and thus create an infinite number of unique utterances. This **innatist** position paralleled the general cognitive theory of **Jean Piaget** (1896–1980), who was born in Switzerland. A graduate of the University of Neuchâtel in biological sciences, his studies of cognitive abilities at different ages led him to posit universal developmental stages of child development. Piaget saw development as an internal process of *assimilation, accommodation*, and *restructuring*. He largely ignored the role of the parent, teacher, or context in the development that occurred through encounters between the child and his/her material surroundings. Piaget did not apply his theory to language learning, but we can see the application: **A child assimilates language by listening to it, accommodates what is heard in the LAD, and restructures it to formulate unique communication.** According to the innatist view, language is considered an "in-the-head" phenomenon, in which language is processed internally, with the forms and rules inferred from the input.

In the 1980s, **Stephen Krashen** developed a theory that argued that learning a second language (L2) is a cumulative process involving the incorporation of new grammatical forms into a developing system (Krashen, 1982; Krashen, 1985; Krashen & Terrell, 1983). He developed a comprehensive theory of second language learning comprised of **five hypotheses**.

1. Acquisition/Learning

Acquisition is a natural process of developing a language, as when the child acquires the first language, or an older person assimilates a second language by being immersed in it. **Learning** is a conscious process in which one is learning "about" the language through grammar rules and vocabulary study.

2. Natural Order

Research on first language (L1) acquisition found that there is a natural order in which a child acquires the language. An infant begins cooing, then babbling, then producing single words, followed by two-word root word phrases. Research shows that the development of various morphemes that qualify root words follows a set sequence. For example, the third person singular -s is acquired later on; whereas, the -ing marker (progressive tense) is acquired early on. Thus, certain grammatical rules and structures are acquired before others.

3. Input

Language develops internally when the learner encounters the language in the environment, and infers the rules to be able to understand and use the language. Thus, the role of input is essential and should be a little beyond the current capacity of the learner which is represented as ($i + 1$); (i) represents the student's current level of proficiency and (+ 1) represents input that is slightly above the student's level. Students are able to improve and progress along a natural order when they receive second language input that is one step beyond their current stage of linguistic competence.

4. Monitor

The learner employs internal processes to extract the rules of the language to gain proficiency. An internal monitor alerts the learner to errors and indicates how to self-correct. According to Krashen, the acquisition system is the utterance initiator, while learning monitors or edits. The monitor acts in planning and correcting when ELs have met three specific conditions: have sufficient time, focus on form or think about corrections, and know the rules (Krashen, 1987).

5. Affective Filter

The affective filter is like a "screen" that controls how much comprehensible input gets through to the learner. Emotional factors play a major role in the learner's ability to acquire a second language. Krashen stipulates that high motivation, self-confidence, a good self-image, and a low level of anxiety support success in second language acquisition. Low motivation, low self-esteem, and high levels of anxiety raise the affective filter. This filter acts like a mental block and prevents comprehensible input and language acquisition.

PAUSE AND REFLECT

1. Bearing in mind Krashen's hypotheses, interview a mainstream Pre-K–12 teacher and inquire about the approaches or methods s/he uses to support the proficiency and the academic content of ELs. Ask for the rationale for the approach and strategies and how they are effective for ELs.

2. Based on your findings, write a reflection on how knowledge of Krashen's hypotheses affect teaching and ELs' learning.

Interactionists, such as Doughty and Long (2003), took a step beyond Krashen, as they agreed that meaningful, comprehensible input is necessary, but acquisition occurs during interaction. Their view entailed a "between-heads" approach. When learners interact with others, they negotiate meaning, and in the process of clarifying, simplifying, repeating, and using modifications in interactions, new forms are learned. **In other words, when language is adjusted in conversation, input becomes comprehensible, making language learning possible.** Researchers, such as Krashen and Long, referred to language acquisition as neither taught nor learned; it emerges as a learner incorporates a universal set of innate linguistic principles. **Acquisition** is largely an *unconscious* process, a term attributed to Noam Chomsky, who challenged the behavioral view of language learning in the late 1950s. Acquisition relies on both the learner noticing the form and consciously or unconsciously putting it to use.

An alternate view of learning is presented in **sociocultural theory (SCT)**. About the same time Piaget was developing his theory of development in Switzerland, **Lev Vygotsky** (1896–1934) was looking at development from a very different perspective in his native Russia. Vygotsky was not trained in science but studied law, literature, linguistics, and the psychology of art. His studies of child learning acknowledged the sociocultural milieu of the learners. Only in the latter part of the 20th century did Vygotsky's writings become translated into English and thus available to North American scholars and practitioners alike. For Vygotsky, learning was not only an internal process, but was also happening in the interaction of the child with others and with the environment. In other words, from the earliest stages of development, children are enculturated through mediation of language, and interaction within a culture contributes to shaping higher mental processes. See **Table 5.1** for an overview of the two theorists.

	Piaget (1896–1980)	**Vygotsky (1896–1934)**
Learning:	Innate ability: child goes through a set of stages of cognitive development	Both internal and external: learning happens through interaction with others and the environment
Characteristics:	"In-the-mind" phenomenon; solo mind evolves (maturation)	Collaborative/social phenomenon scaffolded by adults and peers
Key concepts:	Assimilation, Accommodation, Restructuring	Mediation, Internalization, Zone of Proximal Development (ZPD)

Table 5.1   Two Theories of Cognitive Development: Piaget vs. Vygotsky.

Mediation is the core concept of Vygotsky's theory. The mediation process occurs within a specified *context* in which learning and development depend on the learners' experiences and interaction with objects and with others in the environment. Mediation leads to *internalization,* defined as "the internal reconstruction of an external operation" (Vygotsky, 1978, pp. 28–29). Vygotsky noted how a child's mental operations begin on the outside through interactions with parents, siblings, and others, and then go "underground." As young children interact with parents or older siblings, their interaction provides a **scaffolding** to assist toward functioning more independently. Although the term scaffolding did not originate from Vygotsky himself, but from Jerome Bruner and others (Wood, Bruner, & Ross, 1976), it is compatible with Vygotsky's concept of **zone of proximal development (ZPD)**. Two types of learning occur. One is that of elementary functions, similar to conditioning in animals. For example, after touching a hot stove, a child learns not to touch it again! The second type of learning relates to higher mental functions and occurs only in human development. The most complex of these higher mental functions is language. Language develops through mediation and internalization and becomes itself a tool for learning. From the very earliest stages of development, children are enculturated through the mediation of language. Interaction within a culture contributes to shaping higher mental processes, contrasting with Piaget who did not consider the impact of culture on mental development. **In the Vygotskyan perspective, language and culture develop simultaneously and are inextricably linked.**

Since the 1980s, James Lantolf and his associates at Penn State University have been advocating for the application of SCT concepts to second language learning. They have noted that the learner already has internalized the first language. The second language offers the opportunity to develop new ways of meaning through collaborative activity. Applying the ZPD to second language, learning "assumes that new language knowledge is jointly

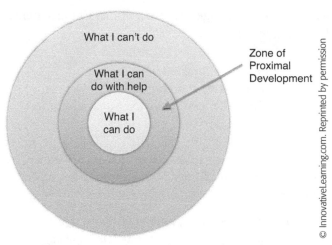

Figure 5.1   Zone of Proximal Development.

constructed through collaborative activity, which may or may not involve formal instruction . . . " (Mitchell, Myles, & Marsden, 2013, p. 227). While the SCT view of language acquisition emphasizes interaction, the process is not one of negotiation, but of actual knowledge creation between the interlocutors in the environment. SCT acknowledges both cognitive processes and the role of input and interaction. See **Table 5.2** for an overview of second language scholars.

Behaviorism	Innatism	SCT
Charles Fries (1887–1967) was an American linguist who taught at the University of Michigan. With his wife, Agnes Carswell, he developed the university's English Language Institute (1941), which pioneered methods and materials for teaching English to foreigners. **Robert Lado** (1915–1995) was one of Fries' students. He was a professor of English and Director of the language institutes at the University of Michigan and Georgetown University. He was one of the co-founders of *Teachers of English to Speakers of Other Languages* (TESOL), a professional association with a mission of teaching English to speakers of other languages.	**Stephen Krashen** (1941–) is professor emeritus at the University of California. In the late 1970s, he began promoting the "natural approach" to language teaching, which he detailed in a landmark text co-written with Tracy Terrell. His five hypotheses about language learning have greatly influenced L2 learning theory ever since. He supports bilingual education. **Michael Long** (1945–) is professor of Second Language Acquisition and Director of the School of Languages, Literatures, and Cultures at the University of Maryland. In his research, he documented the importance of interaction between learners and native speakers and among learners themselves.	**James Lantolf** (1947–), a pioneer in applying Vygotsky's sociocultural theory to second language acquisition, received his doctorate from Pennsylvania State University where he is currently professor of Spanish and Linguistics and Director of the Center for Language Acquisition. Lantolf has conducted extensive research on second language learning from the sociocultural perspective, and is also its major theoretician.

Table 5.2   Short Biographies of Second Language Scholars.

The use of idioms illustrates the challenges and frustrations ELs face in learning English, as exemplified by the following idioms:

You're coming out of your shell.
Are you down in the dumps?
You're driving me up the wall.
Shake a leg!

Native speakers of English use such expressions without even thinking; however, ELs are often confused with idioms as they tend to understand only literal meanings of the words. Thus, it is not only academic vocabulary that is a frustration, but everyday expressions.

1. *How can you guide ELs to grasp the meaning of ambiguous language?*
2. *What other tasks might be used with ELs that incorporate language play and collaborative activities?*

Language learning depends not simply on unconscious or incidental learning of new linguistic forms and functions, but also on active engagement of higher mental processes, all of which involve "awareness, abstraction, and control" (Vygotsky, 1986, p. 179). When ELs are actively engaged in their ZPD with the teacher and their peers, they are being directed to a more advanced level of functioning and learning. The zone of actual development expands beyond where it had been, and new skills, knowledge, and language are internalized. Although some researchers argue that ZPD is equivalent to Krashen's notion of ($i + 1$), it is actually quite different; ($i + 1$) *represents what the teacher does __for__ the learner; ZPD represents what the teacher does __with__ the learner.* See **Table 5.3** for summary of SLA theories.

	Behaviorism	**Input**	**Interaction**	**SCT**
Key Names	Fries and Lado	Krashen	Long	Lantolf
Key Concept(s)	Imitation Repetition	Comprehensible Input, ($i + 1$)	Negotiation of meaning	Mediation, Internalization, ZPD Scaffolding
L2 Learning	Language learning is a process of habit formation. Repetition and drills result in language acquisition.	Language learning is an "in-the-head" phenomenon. Language is innate, and its system is rule-governed.	Language learning is a "between-heads" approach. New forms are learned during interaction through negotiation of meaning.	Language is internalized as a result of social interaction. What happens "outside" determines what is "inside" learners' head.
L2 Teaching	Teachers provide a model for students to repeat sounds and memorize phrases and sentences.	Teachers provide input that is slightly higher than the learners' linguistic knowledge ($i + 1$).	Teachers provide opportunities for conversation (e.g., role-plays) and negotiation of meaning.	Teachers provide opportunities for learners to interact with each other, the teachers, and resources to expand their ZPDs.

Table 5.3   Summary of Theories of Second Language Learning.

	Behaviorism	**Input**	**Interaction**	**SCT**
L2 Activities	• Pronunciation (in class or with software) • Repetition of phrases and sentences (from a phrasebook)	• Listening and reading materials adapted to the level of the learner • Extensive reading (not meant for in-depth analysis)	• Role-plays of everyday situations • Debates in which learners explain their opinions and respond to other participants' opinions • Group work	• Small group discussions about unfamiliar vocabulary • Jigsaw activities • Role-plays and scenarios • Group work (see Table 5.4 for more on activities)
Error correction	Errors must be corrected immediately.	Errors are part of a natural process and corrected indirectly.	Errors are handled through negotiation of meaning.	Errors are dealt with implicitly or explicitly depending on the learner.

Table 5.3   Summary of Theories of Second Language Learning (Continued).

NOTE: **Tables 5.2** and **5.3** focus on second language theories. Chomsky and Vygotsky are not included as they influenced L2 scholars but did not propose second language theories.

 Before continuing on with this chapter, respond to the following questions with a partner, in a small group, or on your own.

1. In what way(s) do you learn new vocabulary best? In your own language? In a new language? In what ways do you teach new words to your ELs?
2. Although we don't always realize it, we use metaphorical and figurative language all the time. Make a list of several such expressions (e.g., bubbly person, feeling blue), and share ways to support ELs in understanding and using them appropriately.
3. If you find yourself lost in a new town or on a strange highway and your cell phone is dead, how would you find out where you are and how to reach your destination? How would you guide an EL to find his/her way to your home?
4. How would you design instruction to foster learning while maximizing ELs' independence, but assuring adequate academic and social support?

SCT IN THE LANGUAGE CLASSROOM

You may have noticed that the activities presented in **Table 5.3** for the interactionist and SCT views are similar. In this section, we present SCT activities to help explain the differences between approaches. Studies within the SCT theoretical framework show that mediation, object-, and self-regulation, not only contribute to successful completion of the task, but crucially to real language development (i.e., internalization). According to SCT, the dialogic interaction among students reveals what and how new knowledge comes to be internalized when they are engaged in challenging tasks. Thus, **language is best learned in realistic communicative context in which ELs are invested in doing something that interests them and challenged to overcome language difficulties.**

The activities in the SCT classroom rely on group processes rather than teacher direction, although teachers need to initiate these in such a way that students are successful. Teachers should plan and manage tasks carefully in order to guarantee that students are challenged and responsible for their own learning. Students should understand how to complete the task, using a range of internal (e.g., prior knowledge, the first language) and external (e.g., keys on a map, dictionaries, other people) resources. **Table 5.4** presents two sample activities with explanations on how theory and research provide a framework for these activities.

SCT Activity	SCT Framework
Activity 1: The teacher selects two similar documents with some missing information on each one: maps, recipes, bus schedules (or the like), then assigns two learners to use the new language to create two identical documents. For example, two novice Swahili learners engaged in a map jigsaw task involving two similar versions of a map of East Africa need to identify different features indicated with either a symbol and a name, or just a symbol (towns, lakes, mountains, etc.), and either ask questions or tell each other about those features. Ask: mountain, north, Tanzania Tell: Nairobi, town, Kenya, middle Kenya The participants are able to devise their own interesting ways to succeed in the task and share those strategies to use in the future.	In a study involving this activity, the analysis of task performance revealed a continuous struggle to agree on the format of the dialogue, the means of moving around the map, and the use of signals, such as rising intonation to indicate questions (Platt, 2004). Helping (or occasionally impeding) each other in various ways, learners created a dialogue using their own made-up version of Swahili, completing the task, and enjoying themselves. They realized that their achievement was considerable despite their novice status as Swahili learners. Even at the earliest stages of L2 development, learners use a variety of solutions to communication problems without having access to a large vocabulary and with only rudimentary knowledge of structure. They use words, phrases, gestures, intonation patterns, emphasis, pointing to task materials, etc. Or, they may just switch to L1.
Activity 2: In a reading class, ELs can be asked to read a text individually and identify unfamiliar vocabulary in the text and write the words on index cards. The learners are then assigned in groups to discuss the words. When they exchange their index cards, they identify the words that they know on their classmate's cards and teach their classmates the words they know. They may also find words that none of the group members know. In addition to speaking with one another, they can use other resources available to learn in the classroom, such as the teacher and the dictionary, to discover the meanings of any unknown vocabulary together.	When given the opportunity to focus on vocabulary and work collaboratively, ELs may *construct* word knowledge together. A study on vocabulary learning showed that ELs internalized knowledge of the form, function, and meaning of words they constructed collaboratively in conversations (Mendoza, 2004). The group activity provides the scenario for learners to internalize and discuss word meanings. The process of vocabulary learning is gradual and cumulative, so teachers should encourage ELs to assist one another through their respective ZPDs. During these dialogues, they should use a variety of resources to make themselves understood and even assist their classmates (mediation), which leads to *internalization*.

Table 5.4   Activities Based on the SCT Theoretical Framework.

MS. WOODWARD'S INSIGHTS ON SLA THEORIES

Behaviorist Approach: Ms. Woodward and her colleagues often observe ELs repeating and mimicking their peers in small group activities. They acknowledge that these strategies can be helpful in acquiring a language, especially when it comes to the sounds of the language. Ms. Woodward is also aware that repetition is essential to learning and in enhancing students' listening skills. Identifying similarities and differences between ELs' languages can also be useful. She understands that a language has a unique set of patterns and grammar rules. Thus, she is attentive to the relationships between English and the native languages of her ELs and to possible learning difficulties for them based on their L1. Ms. Woodward remembers some Spanish grammar rules from her high school classes and can use that knowledge when working with ELs. However, she knows learning a language exclusively through behaviorist methods does not work, as she cannot speak Spanish after studying it for four years in high school. Ms. Woodward recalls memorizing vocabulary and verb tenses in her Spanish classes, yet, quickly points out that she cannot recall much of it. She recounts having conversations outside of school and joking about speaking Spanish by adding in "Spanglish" or slang she picked up from her peers; she is not, by any means, proficient in Spanish.

© Iakov Filimonov/Shutterstock.com

Innatist View: Ms. Woodward visualizes the LAD as an internal "black box" where ELs interpret the rules of the English language that they hear in the classroom and produce these words and sounds to demonstrate their proficiency and academic knowledge. She recognizes that the innatist theory is built on the premise that learning a language is inborn; yet, experience using the English language is necessary. In looking at Krashen's (2003a, 2003b) theory, Ms. Woodward can see that ELs acquire the English language through meaningful interactions in the classroom and are often not even aware of their proficiency. Thus, she continuously seeks ways to provide meaningful learning opportunities for ELs to acquire English proficiency and the academic content. In the classroom, teachers must provide the appropriate input; so, Ms. Woodward includes plenty of visuals, often paraphrases, enunciates her speech, and is aware of her use of idioms. She is mindful that ELs acquire proficiency and literacy through an understanding of the language, or simply stated, **ELs should be challenged through high expectations and varied practical opportunities to enhance their English skills and academic knowledge. In addition, Ms. Woodward strives to lower the anxiety and stress levels of her students, while at the same time increase their motivation and self-confidence.** She understands that if ELs are overwhelmed with vocabulary and grammar concepts in English, there are limited opportunities to grasp the academic content. Reflecting on Vinn, he always seems more confident when working collaboratively in small groups where he has time to practice. Although he is an outstanding student, Vinn still shows signs of hesitancy and a lack of confidence with math problems and science lab experiments. Yet, when working with a partner or small group, Vinn's anxiety seems to diminish. Thus, Ms. Woodward easily connects Krashen's (2003a, 2003b) affective filter hypothesis to her teaching style.

SCT Perspective: Ms. Woodward discovers that being knowledgeable about SCT is a comprehensive way of thinking about how languages are learned and a way to promote multiple opportunities for ELs to develop the necessary academic and social skills in English. She uses scaffolding strategies, such as pre-teaching, problem-solving, and graphic organizers. She recognizes that each student has the potential of expanding his/her ZPD in the classroom through interaction with peers, the teachers, and the resources available to them. Thus, she strives to plan lessons in which students will be engaged in a way that each student is directed to higher levels of understanding of content and linguistic proficiency. Ms. Sereda, one of Ms. Woodward's colleagues, also values SCT. She recounts learning French for three years in high school through memorization of grammar and lists of vocabulary words. Perhaps if she had the opportunity to "know" French versus learn "about" the language, she would be more confident and fluent. In not being able to speak French today, she certainly realizes the need to plan lessons in which the vocabulary, or academic language, is seamlessly interwoven into relevant and engaging activities. She focuses on creating a classroom environment where all students are motivated to learn the content and skills to demonstrate their knowledge through class activities, projects, and assessments. Ms. Sereda's students are continuously engaged in their learning experiences, which gives them new strategies and skills they can use as they continue learning and developing. Vinn's sister, Marta, needs more than just attention to linguistic forms and functions. She relies on various psychological tools, such as gestures, her first language, memory techniques, and decision-making processes as she internalizes classroom experiences and becomes more proficient in English. Marta's learning and development depend on classroom negotiations, mediations, and experiences.

LEARNER CHARACTERISTICS

Whichever theoretical lens Ms. Woodward and her colleagues look through, it can be easily seen that the circumstances and the processes of learning a second language are quite different. Learning a first language is mostly an unconscious process that happens in the normal course of development. If you've ever learned a second (or third) language, you know it's anything but unconscious. It's hard work. And it often occurs in a teaching/learning environment, not in the natural environment of the child growing up. You know that you are different from that infant you were when you learned your first language. There are personal characteristics that come into play when learning a second language, as well as a developed linguistic/cultural system already in place within the learner.

The diversity of those who are learning a second language plays a determinant role in the success of the learning process. Krashen recognized this when he included the **affective filter hypothesis** in his model of second language (L2) acquisition. The characteristic that he highlights in this hypothesis is anxiety. Other elements to consider are the learner's age, language learning aptitude, attitudes and motivation, personality, the nature of the L1, and the factors related to culture. In addition, second language learners in the classroom may be at different stages of language acquisition, necessitating accommodations at each stage. The stages of language acquisition are derived from Krashen's work and can help teachers think in terms of what the learners are able to do at each stage. See **Table 5.5.**

Stages	Characteristics	Considerations
1	**Pre-Production:** This is also known as the silent period. It may last up to six months. English language learners may have up to 500 words in their receptive vocabulary, but they are not yet ready to speak.	Teachers can encourage short responses, but should not try to force students to speak. Total Physical Response (TPR) (1983) activities are good at this stage.
2	**Early Production:** Students can usually speak in one- or two-word phrases. They can use short language chunks that have been memorized, although these chunks may not always be used correctly.	Teachers encourage students to speak by asking yes/no and short answer questions, as well as providing many opportunities for learners to hear and produce language chunks, such as "How are you?"; "May I get a book from the library?"
3	**Speech Emergence:** Students have developed a vocabulary of about 3,000 words. They can communicate with simple phrases and sentences.	Learners are able to participate more fully in role-plays and collaborative activities. In presenting content area topics, access to the L1 helps learners to understand the concepts while acquiring the English vocabulary to express them.
4	**Intermediate Fluency:** English language learners at the intermediate fluency stage have a vocabulary of 6,000 active words.	Learners are fully capable of interacting on the social level, so there may be a tendency to think that they have mastered the language. Teachers must continue to monitor that learners are understanding content.
5	**Advanced Fluency:** It takes students from 4–10 years to achieve proficiency in a second language. Student at this stage will be near-native in their ability to perform in content area learning.	Special attention must be paid to written language as this is the skill that is most difficult to master.

Table 5.5   Stages of Second Language Acquisition.

The major difference in first and second language learning resides in the learner, not in the theory. Let's look at the language learner through the proficiency descriptors by WIDA. What most obviously distinguishes the L2 learner is **age**. All infants begin the learning process at approximately the same age, while second language learners' starting points vary greatly. Some children learn more than one language from birth. They are not considered to be L2 learners, but are bilinguals. But if a child is introduced to a new language as a toddler, then the child is learning a second language. It is generally agreed that an early start results in more proficient learning, though some researchers point out that an adult with more developed cognitive processes is better able to learn some aspects of the language than a young child.

Aptitude is another factor in the ease with which a person learns a language. Carroll (1983) noted four characteristics that help in gaining proficiency in a language:

1. phonetic coding ability that allows one to perceive and remember distinct sounds associated with symbols;
2. grammatical sensitivity to the function of lexical elements in a sentence;
3. rote learning ability to learn and retain word meanings; and,
4. inductive learning ability to infer the rules governing the structure of a language.

Attitudes and **motivation** are key to success in learning a language. Does the individual want to learn the language? How does the person feel about people who speak the language? Oftentimes in the classroom you will find children who are brought to this country by their parents and are angry at being taken away from their home and friends. This can set up a situation in which the child reacts negatively to the language and the people who speak it. They are not motivated to learn. Teachers have a great impact on motivation by respecting the child and making learning the language a fun and interesting activity.

The anxiety that Krashen mentions is linked to attitude, motivation, and personality. Adjusting to a new life is stressful, and the stress can impede learning. A child with an outgoing personality may have an easier time than a more introverted individual. An optimist will see the situation differently from a pessimist. The level of **self-confidence** also impacts the learning process. In the classroom, ELs bring a wealth of knowledge about their native language and culture that they can share with everyone, that is teachers and other students. The teacher has the opportunity to help students build self-confidence by recognizing the contributions they make.

Generally, learners whose first language resides in the same language family as the language they are learning may have an easier time. The roots of English lie in the Germanic branch of the **Indo-European** family, along with Dutch, German, and Swedish, among others. Learners will find similarities in structure and vocabulary. Another branch of Indo-European is Latin, which includes Spanish, Italian, Portuguese, and French, among others. English was developing in the times of the Roman Empire, when Latin spread throughout the European continent and was the language of government and academia. Many terms made their way from Latin into English, thus the strong influence of Latin-root words in academic English today. Most of the languages in the Indo-European family use an alphabetic writing system, facilitating literacy among learners from these languages. Languages such as Mandarin, Japanese, and Korean employ a logographic system, creating more difficulty in acquiring literacy.

In the classroom, Ms. Woodward and her colleagues need to be aware of the characteristics of each learner and of the factors related to the native language and culture. At the same time, learners may all be at different stages in the learning process. Some come with very little knowledge of the L2, while others have had varying degrees of exposure. **Table 5.5** outlines the stages of language acquisition (derived from Krashen's work) and includes some considerations for teachers. **Tables 5.6** and **5.7** provide an overview of the WIDA Performance Definitions for Listening, Speaking, Reading, and Writing within sociocultural contexts.

WIDA Performance Definitions—Listening and Reading Grades K–12

Within sociocultural contexts for processing language . . .

	Discourse Dimension	Sentence Dimension	Word/Phrase Dimension
	Linguistic Complexity	Language Forms and Conventions	Vocabulary Usage
Level 6—Reaching	English language learners will process a range of grade-appropriate oral or written language for a variety of academic purposes and audiences. Automaticity in language processing is reflected in the ability to identify and act on significant information from a variety of genres and registers. English language learners' strategic competence in processing academic language facilitates their access to content area concepts and ideas.		
	At each grade, toward the end of a given level of English language proficiency, and with instructional support, English language learners will process...		
Level 5 Bridging	• Rich descriptive discourse with complex sentences • Cohesive and organized, related ideas across content areas	• A variety of complex grammatical structures • Sentence patterns characteristic of particular content areas	• Technical and abstract content-area language • Words and expressions with shades of meaning across content areas
Level 4 Expanding	• Connected discourse with a variety of sentences • Expanded related ideas characteristic of particular content areas	• Complex grammatical structures • A broad range of sentence patterns characteristic of particular content areas	• Specific and some technical content-area language • Words or expressions with multiple meanings across content areas
Level 3 Developing	• Discourse with a series of extended sentences • Related ideas specific to particular content areas	• Compound and some complex grammatical constructions • Sentence patterns across content areas	• Specific content-area language and expressions • Words and expressions with common collocations and idioms across content areas
Level 2 Emerging	• Multiple related simple sentences • An idea with details	• Compound grammatical structures • Repetitive phrasal and sentence patterns across content areas	• General content words and expressions, including cognates • Social and instructional words and expressions across content areas
Level 1 Entering	• Simple statements or questions • An idea within words, phrases, or chunks of language	• Simple grammatical constructions (e.g., commands, Wh- questions, declaratives) • Common social and instructional forms and patterns	• General content-related words • Everyday social, instructional, and some content-related words and phrases

Table 5.6 WIDA Performance Definitions: Receptive.

WIDA Performance Definitions—Speaking and Writing Grades K–12

Within sociocultural contexts for language use . . .

	Discourse Dimension	Sentence Dimension	Word/Phrase Dimension
	Linguistic Complexity	Language Forms and Conventions	Vocabulary Usage

Level 6—Reaching

English language learners will use a range of grade-appropriate language for a variety of academic purposes and audiences. Agility in academic language use is reflected in oral fluency and automaticity in response, flexibility in adjusting to different registers and skillfulness in interpersonal interaction. English language learners' strategic competence in academic language use facilitates their ability to relate information and ideas with precision and sophistication for each content area.

At each grade, toward the end of a given level of English language proficiency, and with instructional support, English language learners will produce . . .

	Discourse Dimension — Linguistic Complexity	Sentence Dimension — Language Forms and Conventions	Word/Phrase Dimension — Vocabulary Usage
Level 5 Bridging	• Multiple, complex sentences • Organized, cohesive, and coherent expression of ideas characteristic of particular content areas	• A variety of complex grammatical structures matched to purpose • A broad range of sentence patterns characteristic of particular content areas	• Technical and abstract content-area language, including content-specific collocations • Words and expressions with precise meaning across content areas
Level 4 Expanding	• Short, expanded, and some complex sentences • Organized expression of ideas with emerging cohesion characteristic of particular content areas	• Compound and complex grammatical structures • Sentence patterns characteristic of particular content areas	• Specific and some technical content-area language • Words and expressions with expressive meaning through use of collocations and idioms across content areas
Level 3 Developing	• Short and some expanded sentences with emerging complexity • Expanded expression of one idea or emerging expression of multiple related ideas across content areas	• Simple and compound grammatical structures with occasional variation • Sentence patterns across content areas	• Specific content language, including cognates and expressions • Words or expressions with multiple meanings used across content areas
Level 2 Emerging	• Phrases or short sentences • Emerging expression of ideas	• Formulaic grammatical structures • Repetitive phrasal and sentence patterns across content areas	• General content words and expressions • Social and instructional words and expressions across content areas
Level 1 Entering	• Words, phrases, or chunks of language • Single words used to represent ideas	• Phrase-level grammatical structures • Phrasal patterns associated with familiar social and instructional situations	• General content-related words • Everyday social and instructional words and expressions

Table 5.7   WIDA Performance Definitions: Expressive.

In this chapter, we took you on a brief journey through the principal second language learning theories that have developed since the mid-1900s, based on general theories of development, from behaviorism to innatism to sociocultural theory. While there is an historical sequence to the emergence of theories, **no single theory accounts for all the aspects of learning a second language.** When developing curricula, methods, and activities for working with learners, draw on aspects of each theory. The audiolingual method is often used in teaching and learning the sounds of the language. Since the L1 is always present in the learner's mind, **contrastive analysis** helps students to see relationships between the native language and the L2.

The more language the learner is exposed to, the better. The ideal setting for learning a language is to reside in a country or region where the language is spoken, thus maximizing exposure. In the U.S. classroom, teachers need to be aware of offering ELs language exposure that is comprehensible yet challenging ($i + 1$). Interactionists added the element of interaction to the innatist position. It is not only input that leads to acquisition, but also the interplay among speakers.

The **Sociocultural theory (SCT)** reminds us of the fundamental relationship of language and culture, as well as the collaborative nature of learning. The curicula must have a strong cultural component, while cooperative activities lead to the construction of knowledge as students work together. SCT places emphasis on what the learner can achieve through interaction with peers, teachers, and the environment. The role of the teacher in scaffolding is crucial in helping learners expand their ZPDs.

Drawing on theories to understand second language learning, and how best to structure learning environments to facilitate learning, is one tool teachers have to help students succeed. The other tool is being aware of the characteristics of learners that influence their learning process. **Age, language learning aptitude, attitudes and motivation, personality, the nature of the L1, and factors related to the learner's culture all play a fundamental role in success.** Teachers, like Ms. Woodward, must be keen observers to know how to engage with their students in ways that will make them feel comfortable and confident.

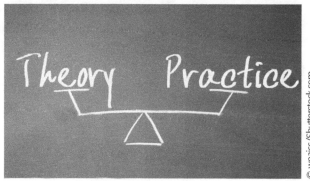

Learning a second language opens doors not only to a new way of speaking, but also to new ways of seeing and understanding the world. A classroom is deeply enriched with the presence of students from other cultures and languages. In U.S. classrooms, English learners are an asset, not a burden. Creating a positive classroom environment involves more than simply making every student feel happy and comfortable. It should be a place where ELs make the transition from *"learning a language to using it"* to *"using it to learning it."* The ultimate goal is for every teacher to have a thorough understanding of ways to meet their needs and to give them the tools to be successful in the classroom and in life.

LITERACY STRATEGY: STORY MAPPING

Directions: Fill in each circle with two or three words to describe each of the concepts of the Sociocultural Theory.

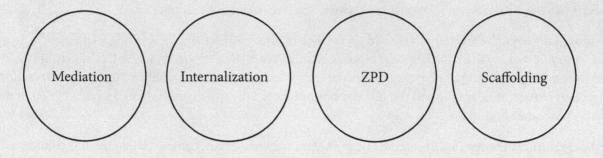

Mediation   Internalization   ZPD   Scaffolding

Tips for Use with ELs: This activity is a way of visually representing the main ideas of a chapter. Students should be able to either act out or orally explain the assigned reading through this visual and later on use it to write a summary. It may also be used to identify the beginning, middle, and ending of a story.

Extended Thinking and Synthesis Questions

1. Contrast Krashen's concept of (*i* + 1) with Vygotsky's ZPD. Do you think of them as similar or different?

2. How do the major theories discussed in this chapter (Behaviorism, Input, Interaction, SCT) relate to your own thinking about teaching students, particularly ELs?

3. Find a comic strip that makes use of a pun. Explain the meaning to a classmate. What might make the pun difficult for an EL?

4. Plan a class debate on how interaction optimizes language learning opportunities for ELs. In preparation, review theories and research on second language acquisition and bilingualism. Your debate might include the following:
   A. how knowledge of language as a system (phonology, morphology, semantics, syntax, and pragmatics) supports ELs;
   B. varied proficiency levels of ELs and the effects on the classroom;
   C. the role of ELs' home language and cultural backgrounds in the classroom;
   D. the sociocultural, sociopolitical, and psychological variables to support ELs;
   E. several ways educators should model using English appropriately;
   F. the role of individual learner variables and learning styles.

REFERENCES

Abrams, J. & Ferguson, J. (2004). Teaching students from many nations. *Educational Leadership, 62*(4), 64–67.

Adger, C. T., Snow, C. E., & Christian, D. Eds. (2002). *What teachers need to know about language.* ERIC Clearinghouse on languages and linguistics: The Center for Applied Linguistics.

Alvermann, D. E., & Phelps, S. F. (2005). *Content reading and literacy: Succeeding in today's diverse classrooms.* Pearson Education, Inc.

Ariza, N. E., Morales-Jones, C. A., Yahya, N., & Zainuddin, H. (2002). Phonology. Why *TESOL? Theories and Issues in Teaching English as a Second Language for K–12 teachers* (2nd ed.) (pp. 49–60). Florida Atlantic University.

Au, K. H. (2000). Literacy instruction for young children of diverse backgrounds. In D. S. Strickland & L. M. Morrow (Eds.) *Beginning reading and writing* (pp. 35–45). International Reading Association.

August, D., & Shanahan, T. (Eds.) (2006). *Developing literacy in second-language learners: Report of the national literacy panel on language-minority children and youth.* Lawrence Erlbaum.

Axelrod, A. (1994). *Pigs will be pigs.* Four Winds Press.

Baca, L. et al. (1994). Language minority students: Literacy and educational reform. In *Literacy: A redefinition.* Ed. N. Ellsworth et al., 1–21. Lawrence Erlbaum.

Beers, K. (2003). *When kids can't read: What teachers can do.* Heinemann.

Bloome, D., Carter, S., Christian, B., Otto, S., & Shuart-Faris, N. (2005). *Discourse analysis and the study of classroom language and literacy events: A microethnographic approach.* Erlbaum.

Braxton, B. (2001). Creating classroom community. Rethinking our classrooms. *Rethinking Our Classrooms: Teaching for Equity and Justice,* 2, 163–166. Rethinking Schools, Ltd.

Brown, H. D. (2000). *Principles of language learning and teaching* (4th ed.). Addison Wesley Longman, Inc.

Brown, H. D. (2007). *Teaching by principles: An interactive approach to language pedagogy* (3rd ed.). Pearson Education, Inc.

Carroll, J. B. (1983). *Psychometric theory and language testing.* In J. W. Oller, Jr. (Ed.), *Issues in language testing research* (pp. 80–107). Newbury House.

Chomsky, N. (1972). Stages in language development and reading exposure. *Harvard Educational Review,* 42, 1–33.

Doughty, C. & Long, M. H. (2003). *Handbook of second language acquisition.* Blackwell.

Drucker, M. J. (2003). What reading teachers should know about ESL learners. *The Reading Teacher, 57*(1), 22–29.

Freeman, Y., Freeman, D., & Mercuri, S. (2005). *Dual Language Essentials for Teachers and Administrators.* Heinemann.

Freeman, Y. S., & Freeman, D. E. (2008). *Academic language for English language learners and struggling readers.* Heinemann.

Freire, P., & Macedo, D. (1987). *Literacy: Reading the word and the world.* Bergin & Garvey.

Friend, L., & Cook, M. (2006). *Interactions: Collaborative skills for school professionals* (5th ed.). Allyn & Bacon.

Fry, R. (2005). How far behind in math and reading are English language learners? Report from the Pew Hispanic Center, Washington, DC.

Galda, L., & Cullinan, B. E. (1991). Literature for literacy. In J. Flood, J. Jensen, D. Lapp, and J. Squire (Eds.). *Handbook of research on teaching the English language arts* (pp. 528–534). MacMillan.

Gandara, P., Maxwell-Jolly, J., & Driscoll, A. (2005). *Listening to teachers of English language learners.* Center for the Future of Teaching and Learning.

Garcia, E. E., Jensen, B. T., & Scribner, K. P. (2009). The demographic imperative. *Educational Leadership, 66*(7), 8–13.

Garcia, G. G. (Ed.) (2003). *English learners: Reaching the highest level of literacy.* International Reading Association.

Gardner, H. (1983). *Frames of mind: The theory of multiple intelligences.* Basic Books.

Garton, A., & Pratt, C. (1989). *Learning to be literate: The development of spoken and written language.* Basil.

Gibbons, P. (2002). *Scaffolding language, scaffolding leaning: teaching second language learners in the mainstream classroom.* Heinemann.

Gibbons, P. (2009). *English learners, academic literacy, and thinking.* Heinemann.

Govoni, J. M. (Ed.) (2008). *Perspectives on teaching K–12 English language learners* (2nd ed.) Pearson Custom Publishing.

Graves, M. F., & Fitzgerald, J. (2003). Scaffolding reading experiences for multilingual classrooms. In G. G. Garcia (Ed.). *English learners: Reaching the highest level of English literacy* (pp. 96–124). International Reading Association.

Kinsella, K. (2009). *Tools for maximizing cognitive and linguistic lesson engagement for English learners.* TESOL Conference, Denver CO.

Krashen, S. (1982). *Principles and practices in second language acquisition.* Pergamon.

Krashen, S. (1985). *The input hypothesis: Issues and implications.* Longman.

Krashen, S. (1996). *Under attack: The case against bilingual education.* Language Education Associates.

Krashen, S. (2003a). *Explorations in language acquisition and use.* Heinemann.

Krashen, S. (2003b). Three roles for reading for minority-language children. In G. G. Garcia (Ed.). *English learners: Reaching the highest level of English literacy* (pp. 55–70). International Reading Association.

Krashen, S., & Terrell, T. (1983). *The natural approach: Language acquisition in the classroom.* Pergamon Press.

Krashen, S. D. (1981). *Second language acquisition and second language learning.* Pergamon Press.

Krashen, S. D. (1987). *Principles and practice in second language acquisition.* Prentice Hall.

Krashen, S. D., & Terrell, T. D. (1983). *The natural approach: Language acquisition in the classroom.* Prentice Hall Europe.

Lantolf, J. P. (1994). Sociocultural theory and second language learning: Introduction to the special issue. *The Modern Language Journal, 78*(4), 418–420.

Lantolf, J. P. (2000). Introducing sociocultural theory. In J. P. Lantolf (Ed.). *Sociocultural theory and second language learning* (pp. 1–26). Oxford University Press.

Lantolf, J. P., & Thorne, S. L. (2006). *The sociogenesis of second language learning.* Oxford University Press.

Lardiere, D. (2009). Some thoughts on the contrastive analysis of features in second language acquisition. *Second Language Research, 25*(2), 173–227.

Lightbown, P., & Spada, N. (2006). *How languages are learned* (3rd ed.). Oxford University Press.

Lucas, T., & Grinberg, J. (2008). Responding to the linguistic reality of mainstream classrooms: Preparing all teachers to teach English language learners. In M. Cochran-Smith (Ed.). *The handbook of teacher education: Enduring questions and changing contexts* (3rd ed.) (pp. 606–636).

Mendoza, M. B. (2004). Collaborative Construction of Word Knowledge in Vocabulary-related group activities in the ESL Classroom. Phd dissertation, Florida State University, Tallahassee, FL.

Mitchell, R., Myles, F., & Marsden, E. (2013). *Second Language Learning Theories* (3rd ed.). Routledge.

Nieto, S. (2000). *Affirming diversity: The sociopolitical context of multicultural education.* Longman.

Nunan, D. (2000). *Language teaching methodology.* Pearson Education, Inc.

Platt, E. J. (2004). "Uh uh no hapana": Intersubjectivity, meaning, and the self. In J. K. Hall, L. Marchenkova, & G. Vitanova (Eds). *Dialogue with Bakhtin and second language learning.* Lawrence Erlbaum Associates.

Skinner, B. F. (1957). *Verbal behavior.* Appleton-Century Crofts, Inc.

Swain, M. (1985). Communicative competence: Some roles of comprehensible input and comprehensible output in its development. In Gass, S. and Madden, C. (Eds.), *Input in Second Language Acquisition* (pp. 235–256). Newbury House.

Swain, M. (2000). The output hypothesis and beyond: Mediating acquisition through collaborative dialogue. In J. Lantolf, (Ed.) *Sociocultural Theory and Second Language Learning* (pp. 97–114). Oxford University Press.

Vygotsky, L. S. (1978). *Mind in society: The development of higher psychological processes.* Harvard University Press. (Original manuscripts [ca. 1930–1934]).

Vygotsky, L. S. (1986). *Thought and language.* (translated by A. Kozulin) MIT Press. (Original work published in 1934).

Wood, D., Bruner, J., & Ross, G. (1976). The role of tutoring in problem solving. *Journal of Child Psychology and Psychiatry,* 17, 89–100.

WEBSITE RESOURCE

WIDA
Link: https://wida.wisc.edu/

5A
Activity!
STAGES

The stages of language acquisition based on Krashen's work in Table 5.5 provide a useful guide when planning lessons that include interaction. Think of a lesson topic you plan to teach. Write scripted questions and plan speaking and/or writing activities that are appropriate for each stage.

Lesson topic: _____

STAGE 1
Pre-Production

STAGE 2
Early Production

STAGE 3
Speech Emergence

STAGE 4
Intermediate Fluency

STAGE 5
Advanced Fluency

5B

Activity!

THEORIES

Studying language learning theories might seem lofty and out of touch, but just the opposite is true. Effective teachers identify with certain theories that reflect their own approach to teaching. Jot down aspects of these theories you find applicable for your own classroom. Discuss.

Behaviorism

Input

Interaction

Sociocultural

5C
Activity!
ATTITUDE

Attitude and motivation are linked to success in language learning. How will you foster a positive attitude, increase motivation, and reduce anxiety for your ELs?

I will foster positive attitudes by . . .

I will increase motivation by . . .

I will reduce anxiety by . . .

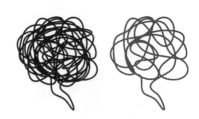

5D
Activity!
WIDA

Refer to WIDA Performance Definitions for **Listening & Reading K-12**. Choose either Discourse Dimension, Sentence Dimension, or Word/Phrase Dimension. Choose a grade level and topic. Write a corresponding activity for each of the five levels.

I choose the _____ Dimension.

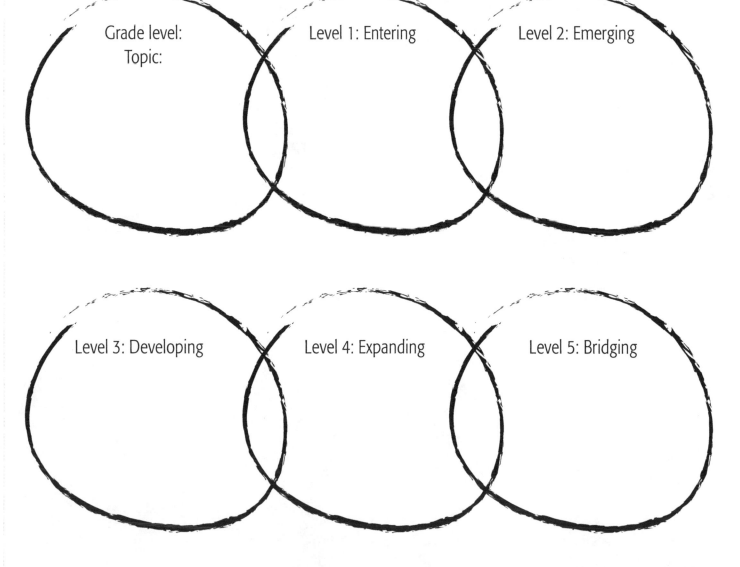

Grade level:
Topic:

Level 1: Entering

Level 2: Emerging

Level 3: Developing

Level 4: Expanding

Level 5: Bridging

5E
Activity!
WIDA

Refer to WIDA Performance Definitions for **Speaking & Writing K-12**. Choose either Discourse Dimension, Sentence Dimension, or Word/Phrase Dimension. Choose a grade level and topic. Write a corresponding activity for each of the five levels.

I choose the _____ Dimension.

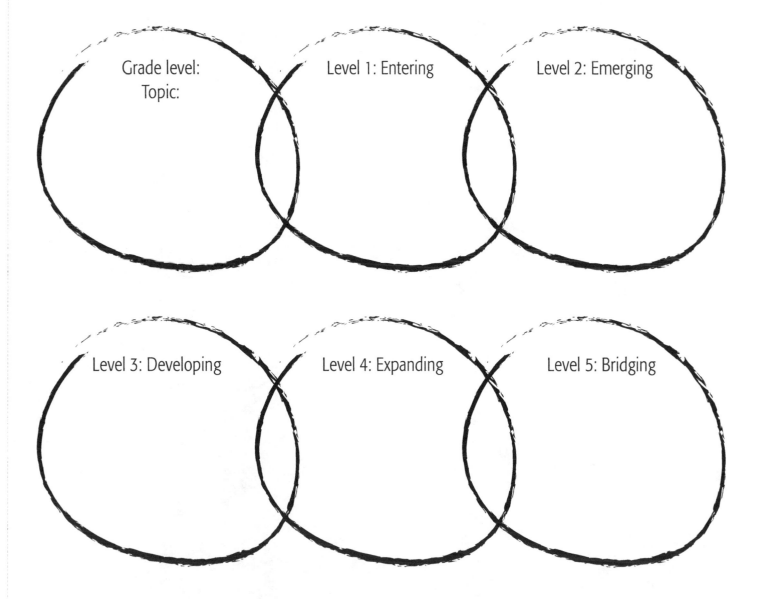

Grade level:
Topic:

Level 1: Entering

Level 2: Emerging

Level 3: Developing

Level 4: Expanding

Level 5: Bridging

5F Activity!

SLA

Name: _____

Scenario: You're in your first year of teaching, and it's the day before winter break. The principal brings you a new student—Carlos from Mexico. He speaks no English. What are the first three things you will do to help Carlos as soon as the principal leaves? Then, jot down what you'll be researching during your winter break.

1

2

3

_____
_____
_____
_____
_____
_____
_____
_____
_____

Section Four

ESOL Methods, Curriculum, and Materials Development: Planning and Implementation

Introduction

 LITERACY STRATEGY: TEACH THE TEXT BACKWARDS

(1) Skim through Chapter 6.
(2) Review the **bold-faced** and *italicized* words.
(3) Preview the questions at the end of the chapter.
(4) Read Chapter 6.

Tips for Use with ELs: The purpose of this strategy is to introduce new concepts or terms, preview the vocabulary, and assign a class reading. It provides a framework for what students will be reading and more insight into what they are about to read.

LITERACY STRATEGY: WORDSPLASH

(1) Below is a set of words and phrases you will be reading about in this section.
(2) Review the list and write a brief definition for the words and phrases you already know—without looking up the definitions.
(3) After reading Chapters 6 and 7, add to your descriptions.
(4) Share three definitions that you elaborated on after reading the chapters.

Strategies to Improve Literacy Skills of ELs with Learning Disabilities

LEAPS Act

State Seal for Bilingualism

Audiolingual Method

Total Physical Response (TPR)

Universal Grammar Theory (UGT)

Direct Method

Grammar-translation method

Differentiated Instruction

Suggestopedia

ZPD

Benefits of Bilingualism

Bilingual Special Education

Communicative Language Teaching (CLT)

Natural Approach

Bilingual Education

Bilingual

Types of Assessment of ELs with Learning Disabilities

Tips for Use with ELs: Wordsplash is a strategy that enables ELs to preview the academic language prior to instruction. Their prior knowledge and experiences may be demonstrated through their initial definitions. It is a simple but practical activity to reinforce literacy skills and academic vocabulary. As a teacher, consider using www.wordart.com to create a word cloud.

TEACHER VIGNETTE: MR. SCHROEDER, MS. LI, AND MS. WU, MIDDLE GRADES, MINNESOTA

Mr. Schroeder, Ms. Li, and Ms. Wu met at college during freshman orientation and stayed friends beyond their college studies. Each majored in teacher education in the respective areas of math, science, and English.

Mr. Schroeder's interests lie in solving math problems and formulating theoretical equations; he pursued math education with the goal of becoming a professor. During his college days, he earned awards for his computational analysis skills. As a middle school teacher, he enjoys math club and sharing his passion for numbers with his students.

Ms. Li speaks fluently in Mandarin Chinese and English. Her parents sent her to elementary school in the U.S. when she was eight years old. She lived with her cousins and spent much of her time reading about NASA and its space exploration programs. She has always been intrigued with the solar system, earth/space exploration, and scientific inquiry. Her goal during college was to become a middle grades science teacher, and she now makes it her mission to find relevant lessons on scientific breakthroughs and discoveries.

Ms. Wu was born in the U.S. and spent summers in Taiwan with her family. She speaks English and Chinese fluently and aspires to teach English as her lifetime career. She was an avid reader as a young child and now seeks to inspire middle grade students to read literary novels.

These educators are in their third year of teaching at a middle school in **Minnesota** where there is a large population of English learners (ELs). The top languages spoken in the community are Spanish, Somali, and Hmong. In addition, the state serves many refugees from Somali, Burma, Bhutan, Iraq, and Ethiopia. The **Learning English for Academic Proficiency and Success (LEAPS) Act** of 2014 provides support for ELs, accountability for Students with Limited Interrupted Formal Education (SLIFE), and the seal for bilingualism and multilingualism. All educators are responsible for providing instruction that is beneficial to students'

learning, including the academic and language needs of ELs. In Minnesota, programs such as pull-out, ESL instruction, dual language, and immersion are offered. (See the Minnesota Department of Education website for further information.)

All three teachers are qualified to teach ESL as they graduated with sufficient hours to earn an ESOL endorsement. They have attended numerous workshops on ESL strategies and assessments and reflect on their studies. *Mr. Schroeder* is competent in speaking about the WIDA standards, descriptors, and approach. During the summer of 2020, he obtained his certification in CLIMBS (Content and Language Integration as a Means of Bridging Success), a learning curriculum offered by WIDA to support teachers in integrating content and language standards for ELs. He is a trainer for the state. His expertise lies in lesson planning to support ELs in comprehending mathematical concepts. (See WIDA website for more information.)

Ms. Li is interested in pursuing her studies in bilingualism. DeJong (2011) reported, if schools choose to have bilingual or multicultural competence as a goal, they must consider how to identify and assess the bilingual skills they want to develop as part of their programs. Herrera, Perez, and Escamilla (2014) noted, **the more aware teachers are of students' second language proficiency levels, the better they are able to plan appropriate lessons.** With this in mind, Ms. Li seeks to identify factors for possible reasons why ELs struggle in the classroom. She aspires to make science a meaningful experience and establish connections between lessons and students' lives.

As for *Ms. Wu*, along with her passion for teaching English literature, she has been an avid researcher on historical ways of teaching and learning a second (or third) language. Methods that were once cutting edge have, for the most part, been replaced with technological tools and practices; yet, there are some methods still prominent in today's classrooms. In the 19th and 20th centuries, *grammar-translation*, the *direct method*, and the *audiolingual method* were optimal practices and still used widely.

The **grammar-translation method** is based on the teaching of Latin, that is, through memorization of grammar rules and translation exercises. Speaking activities are not practiced. The primary focus of the grammar-translation method is on developing students' minds in a deductive manner through grammar, hence its name. In today's classrooms, the explicit instruction of academic language, or the teaching of science terms, illustrates this method.

Characteristics of the **direct method** are those of motivating students through "direct" usage of words and phrases in the target language, such as visuals to introduce new vocabulary with a focus on speaking and listening skills. This method is observed in today's classroom through the usage of WIDA's sensory and graphic supports (i.e., manipulatives, pictures, graphics, and timelines), to directly connect academic vocabulary in English without translations.

The **audiolingual method** met the need for proficiency in foreign languages soon after World War II. It was influenced by behaviorists, as language was regarded as a mechanical habit. This inductive approach does not allow for creativity; yet, it focuses on cultural learning. Students learn language through memorization of dialogues and drills. In today's classrooms, this method is seen in language labs and through the use of technological tools, such as audio software programs and apps.

The 1970s and 1980s furthered second language learning through the emergence of transitional and eclectic strategies that often embraced more than one theory. *Total physical response (TPR), suggestopedia,* and the *natural approach* emerged and still are present in teaching today.

TPR, developed by James Asher, is popular in language classrooms where teachers provide a set of commands in the language and students complete the actions (e.g., "stand up" or "open your books to page 21"). Students follow directions by the teacher without language translations. Teachers who ask students to show a "thumbs-up" if they understand a concept are modeling TPR.

Suggestopedia, developed by Georgi Lozanov, is an inductive way of learning based on a comfortable, relaxed classroom environment. Music, such as classical, is used to lower anxiety and appeal to students' subconscious in learning. This is observed in today's classroom when music is played during instruction or when students are working independently to complete an assignment or project.

The **natural approach**, developed by Krashen and Terrell in the late 1970s, emphasizes comprehensible input ($i + 1$) for students to acquire the language naturally and in meaningful ways. Neither direct instruction nor memorization of vocabulary and grammar are characteristics. Examples may include when students talk about ideas, perform tasks, or solve problems. There is less emphasis on teacher talk. However, this approach has been criticized over the years by researchers.

Along with the natural approach, **communicative language teaching** (CLT) began in the 1980s as a way to view language learning through authentic and meaningful communication. For example, an emphasis is placed on student interaction. Poole (2014) reported that language acquisition gave birth to eclectic views and, as a result, multiple approaches were introduced. CLT is one method to foster communication and build on ELs' language acquisition skills.

The 1980s and 1990s brought about the **universal grammar theory** (UGT) spearheaded by the well-known linguist, Noam Chomsky, who brought to light the notion that all languages have similarities and differences. The similarities, such as verbs and nouns, were considered universals of language. His focus was that the brain naturally has universals which direct the acquisition of language. This led to the belief that everyone is predisposed to learning a language. This nativist view brought a new dimension to language learning.

A subsequent development brought about the **attention theories**, which in contrast to UGT, held that language learning is similar to learning any content. The focus is on linking materials to be learned with existing schemata of a learner, as seen in the teaching of reading. Other innovative ways to promote ELs' proficiency and academic language observed over the years are cooperative learning and the use of multiple intelligences and technological tools.

Technology is a means for ELs to interact in English in a safe environment and be strategic risk-takers as they mediate their language development. Ban and Summers (2014) shared that technology-enriched lessons promote autonomous learners and allow ELs to participate on a more equal footing. Vygotsky's concept of the **Zone of Proximal Development** (ZPD) supports the use of technology enhanced activities in the classroom as learning is determined by what a learner can do with appropriate assistance or mediation. As technology continues to provide new language tools, ELs will have increased opportunities to improve their English acquisition.

Differentiated instruction is yet another approach that affords multiple opportunities for taking in information and understanding concepts and ideas in the classroom. It is an approach that supports the *Lau v. Nichols* court ruling with its basis on three concepts; that is, students have different learning profiles; are active learners, decision-makers, and problem-solvers; and are involved in "making meaning." An example of a collaborative learning activity is a **WebQuest** or an inquiry-based activity. A WebQuest consists of an introduction, task, process, evaluation, and a conclusion. ELs can work in groups to solve a problem appropriate to their language proficiency and cognitive abilities.

PAUSE AND REFLECT

Teachers use a variety of technologies in the classroom today. Research ways to use technology to assign homework, keep parents informed, and for class projects. Share your findings with a classmate. Then, choose which technological tools (websites, apps, URLs, videos, computer activities) you believe are most appropriate to support ELs' proficiency.

Mr. Schroeder, Ms. Li, and Ms. Wu have vast knowledge about teaching and assessing ELs; however, their overall focus is to teach and assess every student in their respective classrooms. It is evident that teachers must be able to adapt to a combination of methods and strategies to meet the needs of all students. Words such as "*meaningful, cognitively demanding, rich academic language, complex language structures, and context-rich*" are often referenced in the field. The importance of these terms is that day-to-day and academic vocabulary should be presented in practical and appropriate ways. A quotation attributed to the well-known anthropologist, Margaret Mead (1901–1978) reads, "*Never doubt that a small group of thoughtful committed citizens can change the world. Indeed, it is the only thing that ever has.*" This quotation reinforces the concept that every teacher makes a difference. Similar to the starfish story, where a little boy throws starfish back into the water one-by-one and, when asked "why," he shares that it makes all the difference in the world to each starfish that survives. Mead's quote and the actions by the little boy provide a mindset for educators in meeting their responsibilities and the needs of their students.

The U.S. is a multilingual nation with diverse learners enrolled across all grade levels. Research shows that school enrollment of students who speak a language other than English at home continues to rise. Methods and strategies are available to support teaching and learning; yet, differentiating between a language difference and a learning disability is still a challenge.

© Sogno Lucido/Shutterstock.com

In Chapter 6, the authors explain the personal, social, economic, and cognitive benefits of being bilingual. They describe **bilingualism** as a way to foster more tolerance of differences, promote more openness to diverse ways of thinking, and become proficient in two (or more) languages.

In Chapter 7, the authors emphasize the role of educators in making decisions to meet the needs of students who are learning to read and write in their L1 and L2 and who may have a **learning disability**. The case study of Griselda, a 10-year-old student from the Dominican Republic, provides a practical and explicit example.

PAUSE AND REFLECT

Take a moment and think back to the teaching styles of your elementary and secondary teachers. Did they fit your needs? Did you favor one style over another? If so, explain. What ways were most beneficial to your learning? How do you know?.

Bilingualism in the Classroom

Oneyda Paneque and Teresa Lucas

© donskarpo/Shutterstock.com

Before reading Chapter 6, check your knowledge about bilingualism by indicating if you believe the following statements are **True** or **False**.

		True	False
1.	It's unusual for people to be bilingual.		
2.	Real bilinguals have no accent in their different languages.		
3.	Bilinguals are born translators.		
4.	Mixing languages is a sign of laziness by bilinguals.		
5.	Bilingualism will delay language acquisition in children.		
6.	Parents should be encouraged to continue to speak the language spoken at home when the school language is different.		
7.	Skills learned in a first language (L1) often transfer to learning in a second language (L2).		
8.	Teachers should never mix languages in the classroom.		
9.	Children who are bilingual from birth experience enhanced cognitive development.		
10.	U.S. teachers should emphasize that children should only speak English if they want to do well in school.		

HISTORICAL PERSPECTIVE

The United States has always been a multilingual nation. Before the British christened New York, Dutch was the language of choice in the city, then called *Nieuw Amsterdam*. The French populated a large swath of the Mississippi Valley, especially New Orleans. The West and Florida were considered home for Spanish speakers. And, of course, the original inhabitants of the continent spoke a wide variety of languages, around 250 in the present area of the 48 contiguous states.

The British were the dominant settlers and the founders of the 13 colonies that joined to form our nation. So, English became the language of choice. As a nation of immigrants, however, the multilingual nature of the country continued, although the languages spoken varied over time. Among traditional immigrant languages were Italian, Yiddish, Polish, and Greek, while today Spanish is the most widely-spoken immigrant language. Also on the rise are Chinese, Arabic, Hindi, Tagalog, Telugu, and Vietnamese. In fact, in 2018, more than 67 million residents in the U.S. spoke a foreign language at home (Zeigler & Camarota, 2019).

A widely repeated joke about languages reveals an attitude that persists among traditional English-speaking Americans. It goes like this:

> What do you call a person who speaks many languages?
> *Multilingual*

> What do you call a person who speaks two languages?
> *Bilingual*

> What do you call a person who speaks one language?
> *American*

The story in most of the world is different. In Europe, the European Day of Languages celebrates multilingualism and encourages people to learn languages. Recognizing that "linguistic diversity is a tool for achieving greater intercultural understanding and a key element in the rich cultural heritage of our continent, the Council of Europe promotes plurilingualism throughout Europe" (European Day of Languages, n.d., p. 4). In African countries, it is common for people to speak several indigenous dialects as well as the language of the former colonial power.

The United States is proud of its history as a "melting pot," signifying that immigrants come to this country and soon blend into the American culture. While adults might continue to speak their native language and engage in the cultural traditions of their homeland, students have often been encouraged by their teachers, and even their parents, to eschew the language and culture of their ancestors, and to learn English and American customs so that they can be successful in their families' adopted land. For many years, schools placed non-English-speaking immigrant students in classes of their age group offering no special consideration to them as they struggled to learn English and adapt to the dominant culture. The attitude was "sink or swim."

The established practice changed in 1968 with the passage of the **Bilingual Education Act (BEA)** (Title VII of the Elementary and Secondary Education Act). The BEA celebrated linguistic and cultural differences and promoted the implementation of bilingual programs in schools. Massachusetts and California led the way in creating curricula that encouraged English learners to also develop their native language.

In 1978, however, an amendment was passed to the BEA that stressed the transitional nature of native language instruction, emphasizing only the development of English language skills, and not the maintenance of a native language. Some programs were called "English as a second language" rather than bilingual. In 1998, California passed Proposition 227, which required schools to teach English learners in special classes taught only in English, effectively eliminating bilingual instruction.

Are we headed in the right direction? You be the judge after looking at the evidence that points to the benefits of bilingualism.

1. *U.S. English* (https://www.usenglish.org) is a citizens' action group dedicated to passing a law declaring English the official language of the United States. Do you think this is a good idea? Why or why not?

2. Go to the ¡Colorín Colorado! website and read an article on bilingualism and English language acquisition. Summarize your findings.

3. If you speak another language, explain how knowledge of your first language helped you in learning the second.

BENEFITS OF BILINGUALISM

Being bilingual affords personal, social, economic, and cognitive benefits. Traveling to other countries is much richer when you know the language that is spoken. Families who strive to maintain their heritage language through generations maintain stronger relationships. Knowing the language of another culture offers opportunities to build relationships with a diversity of people. Furthermore, bilinguals tend to be more tolerant of differences and more open to diverse ways of thinking.

There are economic advantages to being bilingual. A study by the University of Florida found that fully bilingual Hispanics earn an average of nearly $7,000 more per year than their peers who speak only English and that corporations could not find enough fully proficient bilingual employees (Fradd & Lee, 1998). In Canada, people who speak English and French have an income nearly 10% higher than those who speak only English, and 40% higher than those who speak only French. According to the recruiting firm Korn/Ferry International, 9 out of 10 headhunters in Europe, Latin America, and Asia say that being bilingual is crucial for success in today's business environment. In one major study, researchers reported the need for bilingual employees doubled in the U.S. in a five-year period with an increased demand for Chinese, Spanish, and Arabic (New American Economy, 2017).

Recent neuroscience research offers proof of a more fundamental reason for learning more than one language—**being bilingual results in a host of cognitive benefits**. As the evidence mounts, educators will find themselves advocating not only for encouraging English learners to develop their native language along with learning English, but also for native English speakers to learn a second language, starting from an early age. Myths that suggested that learning more than one language slows language and cognitive growth and confuses children have been proven wrong by studies that show that learning two languages actually improves cognitive function.

Bilingualism appears to promote divergent, creative thinking. Several studies (Rodriguez, 2014) revealed that fluent bilingual children are better at being able to think creatively and come up with original solutions to problems. They examine situations from different perspectives and are better divergent thinkers. In addition, bilingual children seem to have better metalinguistic skills and a deeper understanding of how language works. Furthermore, studies of bilingual education programs (Oller & Eilers, 2002) that control for socioeconomic status and program quality, found that bilingual students perform academically as well as or better than monolingual students.

Bilingualism appears to offer an advantage in performing cognitive memory tasks in adults. In three research studies conducted by Bialystok et al. (2004), bilingual adults outperformed monolingual adults on memory tasks often associated with mental decline due to aging. Their findings suggest that the flexibility and complexity required to negotiate two languages contributed to heightened mental agility among bilingual adults.

© zentila/Shutterstock.com

Although children learning two languages simultaneously sometimes get confused, this confusion is not permanent. **Bilingualism does not cause language delays or emotional disorders**. Children with disabilities become bilingual if they grow up in a bilingual environment (Baca & Cervantes, 2004). Yet, families of children with disabilities usually are advised by educators to speak only English to their children. Often, this recommendation is made for the convenience of the education profession and others in the school where English is the primary language spoken, not because it is necessarily best for the child and family. Bilingual students with disabilities often get the short shrift, in terms of services they receive, both because of the limited number of bilingual special education professionals and the high probability of coming from a low-income family.

The benefits of being bilingual continue throughout life, even for those who learn a language later in life. In one study of 44 elderly Spanish-English bilinguals, scientists found that individuals with a higher degree of bilingualism—measured through a comparative evaluation of proficiency in each language—were more resistant than others to the onset of dementia and other symptoms of Alzheimer's disease: the higher the degree of bilingualism, the later the age of onset.

CONCEPTS FOR TEACHERS

After considering the benefits of bilingualism, let's go back to the question of whether measures to enforce "English only" policies are taking education in the right direction. Here are some terms relevant to the discussion. We understand that **bilingualism** means some degree of proficiency in two (or more) languages. When children learn two (or more) languages from birth, this is *simultaneous bilingualism*. If a second language (L2) is added at some point after the process of acquiring the first, or native language (L1), the process is *sequential* bilingualism. When an individual maintains the development of their L1 while acquiring proficiency in an L2, the process is referred to as *additive* bilingualism. If development of the L2 results in the weakening, or even loss of the L1, *subtractive* bilingualism is the result. A person demonstrating near equal proficiency in two languages is a *balanced* bilingual. A *dominant* bilingual shows preference for one language over the other. There are many degrees of dominant bilingualism, determined by how fluent a person is on the continuum of language skills as measured by listening, speaking, reading, and writing fluency in each language. The degree of fluency is affected by interaction variables, such as topic, relationship of participants, and the setting or context in which language interactions take place (Baker, 2001).

Traditionally, educators have looked at bilingual children and seen them as dealing with two autonomous language systems that work independently from each other. This has led to the development of programs that keep strict boundaries in the use of each of the languages, even when the programs are bilingual. In the mainstream classroom in the U.S., the emphasis has been on "English only." Allowing children to access their first language is seen as detrimental to the acquisition of English. *Code-switching*, defined as the use of elements from two different languages or dialects within the same conversation, or even the same sentence, has been frowned upon.

In many parts of the U.S., the language debate has shifted from bilingualism as a *problem* to bilingualism as a *resource*. The U.S. Department of Education indicated in 2015 that it is important for all students, English language learners and native English speakers alike, to gain critical 21st century language and cultural skills. This can be done by creating clear and accessible paths to bilingualism and biliteracy in schools.

While there is a renewed interest in providing bilingual education, the models often continue to follow the practice of keeping the languages separate. But according to Jim Cummins' Interdependence Hypothesis, the interplay between a student's first and second languages allows for the transfer and reinforcement of academic content and deeper learning concepts (Cummins & Swain, 1986a, 1986b: Cummins, 2003). Bilinguals develop one linguistic repertoire with two languages, not two separate language systems. The concept of *translanguaging* offers a vision of a pedagogy that is "an approach to bilingualism that is centered not on languages . . . but on the practices of bilinguals that are readily observable" (Garcia, Johnson, & Seltzer, 2016, p. 15).

Garcia, Johnson, & Seltzer (2016) described the experience of Carla, a teacher of a 4th grade English-Spanish bilingual class in New Mexico. Though the school adhered to the policy of keeping the languages separate, Carla found the children were always using both languages to make meaning. Instead of policing language use, she decided to "encourage students to use their entire language repertoire to learn and demonstrate what they learned" (p. 4). When engaging in challenging content, Carla's students worked together to understand the concepts, utilizing both languages. In checking for understanding of a reading, students responded to comprehension questions in the language of their choice. With native speakers of both English and Spanish communicating in a natural manner using their linguistic resources, all students benefited.

By allowing the natural use of the language resources that students possess, teachers allow for the important process of *skill transfer.* We look at this concept next.

 Search the Internet for current research articles on bilingualism. After reading at least three articles, choose one to summarize in a concise way to show your understanding of the role of bilingualism in schools today. Include your resources.

PRINCIPLES OF SKILL TRANSFER

Transfer of learning is a basic concept studied by educational theorists since the beginning of the 1900s (Thorndike, 1913). The basic premise is that learned skills can be transferred to new skills and situations. The likelihood of a successful transfer depends on the similarities and differences between the old and new skills or the situations. Thorndike and his followers held a behaviorist perspective focusing on the stimulus-response patterns of skills and situations that were very similar. The cognitive psychologists, such as Bransford and Schwartz (1999), looked at how new learning builds on prior learning.

Transfer of learning may involve skills, knowledge, understanding, behaviors, and attitudes. In language learning all of these elements are important. Seven factors that affect transfer are:

a. meaningful learning experiences are necessary as opposed to rote memorization;
b. thorough knowledge leads more likely to transfer;
c. similarity between the two situations fosters probability of transfer;
d. general principles and rules are more easily transferred than specific facts and information;
e. the number and types of examples and opportunities to practice increase the likelihood that knowledge and skills will be applied in new situations;
f. the longer the time interval between old and new learning decreases the likelihood of transfer; and
g. transfer of learning increases when the circumstances promote and expect transfer (Ormod, 2012).

The original concept of transfer of learning has evolved and been applied to different learning situations. Specifically, the transfer of language skills between languages a person knows is referred to as **cross-linguistic transfer**. Usually learners transfer knowledge and skills from their first language to their second language. Indeed, one of the variables that affects second language acquisition is the degree of fluency of a learner's first language. Thus, developing and maintaining a first language promotes learning a second. Transfer can also occur from the second language to the first if the initial learning occurs in the second language and is then transferred to the first language. For example, imagine a person moves to another country as a young adult and learns the language there. As she learns the language, she also engages in new activities, such as skydiving. She learns about skydiving in the new language, and then transfers the knowledge about that activity to her first language.

Cross-linguistic transfer is fluid. It can occur in oral or written language skills. Successful transfer requires initial learning of one language to support the transfer. Transfer may not be automatic. Emergent bilinguals need to learn to transfer skills and learning behaviors. **Teachers need to learn how to assist students in transferring skills, knowledge, and behaviors from one language to another.**

PAUSE AND REFLECT

It might be surprising to you that transfer from one language that you know, to another that you don't know, can actually support your understanding of the unknown language. See how much German you understand in the following text.

Die familie hat eine Mutter, Lisa.
Der Vater heisst Hans.
Sie haben drei Kinder.
Angela ist ein Madchen. Sie hat 14 Jahren.
Johann ist einer Junge. Er hat 12 Jahren.
Claudia ist ein Madchen. Sie hat 7 Jahren.
Alles wohnen en einen Haus en Dusseldorf.
Sie sind sehr frohlich.

The family has a mother, Lisa.
The father's name is Hans.
They have three children.
Angela is a girl. She is 14 years old.
Johann is a boy. He is 12 years old.
Claudia is a girl. She is 7 years old.
They all live in a house in Dusseldorf.
They are very happy.

TEACHING FOR TRANSFER

According to the findings of the National Literacy Panel on Language Minority Children and Youth reported by August and Shanahan (2006), there is evidence in support of transfer of knowledge from the first language to the second. The areas identified are word reading, spelling, vocabulary with cognates, reading strategies, and writing. **Findings suggest that ELs who have a chance to learn and become fluent in two languages progress better than ELs who are in English-only classrooms.** The same is true for ELs who move to English instruction before they are fully developed in their first language oral skills.

Teachers should help their students become bilingual by encouraging them to speak their native language and supporting their parents to speak and read to them in their first language. Parents sometimes worry that their children will not learn English and become successful, so they tell their children to speak English. Teachers have to educate the parents so they understand that full development of the L1 is the basis for learning English as a second language. They also need to point out to parents the personal, social, economic, and cognitive benefits of being bilingual.

Teachers should have genuine interest in the languages represented in the classroom and make an effort to learn about the cultures of their students. They can make attempts to acquire basic vocabulary of the languages. ELs will be more comfortable speaking in their L1 if they know their language and culture are respected. Teachers can view students as resources for teaching their classmates about their languages and cultures.

Many teachers label the items in the classroom to help ELs learn English. The labels can include two or more languages, so that English speakers learn the vocabulary of a second language. Classroom rules can be posted in two languages, along with common phrases needed every day. The morning routine can rotate between two languages, even if the teacher is not fluent in the second language. There should be books and technological resources available in multiple languages. Teach songs in the languages and show movies. Family members can be invited to speak.

An atmosphere of excitement in knowing more than one language is the key to motivating children to develop their multilingual capabilities. These capabilities will serve them throughout their lives.

 KWL ACTIVITY

Summarize what you have learned from the readings, questions, and activities in this chapter by completing the K-W-L-A chart.

K (What I Now Know)	W (What I Want to Know)	L (What I Learned)	A (How I Plan to Apply What I Learned)

Extended Thinking and Synthesis Questions

1. Bilingualism and multilingualism are not uncommon in many countries, yet many U.S. Americans are satisfied with knowing only English. What do you think are factors that lead to this attitude?

2. Discuss examples of situations in which you have experienced a benefit of being bilingual or in which you wish you had known another language.

3. How might being bilingual have an influence on a person's creativity and ability to solve problems?

4. Garcia et al. (2016) describe a scenario in which a teacher uses the translanguaging approach in her classroom. What advantages and disadvantages can you see in this approach? Describe another way in which translanguaging might be employed in a classroom.

5. What is the relation between translanguaging and language transfer?

6. Research methods of SLA, and choose one method that you believe will support your teaching style. Describe the method, and then provide an example of how this method is valuable to your teaching.

7. Identify one of the teachers, Mr. Schroeder, Ms. Li, or Ms. Lu. Refer back to their interests and content area of teaching. Based on the methods and strategies presented in the textbook, identify one that would be beneficial to the teacher. Explain your rationale for choosing the teacher, the method, and the benefits of this technique.

8. In addition to the suggestions you have read thus far in supporting bilingualism, describe specific ways to motivate ELs to continue to develop their first language.

9. The topic of bilingualism has been around for many years in the profession. What is your understanding of the benefits of being bilingual? How will you support your ELs and their families in maintaining their first language at home?

10. Design a PowerPoint presentation, YouTube video, podcast, Prezi, or slide show to present to your school community on the benefits of being bilingual. Include specific ways how teachers can guide ELs to maintain their first languages. Provide examples of how teachers can reinforce bilingualism in the classroom.

REFERENCES

August, D. & Shanahan, T. (2006). *Developing literacy in second-language learners: Report of the National Literacy Panel on Language-Minority Children and Youth.* Lawrence Erlbaum Associates.

Baca, L. M., & Cervantes, H. T. (2004). *The bilingual special education interface* (4th ed.). Prentice-Hall.

Baker, C. (2001). *Foundations of bilingual education and bilingualism* (3rd ed.). Multilingual Matters.

Ban, R., & Summers, R. (2014). Expanding teacher knowledge: Using technology with English learners. In *Preparing the way: Teaching ELs in the prek-12 classroom.* Govoni, J. (Ed.). Kendall Hunt Publishing Company.

Bennett, C.I. (2011). *Comprehensive multicultural education: Theory and practice* (7th ed.). Pearson Education, Inc.

Bialystok, E., Craik, F. I. M., Klein, R., & Viswanathan, M. (2004). Bilingualism, aging, and cognitive control: Evidence from the Simon Task. *Psychology and Aging, 19,* 290–303.

Blom, E., Boerma, T., Bosma, E., Cornips, L., & Everaert, E. (Apr. 21, 2017). Cognitive advantages of bilingual children in different sociolinguistic contexts. *Frontiers in Psychology.*

Bransford, J. D., & Schwartz, D. L. (1999). Rethinking transfer: A simple proposal with multiple implications. *Review of Research in Education, (24)* 61–100. American Educational Research Association.

Crawford, A. (2003). Communicative approaches to second language acquisition: The bridge to second-language literacy. In G.G. Garcia (Ed.). *English learners: Reaching the highest level of English literacy* (pp. 152–181). International Reading Association.

Cummins, J. (2003). Reading and the bilingual student: Fact and friction. In G.G. Garcia, (Ed.). *English learners: Reaching the highest level of English literacy* (pp. 2–33). International Reading Association.

Cummins, J., & Swain, M. (1986a). *Bilingual education and bilingual special education.* Longman.

Cummins, J., & Swain, M. (1986b). *Bilingualism in education: Aspects of theory, research, and practice.* Longman.

DeJong, E. (2011). Foundations for multiculturalism in education: From principles to practice. Caslon Publishing.

Espino-Calderón, M., & Minaya-Rowe, L. (2003). *Designing and implementing two-way bilingual programs: A step-by-step guide for administrators, teachers and parents.* Corwin Press, Inc.

Espinosa, L. M. (2010*). Getting it right for young children from diverse backgrounds: Applying research to improve practice.* Pearson Education Inc.

European Day of Languages. (n.d.). (2020). http://edl.ecml.at/

Garcia, O., Johnson, S. I., & Seltzer, K. (2016). The translanguaging classroom: Leveraging student bilingualism for learning. Caslon Publishing.

Govoni, J. M. (Ed.) (2018). *Preparing the way: Teaching ELs in the pre-k-12 classroom* (3rd ed.). Kendall Hunt Publishing Company.

Herrera, S. G., & Murry, K. G. (2005). *Mastering ESL and bilingual methods: Differentiated instruction for culturally and linguistically diverse (CLD) students.* Pearson.

Herrera, S. G. Perez, D. R., Escamilla, K. (2014). (2nd ed.). *Teaching reading to English language learners: Differentiated literacies.* Pearson Education.

Jimenez, R. T. (2001). "It's a difference that changes us": An alternative view of the language and literacy learning needs of Latina/o students. *The Reading Teacher, 54*(8), 736–742.

Johnson, A. (2010). *Teaching mathematics to culturally and linguistically diverse learners.* Pearson Education Inc.

Kamenetz, A. (Nov. 29, 2016). *6 potential brain benefits of bilingual education.* NPR. https://www.npr.org/sections/ed/2016/11/29/497943749/6-potential-brain-benefits-of-bilingual-education

Magiera, K., & Zigmond, N. (2005). Co-Teaching in Middle School Classrooms Under Routine Conditions: Does the Instructional Experience Differ for Students with Disabilities in Co-Taught and Solo-Taught Classes? *Learning Disabilities Research and Practice, 20*(2), 79–85.

Mead, M. Quotes at https://www.goodreads.com/quotes/1071-never-doubt-that-a-small-group-of-thoughtful-committed-citizens

Menken, K., & Antunez, B. (2001). *An overview of the preparation and certification of teachers working with limited English proficient (LEP) students.* National Clearinghouse for Bilingual Education

New American Economy. (2017). *Not lost in translation: The growing importance of foreign language skills in the U.S. job market.* http://www.newamericaneconomy.org/wp-content/uploads/2017/03/NAE_Bilingual_V9.pdf

Oller, D. K., & Eilers, R. E. (2002). Balancing interpretations regarding effects of bilingualism: Empirical outcomes and theoretical possibilities. In D. K. Oller & R. E. Eilers (Eds.), *Language and literacy in bilingual children* (pp. 281–292). Multilingual Matters.

Ormod, J. E. (2012). *Human learning.* Pearson.

Ovando, C., Collier, V., & Cooms, M. (2003). *Bilingual and ESL classrooms: Teaching in multicultural context* (3rd ed.). McGraw-Hill.

Palmer, D. K. (2009). Middle-class English speakers in a two-way immersion bilingual classroom: 'Everybody should be listening to Jonathan right now...' *TESOL Quarterly*, 43, (2) 177–202.

Poole, G. (2014). Maximizing learning in an ESOL-infused classroom: Instructional dynamics and management. In *Preparing the way: Teaching ELs in the prek-12 classroom.* Govoni, J. (Ed.). Kendall Hunt Publishing Company.

Rodriguez, D. (2008). Preparing Latina teachers for special education programs. *Essential Teachers, 5* (2) 28–30.*Childhood Education 80*, 121–127.

Rodriguez, D. (2014). *The bilingual advantage*: Promoting academic development, biliteracy, and native language in the classroom. Teachers College Press.

Schuman, D. (2004). *American schools, American teachers: Issues and perspectives.* Pearson Education, Inc.

Schumm, J., & Vaughn, S. (1995). Getting ready for inclusion: Is the stage set? *Learning Disabilities Research & Practice*, 10, 169–179.

Thorndike, E. I. (1913). *Educational Psychology* (Vols. 1 and 2). Columbia University Press.

Wilson, G., & Michaels, C. (2006). General and Special Education Students' Perceptions of Co-Teaching: Implications for Secondary-Level Literacy Instruction. *Reading and Writing Quarterly*, 22, 205–225.

Yong, E. (Feb. 10, 2016). The bitter fight over the benefits of bilingualism. *The Atlantic.*

Zeigler, K., & Camarota, S. A. (2019). *67.3 Million in the United States spoke a foreign language at home in 2018.* Center for Immigration Studies. https://cis.org/Report/673-Million-United-States-Spoke-Foreign-Language-Home-2018

WEBSITE RESOURCE

WIDA
Link: https://wida.wisc.edu

6A
Activity!
BILINGUAL

Is anyone in your family bilingual? How about your ancestors? Do you know which languages they spoke? Ask your parents and grandparents about your ancestry and linguistic diversity. Identify the languages spoken, and reflect further here.

Languages spoken on my mother's side:

Languages spoken on my father's side:

Do you speak any of these languages? Do you know any words from these languages? Reflect on whether or not you would want to learn and know these languages from your family tree...

6B

Activity!

BILINGUAL

Time to walk in someone else's shoes. Watch a TV show or movie in another language that uses English subtitles. Jot down the positive (rewarding) experiences and the negative (challenging) experiences. Does this inspire you to learn another language or deter you?

Name of movie:_____

(+)

(−)

6C
Activity!
BILINGUALISM

Name: _____

Cross-linguistic skill transfer can help ELs become bilingual, but transfer is not always automatic. Examine the principles of skill transfer, and then describe actions you can take to assist students in transferring knowledge, skills, and behaviors from their L1 to English.

What I can do to facilitate skill transfer:

6D
Activity!
BILINGUALISM

Cognates provide one of the greatest benefits for many who are bilingual. Unfortunately, not all languages share cognates with English. Here are some near perfect cognates from French and Spanish. Write the corresponding English word. Discuss.

French to English

nombre

raison

logique

ordinaire

horreur

musique

Spanish to English

contrario

glorioso

acción

cómico

acto

delicioso

Jot down any other cognates you know . . .

6E
Activity!
BILINGUAL

Some teachers label items in their classrooms in English to support ELs. Still others add other languages to foster positive attitudes toward bilingualism. Choose another language you'd like to introduce or support in your classroom. Look up the translation for each object. Add the word in one or more languages. Example: desk (English)/ bureau (French). You can cut these out and use as labels in your own classroom someday.

Language:_____

desk	**window**	**computer**
door	**chair**	**wall**
book	**whiteboard**	**teacher**
pencil	**notebook**	**phone**

Making the Connection to Literacy: ELs With Learning Disabilities

Diane Rodriguez and Esmeralda Rodriguez

 LITERACY STRATEGY: KWL

1. Fill in the chart below with what you **know** about ELs who may have a learning disability.
2. Fill in the second column with questions or considerations about what you **would like to know**.
3. After reading Chapter 7, refer back to the last column and fill in **what you learned** about ELs with learning disabilities.

| K
What I Know | W
What I Want to Know | L
What I Have Learned |
|---|---|---|
| | | |
| | | |
| | | |
| | | |
| | | |
| | | |

Tips for Use with ELs: The KWL strategy is a way to gauge ELs' background knowledge on the content presented in class. It can be used before and after a reading or class activity. Research shows an increase in learning when students access what they already know about a topic or content area.

(Adapted from Vacca and Vacca, 1996)

The field of bilingual special education has been controversial and challenging for decades. Among the many difficult issues, the most fundamental question is: *Do students who are acquiring a second language have a learning disability, or do they have a language difference?* First, we present a few definitions related to English learners (ELs) with disabilities.

Bilingual Education: The medium of academic instruction is in two languages. The Bilingual Education Act has been amended several times since 1968 when the law was passed. Presently, English as a second language is an integral component of many bilingual programs.

Bilingual Special Education: The instruction of academic content is in two languages (English and the native language) with a specifically designed program to meet the needs of learners who are acquiring a second language and who have a disability.

English Learner (EL): This is an individual who is acquiring a second language and living in a bilingual world; the native language is spoken at home and the second language (English) at school.

Disabilities: IDEA defines a child with a disability as: having an intellectual disability, a hearing impairment (including deafness), a speech or language impairment, a visual impairment (including blindness), a serious emotional disturbance (referred to in this part as "emotional disturbance"), an orthopedic impairment, autism, traumatic brain injury, an other health impairment, a specific learning disability, deaf-blindness, or multiple disabilities, and who, by reason thereof, needs special education and related services. Over time, lawmakers have revisited this law, and **Public Law 94-142** was reauthorized in 1990, 1997, and 2004. In 1975, the law passed as the **Education for all Handicapped Act**, which set the rules and guidelines for special education. This law is called the Individuals with Disabilities Education Act.

English Learners with Disabilities: This is an individual who is acquiring a second language and identified as having a disability according to the Individuals with Disabilities Education Act (**IDEA**). This learner lives in a bilingual world; the native language is spoken at home and the second language (English) at school.

There have been numerous questions regarding what teachers should do when faced with determining whether a student has a learning disability or a language difference. Read the following teacher's reflection, which illustrates the complexity in today's mainstream classrooms. Note: This writing includes acronyms, such as **EC**—Emotionally Challenged; **L1**—first language; **L2**—second language; **SIOP**—Sheltered Instruction Observation Protocol (a model developed to assist with the teaching of English learners); and **AR**—Accelerated Reader. The following journal entry sets the stage for learning about ELs who may have learning disabilities.

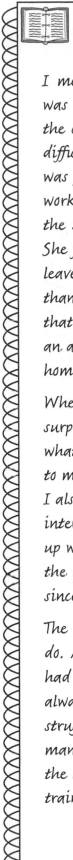

TEACHER REFLECTION

I met with several teachers each week to assist with the work of a student who was emotionally challenged (EC). One student who came to my attention during the conversation was an EL, but not identified as EC. The student was having some difficulties completing her work and staying on task. She avoided tests. Thus, she was failing. The teacher came to me looking for answers. I reviewed the student's work, completed several observations, met with the teachers involved, and spoke to the student. I discovered that the student feared that she would "really mess up." She felt that if she acted as if she did not know the information, the teachers would leave her alone, and she would not have to do the work. It was better not to attempt than to fail. By working with the other teachers, I was able to set up modifications that could possibly help her feel successful and provide an opportunity for her to be an active participant. I also provided resources to help her with organization, such as homework assignment sheets, a bilingual dictionary, and translation services.

When this student's case was first brought to my attention, I felt confused and surprised. I was not aware that this student was in trouble. I found myself wondering what had been done before and how could I best help her now. Several concerns came to mind, such as language barriers, cognitive ability, text availability, and skill level. I also needed to take into account the teacher and how this teacher and student were interacting. The student indicated that she felt "dumb" because she could not keep up with the other students. She also thought the teacher did not understand her. And the teacher thought he was failing to meet her needs and did not know what to do since everything he attempted to do failed thus far.

The teacher was happy to accept my help. I wondered why he did not know what to do. After all, he was a certified special education teacher. I thought most teachers had a basic understanding of how to work with ELs. But I found out that this is not always the case. Some teachers, even those who have been teaching for many years, struggle. Other teachers just want to teach the way they have for years. I attended many professional development trainings to become a better teacher, even if only for the benefit of one student. I do not understand why some teachers don't take district trainings more seriously.

For example, because of the time I spent in Europe and my experience in ESOL training, I am learning to adjust my bias that students should speak in English. I was taught that if you live in a new country, then it is your job to learn the language. I learned to live in both worlds. Now, I am sometimes frustrated with my students because they do not sufficiently demonstrate that they are working toward their goals. When I am working with my ELs, I have to make a conscious effort not to put my own childhood experiences onto them. In attending trainings, I discovered that students do not have to separate their language skills.

They can think in L1 and translate in L2 with practice. But I do not remember this taking so many years. I keep looking for ways to help my students. This means taking classes and attending ESOL workshops while trying to encourage my peers to do the same. At each session, I discover at least one beneficial strategy. An example of this was the recent SIOP training; I was able to learn new activities to share with my students to help them learn the academic vocabulary. In addition, I was able to work with this teacher and show him how to do illustrations for student readings. This came into play for several students who read a book, but failed the AR test. I set up illustrations as an alternative means of assessment. By doing this, the students were able to demonstrate their understanding of the book they just read.

I will continue to blend the past and present, and, in doing so, I hope to encourage ELs to make the best of both worlds. By learning about cultural groups and identities, students can flourish in both. They need teachers to guide them. To help with this, there should be multilevel opportunities to practice both L1 and L2 in both oral and written ways. I struggled learning Spanish, which amused my students; now they help me to learn their native language.

Lorraine Smith, Teacher

Asheville, North Carolina

PAUSE AND REFLECT

1. According to Ms. Smith, what challenges do ELs with learning disabilities face?

2. Are there ELs with learning disabilities in your classroom? If so, what accommodations are provided?

3. If you were placed in a field experience with Ms. Smith, what suggestions would you make to plan instruction to support ELs with learning disabilities and promote a student-centered environment?

4. How does the type of disability, coupled with the difficulties of learning a new language, further challenge the student? The teacher?

CONNECTING WITH INSTRUCTION

English learners with learning disabilities live in a bilingual and bicultural world. Educators must be able to focus on strengths rather than learning disabilities. In order to connect academic language and content, ELs should be exposed to relevant curriculum materials. An effective curriculum provides quality literature and purposeful ways to incorporate reading as a means to foster language. Students, including ELs with learning disabilities, should be encouraged to develop an appreciation of the written word and a desire to read. For example, teachers, like Ms. Wu and Ms. Smith, ensure that the quality and content of reading materials are engaging and relevant.

An effective pedagogical approach is to integrate language, content knowledge, and literacy learning objectives and **distinguish between language differences and language disorders.** Some similarities between English learners and behaviors associated with learning disabilities are presented in **Table 7.1.**

Establishing connections between ideas in a passage to a student's personal experience is important. **ELs with learning disabilities may have difficulty in decoding skills, fluency, comprehension, and in showing an appreciation of learning to read.** Thus, teaching basic reading skills is important in developing English and literacy skills.

Behaviors Associated With Acquiring a Second Language	Behaviors Associated With Learning Disabilities
Difficulty following directions	Difficulty following directions
Difficulty distinguishing between sounds not in L1	Difficulty with phonological awareness
Confusion with sound-symbol correspondence when different than L1; Difficulty pronouncing sounds not in L1	Slow to learn sound-symbol correspondence
Difficulty remembering sight words when word meanings not understood	Difficulty remembering sight words
May understand more than can convey in L2	Difficulty retelling a story in sequence
Confused by figurative language	Confused by figurative language
Slow to process challenging language	Slow to process challenging language
May have poor auditory memory	May have poor auditory memory
May have difficulty concentrating	May have difficulty concentrating
May seem easily frustrated	May seem easily frustrated

Table 7.1   Similarities between ELs and Behaviors Associated with Learning Disabilities.

To connect ELs with learning disabilities to academic language and content, the first step is to get to know their biographies. Herrera (2016) discussed the need for teachers to understand culturally and linguistically diverse student biographies as they assimilate to new surroundings. She explained the implications of adapting to a new educational system and ways of coping with a school's culture. Herrera designed a biography card with information on first and second language proficiency in writing and reading. More examples are available at: https://education.wm.edu/centers/sli/events/ESL%20101/cld-student-biography-card.pdf for examples. **See Figure 7.1**.

Student Information	L1 Proficiency	L2 Proficiency	Prior Schooling	Academic/ Assessment Consideration
Name: Age: Grade: Born: Time in USA:	Oral: Writing: Reading: Based on: __Observation __Test __Both	Oral: Writing: Reading: Based on: __Observation __Test __Both	Parental Support	*dare to be different*

Figure 7.1   Sample information from a Student Biography Card.

LITERACY AND ENGLISH LEARNERS WITH DISABILITIES

Knowledge of literacy begins at home and may start with a picture book to introduce the graphic representations of meaning. The interpretation of drawings is an integral part of literacy, just like listening to a story to expand on vocabulary. Children who have had stories read to them draw upon a wider range of vocabulary when talking about topics that come up in class. Learners do not become literate solely for the purpose of school; rather, they become literate to do well in life. Literacy is a a profoundly important part of achieving that goal. Being literate opens doors to knowledge, people, and to opportunities (Evans, 2014).

 Brainstorm ways to create supportive, accepting classrooms for ELs with learning disabilities to become literate in English. Select at least two pieces of culturally responsive and age appropriate literature to guide your classroom instruction.

> **Possible answers:**
>
> 1. Emphasize the mechanics of reading and writing. Provide ample opportunities for ELs with learning disabilities to master the necessary skills for decoding a written message in order to discover its meaning. Involve them in encoding a spoken message in writing as this promotes letter formation, spelling, and punctuation.
> 2. Teach ELs with learning disabilities to cope with the literacy demands encountered in everyday life. Ensure that they are able to read instructions.
> 3. Practice reading and writing for multiple purposes. Take the opportunity to teach the different purposes and types of reading and writing. ELs with learning disabilities improve their ability to comprehend content from a variety of sources, including textbooks, software, apps, and Internet resources.
> 4. Recognize the close relationship between language use and the way in which knowledge is constructed, modified, and extended through practice. Encourage personal construction, evaluation, and reconstruction of knowledge.

According to Herrera, Perez, and Escamilla (2015), English learners "approach literacy from the basis of their own exposure to and experiences with text, and often, these experiences are less formal than those traditionally valued in U.S. classrooms" (p. 23). To develop effective instruction for ELs with learning disabilities, teachers should consider experiential knowledge of text and formal literacy practices. Lack of such knowledge impacts the rate and speed at which an EL with a learning disability learns to read. Herrera, Perez, and Escamilla identified common understandings that frequently transfer from an EL's native language to a second language as follows:

- knowledge
- literacy as symbolic
- literacy as communicative
- phonological awareness
- alphabetic and orthographic awareness
- concepts about print
- habits and attitudes
- self-esteem

CASE STUDY: GRISELDA

Griselda is a 10-year-old student who is placed in a first grade Dual Language (Spanish–English) class. She was born in the Dominican Republic. There are several behaviors the teacher notices as Griselda enters the classroom: she is very shy; she does not speak in her native language or in English to other students or school personnel; and she barely makes any eye contact. Even though classes are taught in Griselda's first language, Spanish, she barely communicates with her peers, even when asked questions. When she does answer, she typically whispers, responds with a simple yes or no, or just nods her head.

Because Griselda is relatively new to the country, information about her previous education, culture, and family background are gathered through parent-teacher communications. This is essential in documenting her specific needs. The teacher has created a rapport with her parents to determine if further evaluation is needed. In the process, her parents are fundamental in providing the necessary information about her educational experiences. ·

According to Griselda's parents, she is timid and quiet. Griselda attended a public school in the Dominican Republic, but the paperwork does not include information about her academic performance. In comparison to her younger sister, Griselda's parents comment that she was progressing at a slower pace and had difficulties in reading at home. While they tried different strategies to improve her reading and writing skills, they continued to notice that she made little progress.

When Griselda enters the classroom, her reading level is assessed using the Developmental Reading Assessment (DRA); her scores show that she is reading at a DRA level 1 in Spanish and DRA level A in English. In math, she is able to count up to 5 but repeats the numbers. In order to improve Griselda's reading, math, and writing skills, she is introduced to various activities to acquaint her to the school curriculum. For example, she is placed in a small group setting to learn phonics in both English and Spanish. Griselda is taught using word walls and visuals to connect meaning to the academic language. Echo reading is practiced at least twice a week, and guided reading is used with direction from her teacher and classmates.

Griselda's case study provides an example of how teachers must collaborate with parents to assess ELs' learning. **Figure 7.2** provides examples of behaviors that are closely associated with both ELs and ELs with learning disabilities. **Because of language differences, ELs often show similar behaviors that are closely associated with students with learning disabilities**. However, students' backgrounds, linguistic skills, schooling experiences, and academic development are important to understand before referring an EL for evaluation. In Griselda's case, all of these factors are considered.

Since she is relatively new to the country and to the school culture, she demonstrates behaviors that are both reflective of ELs and ELs with special needs. For example, Griselda has trouble understanding English in class because she is new to learning the language. She is more than likely at the WIDA developmental level of "emerging" or at the beginning level of SLA.

In addition, she is learning how to adjust to the school environment, academic and social language, and the culture of the classroom. Most of the time she is confused about the structure and discipline in the classroom; for example, during guided reading, Griselda often seems confused and forgets what she sees in a book. During one-on-one reading, Griselda demonstrates limited reading comprehension and word decoding skills.

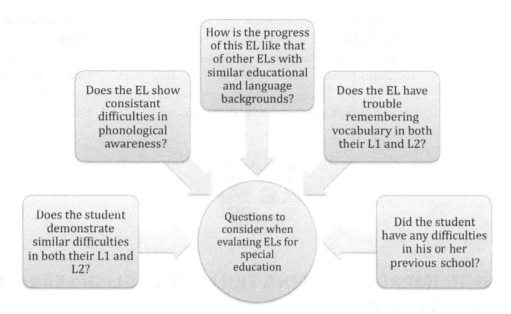

Figure 7.2   Similarities between ELs and behaviors associated with learning disability.

Griselda's behaviors are similar to ELs without learning disabilities. **Research studies show ELs display signs that are easily mistaken as learning disabilities**. For example, ELs may exhibit limited phonological awareness skills and word recognition skills; vocabulary awareness may be poor compared to monolingual students; and ELs may demonstrate poor reading comprehension skills (Fraser, Adelson, & Geva, 2014). According to these researchers, ELs without learning disabilities show improvements over time in recognizing unfamiliar words, grammar, vocabulary, and oral language skills.

In Griselda's case, she has difficulty identifying letters and vowel sounds and finding initial and final sounds. In math, Griselda has trouble remembering numbers and difficulty counting numbers less than 10. She is often confused with basic computations and counting. Socially, Griselda's interaction and communication skills are minimal; she has a tendency to make sounds or say a few words to express herself.

Compared to other ELs, Griselda is performing at a similar academic pace based on her educational and language background. During guided reading, she often becomes confused, and this causes her some frustration. Many times, she has trouble remembering sight words and decoding. She also shows limited comprehension skills and difficulties in verbally describing characters in a story or even recalling the plot or main events. Over time, Griselda learns the sounds of vowels and letters; however, blending sounds and remembering sight words are challenging and difficult concepts to grasp.

ELs with learning disabilities develop their skills at a different level than their peers. They typically have reading comprehension problems and show little progress in the "written text" (Fraser, Adelson, & Geva, 2014). These same problems are exhibited in their L2, and can be found in their L1. Griselda shows limited comprehension skills in both her L1 and L2 language and demonstrates social and linguistic difficulties.

To assist ELs with such learning disabilities, the use of explicit instruction to improve phonological awareness is needed. Response to intervention (RTI) is a method that is useful to assess students. Imagine Learning to support students' literacy is another popular resource. The link is: https://www.imaginelearning.com/. To improve vocabulary, students should practice reading and writing using "explicit vocabulary instruction" to guide them in acquiring new words and improve their reading and listening comprehension skills (Fraser, Adelson, & Geva, 2014). With her teacher's guidance and knowledge of ESOL strategies, Griselda should continue to improve academically.

STRATEGIES TO IMPROVE READING SKILLS OF ENGLISH LEARNERS WITH LEARNING DISABILITIES

As Ms. Wu and Ms. Smith would agree, educators are continuously faced with decisions on how to create lessons that will meet the needs of all students. There is an even greater challenge in finding ways to meet the needs of ELs who are identified as having a learning disability. Ms. Wu discovered in her historical research on second language methods that **differentiation** provides scaffolds that meets students' needs and prevents falling behind academically (Echeverria, Frey, & Fisher, 2015). Evans (2014) reported that schools play a major role in the social, psychological, linguistic, and academic development of students. Both words and experiences, the building blocks of literacy, are pivotal. It is this expansive view of literacy, beyond the nuts and bolts of standards, that allows connections between school and home cultures. The principle question is, *"How do you teach ELs with learning disabilities to read and write in English?"*

Assessing, understanding, and knowing ELs' reading abilities in their native languages and understanding their cultural backgrounds are the first steps. Orosco et al. (2013) reported that it is important to provide direct and explicit instruction to draw on background knowledge, schema, and language. In a study by Allor et al. (2010), 25 students were taught through explicit instruction in which 60% improved in the areas of phonemic awareness, phonemic decoding, and word identification. Reed (2013) found that four adolescent ELs with learning disabilities improved on letter sound and recognition through explicit instruction.

Evans (2014) reminded us that children typically have a vocabulary of approximately 5,000 words by the time they are five years old. They have been making sense of their world from the day they were born by learning how to label the items in their environment, learning a language to negotiate relationships, and gaining exposure to literacy through structured and unstructured means. By age five, they have been exposed to different types of language and literacies. **School signals the beginning of formal academic literacy**. If students are exposed to print, understand story structure, know how to use pictures to scaffold comprehension, have a well-developed vocabulary, realize that print carries meaning, and recognize that literacy can be used for many different purposes, they are further along in academic literacy. Yet, bear in mind that SLIFE may not have these same schooling opportunities, and these students present another challenge to teaching and learning. SLIFE must develop age-appropriate literacy skills, and their participation in formal education may not be complete or even existent; they need to develop the ability to think in cognitively different ways than they have been accustomed to (DeCapua & Wintergerst, 2016; DeCapua & Marshall, 2011; 2013). ELs with learning disabilities bring yet another dimension to the classroom.

Research supports the development of literacy in a student's native language (Cummins & Swain, 1986; Krashen, 1996; 2003; Spangenberg-Urbschat & Pritchard, 1994). A key factor is that the home or native language must be considered as a vehicle for literacy instruction or, in cases where this is not possible, as an important source of information about the literacy abilities that students bring to becoming literate in English. Theories have attested to the importance of prior knowledge and rich literacy-related experiences for the acquisition of literacy in schools. The **Schema theory** maintains that a reader's level of comprehension of a text is dependent upon the interaction between the reader's background knowledge and the information in the text itself. **When students have experiences that more closely mirror the cultural expectations of the school, the path to literacy is already paved.** However, when they come to school with prior experiences that are quite different from the school's expectations, they have less to draw upon to make sense of instruction. ELs, including those with learning disabilities, are far from blank slates when they arrive at school. They bring linguistic, academic, emotional, cultural, and personal characteristics that may either assist or impede their transition into the literate environment of the school (Abrams & Ferguson, 2004).

Cummins (2003) identified **three dimensions of language proficiency**, each one enabling students to engage in certain school-related functions. Taken together, they form the linguistic framework needed for school achievement. These three dimensions are conversational fluency, discrete language skills, and academic language proficiency. At times concurrent, interdependent, and independent, all three dimensions are essential to English learners' ability to acquire literacy within a school environment.

Conversational fluency is described as the ability to carry on conversations using high-frequency vocabulary and simple grammar. This type of fluency is often developed within one to two years. **Discrete language skills** include phonemic awareness and the ability to decode. Many of these skills are also learned early, and often concurrently with basic vocabulary and conversational fluency. Students continue to develop as they progress through their schooling, increasing in sophistication when exposed to more complex language. As ELs progress through grade levels, they encounter more low-frequency words, complex syntactic structures, and abstract language. They are required to navigate more complex academic language and content texts and to apply their language skills to sophisticated writing tasks. This process is called **academic language proficiency**.

The three dimensions might be seen as a triangle of literacy for ELs. Literacy will not happen effectively if one of these elements is missing. ELs must have oral language abilities as a foundation for understanding print. They must have the ability to decode text and be able to gain comprehension of simple and complex texts, as well as create them in written form. **Therefore, classrooms play a prominent role in the socialization and development of conversational fluency**.

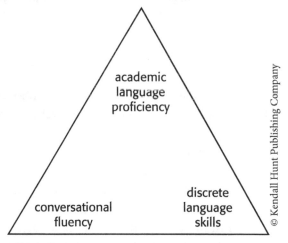

Figure 7.2 Three Dimensions of Language Proficiency.

Evans (2014) reported that recognizing divergent ways of thinking about literacy instruction is important; yet, setting up camp squarely in one methodology or another is counterproductive to the goal of assisting ELs (and ELs with learning disabilities) in becoming literate in English. The array of learning styles, background experiences, motivations, and interests of ELs in schools in the U.S. precludes a one-size-fits-all approach to literacy. Students need the **top-down** processes that engage higher order thinking; they need the **bottom-up** processes that provide access to the printed word. They need to be able to predict what will happen next in a story and to be able to learn from expository text. Using a variety of teaching strategies will guide ELs with learning disabilities to understand how to put their ideas together in writing.

As you may recall, Krashen's (1992) theory of **comprehensible input** explains the key to language acquisition being that ELs understand the messages they receive; whereas, Vygotsky's **zone of proximal development** is the level at which a task becomes doable when scaffolded in some way by an instructional approach or materials. Modification of academic language and classroom instruction make the language more comprehensible. Providing authentic, meaningful opportunities to engage in literacy is beneficial to all students, including ELs with learning disabilities.

Students who are able to use their L1 literacy knowledge in their L2 are able to decode unknown words more than those who do not use their L1 (Cummins, 1989; Jimenez, 1997; Rodriguez, Carrasquillo, & Lee, 2014). Therefore, **scaffolding literacy skills** from L1 to L2 is instrumental in the success of reading comprehension for ELs with learning disabilities. Another strategy is the **usage of cognates** to draw from words ELs already know, and use them to find meaning in the vocabulary of L2. When teachers use cognates, this bridges strategies to increase literacy skills of ELs. For example, Rodriguez, Carrasquillo, & Lee (2014) suggested the following action words in teaching cognates to English learners whose L1 is either Spanish, Portuguese, or Haitian Creole.

English	Spanish	Portuguese	Haitian Creole
Describe	Describir	Descreva	Dekri
Define	Definir	Defina	Defini
Analyze	Analizar	Analise	Analize
Evaluate	Evaluar	Avalie	Evalye
Apply	Aplicar	Aplique	Aplike
Clarify	Clarificar	Esclareça	Klarifye
Connect	Conectar	Conecte	Konekte
Interpret	Interpretar	Interprete	Entrprete
Compare	Comparar	Compare	Konpare

Other plausible suggestions are to use phonological awareness with different types of readings, use students' L1 and L2 languages to teach comprehension skills, and improve literacy skills in their L1 (Klingner, Artiles, & Barletta, 2006). More examples include incorporating read-alouds to connect students' knowledge and using culturally relevant books to provide a space where ELs with learning disabilities add information to the lesson (Nguyen, 2012). Another strategy is **scaffolding**, such as mediated scaffolds, task scaffolds, and material scaffolds to improve students' knowledge about the lesson (Herrera, 2010; Nguyen, 2012). These include using sentence starts, story maps, regulation of task, and gradually minimizing the assistance from the teacher or peer until ELs can do the work independently (Herrera, 2010; Nguyen, 2012). When teaching ELs with learning disabilities, it is important to provide strategies that unify their culture, language, and prior knowledge.

 PAUSE AND REFLECT

Share ways to ensure a successful literary experience for ELs with learning disabilities in promoting a student-centered learning environment.

Teachers who teach literature must base instructional methods on a variety of curricular circumstances, including content genre, integration, flexibility, and student characteristics (e.g., growth, receptive abilities, and expressional abilities). **Educators must understand the academic, motivating, and affective capabilities of ELs with learning disabilities to make appropriate instructional decisions.** For example, if the vocabulary or sentence structure of a story is too difficult, they may find it boring, and the lesson will be deemed as not being linguistically appropriate. Therefore, content must be personal, meaningful, and relevant (Lovell, 2018). **When teachers have multiple literature genres from which to choose, ELs with learning disabilities are enriched through a variety of reading materials.**

© Rawpixel/Shutterstock.com

Literature styles may include historical fiction, realistic fiction, fantasy, nonfiction, autobiography, biography, graphic novels, poetry, and plays. If various forms of literature become an integral part of the curriculum, consideration must also be given to how integration is accomplished. Just as overall planning requires discussions about experiments, field trips, and technological resources, so, too, does it require decisions about literacy experiences that enrich ELs and supplement other curriculum areas. **ELs with learning disabilities are often more successful when teachers scaffold language sensitive content instruction.** Planning individual adaptations and keeping in mind multiple instructional objectives is essential in providing supportive learning environments.

ELs need to understand letter recognition, phonemic awareness, word identification, syntactic analysis, discourse level analysis, and schema level analysis. In addition, ELs with learning disabilities must be provided opportunities and encouragement to explore areas of their own interests and to discover new ones through individual reading. This lays the foundation for greater appreciation and understanding of academic content and language. Create opportunities to develop metacognitive skills necessary to comprehend a story, regardless of literacy level. For example, provide support in reading different genres, and build on prior knowledge.

Just like other students, ELs with learning disabilities benefit from expressive activities that develop both oral and organizational skills; for example, dramatize a scene from a favorite story. Activities related to books and stories enhance the reading experience in two ways. First, by using or applying the information or ideas gained from a story, students clarify their understanding of the story. This helps them to make the meaning more personal and increase enjoyment of learning (Herrera, Perez, & Escamilla, 2015). Second, given that enthusiasm is contagious, even reluctant readers increase their motivation to read when they see their peers having a good time with books. Of vital importance are expressive activities that provide a natural vehicle for purposeful practice of oral and written language skills and abilities. **Beneficial strategies to promote language development include, planning diverse reading and writing tasks, creating opportunities to discuss readings, and presenting expressive activities related to readings.**

PAUSE AND REFLECT

1. Explain ways that student centers assist ELs with learning disabilities.

2. Brainstorm ways to develop a supportive learning environment for ELs with learning disabilities. Include strategies or activities to improve reading, writing, listening, and speaking.

Another type of activity to promote literature is **storytelling**, which is a particularly useful tool with younger students. A storyteller communicates his enthusiasm to the listener. A well-stocked school may contain files of book jackets, pictures, white boards, computers, software, apps, and other resources. Instead of using technical terms for elements of a short story (e.g., plot, setting, point of view), ask "*Where did the story take place? Who told the story?*" By using familiar words in questions, ELs are better able to understand the story and increase their understanding of the big ideas by interconnecting outside stories related to family and inside stories related to the classroom. iPad applications or tablets can individualize instruction, facilitate engaged oral storytelling, and record learners on digital video. Technologically savvy teachers create their own iOS (iPad, iPhone, iPod Touch) and Android apps to provide unique learning experiences.

© Edward Lara/Shutterstock.com

Book reports provide practice in speaking and writing. Oral activities may take a variety of forms; for example, ELs may read a particular event to the class, dramatize a scene, or set up a panel. Other literacy materials include **drawing illustrations** for a story, using an app to design a picture, or making a mobile that depicts characters in a book. In addition, **poetry** offers a unique way to express ideas and feelings. It stimulates the imagination and provides an outlet for emotions. It motivates students to express their own creativity, and it shows them the beauty and expressiveness of the language. When teaching literature, consider ELs' responses to literature and draw on interactive activities beneficial to students as they construct meaning (Herrera, Perez, & Escamilla, 2015). This includes comprehension of what the story means, followed by transfer of meaning to extant circumstances. If predetermined results of reading comprehension are feasible for students, then ELs with learning disabilities are capable of these results when consideration is given to and adjustments are made for their sociocultural, cognitive, linguistic, and academic knowledge.

The use of **direct instruction** is encouraged within instructional objectives; in this way, prior knowledge is activated to determine what students already know about the subject. In addition, teachers should read aloud to the group; re-read as students follow along, and ask individual students to take turns reading words or sections and answering questions. These instructional approaches provide sensitivity to ELs' first languages and cultures and allow them to learn English systematically and cumulatively, moving from concrete to abstract levels of language development in a spiraling fashion (Rodriguez, 2018). In all

cases, it stresses the primacy of oral skills in the development of overall communicative linguistic competence in understanding, speaking, writing, and reading in English.

The ability to read in English is critical to ELs with learning disabilities for their long-term success. Reading includes activities that involve topics and experiences related to what exists around students. Real world settings motivate students to get involved in the process. When reading is relevant, students want to read and feel curious about finding out about new information. **Establishing connections** between ideas in the text and ELs' experiences is more meaningful when considering their interests, cultural backgrounds, and background knowledge.

Language acquisition is optimal when input is provided that is comprehensible, interesting, relevant, grammatically sequenced, and presented in sufficient quantity (Krashen, 1983). In brief, language is acquired when you understand it. A central feature of **Piaget's developmental view** of thinking and learning is the premise that learning and thinking involve the participation of the learner, whether in relation to objects or social relationships. When ELs with learning disabilities are thinking and learning, that is, when their intelligence is developing, they are going through the process of assimilating their experiences and integrating them into their mental or cognitive structure. Concepts already learned in their native language are transferred into English and developed as they engage in classroom activities. **Take advantage of language**

strengths and of the valuable knowledge ELs bring to the classroom. Have an understanding of reading goals. Determine the environment conducive to reading growth and what types and uses of assessment data are instrumental to ELs' development. Perhaps the best recommendation for working with ELs with learning disabilities is to be knowledgeable in the areas of phonics, vocabulary skills, and whole language approaches in their first and second language. **In order for ELs with learning disabilities to be successful in reading, teachers must support oral language proficiency in English that scaffolds literacy development.** In addition, teachers should be able to recognize congruence between first and second language and ELs' learning styles and interests.

There is no doubt that all teachers need to be knowledgeable about second language reading strategies for word recognition and comprehension and how to determine the cultural relevance of academic content. Teaching requires knowledge, coupled with a favorable disposition, to connect instructional content to sociocultural knowledge, cognitive knowledge, linguistic knowledge, and academic knowledge of ELs with learning disabilities. Listening to books will build a schema for stories and increase their knowledge of the world. **Educators should match the language proficiency level with the difficulty level of the text and determine the background knowledge needed for higher levels of comprehension.**

ASSESSMENT OF ENGLISH LEARNERS WITH LEARNING DISABILITIES

According to Rodriguez and Anoysa (2020), assessments of ELs with learning disabilities should determine where students are on a developmental skills continuum and provide feedback for personal growth. Additionally, evaluation data should be used to determine the effectiveness of instructional strategies and interventions for all learners. **There is a constant need to properly assess ELs with learning disabilities.** Traditional assessment is not sufficient.

Teachers should think outside the box to determine learning outcomes and objectives for ELs with learning disabilities, and assess ELs' proficiency in speaking, listening, reading, and writing, both formally and informally. Authentic assessment provides information on academic growth and overall strengths of students. However, this is often not feasible; therefore, educators must consistently strive to seek a curriculum that promotes best practices and evidenced-based strategies to plan a supportive learning environment for all students.

ELs have historically been over- and underrepresented in special education; therefore, assessment procedures need to be carefully followed (August, 2018). Educators must distinguish if an an EL is having difficulty absorbing classroom material because of a learning disability or in acquiring a new language. To successfully assist ELs at-risk, trained teachers should begin by screening all ELs for reading difficulties. To avoid concerns of validity, examiners should have a similar cultural background to students whose scores are being standardized (Sciuchetti, 2017).

Additionally, data documenting student progress is to be collected multiple times a year to analyze if ELs with learning difficulties are developing the skills needed to flourish academically (August, 2018). It is recommended that instruction is consistently adjusted to present ELs with material that is culturally and linguistically appropriate (Li et al., 2018). Specific reading skills are assessed based on different grade spans (August, 2018).

Phonological skills are examined from kindergarten through first grade by utilizing exercises that evaluate a student's ability to follow basic phonic rules. From second through fifth grade, students should be able to read texts fluently and process information to correctly summarize the content presented. It should be stressed that these grade spans were created with the assumption that ELs being assessed have started U.S schooling in kindergarten. Teachers must be cognizant of this and consequently modify instruction to fit the personalized needs of all ELs. Mishandling this crucial step can initiate inappropriate special education referrals that contribute to the marginalization of culturally and linguistically diverse students (Sciuchetti, 2017).

If certain ELs remain unable to make progress, teachers should then decide if that student is to be referred to special education using formative data from screening and progress monitoring (August, 2018).

It is important to note that oftentimes, bilingual special education teachers are under-resourced by their school districts (Rodriguez & Rodriguez, 2017). This is a disadvantage that directly affects their proactiveness to create nurturing environments for their students. Teachers are encouraged to use their knowledge of research-based approaches along with their creativity to determine how to assist ELs with learning disabilities.

📖 LITERACY STRATEGY: CHARACTER FRAMES

(1) Skim through this chapter once again.
(2) List characteristics of ELs with disabilities in the first column.
(3) Google ways to support ELs with learning disabilities, and add this research to your second column.

Characteristics of ELs with Learning Disabilities	Research Says...

Tips for Use with ELs: In this strategy students are able to select and describe text from a reading and justify their responses. It is a way to compare or contrast two elements, ideas, story characters, and more.

Extended Thinking and Synthesis Questions

1. Google *Bloom's Taxonomy of Educational Objectives* and *Webb's Depth of Knowledge*. Share how knowledge of these resources supports ESOL curriculum and materials development.

2. In class, participate in the "Lead Me Blindfolded" activity in which a classmate is blindfolded and another walks the classmate around the room providing clues as to where to walk to avoid stumbling into furniture. Discuss this experience as the one blindfolded and as the leader. Compare how you felt in this activity and how ELs with learning disabilities might feel in a mainstream classroom.

3. Make a list of technological resources (software, Internet, apps, media, etc.) that may be used to enhance instruction for ELs with learning disabilities.

4. Refer back to your KWL chart at the beginning of this chapter, and fill in the third column on what you now know about teaching ELs with learning disabilities.

REFERENCES

Abrams, J., & Ferguson, J. (2004). Teaching students from many nations. *Educational Leadership*, 62(4), 64–67.

Allor, J. H., Mathes, P. G., Roberts, J. K., Cheatham, J. P., & Champlin, T. M. (2010). Comprehensive reading instruction for students with intellectual disabilities: Findings from the first three years of a longitudinal study. *Psychology in the schools*, 47, 445–466.

August, D. (2018). Educating English language learners: A review of the latest research. *American Educator, 42*(3), 4.

Chu, S., & Flores, S. (2011). Assessment of English language learners with learning disabilities. *Clearing House: A Journal of Educational Strategies, Issues and Ideas, 84*(6), 244–248.

Cummins, J. (1989). *Empowering minority students.* California Association for Bilingual Education.

Cummins, J. (2003). *Language, power, and pedagogy: Bilingual children in the crossfire.* Madrid: Ediciones Morata, S.L.y Ministerio de Educacion, Cultura y Deporte. (translated by Pablo Manzano).

Cummins, J., & Swain, M. (1986). *Bilingualism in education: Aspects of theory, research and policy.* Longman.

DeCapua, A., & Marshall, H. (2011). *Breaking new ground: Teaching new students with limited or interrupted formal education in secondary schools.* University of Michigan Press.

DeCapua, A., & Marshall, H. (2013). *Making the transition to classroom success: Culturally responsive teaching for struggling language learners.* University of Michigan Press.

DeCapua, A., & Wintergerst A.C. (2016). *Crossing cultures in the language classroom* (2nd ed.). University of Michigan Press.

Echevarria, J., Frey, N., & Fisher, D. (2015). What it takes for English learners to succeed. *Educational Leadership, 72*(6), 22–26.

Evans, L. (2014). Applying literacy strategies for ELs in the classroom. In *Preparing the Way: Teaching English learners in the Pre-K–12 classroom.* (2nd ed.) Govoni, J. (Ed.). Kendall Hunt Publishing.

Fraser, C., Adelson, V., & Geva, E. (2014). Recognizing English Language Learners with Reading Disabilities: Minimizing Bias, Accurate Identification, and Timely Intervention. *Perspectives on Language and Literacy, 40*(4), 11–17.

Herrera, S. G. (2016). *Biography-driven culturally responsive teaching.* Teachers College Press.

Herrera, S. G., Perez, D.R., & Escamilla, K. (2015). *Teaching reading to English language learners: Differentiated literacies* (2nd ed.). Pearson.

Hoover, J. J., & Patton, J. R. (2005). Differentiating curriculum and instruction for English-Language Learners with special needs. *Intervention in School and Clinic, 40*(4), 231–235.

Imagine Learning. (2020). https://www.imaginelearning.com/

Jimenez, R. T. (1997). The strategic reading abilities and potential of five low-literacy Latina/o readers in middle school. *Reading research quarterly, 32*(3), 224–43.

Klingner, J., Artiles, A., & Barletta, L. (2006). English language learners who struggle with reading. *Journal of Learning Disabilities, 39*(2), 108–128.

Krashen, S. (1992). Fundamentals of language acquisition. Laredo Publ. Co.

Krashen, S. (2003). *Explorations in Language Acquisition and Use.* Portsmouth, NH: Heinemann.

Krashen, S. (2004). *The Power of reading.* Heinemann.

Krashen, S. (2008). *The Case For Libraries and Librarians. Submitted to the Obama-Biden Education Policy Working Group.* (The Case For Libraries and Librarians).

Krashen, S. (2015). Fact or fiction? The plot thickens. *Language Magazine, 15*(3).

Krashen, S., & Terrell, T. (1996). *The natural approach: Language acquisition in the classroom.* Janus Book Pub.

Li, C., Kruger, L. J., Margaret, B., Kimble, E., & Kalyani, K. (2018, October). The unintended consequences of high-stakes testing on English-language learners: Implications for the practice of school psychology. *In School Psychology Forum, Research in Practice* (Vol. 12, No. 3, pp. 79–90). National Association of School Psychologists.

Lovell, C. (2018). *Taking off the wrapper: Identifying and serving gifted English learners.* In J.M. Govoni (Ed.) Preparing the way: Teaching ELs in the pre-k-12 classroom (3rd ed.). (pp. 213–236). Kendall Hunt Publishing Company.

Mitchell, C. (July 31, 2019). Ways to better serve often-misunderstood English-learners with disabilities. *Education Week.*

Nguyen, H. T. (2012). General education and special education teachers collaborate to support English language learners with learning disabilities. *Issues in teacher education, 21*(1), 127–152.

Orosco, M. J., Swanson, H. L., O'Connor, R., & Lussier, C. (2013). The effects of dynamic strategic math on English language learners word problem solving. In the *Journal of Special Education, 47,* (96–107).

Reed, D. (2013). The effects of explicit instruction on the reading performance of adolescent English language learners with intellectual disabilities. *TESOL quarterly, 47*(4), 743–761.

Rodriguez, A., & Rodriguez, D. (2017). English learners with learning disabilities: What is the current state? *Insights into Learning Disabilities, 14*(1), 97–112.

Rodriguez, D. (2018). *Making the connection to literacy: English learners with disabilities.* In J.M. Govoni (Ed.) Preparing the way: Teaching ELs in the pre-k-12 classroom (3rd ed.). (pp. 193–210). Kendall Hunt Publishing Company.

Rodriguez, D., Carrasquillo, A., & Lee, K.S. (2014). *The bilingual advantage: Promoting academic development, biliteracy and native language in the classroom.* Teachers College Press.

Sciuchetti, M. B. (2017). Addressing inequity in special education: An integrated framework for culturally responsive social emotional practice. Psychology in the Schools, 54(10), 1245-1251. Spangenbeng-Urbschat, K. & Pritchard, R. (1994). (Eds.). *Kids come in all languages: Reading instruction for ESL students.* Newark, Del: International Reading Association.

Tam, K. Y., & Heng, M. A. (2005). A case involving culturally and linguistically diverse parents in prereferral intervention. *Intervention in school and clinic, 40(4),* 22–23. Zwiers, J., & Crawford, M. (2009). How to start academic conversations. *Educational Leadership,* 66(7), 70–73.

Zwiers, J.,& Crawford, M. (2009). How to start academic conversations. *Educational Leadership, 66*(7), 70–73.

WEBSITE RESOURCES

CLD (Culturally Linguistically Diverse) Student Biography Card
Link: https://education.wm.edu/centers/sli/events/ESL%20101/cld-student-biography-card.pdf

Individuals with Disabilities Education Act (IDEA)
Link: https://sites.ed.gov/idea/

Selected Instructional Aids from Biography-Driven Culturally Responsive Teaching
Link: http://docshare01.docshare.tips/files/26143/261436757.pdf

7A
Activity!
IDEA/SLD

Name: _____

The Individuals (alphabetize) with Disabilities Education Act (IDEA) defines a specific learning disability (SLD) as "a disorder in one or more of the basic psychological processes involved in understanding or in using language, spoken or written, that may manifest itself in the imperfect ability to listen, think, speak, read, write, spell, or to do mathematical calculations." In each category, list anticipated challenges when working with an EL with a specific learning disorder.

READING (DYSLEXIA)

WRITING (DYSGRAPHIA)

LISTENING

SPEAKING

REASONING

MATH (DYSCALCULIA)

7B

Activity!

SLD

Research the term "specific learning disabilities" and create a list of possible signs and characteristics of SLDs and corresponding instructional strategies and teaching tips. Jot down any websites that are especially useful, and be sure to bookmark them on your computer for future reference.

SIGNS/CHARACTERISTICS	STRATEGIES/TEACHING TIPS

7C
Activity!
WORDLESS

Wordless picture books have proven themselves to be valuable tools for English learners as well as ELs with SLDs. Think about it...they are useful for any language, allow for expression and storytelling and they support communication skills. Choose your favorite wordless picture book, or select one from this site: https://readingrockets.org/booklists/our-favorite-wordless-picture-books. Use your creativity to come up with activities to engage ELs with SLDs.

Title:

Author:

Age range: _____

Activities:

_____

_____

_____

_____

_____

_____

_____

_____

7D
Activity!
INTEREST

Think about the grade level you hope to teach, and take this opportunity to develop an interest inventory for your students. Remember, open-ended questions give them room to expand on their thoughts.

Interest Inventory Ideas

7E

Activity!

DISABILITIES

Name: _____

Regularly assessing ELs with learning disabilities is essential to provide feedback, modify instruction, and reteach when necessary. This all begins with writing appropriate language objectives and content objectives Draft appropriate objectives and assessments for an EL with learning disabilities. Discuss with a classmate.

Subject & grade level: _____ Lesson Topic: _____

Language objectives(s):

Content objective(s)—must be specific and measurable:

Brainstorm possible assessment methods for both types of objectives:

I can assess language objectives by:

I can assess content objectives by:

7F

Activity!

DISABILITIES

ELs with learning disabilities are more successful when teachers scaffold instruction. This is especially true when content and instruction are language-sensitive. Brainstorm a lesson, and identify the language skills you may need to scaffold to ensure these students can master the subject content (e.g., math, social studies).

Subject & grade level: _____ Lesson Topic: _____

Content objective(s)—must be specific and measurable:

Think about the language students need to access content...

Academic Language:

measure

determine

objective

compare

Subject Vocabulary:

capital

map

distance

legend

List academic vocabulary & content vocabulary:

Academic language they will need to know:

Content/subject vocabulary:

7G

Activity!

PERSONAL

Research tells us again and again that teachers should endeavor to make lessons personal, meaningful, and relevant to help students form a connection to the content they are learning. This is especially important for ELs with learning disabilities. Now is the time to think about how you will accomplish this. Choose a topic or concept you will teach, and brainstorm ways to do this.

Topic/concept: _____

Personal: How does this relate directly to the student?

Meaningful: How does this move the student on a personal level?

Relevant: How does this impact the student's life right now?

7H

Activity!

INTERImp

INTEREST

Name: _____

One way to help students make connections to content is planning instruction in which the student has an interest. Take the interest inventory below, and then design an interest inventory you will share with your students on the back.

Favorite subject?_____ Favorite food? _____

Favorite movie? _____

Favorite book? _____

Favorite song/singer? _____

I'd like to be...

If I could, I would...

My wish for the world is...

My favorite place to visit is...because...

If I had a million dollars I would...

My hobbies and interests include...

71
Activity!
CALP

Name: _____

Cognitive Academic Language Proficiency (CALP) is essential to ELs' success, although it is acquired much differently than Basic Interpersonal Communication Skills (BICS), which includes conversational fluency and discrete language skills. Think about the grade level you hope to teach and a subject you will teach. Brainstorm a list of academic language your ELs will be expected to learn. How will you ensure this?

Grade level: *Subject:*

Academic language:

99

Taking Off the Wrapper: Identifying and Serving Gifted English Learners

Cindy Lovell

LITERACY STRATEGY: FIRST LINES

(1) Read the "first lines" of several paragraphs in Chapter 8.
(2) Write down your predictions on the status of ELs in gifted education across the nation.
(3) Share your predictions with a classmate.
(4) After reading the chapter, revisit your predictions and share what you learned.

Tips for Use with ELs: This pre-reading strategy enables students to make predictions about what they are about to read by focusing on the "first lines" of the text. As ELs begin to read the story, poem, or piece of literature, they can revise their predictions to demonstrate their understanding of the reading. It is a comprehension strategy that can be done individually or in small groups. See Reading Rockets website for further information.

In teacher education programs, it is generally understood that *how* professors teach is actually *what* they teach; their subject matter emphasizes the most effective teaching methods, so they model strategies in their own classrooms—and elsewhere. It's a matter of practicing what you preach. It is not limited to knowledge and skills, but also includes dispositions. In fact, a teacher's disposition, or attitude, may be the most critical component of all. *So, what does this have to do with gifted English learners?* Here is a short story about an error in judgment that may begin to answer this question.

I had just earned my PhD at the University of Iowa, where I specialized in ESOL and Gifted Education. And if I learned nothing else, I learned that we must look past accented English, incorrectly conjugated verbs, and cultural differences that might camouflage a gifted learner. I was a champion of this underidentified and underserved group—the gifted English learner—and I intended to put my newfound knowledge and passion to work. I accepted a position at my alma mater, Stetson University in DeLand, Florida, and got to work. Since I had done my graduate work at the Belin-Blank International Center for Gifted Education and Talent Development at the University of Iowa, I immediately established a satellite center at Stetson offering above-level testing for Florida's students through the High Achieving Talented Students (HATS) Program. The Belin-Blank Center invites eligible students (those who score at the 95th percentile or higher on a standardized grade-level assessment) to take an above-level test in order to better assess their true levels of achievement, and therefore to provide accurate and meaningful information to classroom teachers to better meet the academic needs of these high achievers. After all, mastering grade level material does not necessarily mean that that's all students have learned. Fourth-, fifth-, and sixth-grade students who qualify are invited to take the eighth-grade level I-Excel test. Seventh-, eighth-, and ninth-grade students take the ACT (Belin-Blank Center, 2020). I sent materials throughout the state of Florida to eligible students, along with a congratulatory letter for earning this special invitation. Parents phoned or emailed me with questions, and many registered their children for these tests. Most recognized it for the opportunity and honor it was. Others saw no value in having their children take such an advanced test. I had all types of communications with all kinds of parents. One afternoon, I decided to walk across campus to get a soda. Just as I stepped onto the road, a small pickup truck pulled alongside me. A woman thrust a piece of paper at me and said, "I'm looking for this person." The paper was the aforementioned letter I had sent out, and I was the person she was looking for, so I waved her into the parking lot. She exited the truck and told me she was in a hurry. She said she was a custodian in Orlando and was on her lunch hour, and she had driven to Stetson in order to meet me and make sure that her son was registered for the test. We went into my office where she asked me to look over the application and make sure she had filled it out correctly. Her English was not the best, but we managed to communicate. I explained that she must mail a copy of her son's scores along with the registration—or so I tried to do. She did not fully understand, so I offered to call her son's school and arrange to have the scores sent home with him. The secretary who answered knew the woman well. "She's a wonderful mother!" the secretary exclaimed. "She's so supportive of her son's education." The scores were arranged, and the mother, although clearly in a hurry to get back to her custodial work before her lunch

> hour was over, hesitated at my door. "Do you know a place I can learn better English?" she asked. Feeling proud of myself for taking time from my very important break, I compiled a list of phone numbers of various literacy initiatives and other resources for her. After all, I was the champion of English learners, and here I was giving this friendly custodian a chance to really polish her English and advance a little. What a great person I was! She clutched the paper and scanned it, looking determined and happy. She smiled and thanked me before rushing out the door. "Thank you," she said sincerely. "You see, in my country, I am a physicist, but here, my English is not good enough."
>
> Cindy Lovell, Teacher
>
> Stetson University

I sat at my desk for a long while afterward feeling rather small. "*In my country, I am a physicist.*" That's what she said. But here in my country, she is a custodian wearing a khaki uniform and forfeiting her lunch hour to be sure her son would benefit from an opportunity. I still cringe each time I share this story, but it's important. It's about labels and wrappers and disguises and clichés. It's about not judging a book by its cover. A physicist. A custodian. And only one thing separated these two careers—the barrier of language. I should have known better.

TEACHER VIGNETTE: MRS. ALLEN, 4TH GRADE, FLORIDA

Mrs. Allen is a non-traditional college student completing her bachelor's degree in Elementary Education in Florida. She has two teenage children of her own and enjoyed volunteering in their classrooms when they were in elementary school. She is thrilled to be fulfilling her dream of becoming a teacher and especially excited because she has just begun student teaching in a fourth-grade classroom in Marion County. She has been learning the rules, routines, and procedures of the classroom while "kid watching" and getting to know the students. Her cooperating teaching, Mrs. Esposito, provided a list of the 22 students with comments about each. Most comments specifically addressed academic issues, but some were more personal. For instance, Guillermo's father died over the summer in a work-related accident. Guillermo attends weekly

© Nadino/Shutterstock.com

counseling sessions at the school to help him cope with his grief. Kenny's father is incarcerated at the Santa Rosa Correctional Institution, a five-and-a-half-hour drive one-way. Mrs. Esposito confided to Mrs. Allen that if Kenny had a bad day, it would likely be on a Monday after he and his mother had made the trip to visit his father over the weekend. This seems understandable to Mrs. Allen who can't help but notice the somberness of both boys.

There are other concerns for her to ponder. Eighty percent of the students qualify for free or reduced lunch. Two children are actually homeless. Suddenly, the wide range of reading and math levels pale in comparison to the personal challenges some of these students face. The old saying, "You can't judge a book by its cover" occurs to Mrs. Allen; she realizes she will need every possible resource to be an effective educator not only for these students, but for all of her future students as well. Mrs. Esposito's list includes four English learners; two are native Spanish speakers, one speaks Finnish, and the other speaks Russian. According to Mrs. Esposito's notes, the four are making adequate progress.

Teachers are expected to work diligently to reduce personal biases and make appropriately challenging education accessible for all students from diverse backgrounds and at varying English proficiency levels. **Effective educators possess not only the knowledge and skills to reach students, but also the right disposition—an attitude that is positive, nurturing, and includes high expectations for all students** (Lovell, 2009). Mrs. Allen is determined to learn as much about her students as she can and make every accommodation possible in order to provide appropriate challenges and support. She knows she will be relying on Mrs. Esposito for guidance and can always ask her university professors for ideas and feedback. She expects to be challenged in new and exciting ways and commits herself to learning all she can from her internship experience.

'GIFTED ENGLISH LEARNER' IS NOT AN OXYMORON

English learners can be gifted, although of the 3 million gifted students in the U.S., relatively few are ELs. Seventeen-year-old Alejandra Galindo was identified as a gifted EL in fourth grade. *"It's just kind of hard to not see people who look like me in my classes,"* she says. *"I'm a minority in the gifted world"* (Sanchez, 2015, p. 2).

To fully prepare oneself and avoid the pitfalls of stereotypes and the high hurdle of low expectations that may hinder recognizing and serving gifted English learners, there are five critical topics for educators to explore: (a) perceptions and misperceptions about gifted students; (b) perceptions and misperceptions about ELs; (c) the underrepresentation of ELs in gifted programs; (d) identifying gifted ELs; and (e) serving gifted ELs in the mainstream classroom.

Teachers of gifted students do not identify gifted children; they teach gifted students who have already been identified by someone else. It is the regular classroom teacher who typically nominates a child to be tested for any exceptionality, including gifted. However, teachers of the gifted are usually the only educators with training in gifted. The irony is frustrating at best and irresponsible at worst. Schools of education infrequently touch on the topic of gifted students in teacher education programs. Since most teachers are not adequately trained in gifted, they are unqualified to identify and/or teach gifted children. It is even more challenging when those students are learning English. Most classroom teachers, in the absence of training in gifted characteristics, rely on their instincts and experiences. In the last two decades, school districts across the country have made greater efforts to identify and serve gifted ELs (Florida Department of Education, 2020; NAGC, 2020); however, some leading educators perceive the lack of gifted training as a national crisis, claiming teachers should be trained as academic talent scouts (Finn & White, 2015).

In 2015, under ESSA (Every Student Succeeds Act), federal legislation was updated with two new requirements for states regarding gifted students. First, all state report cards must include achievement data for high achieving students. Prior to this change, states only reported on students who performed at proficient levels or below. Second, when requesting Title II professional development funding, states must explain how they plan to improve educators' abilities with regard to identifying and serving gifted students in the classroom. Both of these requirements impacted school districts in similar ways; districts must collect and disaggregate achievement data on all students, and ESSA explicitly stated that the term "all students" includes gifted students (ESSA, 2015). Many states have specifically addressed the underrepresentation of ELs in gifted programs.

Across the United States, educators recognize the lost potential in not identifying and serving these children. They face the challenge of identification with varying approaches, but

teacher nominations followed by standardized tests remain the most common tool. One study examined the effectiveness of screening all students for gifted (instead of those nominated by teachers only) to see if this approach would yield more gifted English learners (Card & Giuliano, 2015). It did. In fact, prior to universal screening, approximately two percent of identified gifted students were ELs; after screening was provided for all, that number increased to five percent. Other notable increases achieved through universal screening included: Plan B, 17%; female, 2 %; black, 5%; Hispanic, 11%; and those eligible for free and reduced lunch, 15%. Sadly, the district that proved successful using universal screening scrapped the program due to budget woes (Card & Giuliano, 2015). This meant the burden of gifted identification shifted back to the teacher nomination process.

Gifted identification practices vary widely from one location to the next because policies and procedures are developed at the state and local levels, but some form of standardized testing is almost always used once the teacher begins the nominating process. Because tests are almost always in English, they may inadvertently be measuring English language ability rather than academic or intellectual ability (Matthews, 2013). With more states pushing to identify and serve gifted ELs, but being unwilling or unable to provide universal screening for all students, the challenge will continue to be placed upon classroom teachers to recognize characteristics of giftedness in students whose first language is not English. *And wouldn't every teacher want to do this?* There is nothing more frustrating than to review and revisit material mastered over and over again—in any language. That is what many unidentified gifted students experience every day in classrooms around the country.

PERCEPTIONS AND MISCONCEPTIONS ABOUT GIFTED STUDENTS

Before tackling the issue of identifying and serving gifted ELs, every teacher must first get past the barrier of gifted. Yes, giftedness can be a barrier. Some professors of education tend to dismiss giftedness with a comment such as, "*Oh, the gifted kids. Well, they're smart, and they'll do okay no matter what, so we'll skip this chapter and focus on the kids who really need extra attention.*" It is with this attitude that schools of education do more disservice to gifted learners than just about anyone else, despite mountains of research that show gifted students require more rigor, depth, and breadth in their curriculum along with trained educators who can deliver the curriculum in engaging and challenging ways (Colangelo, Assouline, & Gross, 2004).

Research, as well as common sense, tells us that there are learners of all intellectual abilities. Let's examine the concept of I.Q., a criterion typically used in conjunction with other criteria when identifying gifted students. Most school districts establish an I.Q. of 130 as an acceptable criterion for admission to a gifted program. Similarly, schools accept the I.Q. of 70 as the primary criterion for mental retardation. Remember, the average I.Q. is 100. A standard deviation is 15 points. Therefore, an I.Q. of 70 is two standard deviations *below* average, and an I.Q. of 130 is two standard deviations *above* average. Few educators would disagree that a child whose I.Q. is two standard deviations *below* the norm requires specialized instruction. Now, consider someone with an I.Q. of 130 or above—two standard deviations *above* the norm. *Wouldn't it be logical to assert that this student, too, would benefit from a specialized learning environment?*

Gifted students often lament that they lose precious time sitting and waiting for others to catch up. It is illogical at best and immoral at worst. *What possible justification is there for holding students back and making them work at a slower pace when research clearly shows they require depth, breadth, and a faster pace of instruction?* **Because gifted students appear "normal" and do not fit a stereotypical image, teachers often erroneously assume that they do not have any special needs.** Nothing could be further from the truth. U.S. classrooms attempt to be the great equalizer, the place where everyone gets an equal opportunity. This is a noble concept, but "equal" and "fair" are not synonymous.

  Would you ask a student whose I.Q. is 70 or 75 and who cannot read on grade level to be on the same page in the textbook as an average student whose I.Q. is around 100? Or, would you break down the assignment into realistic and manageable steps?

Next, consider another student whose I.Q. is 125 or 130, one who may have already finished the book. Bear in mind that gifted students are consistently asked to repeat, revisit, and review material they have long ago mastered. This may be "equal" but how is this "fair?"

When we ask students to be on the same page in math and to read the same novel at the same pace, we are treating them equally, but we are certainly not treating them fairly.

Teachers must get past the notion that "equal" and "fair" are the same in the classroom. They are not. And any teacher expecting a student with an I.Q. of 75 or 80 to keep up with the rest of the class would be criticized and perhaps even dismissed. However, teachers do the reverse to gifted students all the time, and no one makes a fuss. Many feel that singling out students as "gifted" and giving  them special treatment makes others feel badly. Americans value excellence in sports, music, acting, and other areas of performance, but academic excellence is often dismissed. When gifted students are asked to sit quietly and wait for others to catch up, what values are we really embracing?

I.Q. is not and should not be the sole criterion for identifying gifted students. However, it is a valid and reliable instrument with academic value. I.Q. tests, however, cannot be administered in every language that teachers will encounter. Therefore, other criteria for identification must be considered. But first and foremost, teachers must dispel any misperceptions held about the concept of giftedness. Noted gifted education expert Nicholas Colangelo said it best: "*By the phrase 'all children are gifted' it is meant that all children are of value, all can do more if encouraged, and all have untapped potential, I am in your camp. But if the phrase means that all kids can do calculus in sixth grade, all students can achieve a composite score of 32 on the ACT … that all students can be piano virtuosi, or play professional basketball, then I am gone from the group*" (2002, p. 8). Yes, all students possess areas of strength, and teachers should always teach to students' strengths, never to their weaknesses. But, to confuse strengths with giftedness does a terrible disservice to students who are truly intellectually gifted. Mrs. Allen is aware that the school where she is student teaching includes self-contained gifted classrooms, and she hopes she'll have the opportunity to at least observe in the fourth-grade gifted classroom during her internship. She is naturally curious about same-age students working at a faster pace on more in-depth material.

PAUSE AND REFLECT

1. Would you agree that a student whose I.Q. is 70 requires certain modifications and adaptations in instruction? How does this concept apply when considering a student whose I.Q. is 130?

2. Think about your own teacher education program. How much time has been spent studying about gifted students? *A Nation Deceived: How Schools Hold Back America's Brightest Students* is a highly respected meta-analysis published in 2004 and endorsed by the National Association for Gifted Children that reveals how public schools and Schools of Education hold back gifted students. Review the 2015 follow-up to see if anything surprises you. Study available online: http://www.accelerationinstitute.org/nation_deceived/

3. Stereotypes about gifted students are not always positive. Review "Myths about Gifted Students" on the NAGC website, and discuss the one that most surprises you. URL: http://www.nagc.org/resources-publications/resources/myths-about-gifted-students.

4. See if you can volunteer and/or observe in a gifted classroom in your district. What did you learn that you could apply in your own classroom someday?

PERCEPTIONS AND MISCONCEPTIONS ABOUT ELs

Educators often believe that ELs do not want to learn English. Mrs. Allen had frequently heard people in her community complaining about this very idea. However, there is no evidence to support this myth. Realistically, there are two types of barriers that prevent ELs from achieving academic success, both erected by educators: language and cultural barriers (Lovell, 2008, 2018). Certainly, teachers are trained to provide corrective feedback when students err, but *can certain mistakes distract from the actual lesson at hand? Will a mispronounced word or an incorrect verb tense, albeit subconsciously, affect teachers' expectations regarding the intellectual abilities of an EL?* It can and does. From accented English to incorrect word choice to the inevitable blank stares, ELs typically generate more language errors than their English-speaking classmates. This is to be expected, but how does this inform a teacher's impressions? **Unfortunately, ELs may possess a vast understanding of important academic concepts, from climate change to evolution to geometry, but their limited proficiency in English creates a barrier for expressing their knowledge.**

Imagine the frustration ELs must feel, much like the physicist described at the beginning of this chapter. Picture yourself taking math and science classes in a foreign language. How would you fare? Teachers who are trained to work with English learners are expected to listen beyond mistakes, but this can present a number of challenges. The brain naturally collects and categorizes responses as correct or incorrect, focusing more on mistakes and causing one to form instant judgments. This is where corrective feedback typically occurs; however, excessive errors in pronunciation and conjugation can cause educators to misperceive ELs' actual abilities. If there is a focus on language errors versus comprehension, two critical events occur. First, by unwittingly focusing on the less important emphasis—the language error itself—it could undermine students' confidence in their abilities.

Fernando: (explaining photosynthesis): *The plant growed toward the sun.*

Teacher: *No, Fernando! The plant* **grew** *toward the sun.*

Second, the most important point is completely missed, that Fernando had mastered the content. If he can explain the concept of photosynthesis, even in imperfect English, he is right where he is supposed to be. The correct response would have been:

Teacher: *Yes! The plant* **grew** *toward the sun. Can you explain why?*

This would give Fernando the opportunity to elaborate on the concept, and the teacher the opportunity to provide corrective feedback in a non-threatening manner. Focus on strengths, probe for elaboration, and model correct language.

It may be painful to admit, but everyone harbors some type of preconceived notions, even biases, about certain groups of people, especially when significantly different from oneself. Effective classroom teachers must constantly reflect on their beliefs and be willing to change them as they 'unlearn' their biases and prejudices. One of the most famous passages in American literature speaks to the importance of unlearning biases. Consider Mark Twain's character, *Huckleberry Finn*. Huck was raised to believe that enslaved Blacks had no feelings for their children, that it was acceptable to split families apart and sell them at an auction, never to be reunited. This myth was promoted in states that legalized slavery for obvious financial reasons. However, when Huck helped Jim, a runaway slave, he got to know Jim as a *man* and realized that *slavery* was simply a condition, not a true characteristic or representation of Jim. As Jim, a man and father, lamented the loss of his wife and children, Huck began to 'unlearn' what a racist society had taught him. "*I do believe he cared just as much for his people as white folks does for their'n. It don't seem natural, but I reckon it's so,*" said Huck (Twain, 1885, p. 207). In similarly painful passages, Mark Twain reveals the paramount importance of unlearning cultural biases and prejudices. **Ignorance of other cultures adversely affects our expectations of culturally diverse students.** Educators must arm themselves with facts and personal experiences so they can identify their biases and work to eliminate their own prejudices (*Remember the physicist disguised as a custodian!*).

Equal treatment is not necessarily fair treatment; however, all educators must treat students equitably and remove cultural barriers for this to occur.

When students hail from different cultures, teachers must not make negative assumptions, but instead value those differences that make everyone unique. In fact, acknowledging and incorporating cultures is an accepted teaching strategy for reaching ELs. Some children are poor; this is especially true of refugees and larger populations of migrant workers whose children transit through school systems. *Can children of migrant workers be expected to afford school supplies, field trip fares, or daily lunch money? Can their impoverished state impact teachers' attitudes and expectations?*

 How does poverty affect attitudes and expectations in your school community? What resources are available to assist students living in poverty? SLIFE? How will you plan your instruction for students with limited formal schooling (LFS)?

As you know, ELs come from diverse countries and speak hundreds of different languages. Some arrive with a strong educational background in their native language. Others speak little to no English and may be illiterate in their own language. Some have perhaps never attended school before.

Others are multilingual, affluent, and well traveled. Still others help their parents pick crops after school. And, although some do participate in gifted programs, there are cultural disparities that must be acknowledged. Caucasian and Asian (or Asian American) children tend to be statistically overrepresented in gifted programs, while Hispanic and Black children tend to be underrepresented. A main cause of this phenomenon is arguably the overreliance on I.Q. tests for screening purposes. Of course, teachers must nominate students for screening in the first place. There is tremendous variance in cultural backgrounds. A student's culture is a critical component of identity and should be valued as such. It should not be a predetermining factor as to whether educators view an individual as gifted or learning disabled. As Linnea Van Eman, gifted coordinator for the Tulsa (Oklahoma) School District, said, *"We need to push back against this perception that giftedness has to look a certain way"* (Sparks & Harwin, 2017, p. 3).

Multilingual students have the advantage over monolingual students in the long run. *"New studies are showing that a multilingual brain is nimbler, quicker, better able to deal with ambiguities, resolve conflicts and even resist Alzheimer's disease and other forms of dementia longer"* (Kluger, 2013, p. 2). Teachers should not only value a student's native culture from a perspective of respect, but also recognize the academic value that comes with being bilingual or multilingual. With more than 7,000 languages in the world, the range of cultural and linguistic backgrounds presents a challenge for educators, but it also offers rewards. Teachers must become more aware and must thoughtfully respond to the diversity of their students. Teacher attitudes toward ELs range from outright resistance and rejection to the acceptance and valuing of everyone. In states with large EL populations, such as California, Florida, Arizona, and Texas, teachers who are unwilling to embrace the challenge are especially susceptible to predisposed negative attitudes toward ELs. Negative views toward mandated training may be transferred to students since the two are inextricably related. And educators who hold negative views of ELs will have lower expectations and be less likely to recognize their talents. **All teachers must continually revisit their attitudes toward students from diverse backgrounds for any signs of lowered expectations or biases against these students' abilities**. America has always been a nation of immigrants, and as long ago as 1892, Mark Twain wrote a sympathetic letter on this topic, stating:

My sympathies are also with you in your desire & purpose to preserve your native language in your American homes, & keep it alive in the family along with our own American tongue. My sympathies could not fail there, for this movement of yours, so publicly & trustingly expressed, is a high compliment to our free institutions. There are countries where it is a punishable crime for the alien subject to use the speech that was born to him, but in America we do not care what a man talks; for we know that the sentiment back of the words will be American, every time—& deep & strong, too. (Twain, 1892)

Fortunately, several states now require ESOL training in teacher education programs, which greatly lessens new teachers' negative views of ELs. However, gifted training in colleges of education remains haphazard at best, and states are inconsistent in their services for gifted students. The National Association for Gifted Children (NAGC) ranked states for their effectiveness in serving and advocating for gifted students, showing we have a long way to go (2015).

During the second week of her internship, Mrs. Esposito asks Mrs. Allen to take something that was accidentally placed in her mailbox to Ms. Rawlins, the fourth-grade gifted teacher. Mrs. Allen knocks on the door, enters, and is surprised to see a student at the front of the class presumably teaching a lesson in conversational Spanish. Students were engaged, and Ms. Rawlins stood nearby overseeing the actual lesson. Mrs. Allen was fascinated by what she witnessed and immediately asks Ms. Rawlins if she could schedule some observation time in the gifted classroom. She wants to learn more about a student who obviously speaks Spanish as her first language and why that student was teaching the other students.

 What are the current national attitudes regarding ELs and their acquisition of English? How might public opinion on this topic impact student achievement? How will you create a supportive and accepting classroom for ELs? For ELs who may be gifted (whether "officially" identified or not)?

UNDERREPRESENTATION OF ELs IN GIFTED PROGRAMS

Most educators would agree that ELs are conspicuous by their absence in gifted programs. In recent years, states have sought to address the underrepresentation dilemma, but it has been challenging (El Yaafouri, 2019). The number of ELs participating in gifted programs is growing at a far slower rate than the number of ELs entering U.S. schools. Three factors contribute in varying degrees to the underrepresentation of gifted English learners: (a) inadequate identification procedures, (b) insufficient teacher training, and (c) reluctance by families to advocate for identification. Proponents of gifted education tend to agree that the significant underrepresentation of culturally diverse students in gifted programs is due to inadequate assessment procedures. Because the educational system focuses its attention on the weaknesses instead of the academic strengths of ELs, it may not even occur to classroom teachers that an EL might also be gifted. **And since ELs may not take standardized achievement tests or I.Q. tests, two common screening tools, classroom teachers often become the single most important factor in the identification process.**

Identification Procedures

Teachers are in the unique position to observe students' potential and progress on a daily basis. It is at their behest that the nominating and subsequent screening process is launched. Yet, relatively few educators are trained in gifted education. In fact, those who receive gifted training are typically those who are teaching students who have already been identified as gifted. Beginning teachers often hesitate to nominate students for gifted programs. This is likely due to lack of training, lack of experience, and the distractions inherent to settling into a new role as a teacher. The screening and placement into gifted can take an entire school year. All of these factors can impede the identification of gifted ELs by years. Some will never be identified and served.

PAUSE AND REFLECT

1. Look up how many ELs are enrolled in your school district's gifted program. Discuss with your cooperating teacher and share in class.

2. Search your state's Department of Education website and investigate the Gifted Endorsement process. *How many courses are needed? Where can you take these classes? How long does it take to become endorsed? Can any teacher become endorsed in gifted education?*

3. Research your home state's service to gifted children in the 2018–2019 NAGC report. *How does your state rank compared to other states with regard to "inclusion of underrepresented students in gifted education" (e.g., low SES, ethnicity, disabled, EL, rural)? What impact might this have in your classroom? Report found here:* https://www.nagc.org/2018-2019-state-states-gifted-education

Teacher Training

Cultural sensitivity helps reduce bias while fostering understanding of variations in culturally influenced behaviors. Many teachers of ELs typically hold low academic expectations for these students, and in fact may coddle them and compensate for them out of misdirected concern. Kindergarten and first-grade teachers, where the majority of gifted identification occurs, reported that although they believed certain students were gifted, they would not recommend them for a gifted program until they had mastered "the basics" of kindergarten and first grade. Although their intentions were good, such actions defy a vast body of research, not to mention the laws and guidelines established by most states regarding identification and service. In many states, ELs who are eligible for gifted programs must be identified and served regardless of their proficiency in English. They, like all students, should be considered potential candidates for gifted programs and services from the beginning of their school attendance.

Some teachers feel that ELs must first master English before tackling the challenges of a gifted curriculum, regardless of policies or identification criteria. These erroneous assumptions further discourage the fair representation of ELs in the gifted classroom. Even ELs who have a better-than-average command of English are viewed through the filtered lens of the EL label. The importance of the role of the classroom teacher in the identification of potentially gifted students cannot be overemphasized. Ideally, teacher training must include the realities of gifted. **If reading this chapter is the only exposure to gifted education you receive during your teacher training, it may be time to talk to someone at your university.**

Family Advocacy

Parents of gifted students are typically known for their strong advocacy roles, but the opposite tends to be true for many ELs. Parents and family members may be reluctant advocates for a number of reasons. They may be embarrassed by their own limited English and therefore hesitant to approach a teacher. School, as an authority figure, may be intimidating for some, especially if their status is that of a non-citizen. Depending on prior experiences with official agencies, a school may be the last place parents of ELs can be found. Many do not understand the significance, or they may believe that any label is a risky proposition. Others may worry that their children must first be fluent in English before facing the rigors of a gifted classroom environment, a sentiment expressed by many classroom teachers. With these factors overlapping, it is easier to understand why ELs are continually underrepresented in gifted programs. In fact, when Mrs. Allen observed in Ms. Rawlins's gifted classroom, she was surprised to find that four of the students were English learners, including the girl she had briefly observed teaching Spanish one day. She did not expect to find ELs in a gifted classroom and plans to ask both Ms. Rawlins and Mrs. Esposito about it.

IDENTIFYING GIFTED ELs

Gifted coordinators across the country grapple with the question of how to best recognize gifted ELs. Over the years, the introduction of teacher checklists, quota systems, alternative assessments, and nonverbal instruments like the Naglieri Nonverbal Ability Test (NNAT), Form 6 of the Cognitive Abilities Test (CogAT), and the Raven's Standard Progressive Matrices (Raven) has made slow but steady gains in closing the gap in identification discrepancies between gifted ELs and non-ELs (Lohman, Korb, & Lakin, 2008). In Iowa, districts rely on the ITBS/ITED for primary identification criteria; however, this is augmented by other methods for ELs (Iowa Department of Education, 2008). Regardless of the actual instrument used to identify students, the first stumbling block to overcome will always be the classroom teacher, since the majority of nominations come from this source. Fortunately, ongoing research provides teachers with ways to identify and serve gifted ELs (Iowa Department of Education, 2020). Experiences impact the likeliness of teachers identifying students for gifted screening. If a teacher has previously taught gifted students, has had a family member identified as gifted, or was identified as gifted, this teacher is much more likely to observe gifted traits in students and nominate students for gifted screening. The identification process is subjective as well as objective. Teachers who have identified gifted students reported that they relied upon certain characteristics when nominating students for participation in a gifted program. These characteristics varied somewhat between EL and non-EL. **See Table 8.1**.

Non-EL Gifted	**EL Gifted**
High level/critical thinking	Ability to go above/beyond/in-depth
High verbal/vocabulary	High level/critical thinking
Quick mastery of subject matter	Ability to learn English quickly
Ability to go above/beyond/in-depth	Similar/same traits as non-EL gifted
Unique approaches/perspectives	Quick mastery of subject matter
Questioning/curious	High verbal/vocabulary
Standardized test scores	Questioning/curious
Teacher's intuition	Artistic
Creative/imaginative	Perfectionist/high standards

Table 8.1   Characteristics of Non-EL Gifted and EL Gifted as Reported by Classroom Teachers.

These traits and characteristics are rank-ordered based on the frequency of teachers' responses. Teachers reported other traits, although not in the same high frequency. These included the following:

- High ability in math
- Use of hands-on and manipulatives to explain understanding
- Creative/imaginative
- Use of drama and role play to explain understanding
- Problem-solving ability

Identifying gifted ELs is not an exact science. Indeed, there is no consensus as to the best approach, and most districts have their own criteria and process, inevitably a work in progress that changes from year to year. Ms. Rawlins explains to Mrs. Allen after school one day that she has never personally nominated a child for gifted, even though she is now a teacher of gifted. Rather, she took gifted endorsement classes, which allow her to teach gifted students.

"How are gifted students identified then—especially those learning English?" Mrs. Allen asks. Ms. Rawlins explains that it's a complicated process and varies among districts.

"In my former district," she says, "teachers used a checklist to get things started. I'll give you a copy."

Mrs. Allen reads and rereads the document titled "Gifted Characteristics Checklist for Underrepresented Populations." She begins thinking about the ELs in Mrs. Espositio's class—one in particular. She decides to search online to see if she can find similar assessments and comes across the Scale for Rating Behavioral Characteristics of Superior Students (SRBCSS), also called the "Renzulli Scales." After reading through both, she decides to speak to Mrs. Esposito about Annika, the Finnish student.

1. Review the Gifted Characteristics Checklist for Underrepresented Populations here: https://cms.azed.gov/home/GetDocumentFile?id=550317311130c016dcbfbc85 and the SRBCSS ("Renzulli Scales") here: https://gifted.education.uconn.edu/wp-content/uploads/sites/612/2014/08/Scales-for-Rating-the-Behvioral-Characteristics-of-Superior-Students.pdf

2. Compare and discuss in class.

Regardless of the formalized process used at district levels, the most critical step is that first one taken by the classroom teacher who scratches his or her head and wonders, "*Hmmmm . . . could this child be gifted*?" Once this line has been crossed, a teacher is honor-bound to pursue the identification process, and there is much to consider. First, there are district guidelines that must be followed. This usually means involving certain school personnel, such as the principal, guidance counselor, and other teachers who can substantiate the need for gifted screening through a checklist or some other evaluation. Second, the child and the family are integral to the process. This is an area that can present challenges. Labels can be detrimental, even that of gifted (Szalavitz, 2007). The label of "gifted" carries significant meaning; therefore, the label of "non-gifted," should the student fail to meet the criteria, carries significance as well. The world is full of people who report being "almost gifted" or who "missed it by two points." The way identification is approached can have lasting emotional consequences for students.

Choose words carefully when explaining to parents what is about to happen. In fact, consider refraining from using the label of "gifted" unless absolutely necessary, and if it used, parents should be cautioned about how to talk about this with their children. Instead of saying, "*You might be gifted—we're going to test you and find out*," it would be more prudent to say, "*We're going to see how well you do on some tests in case your teacher needs to make some changes to better suit your needs.*" All of these discussions must be presented to students in developmentally appropriate ways. Having this conversation with parents who speak a different language can also present challenges. They may misperceive the process as something negative and worry that their child is falling behind. Teachers must be extra sensitive when screening students from culturally diverse backgrounds. In every instance, for ELs and non-ELs, tact and restraint must be used. One student who adored her teacher was identified as gifted in the first grade. Her mother, who was simply excited and proud of her, blurted out, "*Now that you're gifted you'll be going to a special school!*" This translated to the child as, "*You're leaving your classroom full of friends and leaving your favorite teacher!*" How did the student react? She threw up! She had "made it" into the gifted program, but what did this mean to her?

And what about the feelings of those other students who "missed it" by a few points? It could be expected that they would hold a negative view of the gifted program in general. Even those of us who understand the arbitrary use of cutoff scores realize that a student with an I.Q. of 126 is an extremely bright child, even if he didn't score the requisite 130 to enter a gifted program. And this brings us to the fifth critical issue regarding gifted ELs: *How do we serve them in the mainstream classroom?*

SERVING GIFTED ELs IN THE MAINSTREAM CLASSROOM

First and foremost, the identification process is imperfect. The process is slow; even if a student ultimately tests into the gifted program, he will likely be in the regular classroom for the bulk of the school year. *So, what do you do?* The underchallenging of gifted students, both ELs and those who are native English speakers, occurs every day in classrooms across the United States. Current scenarios for gifted students in the mainstream classroom include the following exchanges:

Gifted Student: "Teacher, I finished all my work."

Clueless Teacher: "Good! Now you can …

a.   … help someone else at your table."
b.   … get started on your homework."
c.   … read quietly at your seat."
d.   … draw a picture."
e.   … clean out your desk."

Gifted students have long served as "teaching assistants." They are bored and underchallenged, which can lead to disruptive behavior and discipline problems. Or they could become complacent teacher-pleasers. **All educators should endeavor to match the curriculum with each student's level of academic and developmental readiness. This is the essence of differentiation**. Yes, this presents unique challenges, but virtually every educator faces a wide range of student abilities, attitudes, and developmental levels—*physically*, *emotionally*, and *intellectually*—and should therefore prepare for this wonderful challenge (Lovell, 2007).

How can teachers match curriculum, not just to a gifted English-speaking student, but also to a gifted EL? There are several possible effective approaches. The most efficient as well as satisfying is an "options" approach. All lessons involve specific and measurable content objectives—how well a student will accomplish a certain academic task. Mastery of objectives, though, can be demonstrated in any number of ways. Also known as **alternative assessment**, the idea is to encourage students to demonstrate mastery in ways that allow them to show their best efforts. This nurtures imagination and creativity, two very important concepts to intellectual development. If you think that students will take the easy approach, you're right. The "easy" approach is the one where a student can show his or her best work. *Who among us would choose to do otherwise?* Students will be more creative and thorough when given the freedom of choosing their own options for mastery. Consider the concept of photosynthesis again. Some students will explain the process in a written narrative. Others will draw a diagram. Still others will act it out, turning their bodies toward the window with outstretched arms, reaching for the sun. As long as the objective has been mastered, teachers are satisfied as are students.

Another way to present options is the **Yo-Yo approach**. In this case, the options are not directly related to content objectives, but to that perennial dilemma delivered by the high-ability student: *I've finished all my work, now what do I do?* "Yo-Yo" stands for "*You're On Your Own*" and allows you to suggest a number of options for when students have finished an assignment ahead of the rest of the class. A simple bulletin board that can be updated from time to time will suffice.

The standard "silent reading" keeps good company with the more specific "work on favorite food poem for a nutrition unit" and "continue online research for oral history project." The list should be varied and contain several viable suggestions. Students need to learn to be responsible for their learning; it is not up to the teacher to entertain or distract students who have completed their work. By offering choices, students have a voice and get to exercise their ability to monitor their own behavior. Students should also be given the option to suggest their own meaningful activity.

Mrs. Allen notices a "yo-yo" sign like this in Ms. Rawlins' classroom. It makes her think of Annika, the Finnish student who is always the first one done with her work, who carefully looks it over to be sure it's correct, and who then goes on to read quietly while waiting for the others to finish. Annika just started school in the U.S. in the fourth grade. She does excellent work, which is reflected in her grades, and several of her classmates recently referred to her as "the smartest." Mrs. Allen lacks the confidence to approach the subject of Annika with Mrs. Esposito. She doesn't want to appear uninformed, but curiosity finally prevails, so she asks, *"Why isn't Annika in the gifted program?"* Mrs. Esposito, an excellent teacher who received extensive ESOL training, replies, *"Well, Annika is still learning English."*

"But her English is so good," counters Mrs. Allen. *"Could she be gifted even though she hasn't fully mastered English?"*

Mrs. Esposito explains that she employs numerous strategies to support ELs and high achievers. This is a good approach, although her explanation doesn't fully resolve Mrs. Allen's question regarding Annika's potential giftedness.

Implementing effective ESOL strategies typically ensures student engagement, especially if students are relatively low in English proficiency. (These strategies may be less effective with SLIFE students, as you learned in Chapter 3.) Use these strategies to help deliver the lesson, or design extension activities that incorporate these strategies. These may include the following:

- Authentic language (vernacular, slang, idioms)
- Creating pictures, illustrations, posters, visual representations
- Demonstrations
- Games (creating new games or using existing games)
- Graphic organizers, concept maps (with illustrations)
- Hands-on activities, manipulatives
- Interaction to promote discussion and elaborate on ideas
- Music, poetry, rhyme
- Personal, meaningful, and relevant content (justification for "why" they are learning—not because it's on a test; the personal connection to the content)
- Realia, primary documents
- Role playing, dramatization, and pantomime
- Technologies, software, computer-generated presentations
- Use of pictures and illustrations

Effective educators frequently bring their personal interests and strengths into the classroom in appropriate and authentic ways. Their deep knowledge and passion for a topic generates enthusiasm, which can be contagious. My favorite author is Mark Twain. My fourth-grade teacher read a single chapter from *The Adventures of Tom Sawyer,* and I was hooked. He put the book in context, paused as he read, explained passages, and clarified the vocabulary and culture of the mid-1800s.

 1. Do you have a special expertise or passion about a particular topic? How might you integrate this into your classroom teaching in appropriate ways? How will you plan for instruction that embeds assessment and provide for re-teaching as needed?

Mark Twain remains America's most popular author, published in more than 50 languages. Despite the challenges his characters' dialects may present—always spoken in vernacular—readers are drawn to his works for this authentic element. He was the first author to write in a uniquely American voice, and he remains America's literary ambassador to the world. Twain wrote approximately 30 books, but the two most widely read are *The Adventures of Tom Sawyer* (1876) and *Adventures of Huckleberry Finn* (1885). These are frequently taught in schools around the world—*Tom Sawyer* for elementary and middle school students, and *Huckleberry Finn* for older students. Twain wrote dozens of essays and short stories that also lend themselves to the Pre-K-12 classroom, and much of his work consists of non-fiction primary sources that meet the Common Core State Standards.

Go to Activity
8E

Tom Sawyer

United States 8c

© AlexanderZam/Shutterstock.com

One aspect of Twain's writing that gives educators pause offers perhaps the best reason for teaching Twain: controversy. Twain's most famous work, *Adventures of Huckleberry Finn*, presents an uneducated white boy from Missouri, a slave-holding state, helping a runaway slave during the time of the Fugitive Slave Act of 1850. The main character is based on a real boyhood friend of Twain's: Tom Blankenship. Tom's older brother, Benson, did provide aid to a runaway slave and was condemned by the townspeople for his actions. In *Huckleberry Finn*, the modern controversy of the book began in the 1950s, when leaders of the NAACP took issue with the racial slur used more than 200 times. This controversy prompted some parents to challenge the book, some schools to ban it, many educators to shy away from it, and some publishers to edit it to be more politically correct. Many scholars argue that *Huck* belongs in the classroom in the way Twain originally wrote it. As they are quick to point out, slavery is a *condition*; one's race and ethnicity is not. Twain put the word in the mouths of the people who would use it to *justify* the institution of slavery (Chadwick-Joshua, 1998).

This is why it stands the test of time; it exposes bigotry and racism springing from the hearts of "good" people, "educated" people, and "religious" people. The book challenges the reader to look into his or her own heart.

There is a long history of discrimination against immigrants in America, and many slurs exist and are used to denigrate various groups of people. In today's political climate, slurs have become the lesser of our worries as more Americans are physically assaulted and even murdered solely because of their cultural or religious backgrounds. Students are not blind or immune to this discrimination simply because of their youth. Indeed, many are victims. A book like *Huckleberry Finn* exposes readers to the painful truth of well-intended parents and civic leaders teaching and justifying racism, prejudice, and hatred and an uneducated boy "unlearning" the lies of his society. Twain pokes his readers with a sharp stick as they read the powerful language. It may be uncomfortable to read, and teachers must use sensitivity when reading it with students; but, its power can be transformative, which is why Twain's works frequently appear in gifted classrooms and on Advanced Placement (AP) and International Baccalaureate (IB) reading lists.

Educators have embraced Mark Twain's writing for many reasons, from the authentic dialogue to literary realism to soul-stirring controversy and critical thinking the book provokes. Rafe Esquith, a fifth-grade teacher for approximately 30 years, focused on Twain's coming-of-age books, *Tom Sawyer* and *Huckleberry Finn*. Esquith's students were ELs, and Esquith immersed them into the American culture using literature as a springboard. He has written four best-selling books about teaching, and the evidence of his success is seen in the lives of his students who have gone on to great accomplishments of their own (Esquith, 2004, 2007, 2009, 2013). Esquith's love of excellent literature has been passed on to his fifth-graders.

In addition to Twain, they read **Steinbeck, Salinger, Shakespeare** and others, and not in any watered-down version, but in their original text. In a PBS documentary featuring his class, Esquith's fifth-grade students are seen choking back sobs when Huck makes the moral decision to help Jim run away to freedom, even though Huck believes in so doing he is consigning his mortal soul to Hell. Rather than turn Jim in, as he believes he should (according to the laws and mores of the time), he chooses his own moral path and famously says, *"All right, then, I'll go to hell."* Esquith shared a story that happened during the filming of the documentary, *The Hobart Shakespeareans* (2005), when a student was asked to name his favorite book. The fifth-grader answered . . . "Adventures of Huckleberry Finn." When asked why, the boy responded, "Mark Twain held the mirror up to our nature." Without blinking an eye, this EL was using *Hamlet* to express his own beliefs and thoughts. Apparently, the poet and dramatist Ben Jonson was right: Shakespeare was not of an age, but for all time.

Rafe Esquith was fearless in his quest to maintain a culture of excellence for his fifth-graders. Although many resided in poor Los Angeles neighborhoods where they frequently witnessed violence, and all spoke a language other than English at home, his students defied the cultures of their neighborhoods to excel. The point is, Twain speaks "American," and it can be argued that he does it better than any other author before or since. He is part of our national identity. And his subject matter focuses primarily on human nature, which means his stories resonate with any audience from any culture. This explains why Twain's books remain bestsellers around the world more than one hundred years after his death. This also explains why a 5th grade classroom of ELs consistently engaged with Twain's work.

PAUSE AND REFLECT

What would be a meaningful way to assess your understanding of the content in this chapter? Suggest at least two options.

Educators should endeavor to facilitate instruction that is personal, meaningful, and relevant for all students from all backgrounds. By doing so, students can answer the proverbial question, *"What's in it for me?"* They can endure chapter quizzes and multiple choice tests, but using authentic literature that speaks to meaningful aspects of a student's life will be instantly engaging. And there are creative ways to be sure students are completing their assigned readings. Instead of administering the BOQ ("boring old quiz") after reading the first three chapters, teachers can instead ask students to "cast" the main characters for a current movie version of the work they are reading. When students read with this in mind, rather than wondering what might be on the quiz, they are scrutinizing characters in a different way. And when they are asked to justify their casting choices, teachers see a higher level of critical thinking and engagement.

Implementing effective ESOL strategies as presented in this chapter will encourage engaged and thoughtful responses from gifted ELs. These strategies also lend themselves to appropriate alternative assessment formats in which content mastery can be accurately evaluated. Identification of gifted ELs must never be about quotas or political correctness. This process should simply be about a single student whose high abilities may be camouflaged by a limited proficiency in English, an individual who, if nurtured and encouraged, may grow up possessing the necessary skills and values to make a significant and positive contribution to society. It is in everyone's best interest to cultivate the gifts in all students. **Students can be both an EL and gifted; indeed, many are.** These actions exemplify a classroom that supports learning, embeds assessment, and differentiates learning experiences for all students. After all, it is every educator's responsibility to understand, develop, and implement effective strategies to develop language skills to support learning for all students.

Near the end of her internship in Mrs. Esposito's classroom, Mrs. Allen and Mrs. Esposito agree that Annika should be screened for the gifted program. Before proceeding, they ask Ms. Rawlins to informally observe Annika, and they meet with the district gifted coordinator. Mrs. Esposito shares that she had never considered nominating a student for gifted before, mainly because she was not trained in this area and also because she expected students to have been identified as gifted long before they entered fourth grade. The principal was involved in discussions and felt professional development in this area would be a step in the right direction for the entire faculty.

Not all student teachers would feel comfortable making such a suggestion in the first place, but Mrs. Allen had listened to her 'little voice' and felt Mrs. Esposito would hear her out. One thing she knew going forward: she would strive to hold high expectations for all students and meet them at their unique levels of readiness, whatever those might be. And she would always remember Annika, who despite challenges in learning English, still managed to stand out academically.

Perhaps Mark Twain said it best:

> *"I have traveled more than anyone else, and I have noticed that even the angels speak English with an accent."* (1897, p. 711)

Extended Thinking and Synthesis Questions

1. Take a minute and think about the Academy, Emmy, Tony, and Grammy awards. How about the Super Bowl, the Stanley Cup, and the World Series? Can you name recent contenders or winners? Jot down as many nominees, finalists, and winners as you can. Next, consider the Nobel Prize and the Pulitzer Prize. How many of these nominees and winners can you name? Discuss what this says about societal values regarding intellectual talent versus other talent.

2. Search your state's Department of Education website or contact your local school district to find out the percentage of ELs district-wide and the percentage of ELs in gifted programs. How do the numbers compare? Discuss your reaction to this with a classmate.

3. What do see as the unique curriculum needs for gifted ELs? Does technology play a role in this curriculum? If so, explain.

4. Contact a teacher or administrator in your school or district and ask how and when students are tested for gifted programs. Plan to share results in class.

5. Review a lesson that you prepared. Make modifications to the lesson to make it more appropriately challenging for gifted ELs. Consider the WIDA levels of proficiency in modifying your lessons. Include technological resources (e.g., Web, software, related media) to enhance instruction.

6. Think about famous people who might be considered gifted English learners, such as Arnold Schwarzeneggr, Ang Lee, and Madeleine Albright. Who else comes to mind? Select someone you believe meets the criteria described in this chapter, and write a brief biography supporting your claim.

7. Research the nonverbal instruments like the Naglieri Nonverbal Ability Test (NNAT), Form 6 of the Cognitive Abilities Test (CogAT), and Raven's Standard Progressive Matrices (Raven) online to learn more about these assessments. Share how knowledge of these assessments supports ELs from diverse backgrounds and at varying proficiency levels.

REFERENCES

Belin-Blank Center. (2020). Belin-Blank Exceptional Student Talent Search. https://belinblank.education.uiowa.edu/students/bests/

Card, D., & Giuliano, L. (2015). Can universal screening increase the representation of low income and minority students in gifted education? *NBER Working Paper No. 21519.*

Chadwick-Joshua, J. (1998). *The Jim dilemma: Reading race and Huckleberry Finn.* University Press of Mississippi.

Cloud, N., Genesse, F., & Hamayan, E. (2000). *Dual language instruction: A handbook for enriched education.* Heinle & Heinle.

Cohen, L. M. (1990). *Meeting the needs of gifted and talented minority language students.* ERIC Digest #E480. ERIC Identifier ED321485.

Colangelo, N. (2002, May). *Anti-intellectualism in American society, schools and gifted education.* Paper presented at Sixth Biennial Wallace National Research Symposium on Talent Development, Iowa City, IA.

Colangelo, N., Assouline, S. G., & Gross, M. U. M. (2004). A nation deceived: How schools hold back America's brightest students. The Templeton National Report on Acceleration. The Connie Belin & Jacqueline N. Blank International Center for Gifted Education and Talent Development.

Colangelo, N., & Davis, G. A. (2002). (Eds.) *Handbook of gifted education* (3rd ed.). Allyn & Bacon.

El Yaafouri, L. (2019, Apr. 30). Identifying and supporting gifted ELLs. https://www.edutopia.org/article/identifying-and-supporting-gifted-ells

Finn, C., & White, B. L. (2015). *Failing our brightest kids: The global challenge of educating high-ability students.* Harvard Education Press.

Florida Department of Education. (2020). Gifted education. http://www.fldoe.org/academics/exceptional-student-edu/gifted-edu.stml

Florida Department of Education. (2015). Technical assistance paper evaluation, determination of eligibility, reevaluation and the provision of exceptional student education services.

Frasier, M. (1997). Gifted minority students: Reframing approaches to their identification and education. In *Handbook of gifted education* (2nd ed.), Ed. N. Colangelo and G. A. Davis, 498–515. Allyn & Bacon.

Govoni, J. M. (Ed.) (2008). *Perspectives on teaching K–12 English language learners* (2nd ed.). Pearson Publishing.

Haley, M. H. (2010). *Brain-compatible differentiated instruction for English language learners.* Pearson Education.

Hernandez, A. (2003). Making content instruction accessible for English language learners. In G. G. Garcia (Ed.), *English learners: Reaching the highest level of English literacy* (pp. 125–149). International Reading Association.

Herrell, A. L., & Jordan, M. (2006). *50 strategies for improving vocabulary, comprehension, and fluency: An active learning approach* (2nd ed.). Pearson Education, Inc.

Hill, J. D., & Flynn, K. M. (2006). *Classroom instruction that works with English language learners.* Association for Supervision and Curriculum Development (ASCD).

Hite, C., & Evans, L. (2005). *Mainstream first-grade teachers' understanding of strategies for accommodating the needs of English language learners* (unpublished manuscript).

Honigsfeld, A., & Dove, M. (2008). Co-teaching in the ESL classroom. *The Delta Kappa Gamma Bulletin, 74*(2), 8–14.

Horwitz, E. (2012). *Becoming a language teacher: A practical guide to second language learning and teaching* (2nd ed.). Pearson Education, Inc.

Iowa Department of Education. (2020). *Identifying gifted and talented English language learners.* https://www.educateiowa. gov/sites/files/ed/documents/IdentifyGiftedTalentedELL.pdf/

Kluger, J. (2018, July 18). How the brain benefits from being bilingual. *TIME Magazine.* http://science.time. com/2013/07/18/how-the-brain-benefits-from-being-bilingual/

Levine, L. N., & McCloskey, M. L. (2009). *Teaching learners of English in mainstream classrooms K–8; One class, many paths.* Allyn & Bacon.

Lohman, D. F., Korb, K. A., & Lakin, J. M. (2008). Identifying academically gifted English-language learners using nonverbal tests: A comparison of the Raven, NNAT, and CogAT. *Gifted Child Quarterly 52*(4).

Lovell, C. (1999). *How elementary teachers identify gifted ESOL students.* Unpublished doctoral dissertation, University of Iowa.

Lovell, C. (2001). Even the angels speak English with an accent. *Kappa Delta Pi Record 38*(4), 150–152.

Lovell, C. (2007). "Goldilocks / Baby bear approach to differentiation" in *Understanding Our Gifted, 19*(2).

Lovell, C. (2008). "Gifted ESOL" is not an oxymoron. In *Perspectives on teaching K–12 English language learners* (2nd ed.). Govoni, J. (Ed.). Pearson Custom Publishing.

Lovell, C. (2009). The high hurdle of low expectations. *Mensa Research Journal, 40*(2), 58–59.

Lovell, C. (2018). Taking off the wrapper: Identifying and serving gifted English learners. In J. M. Govoni (Ed.) *Preparing the way: Teaching ELs in the pre-k-12 classroom* (3rd ed.). (pp. 47–60). Kendall Hunt Publishing Company.

Matthews, M. S. (2013). English language learner students and gifted identification. *Duke Digest of Gifted Research.*

National Association for Gifted Children (NAGC). (2020). *2014–2015 State of the states in gifted policy and practice data.* National Association for Gifted Children (NAGC). (2020). *2014–2015 State of the states in gifted policy and practice data.* https://www.nagc.org/information-publications/gifted-state

Nisen, M. (2015, September 15). Tackling inequality in schools' gifted-and-talented programs. *The Atlantic.* https://www. theatlantic.com/education/archive/2015/09/inequality-gifted-programs-schools-testing/405013/

Sanchez, C. (2016, April 11). Gifted, but still learning English, many bright students get overlooked. NPR. http://www.npr. org/sections/ed/2016/04/11/467653193/gifted-but-still-learning-english-overlooked-underserved/

Sparks, S. D., & Harwin, A. (2017, June 20). Too few ELL students land in gifted classes. *Education Week.* http://www. edweek.org/ew/articles/2017/06/21/too-few-ell-students-land-in-gifted.html/

Szalavitz, M. (2007, Feb. 27). Gifted? Autistic? Or just quirky? As more children receive diagnoses, effects of these labels seem mixed. *The Washington Post*, p. HE01.

Twain, M. (1885). *Adventures of Huckleberry Finn.* Webster Publishing Co.

Twain, M. (1897). *Following the equator.* American Publishing Co.

WEBSITE RESOURCES

A nation deceived: How schools hold back America's brightest students.
Link: http://www.accelerationinstitute.org/nation_deceived/

A nation empowered: Evidence trumps the excuses holding back America's brightest students.
Link: http://www.accelerationinstitute.org/Nation_Empowered/

Esquith, R. The Hobart Shakespeareans.
Link: http://www.hobartshakespeareans.org/

Gifted characteristics checklist for underrepresented populations.
Link: https://cms.azed.gov/home/GetDocumentFile?id=550317311130c016dcbfbc85

Gifted services for the culturally and linguistically diverse.
Link: https://sites.google.com/site/gingrichrobertsrodgers/useful-links

Myths about gifted students.
Link: http://www.nagc.org/resources-publications/resources/myths-about-gifted-students/

SRBCSS (Renzulli Scales).
Link: http://gifted.education.uconn.edu/wp-content/uploads/sites/612/2014/08/Scales-for-Rating-the-Behvioral-Characteristics-of-Superior-Students.pdf

8A Activity!

GIFTED EL

Scenario: You are interning in a 4th grade classroom. One of the students is an EL from Puerto Rico who is learning English quickly, although he is shy. The classroom teacher says he is in the process of being evaluated for the gifted program, which can take a long time. She asks you to jot down ways you can support/challenge him academically in this classroom setting ...

_____

_____

_____

_____

_____

_____

_____

_____

_____

_____

_____

_____

8B
Activity!
GIFTED EL

Name: _____

Think about a famous gifted person who would have been considered an EL as a child. This person may be gifted musically, as a writer, or in some other field. Research this person to see what you can learn about his or her childhood. Create a word portrait that includes name, characteristics, etc. Be prepared to share.

8C
Activity!
"G"

Name: _____

Radiolab Presents: G—Go to this website:
https://www.wnycstudios.org/podcasts/radiolab/projects/radiolab-presents-g

The concept of G represents intelligence. Radiolab explored the fascinating history, including numerous missteps, of how researchers have attempted to quantify intelligence. Listen to the first two podcasts in order of their broadcast dates. Jot down key take-aways for each. Then, listen to your choice of one of the other podcasts about G (there are 6 total). List take-aways. (activity continued on back)

G: The Miseducation of Larry P (June 7, 2019)

G: Problem Space (June 14, 2019)

G: Your Choice: _____ (Date: _____)

8C Activity!
"G"

Below, list the main points you feel are most important to consider as you think about a student's level of intelligence. Identify positive and negative aspects. Include any thoughts you have about classroom application.

Understanding the quest for G

(+) Positive...

(−) Negative...

(×) What I can apply...

8D
Activity!
YO-YO

Name: _____

You're On Your Own! By now you have been in plenty of classrooms and have seen strategies used by effective educators. Create your own Yo-Yo Chart below that you can post in your own classroom someday. You can use ideas from the chapter, other classrooms, and your own ideas! Go ahead ... you're on your own!

Cut and save this Yo-Yo chart for your classroom! ✂

- -

YO-YO TIME!

You're On Your Own

YO-YO

Finished with your work? You've checked to be sure it's complete and correct? Good for you! You're on your own time, so choose one of these activities to do next.

8E

Activity!

PASSION

Do you remember a teacher who brought his or her particular passion into the classroom? Maybe it was a science teacher who loved butterflies or a language arts teacher who loved Harry Potter. Think about your own passions and/or interests. Are you a surfer? Art lover? Antiques lover? Music lover? Collector of toy trains? Surely there is some unique area of interest that you can share appropriately with your students. Consider the examples, and then brainstorm how you might bring some excitement to your teaching using your area of passion as a conduit.

Examples:

1. A kindergarten teacher collects teddy bears. She lets her students use them when she teaches sorting skills (color, size, etc.) and other topics. She also lets students choose a bear as a "reading bear buddy" during story time. She finds many ways to bring the fun of her collection into her classroom to engage students.

2. A social studies teacher is an avid Civil War reenactor who does not hesitate to dress up as historical figures when introducing a unit or presenting certain lessons. His knowledge about the subject allows him to facilitate in-depth discussions, and his students remember these highlights more than they would reading about it from the textbook.

What is your passion?

Jot down your favorite areas of interest and ways you can appropriately bring this into your classroom.

8F

Activity!

OPTIONS

Name: _____

Providing options to demonstrate mastery of objectives is a smart and effective way to differentiate and allow students to shine. Consider this objective: Students will provide at least 3 assessment options to correspond to 3 learning objectives (for a total of 9 options). Example: Objective—Students will identify the capitals of all 50 states. Options—1) Complete a matching quiz; 2) Label a map; 3) Create a puzzle of the U.S. states labeled correctly. Write at least 3 options to demonstrate mastery of the objectives shown below.

Objective 1:

Students will describe the setting of the story with a minimum of 6 details.

3 Options:

Objective 2:

Students will explain the differences between birds and mammals with at least 6 details.

3 Options:

Objective 3:

Students will measure to the nearest inch with at least 80% accuracy.

3 Options:

Section Five

ESOL Testing and Evaluation

Introduction

LITERACY STRATEGY: KWL

Prior to reading about ways to use proficiency testing to improve classroom instruction, fill in the first column of the KWL chart to describe what you currently **know** about testing, the WIDA Standards, and ACCESS for ELLs. Next, fill in the middle column on what you **would like to know** about proficiency testing as it relates to your teaching. After reading this chapter, come back to the third column and write what you **have learned**.

K What I Know	W What I Want to Know	L What I Learned

Tips for Use with ELs: A KWL chart taps background knowledge before and after reading. This strategy allows students to share information from their personal experiences and cultures.

TEACHER VIGNETTE: MS. WHITECAGE, 3RD GRADE, MS. JONES, 7TH GRADE, AND MR. BLAKE, 7TH–8TH GRADE, COLORADO

Ms. Whitecage is one of several new teachers recently hired in the Boulder Valley School District. Previously, she taught in an elementary school in Sacramento, California where she earned the Crosscultural, Language and Academic Development (CLAD) certificate. This indicates that she understands how to support ELs in acquiring the English language and is able to teach using strategies for ELs to comprehend the academic content. She is now planning on attending a workshop on Assessment and Evaluation of English learners (ELs) for the Colorado school district. The trainers will be showcasing ways to adapt, analyze, and interpret assessments for ELs. In addition, they will reinforce the need to make informed decisions about language and content learning. A speaker from the WIDA Consortium will

address the Early English Language Development E-ELD standards, levels of English language proficiency, and WIDA performance definitions. Understanding assessment issues is critical across the nation and the Colorado Department of Education Office of Culturally and Linguistically Diverse Education (CLDE) provides numerous professional learning opportunities to educators in promoting equitable access and a well-rounded education for all students. For further information, visit the Colorado Department of Education website at: http://www.cde.state.co.us/cde_english. You will learn that English language learners in Colorado are diverse with Spanish, Vietnamese, Arabic, Russian, and Chinese (Mandarin) being popular languages spoken in schools. Colorado ranks in the top 10 for states with the largest number of EL charter schools. Check out ranking of charter school state-by-state laws (2020) at: https://www.publiccharters.org/latest-news/2020/01/27/new-state-rankings-report-compares-charter-school-laws-state-state

Ms. Jones earned her Master of Arts in Teaching (MAT) with a concentration in science and recently attained Bilingual, Crosscultural, Language and Academic Development (BCLAD) credentialing in California. The BCLAD requires more testing than the CLAD certification but enables Ms. Jones the opportunity to teach in English and her first language, Spanish. She is moving to the Boulder Valley School District in Colorado to teach at a high school where her boyfriend's family has lived for over five generations. The local high school has a high percentage of Hispanic students, and she was recently hired to teach 7th grade science. Her ultimate goal is to guide ELs in becoming more proficient in English and in mastering the science curriculum. Her fluency in Spanish will be an asset in teaching and assessing her students. Gottlieb (2016) reported that *"the context of assessment revolves around the characteristics of the student population, including linguistic expertise and their multicultural resources"* (p. 13).

Mr. Blake graduated with a degree in English with his ESOL endorsement. He has several years of teaching experience but is a new hire at a local middle school outside Boulder, Colorado. Although his transcripts list ESOL coursework, he is still unsure about assessing ELs. The workshop will focus on assessment practices and should prove to be beneficial for Mr. Blake as he begins to designs lessons for ELs to acquire proficiency in English and to achieve grade-level academic content knowledge.

© AJR_photo/Shutterstock.com

The three teachers have between one to five years of experience in the classroom. They seem confident about their teaching and lesson planning strategies. They are ready for the academic year to begin, but right now they are focusing on learning about **ACCESS for ELLs** (Assessing Comprehension and Communication in English State-to-State for English Language Learners). This is a large-scale language proficiency test for K–12 students developed by WIDA in collaboration with the Center for Applied Linguistics (CAL). It was initially administered by three states in 2005 and is a valid and reliable measure of ELs' English language proficiency.

ACCESS for ELLs meets federal legislative requirements under ESSA for monitoring and reporting ELs' progress toward English language proficiency. Each assessment tests in four domains: **listening, speaking, reading, and writing**. Visit https://wida.wisc.edu/ for more information.

Using Proficiency Testing to Improve Instruction: WIDA ACCESS for ELLs

Florin M. Mihai

© donskarpo/Shutterstock.com

PROFICIENCY TESTING

Language **proficiency testing** is typically used to place and exit students from a program. **The primary goal of proficiency testing in U.S. mainstream classrooms is to determine at what level an EL can listen, speak, read, and write in English.** The levels of proficiency for WIDA range from Level 1 (Entering) to Level 6 (Reaching). Díaz-Rico (2014) described proficiency testing as a measure of an individual's overall ability in English, usually independent of an instructional program. By design, proficiency tests assess discrete aspects of 'language' and provide a total score of a student's overall language skills. **In other words, proficiency tests measure ELs' level of English and not academic knowledge.** The scores facilitate teachers in mainstream classrooms to better understand the competency level of ELs in English, which in turn, affects academic performance.

Proficiency tests follow several theoretical trends, and we will review three types: **discrete point, integrated approach**, and **pragmatic tests**. First, **discrete point** tests measure a single or specific component of a language. The skills/discrete points can be combined to form an overview of an individual's language proficiency. For example, if students have expertise in phonology (the sound system), morphology (word structure), or syntax (phrase and sentence structure), they can put these different skills together to form a language. Discrete point tests measure language in small bits, such as *multiple-choice* questions or *fill-in* items. Discrete point tests break down the components of language and examine each part individually. Ms. Jones often gives Friday quizzes on the weekly science terms. She may design fill-in-the-blank statements with a word list to check students' comprehension, or write true/false statements, or simply ask students to spell newly learned science words. Her strategies represent discrete point testing as she assesses by reducing the vocabulary to individual or separate component points around the science lessons.

A second trend is the **integrated approach** where language is combined with academic content. This assessment is in contrast to discrete point as language is believed to be inseparable; that is, language concepts cannot be divided. For example, instead of using vocabulary in isolation, or simply listing vocabulary words, students are asked to listen to a story and retell it so that their understanding of the vocabulary is presented in a more meaningful way. Research shows that students benefit from practical lessons in which they can relate to and apply their own meanings. Mr. Blake wants to make sure his students have appropriate grade-level computer skills in his English classes. He designs a class project that incorporates computers aligned to the 7th grade language arts standards. He assesses students' technological skills, promotes higher level thinking, and makes connections to the content for ELs and all students. He provides an integrative language experience as students use the language skills of listening, speaking, reading, and writing. Other times, he gives *cloze tests* where he leaves out key vocabulary words, and students focus on the grammar, context of statements, and academic words presented in the lesson to complete the assessments. Students have an integrative experience as they consider the context from the lesson. Other times, Mr. Blake promotes *dictation activities* where students write down what they hear, thus integrating their language skills.

In the third trend, language is viewed as a pragmatic skill. **Pragmatic tests** link language knowledge with students' own experiences and world knowledge. These types of tasks seek to be more *real life*. In a story retell, a pragmatic test allows students to ask questions, use their time differently, and make inferences. Moreover, the story itself may have a significant meaning for students, and this might be an opportunity to bring in ELs' varied cultural backgrounds. In Ms. Jones's 7th grade science class, she asks her students to design an alternative way to solve a lab experiment. Ms. Whitecage provides her students with several short stories and asks that they choose one story and create a new ending. In this way, students may respond based on their cultural backgrounds, prior knowledge, and personal experiences. Mr. Blake uses the flipped-classroom approach, where his students watch a lecture at home and then discuss and collaborate in class. His students work at home at their own pace and apply what they learned in the classroom.

THEORETICAL TRENDS OF PROFICIENCY TESTING

- Discrete Point   • Pragmatic Skills   • Integrated Approach

Whatever the philosophical approach, proficiency tests must be feasible as well as **reliable** and **valid**. Some proficiency tests are more suited to large-scale implementation than others. Pragmatic tests are favored from a philosophical standpoint, but not feasible if administered to large populations of students. Proficiency tests tend to be somewhere along a continuum of direct to indirect. This is to say, there are tasks related to actual language use, such as producing an essay to **assess** students' writing skills, and tasks not related to language use, such as assessing writing based on knowledge of grammar. If students have the separate skills to do a holistic task, then they are able to complete a larger, more complex task. For example, if students demonstrate good editing skills, the assumption is that they will write an effective essay. **Determining proficiency provides insight into ELs' language proficiency and their knowledge of academic vocabulary.**

 In your own words, define proficiency testing and its three theoretical approaches. Explain how testing results affect **teacher** planning and classroom strategies.

The primary goal of **former proficiency assessment** was to determine if students were eligible to receive ESOL services. These tests were designed to determine if students had limited English proficiency, and for the most part, this distinction was all they provided. The most sensitive proficiency tests determined to what extent an EL was proficient, but, even then, descriptions of the levels of proficiency tended to be vague and not useful in terms of classroom instruction. Thus, it was impossible to use proficiency test results for anything beyond the purpose of general placement.

© YanLevShutterstock.com

With the requirements of No Child Left Behind (NCLB) Act enacted in 2002, proficiency testing became a much larger need for teachers and administrators. NCLB required annual proficiency assessment and placed rigid responsibilities on school districts. It caused changes and many challenges for schools, parents, and students. **Research shows that testing ELs is more problematic than testing any other group of students.** Historically, ELs underperform in evaluation. As NCLB requirements became unachievable for schools, the passage of ESSA in 2015, afforded more flexibility in testing practices and protocol.

While many tests are used as both proficiency and achievement, this practice does not always result in an accurate measurement for both purposes. Moreover, the EL population tends to be unstable, with ELs moving in and out of schools at a significant pace, either through improvements in their English proficiency or physical movements across states. As a result, more and more states felt the impact of assessment and joined the **WIDA Consortium**. Through this consortium, these issues, among others, are addressed. This chapter briefly addresses the foundation of WIDA as a means to meet the requirements of ESSA and provides an introduction to ACCESS for ELLs.

STAGES OF SECOND LANGUAGE ACQUISITION: A FOUNDATION FOR THE WIDA STANDARDS

The WIDA levels of language proficiency are a continuation of a process based on Krashen's (1981) theory of second language acquisition, which includes five hypotheses. The first states that fluency in a second language is a result of what has been **acquired vs. learned** in an environment that replicates the natural way in which people acquire their first language. **Acquired** is a subconscious process, whereas **learned** is a conscious knowledge about a language. In essence, *acquired* is similar to the process children experience in picking up their first language; *learned* is knowledge of the grammar rules of a language. For example, in Ms. Whitecages's classroom, she encourages her students to use visuals, refer to the word wall, and create stories using the academic vocabulary presented in class. She focuses on repetition, practice, and cooperative learning activities to allow her students to acquire the necessary language skills. She avoids overtly teaching grammar or English rules for spelling.

The second hypothesis introduces the concept of a **monitor**, which serves as an internal set of explicit grammar rules that ELs use when they have time to focus on the accuracy of their utterances, such as when they write in English. The monitor links acquisition and learning. According to Krashen (1981), acquisition is the utterance initiator, while learning monitors or edits. The monitor acts in planning and correcting when ELs have met three specific conditions: (1) they have sufficient time, (2) focus on form or think about correctness, and (3) know the rules (Krashen, 1981). Thus, the internal monitor supports ELs in their acquisition of English. For example, Mr. Blake focuses on the language arts standards in developing his lessons, such as, using punctuation to indicate a pause or break. However, he enhances his lessons so that ELs have opportunities to practice in small groups, check their answers, and edit their responses. He shares that his strategies allow students to be monitors, editors, or supervisors of their learning.

The third hypothesis claims that one acquires language in a predictable or **natural order**. However, this does not imply grammatical sequencing, as Krashen does not support language sequencing, but rather the acquisition of a language. ELs in mainstream classrooms should be provided opportunities to acquire English in a practical and natural learning environment. **Teachers should be able to create and maintain classrooms where ELs acquire English proficiency along with academic knowledge in a practical and positive learning environment.**

The fourth hypothesis introduces the concept of ($i + 1$), or **comprehensible input**, as a condition of second language acquisition, where acquisition takes place with a structure a bit beyond ELs' current level of language competence. According to Krashen (1981), this hypothesis explains how ELs acquire English as a second language. They are able to improve and progress along a *natural order* when they receive second language *input* that is one step beyond their current stage of linguistic competence. For example, if an EL is at stage *i*, then acquisition takes place when exposed to *comprehensible input* that belongs to level ($i + 1$) (Krashen, 1981). **Simply stated, ELs should be challenged through high expectations and varied opportunities to enhance their English skills and academic knowledge.**

The last hypothesis explains the concept of an **affective filter** in which acquisition best takes place in environments where anxiety levels are low. Krashen stipulates that high motivation, self-confidence, a good self-image, and a low level of anxiety support success in second language acquisition. On the contrary, low motivation, low self-esteem, and high levels of anxiety raise the affective filter. This filter acts like a *mental block* and prevents comprehensible input and language acquisition. **If ELs are continuously overwhelmed with vocabulary and grammar concepts in English, then there are fewer opportunities for them to comprehend academic content needed to be successful learners.** This is seen in Ms. Jones' class where she is aware of the high anxiety levels of her students when they are evaluated on lab assignments. She provides ELs with a key list of science terms and has bilingual glossaries available on their desks. She often places an EL with a buddy to complete a lab, especially if it is a detailed experiment. She strives to motivate all students and to promote positive attitudes toward the field of science. Her attempts to lower the affective filters of her ELs are demonstrated through her teaching strategies, safe classroom environment, empowering structure given to students, and opportunities to share with others.

KRASHEN'S THEORY OF SECOND LANGUAGE ACQUISITION:

Acquisition-Learning Hypothesis
Monitor Hypothesis
Natural Order Hypothesis
Input Hypothesis ($i + 1$)
Affective Filter Hypothesis

© Nitr/Shutterstock.com

Krashen and Terrell (1983) developed a teaching approach called the **Natural Approach** based on Krashen's theory of second language acquisition. It has been linked to Krashen's monitor model. See **Table 9.1** for a component of this approach used to foster communication skills.

Characteristics	Time Frame	Teacher Prompts
Has minimal comprehension; does not verbalize; nods "Yes" and "No"; draws and points	0–6 months	Show me … circle the … where is … ? who has … ?
Has limited comprehension; produces one- or two-word responses; participates using key words and familiar phrases; uses present-tense verbs	6 months–1 year	Yes/no questions; either/or questions; one- or two-word answers; lists; labels
Has good comprehension; can produce simple sentences; makes grammar and pronunciation errors; frequently misunderstands jokes	1–3 years	Why … ? how … ? explain … phrase or short-sentence answers
Has excellent comprehension; makes few grammatical errors	3–5 years	What would happen if … ? why do you think … ?

Table 9.1 Second Language Acquisition.

Reflect on how knowledge of Krashen and Terrell's four stages of language acquisition (see Table 9.1) affects teaching and learning. Review TESOL's Proficiency Standards Framework (https://www.tesol.org/docs/books/bk_prek-12elpstandards_framework_318.pdf?sfvrsn=2). Compare Krashen and Terrell's proficiency stages with the TESOL language proficiency levels. How will knowledge of both phases of proficiency increase ELs' academic and social skills?

THE WIDA STANDARDS AND LANGUAGE PROFICIENCY LEVELS

With the assistance of a Department of Education grant, the WIDA Consortium was established with the purpose of promoting educational equity and academic achievement for ELs. The first product of WIDA was a set of standards for English language proficiency (ELP) in 2004, which were revised in 2007, and again in 2012 revised to English language development (ELD) standards. The most recent revision, in 2020, envisions all students **developing language** and **learning content** together (WIDA: https://wida.wisc.edu/teach/standards/eld/2020).

English Language Development Standard 1:   English language learners communicate for **Social and Instructional** purposes within the school setting.
English Language Development Standard 2:   English language learners communicate information, ideas, and concepts necessary for academic success in the content area of **Language Arts**.
English Language Development Standard 3:   English language learners communicate information, ideas, and concepts necessary for academic success in the content area of **Mathematics**.
English Language Development Standard 4:   English language learners communicate information, ideas, and concepts necessary for academic success in the content area of **Science**.
English Language Development Standard 5:   English language learners communicate information, ideas, and concepts necessary for academic success in the content area of **Social Studies**.
Source: https://wida.wisc.edu/teach/standards/eld

Table 9.2   WIDA ELD Standards.

The WIDA ELD standards address, in terms of organization, five standards listed in **Table 9.2**. They contain the following elements: language domains, grade level clusters, and language proficiency levels with an emphasis on the importance of content as well as language. Take note that WIDA refers to ELs as "multilingual learners" and provides resources to address policy, theory, and practice.

The four language domains (listening, speaking, reading, and writing) define how ELs process and use English. Each standard is divided into six grade-level clusters: K, 1, 2–3, 4–5, 6–8, 9–12. The final element is represented by the six language proficiency levels, each of them with their respective performance definitions as outlined in **Table 9.3**.

Multilingual learners will progress through the following levels:		
	Discourse Level	**Sentence Level**	**Word/Phrase Level**
	Linguistic Complexity	**Language Forms and Conventions**	**Vocabulary Usage**
Level 6—Reaching Language that meets all criteria through Level 5, Bridging		
Level 5 Bridging	• Rich descriptive discourse with complex sentences • Cohesive and organized related ideas	• Compound, complex grammatical constructions (e.g., multiple phrases and clauses) • A broad range of sentence patterns characteristic of particular content areas	• Technical and abstract content-area language • Words and expressions with shades of meaning for each content area
Level 4 Expanding	• Connected discourse with a variety of sentences • Expanded related ideas	• A variety of complex grammatical constructions • Sentence patterns characteristic of particular content areas	• Specific and some technical content-area language • Words and expressions with multiple meanings or collocations and idioms for each content area
Level 3 Developing	• Discourse with a series of extended sentences • Related ideas	• Compound and some complex (e.g., noun phrase, verb phrase, prepositional phrase) grammatical constructions • Sentence patterns across content areas	• Specific content words and expressions • Words or expressions related to content area with common collocations and idioms across content areas
Level 2 Emerging	• Multiple related simple sentences • An idea with details	• Compound grammatical constructions • Repetitive phrasal and sentence patterns across content areas	• General and some specific content words and expressions (including cognates) • Social and instructional words and expressions across content areas
Level 1 Entering	• Single statements or questions • An idea within words, phrases, or chunks of language	• Simple grammatical constructions (e.g., commands, Wh- questions, declaratives) • Common social and instructional forms and patterns	• General content-related words • Everyday social, instructional and some content-related words and phrases

From 2012 AMPLIFICATION OF THE ENGLISH LANGUAGE DEVELOPMENT STANDARDS, KINDERGARTEN-GRADE 12 by WIDA Consortium. Copyright © 2012 by Board of Regents of the University of Wisconsin System. Reprinted by permission.

Table 9.3A   WIDA Performance Definitions Listening and Reading, Grades K–12.

Multilingual learners will progress through the following levels:			
	Discourse Level	**Sentence Level**	**Word/Phrase Level**
	Linguistic Complexity	**Language Forms and Conventions**	**Vocabulary Usage**
Level 6 – Reaching Language that meets all criteria through Level 5, Bridging			
Level 5 Bridging	• Multiple, complex sentences • Organized, cohesive, and coherent expression of ideas	• A variety of grammatical structures matched to purpose and nearly consistent use of conventions, including for effect • A broad range of sentence patterns characteristic of particular content areas	• Technical and abstract content-area language • Words and expressions with precise meaning related to content area topics
Level 4 Expanding	• Short, expanded, and some complex sentences • Organized expression of ideas with emerging cohesion	• A variety of grammatical structures and generally consistent use of conventions • Sentence patterns characteristic of particular content areas	• Specific and some technical content-area language • Words and expressions with multiple meanings or common collocations and idioms across content areas
Level 3 Developing	• Short and some expanded sentences with emerging complexity • Expanded expression of one idea or emerging expression of multiple related ideas	• Repetitive grammatical structures with occasional variation and emerging use of conventions • Sentence patterns across content areas	• Specific content words and expressions (including content-specific cognates) • Words or expressions related to content areas
Level 2 Emerging	• Phrases or short sentences • Emerging expression of ideas	• Formulaic grammatical structures and variable use of conventions • Repetitive phrasal and sentence patterns across content areas	• General content words and expressions (including common cognates) • Social and instructional words and expressions across content areas
Level 1 Entering	• Words, phrases, or chunks of language • Single words used to represent ideas	• Phrase-level grammatical structures • Phrasal patterns associated with familiar social and instructional situations	• General content-related words • Everyday social and instructional words and expressions

From 2012 AMPLIFICATION OF THE ENGLISH LANGUAGE DEVELOPMENT STANDARDS, KINDERGARTEN-GRADE 12 by WIDA Consortium. Copyright © 2012 by Board of Regents of the University of Wisconsin System. Reprinted by permission.

Table 9.3B WIDA Performance Definitions Speaking and Writing, Grades K–12.

The most recent WIDA Standards Framework (2020) provides proficiency level descriptors by grade-level clusters and are available at: https://wida.wisc.edu/sites/default/files/resource/WIDA-ELD-Standards-Framework-2020.pdf. The standards appear in two frameworks that are used for instruction and assessment of ELs. The *first framework* is summative and large-scale. It is geared toward demonstrating ELs' level of language proficiency over an extended period of time. The *second framework* is formative and classroom-based. It is intended to guide learning and instruction on a continuous basis.

After completing the ELP standards in 2004 (revised in 2007, changed in 2012 to ELD Standards, and revised in 2020), the natural step along the way was to develop various assessment instruments for ELs. The large-scale assessment **ACCESS for ELLs** is an acronym for *Assessing Comprehension and Communication in English State-to-State* and measures multilingual learners' language proficiency development in grades 1-12 annually. Its primary purpose is to assess ELs' placement, progress, and achievement. Other assessments through WIDA in the U.S. are WIDA MODEL and WIDA Screener (https://wida.wisc.edu/assess/choosing-assessment). The scores guide teachers and parents of ELs in understanding students' language abilities. The scores provide a snapshot of ELs' listening, speaking, reading, and writing proficiency in English. A proficiency score of 2.7 indicates that an EL is at a proficiency level of 2 (Emerging) and is more than halfway (7) toward achieving proficiency of 3 (Developing). Scores are not comparable across grades. That is, a score of 5 (Bridging) for a 3rd grader and a 5th grader are unique to grade level appropriate content. To view practice items for the assessments, go to the WIDA website at https://wida.wisc.edu/assess/access/preparing-students/practice.

© Vixit/Shutterstock.com

Proficiency testing informs classroom instruction in meaningful and contextual ways. Research shows that in learning academic content, ELs must first be able to interpret the sociocultural context of the classroom. Gottlieb (2016) reported, *"Academic language learning always occurs in a sociocultural context, as do standards, instruction, and assessment"* (p. 30). Ms. Whitecage, Ms. Jones, and Mr. Blake are aware that states have flexibility in assessing ELs under ESSA and are eager to implement strategies in their classrooms based on their upcoming WIDA training. They are focused on determining if proficiency in English is a barrier to learning the academic content. Ms. Jones says that it is up to every teacher to teach and assess in ways that are comprehensible for all students. Ms. Whitecage shares that assessment is more than a grade in a student's record; all types of assessment are powerful in informing teaching and learning. The three teachers are ready to learn more about large-scale and classroom-based assessments.

Entering	Emerging	Developing	Expanding	Bridging	Reaching
Level 1	Level 2	Level 3	Level 4	Level 5	Level 6

Source: WIDA

Extended Thinking and Synthesis Questions

1. Briefly describe how state and national legislation on proficiency assessment affects the classroom today. In your response, describe the role of parents, administrators, guidance counselors, school psychologists, and teachers in meeting these requirements.

2. Design a PowerPoint presentation, a Prezi, or a Google Doc for teachers at your school to enhance their knowledge of the policies and legislative rules in assessing ELs.

3. Go back to the KWL activity at the beginning of this chapter and fill in the last column.

4. Go to ESOL in Higher Ed website to explore further resources, readings, and activities on testing and evaluation in ESOL.

REFERENCES

Abedi, J., Courtney, M., Mirocha, J., Leon, S., & Goldberg, J. (2005). *Language accommodations for English language learners in large-scale assessments: Bilingual dictionaries and linguistic modification* (CSE Tech. Rep. No. 666). University of California's National Center for Research on Evaluation, Standards, and Student Testing.

Abedi, J., Hofstetter, C. H., & Lord, C. (2004). Assessment accommodations for English Language Learners: Implications for policy-based empirical research. *Review of Educational Research, 74(1)*, 1–28.

Bachman, L. F. (1990). *Fundamental considerations in language testing.* Oxford University Press.

Díaz-Rico, L. T. (2014). *The crosscultural, language, academic development handbook: A complete K–12 reference guide* (5th ed.). Pearson Education.

Gottlieb, M. (2016). *Assessing English language learners: Bridges to educational equity* (2nd ed.). Corwin Press.

Koenig, J. A., & Bachman, L. F. (Eds.). (2004). *Keeping score for all: The effects of inclusion and accommodation policies on large-scale educational assessments.* The National Academies Press.

Krashen, S. D. (1981). *Second language acquisition and second language learning.* Pergamon Press.

Krashen, S. D., & Terrell, T. (1981). *The natural approach: Language acquisition in the classroom.* Pergamon Press.

Lachat, M. A. (2004). *Standard-based instruction and assessment for English language learners.* Corwin Press.

Lake, V. E., & Pappamihiel, N. E. (2003). Effective practices and principles to support English language learners in the early childhood Classroom. *Childhood Education, 79*, 200–203.

Reutzel, D. R., & Cooter, Jr., R. B. (2011). *Strategies for reading assessment and instruction: Helping every child succeed* (4th ed.). Pearson Education, Inc.

Rice, D. C., Pappamihiel, N. E., & Lake, V. E. (2004). Lesson adaptations and accommodations: Working with native speakers and English language learners in the same science classroom. *Childhood Education, 80*(3), 121–127.

Rhodes, L. K., & Shankin, N. L. (1993). *Windows into literacy: Assessing learners K–8.* Heinemann.

Vacca, J. L., & Vacca, L. T. (1996). *Content area reading* (5th ed.). Harper Collins.

Whelan-Ariza, E. (2010). *Not for ESOL teachers: What every classroom teacher needs to know about the linguistically, culturally, and ethnically diverse students* (2nd ed.). Pearson Education, Inc.

WEBSITE RESOURCES

California Commission on Teacher Credentialing
Link: www.ctc.ca.gov

Colorado Department of Education
Link: http://www.cde.state.co.us/cde_english

ESSA
Link: www.ed.gov/essa

NCLB. (2001). The U.S. Department of Education.
Link: https://www2.ed.gov/nclb/landing.jhtml

WIDA
Link: https://wida.wisc.edu/

9A
Activity!
PROFICIENCY

Teachers informally assess ELs' English proficiency on a daily basis. Formal proficiency testing is used to place students into programs or exit them from programs. There are 3 theoretical approaches to this. Examine each of these, and write a brief scenario explaining these approaches.

Discrete Point

Pragmatic Skills

Integrated Approach

9B

Activity!

TESTING

Educators use proficiency testing to place ELs into programs and to exit them from programs. Accurate proficiency testing is crucial for appropriate placement. WIDA levels of proficiency build on Krashen's 1981 theory of second language acquisition. Research and briefly describe the five hypotheses that comprise his theory. Briefly describe how you can apply these hypotheses in your class.

Name: _____

1. Acquisition—Learning

2. Monitor

3. Natural Order

4. Input (i + 1)

5. Affective Filter

How to Apply:

9C
Activity!
PROFICIENCY

WIDA provides guides to understand ACCESS for ELLs scores. Visit this link on the WIDA website: https://wida.wisc.edu/assess/access/scores-reports. Review the 3 types of score reports. Identify their intended audience, and briefly describe them here in a "user-friendly" way that you would share with parents/families of ELs, administrators, etc.

Individual Student Report

Audience:

Description:

Student Roster Report

Audience:

Description:

Frequency Report

Audience:

Description:

9D

Activity!

SUPPORT

Scenario: You are teaching a 3rd grade EL. She is at WIDA Level 2 Emerging. You are offered a $500 grant to support this student. What materials would you purchase? Describe the potential benefits of these materials. Consider how parents and others may use these materials to support the EL. Be creative, and spend it all!

Materials	Cost	Benefits	Where to Purchase

ELs and Content Area Assessment: Large-Scale and Classroom-Based Considerations

Florin M. Mihai

© donskarpo/Shutterstock.com

Introduction

In this section, we present the assessment of ELs and its impact on Pre-K-12 schools and communities. Whelan-Ariza (2010) noted that *"assessment can measure content knowledge as well as language proficiency. When used properly, assessment can guide instruction, evaluate the effectiveness of teaching strategies, place students appropriately, determine whether students should enter or exit programs, and diagnose and monitor student progress"* (p. 24). Gottlieb (2016) reported *"accountability for learning rests on students' academic performance; their content area achievement, in large part, is a marker of success in school. For ELs, although language development is a vehicle toward reaching that goal, it often becomes entangled with content in getting there"* (p. 63). Ms. Jones attends to the language skills of her ELs in English and in Spanish. She understands that the majority are Hispanic, and she has access to the school's anecdotal records of cultural experiences and family backgrounds. Her goal is to observe, gather data on their linguistic skills, and modify her lessons accordingly. She realizes that teachers are held accountable for effective strategies and assessment practices. Mr. Blake, on the other hand, is learning about assessment protocol for ELs and intends to differentiate his strategies and measure the learning gains of his students. He recognizes that language proficiency and content knowledge are challenging to discern. He plans to determine if ELs' proficiency in English masks their academic knowledge. He is reminded that just because ELs may lack proficiency in English, this does not mean that they lack intelligence or knowledge. Ariza & Coady (2018) reported, *"Throughout the entire process of teaching and learning, authentic assessment should be ongoing, methodical, and linked to all subjects taught. In this way, the instructor can judge the EL's progress holistically, as well as objectively, and accurately analyze reading, writing, listening, and speaking, cultural knowledge, and communicative competence"* (p. 354).

Ariza and Coady (2018) stated, *"Inappropriate or inadequate testing that leads to misclassification of ELs results in unfair repercussions for students. If an EL is misplaced, insufficient instruction takes place, having a negative effect on student learning and academic achievement. Long-term results may include higher dropout rates, thus perpetuating unequal educational opportunities for ELs"* (p. 336).

Assessment plays a pivotal role in education. The Every Student Succeeds Act (2015) that replaced the No Child Left Behind Act (NCLB) of 2001 requires that all K-12 students be held to high academic standards to be prepared to succeed in college and careers. To measure students' progress toward the high standards, ESSA continues the NCLB requirement of annual statewide assessments. **The WIDA assessment, ACCESS for ELLs, is one testing tool used to monitor ELs' progress in acquiring academic English by measuring ELs' proficiency in listening, speaking, reading, and writing.**

The school community should be able to readily attain information about the English and academic skills of ELs. As you have read, educators must distinguish between ELs' language differences, giftedness, and special education needs. In addition, they must be equipped with a repertoire of accommodations to support ELs of diverse backgrounds and at varying English proficiency levels. The fact is, effective teachers provide opportunities for ELs to be instructed and assessed in comprehensible ways across all content areas. **Teachers determine if academic content has been mastered or if proficiency in English is a barrier to learning.** In this section, we present an overview of testing issues.

TEACHER VIGNETTE: MS. WHITECAGE, MS. JONES, AND MR. BLAKE

Ms. Whitecage, Ms. Jones, and Mr. Blake have some understanding on ways to assess ELs in their classrooms. They are ready to differentiate between ELs' proficiency in English and their knowledge in content areas. Gottlieb (2016) reported, *"When it comes time for assessment, sometimes we have to teach language and content apart"* (p. 64). The three teachers are prepared to report on the growth in English proficiency and on the academic development of ELs. As their confidence grows, so does their enthusiasm. The teachers share their insights on assessing ELs.

Ms. Whitecage compares the WIDA proficiency levels to that of building a house in the mountains. She describes the third-grade curriculum in which all students should be able to read, write, and communicate effectively to that of understanding the construction codes in Colorado. Her story of an alignment is as follows.

"This summer I investigated the construction of a house in the mountains just outside of Boulder, Colorado. Although I was a bit apprehensive, I researched building and safety regulations and sought advice from several contractors in order to comply with codes, permits, and other regulations. All in all, I realized that it was essential to have a clear understanding of the process as every decision would ultimately affect my lifestyle.

*"The WIDA entering level of proficiency can be aligned to the initial process of building my home. Just as I had to research and understand the permitting codes, ELs must understand the cultural and linguistic norms in a school environment. I adapted my plans, just as ELs must adapt to the social and academic language of the classroom. In addition, I could not envision my mountain home without architectural plans, just as ELs cannot learn English and the academic content without support and modifications. Modifications, such as visuals and graphics, are essential in supporting ELs' learning needs. **At the entering level of proficiency, ELs are typically able to produce small chunks of vocabulary, short phrases, and respond to yes/no type questions**. Although they may not be able to produce much English to show their understanding of the academic content, they are able to demonstrate their knowledge through sensory, graphic, and interactive supports* (see WIDA website for examples at https://wida.wisc.edu/).

"At the WIDA emerging level of proficiency, ELs use more academic language and begin to interact in meaningful ways with their peers. Gottlieb and Ernst-Slavit (2014) noted, 'Discourse, sentences, and word/phrases are the building blocks of academic language that vary according to the sociocultural context and situation of language use, or in the case of schools, in each and every classroom' *(p. 114). **ELs are typically able to respond in short sentences, identify facts, sort or describe pictures, and restate facts with visuals and graphics to support their understanding at this level of proficiency**. Thus, their success is dependent upon the strategies available to them in acquiring English in a safe, comfortable, and adaptive environment, just as my success is based on the contractor's implementation of the master plan.*

*"At the WIDA developing level of proficiency, ELs are able to compare and contrast, describe, categorize, or sequence facts and events. In this way, ELs demonstrate their comprehension of the content, just as I seek ways to appreciate the design features of my home. **With ELs schooled in all 50 states, teachers must be knowledgeable about differentiating instruction, modeling in English, providing meaningful lessons, and providing supportive and collaborative learning opportunities.***

"As ELs continue to broaden their language skills, they must demonstrate specific techniques by using a variety of sentences, summarizing, inferring, and analyzing. ELs at the WIDA expanding level of proficiency progress in mastering their language skills to meet the academic demands of the curriculum. My plans advance as I select cabinets, countertops, vanities, flooring, and more. I provide color suggestions and justify my decisions, just as ELs interpret information and find details to support their understanding of the academic content.

"Finally, ELs typically draw conclusions, engage in debates, conduct research, and apply information to new context at the WIDA bridging level of proficiency. They use a variety of sentence structures at varying levels of linguistic complexity, with an extensive vocabulary comparable to that of native English speakers. Their process of acquiring English reaches the point of being independent. It is a time for ELs to demonstrate their proficiency, just as it is time for me to sit back and enjoy my view."

WIDA PERFORMANCE DEFINITIONS

6 – Reaching	• specialized or technical language reflective of the content areas at grade level • a variety of sentence lengths of varying linguistic complexity in extended oral or written discourse as required by the specified grade level • oral or written communication in English comparable to English-proficient peers
5 – Bridging	• specialized or technical language of the content areas • a variety of sentence lengths of varying linguistic complexity in extended oral or written discourse, including stories, essays or reports • oral or written language approaching comparability to that of English-proficient peers when presented with grade level material
4 – Expanding	• specific and some technical language of the content areas • a variety of sentence lengths of varying linguistic complexity in oral discourse or multiple, related sentences or paragraphs • oral or written language with minimal phonological, syntactic or semantic errors that do not impede the overall meaning of the communication when presented with oral or written connected discourse with sensory, graphic or interactive support
3 – Developing	• general and some specific language of the content areas • expanded sentences in oral interaction or written paragraphs • oral or written language with phonological, syntactic or semantic errors that may impede the communication, but retain much of its meaning, when presented with oral or written, narrative or expository descriptions with sensory, graphic or interactive support
2 – Emerging	• general language related to the content areas • phrases or short sentences • oral or written language with phonological, syntactic, or semantic errors that often impede the meaning of the communication when presented with one- to multiple-step commands, directions, questions, or a series of statements with sensory, graphic or interactive support
1 – Entering	• pictorial or graphic representation of the language of the content areas • words, phrases or chunks of language when presented with one-step commands, directions, WH-, choice or yes/no questions, or statements with sensory, graphic or interactive support • oral language with phonological, syntactic, or semantic errors that often impede meaning when presented with basic oral commands, direct questions, or simple statements with sensory, graphic or interactive support

Source: https://wida.wisc.edu/

Ms. Jones decides to develop a rubric to demonstrate the assessment principles she learned in the workshop. In this way, she will be able to make informed decisions about her students' progress in life science and English proficiency. She refers to the WIDA English Language Proficiency Standard of Science and the Colorado Academic Standards for Science to guide her in developing an appropriate rubric for a 7th grade life science lesson aligned to the WIDA proficiency levels.

WIDA English Language Proficiency Standard 4:
English language learners communicate information, ideas, and concepts necessary for academic success in the content area of **Science** (https://wida.wisc.edu/).

Colorado Academic Standard: 1. Life Science:
Individual organisms with certain traits are more likely than others to survive and have offspring in a specific environment (Colorado Department of Education).

Objective: Explain how environmental and genetic factors influence the growth of organisms.

Language Domain: Writing

Ms. Jones plans a lesson for students to demonstrate an understanding of characteristics of an organism to survive and produce offspring in a given environment. Class discussions include environmental factors such as food, light, and water; examples of genetic factors are large breed cattle and species of grass affecting growth of organisms. The objective of her lesson is for students to analyze how environmental and genetic factors influence the growth and survival rate of organisms. Examples of evidence may be drought decreasing plant growth, fertilizer increasing plant growth, or fish growing in big ponds versus in smaller ones. Following is a copy of her rubric.

PROFICIENCY LEVEL/ STUDENT ASSESSSMENT	BELOW EXPECTATION	AT EXPECTATION	ABOVE EXPECTATION
ENTERING **10 Yes/No Questions** Circles 'Y' or 'N' to show which drawings of the factors the evidence belongs	Circles fewer than 3 factors	Circles between 4–6 factors correctly	Circles at least 7 factors correctly
EMERGING **T-Chart** Sorts pictures and definitions of factors provided by the teacher	Identifies and copies 2 factors from the list provided	Identifies and copies 3–4 factors from the list provided	Identifies and copies more than 4 factors from the list provided
DEVELOPING **Graphic Organizer** Creates a visual with environmental and genetic factors that influence growth of organisms with a partner	Creates a visual and writes 1 sentence for each factor	Creates a visual and writes at least 2 sentences for each factor	Creates a visual and writes 3–5 sentences for each factor
EXPANDING **Essay** Writes a paragraph on environmental and genetic factors that influence growth of organisms using textbook diagrams	Writes 1 sentence for each factor	Writes at least 2 sentences for each factor	Writes 3 or more sentences for each factor
BRIDGING **Essay** Writes an essay on environmental and genetic factors that influence growth of organisms using information from class video	Writes 1 sentence to describe each factor	Writes 2–3 sentences to describe each factor	Writes at least 4 sentences to describe each factor

Ms. Jones finds the rubric to be beneficial in clearly understanding the expectations for ELs and in assessing their progress in demonstrating the lesson objective. She will develop more rubrics as she continues to develop science lessons. She is already familiar with using anecdotal notes, checklists, the SOLOM and SWOLM, standards-based scales, portfolios, and other ways to assess performance in the classroom. Brookhart (2013) described rubrics as a coherent set of criteria for students' work that includes descriptions of levels of performance quality on the criteria. Ariza and Coady (2018) shared, *"Teachers can prepare rubrics for ELs according to the objectives they want to achieve. The rubrics can include language and content area skills and can provide feedback to ELs in both areas"* (p. 362). **Rubrics will assist Ms. Jones in distinguishing between ELs' knowledge of science and their English language proficiency level.**

Mr. Blake decides to focus on principles of assessment, various types of assessments, and testing accommodations in looking at large-scale and classroom-based evaluation. Gottlieb (2016) reported that large-scale assessments *"require the use of standard conditions across multiple classrooms and include schools, districts, or states in the*

planning, gathering, analyzing, and reporting of student data" (p. 24). Classroom-based assessment comes from a teacher's presentation of a lesson objective or standard, in other words, an evaluation of how students perform based on teacher instruction. Gottlieb (2016) noted that:

> *"measuring academic achievement as an educational outcome has become intertwined with academic language use. This creates a conundrum for ELs who may have the conceptual base in their home language but have not yet developed the academic language in English to express and apply it."* (p. 31)

Therefore, being aware of the types of assessment is critical in order to make informed instructional decisions. **All teachers must be able to analyze and interpret student data from varied types of measurement.** In addition, scaffolding English language and content assessment is critical in making decisions and advocating for ELs. Díaz-Rico (2020) stated, *"Teachers with a flexible repertoire of assessment strategies can design instruction to provide a range of evidence that ELs are advancing in English proficiency and accessing the core curriculum"* (p. 250).

According to Herrera, Murry, and Cabral (2007, 2013), **assessment** is defined as an extensive range of actions that are used to obtain information about what students know and, more significantly, about how they are able to demonstrate what they know. Assessment offers a comprehensive image about a student's level of knowledge because it combines formal and informal measures and findings that happen inside and outside the classroom. Egbert and Ernst-Slavit (2010) defined **assessment** as the general process of gathering data and described traditional classroom assessments as quizzes, tests, and structured papers. These assessments provide a score to designate how students have mastered individual (discrete) content or language items. Wiggins (2014) claimed that the effective transfer of learning, done with creativity, polish, and grace, is the essence of mastery. He suggested obtaining standards-based scores at least twice a year from school-wide assessments that reflect state and federal requirements. Staehr-Fenner and Synder (2017) defined assessment of ELs as *"more complex than assessing non-ELs. In addition to assessing ELs' content knowledge, it is necessary to assess their acquisition of academic language. As a result, because teachers of ELs are teachers of academic language, all teachers should also assess ELs' academic language"* (p. 233).

 Explain the assessment process used in your school district to evaluate both language proficiency and academic knowledge of ELs.

Wright (2010) noted that assessment is much broader than testing; therefore, it is critical to distinguish between assessment and tests. **Tests** are measurement instruments specifically designed to obtain a specific sample of an individual behavior (Bachman, 1990). Wright (2010) defined a test as a photographic snapshot and a sample of a student's knowledge and ability. Tests are part of assessment, but they are not the only component that should be taken into account when making educational decisions that will positively or negatively affect students' futures.

Boyd-Batstone (2013) stated that there is no single assessment to address the needs of all students. Thus, it is unfortunate for ELs that scores obtained on large-scale tests are often used as the primary measure of academic progress and language development. **These scores represent only a single measurement of ELs' abilities in content areas**. Under the No Child Left Behind Act (2001), replaced by the Every Student Succeeds Act (ESSA) (2015), ELs became part of a school's overall measure of Adequate Yearly Progress (AYP) and, because they often fall into more than one subgroup, are often counted multiple times in a school's overall AYP score. Wright (2010) claimed it is unfair for schools to include EL scores for accountability purposes. He reported that there are unresolved issues related to reliability and validity of test scores for ELs.

Furthermore, large-scale assessments pose a different challenge for ELs based on the test-design philosophy employed by test makers. In earlier years, standardized test designers did not take into account the linguistic and cultural characteristics of ELs when creating these assessments. It is true that ELs taking these tests are allowed access to accommodations and test modifications in an effort to make test results valid and comparable to those of their native English speaking peers. Díaz-Rico (2014) reported that standardized tests, though designed to be fair, are not necessarily well-suited as measures of language ability or achievement for ELs. She cautioned educators to

have a good understanding of the purposes for testing, as well as an awareness and receptiveness to learning from diverse cultures. Whelan-Ariza (2010) also confirmed the need for educators to distinguish if content has been mastered or if the language has interfered with learning. Gottlieb and Honigsfeld (2019) reported, *"If tests can be retrofitted linguistically (as in allowing the use of dictionaries or reading instructions in the students' home language) and logistically (as in special seating arrangements or extra time), then we have equalized the playing field in regards to eradicating the inherent inequities of testing"* (p. 137). In addition, WIDA aligned proficiency testing with language functions, to give teachers access to examples of language use for the classroom.

In addition to troubles with large-scale assessment, content area assessment is also of critical concern. However, Whelan-Ariza (2010) pointed out that assessment of ELs' learning in content areas is often difficult and may cause problems due to the separation of language proficiency and knowledge of content. She emphasized the need for teachers to distinguish between whether ELs have mastered the content or if their lack of knowledge of English is interfering with their learning.

 Why is content area assessment important for ELs in the mainstream classroom?

ASSESSMENT PRINCIPLES

PAUSE AND REFLECT

1. Do tests actually measure what ELs know?

2. Are assessments too expensive to administer?

3. How can teachers assist ELs in developing appropriate test-taking skills?

All teachers need to determine the effectiveness of assessments they use. Before discussing ELs in large scale and classroom-based measurements, an examination of the principles that are closely related to assessment design, implementation, and interpretation are presented. These critical principles are: **validity, reliability, practicality,** and **washback**.

Validity is defined as the extent to which a measure, for example, a test, actually reflects the concept or knowledge that it is intended to measure. In other words, in the case of a math test, does the test measure math knowledge or something else? In the case of ELs, language proficiency can influence validity in numerous ways. Let's take math as an example. Math is considered to be a universal language because it expresses knowledge using numbers that can be understood by many people, regardless of language or culture. Nevertheless, quite a few items on math assessments are word problems for which language proficiency is essential in solving them. To understand ELs' frustration vis-à-vis word problems, let's look at the following item:

ما هو حاصل طرح ثالثة من خمسة؟

This math problem written in Arabic is very simple. Because words are used instead of numbers and symbols, it is very difficult to determine the correct answer if Arabic is unknown. However, the math problem becomes much simpler if the following format is used: '5−3=?'. As word problems become more and more common in both classroom and standardized tests, you can easily understand the frustration for ELs who are required to demonstrate knowledge of math when, in fact, they are tested on language proficiency.

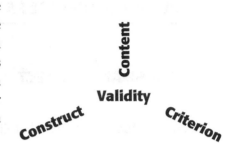

There are several ways of establishing validity. The first is **content validity**, which occurs when the selection of assessment items matches the content that needs to be evaluated. Assessments that display content validity have relevant content and coverage. For example, if you want to test whether or not students can do multiple-digit subtractions, you should use a wide range of numbers and not use only one-digit or two-digit examples in order to make sure students can indeed perform the mathematical operation you want to measure.

The second type of validity is represented by **construct validity**. Theories, hypotheses, and models are all constructs. In chemistry, the periodic table is a construct. *How do you measure whether or not students understand?* One possible way is to design an item in which students have to use the periodic table to determine the number of electrons available for bonding for a specific chemical element.

The third type of validity is **criterion validity**, which is comparing the results of an assessment with another instrument. For example, if a student receives a score of 75 in a classroom-based assessment and an equivalent score on a standardized assessment, then the classroom-based assessment has criterion validity. For ELs, criterion validity is difficult to establish. Whelan-Ariza (2010) pointed out that it is essential to test skills from a global perspective across domains and tasks, and consider the total product, rather than individual sub-skills (e.g., vocabulary, grammar, pronunciation, inferring meaning) of language. Classroom-based instruments often incorporate accommodations that aim to reduce the linguistic burden for ELs. On the other hand, standardized tests rely very heavily on English language proficiency and allow only multiple-choice and short-answer types of questions. In other words, ELs may be able to demonstrate they know the concepts of metal contraction and expansion through a lab experiment, but they might not score high on a multiple-choice test focusing on the same concepts.

Another word for **reliability** is consistency, and it may be defined as the capacity of a test or other form of measurement to be consistent in getting the same results over and over again. If students take the same test on two different occasions, and their scores differ considerably, then the scores cannot be considered a reliable indicator of students' ability. A reliable test should be a test that stays consistent regardless of the time it is administered, the format, or the individuals who grade it. Whelan-Ariza (2010) reported that more than one test is needed to make decisions about ELs' knowledge, achievement, and placement. An overall composite of skills provides the evidence needed to appropriately evaluate ELs.

A test that is reliable is not necessarily valid. Here is an example that illustrates the difference between reliability and validity. Suppose you want to measure the freezing point of water, and you know that the thermometer should read 32° F. If you measure the temperature ten times, and each time the thermometer reads "32," then the measurement is reliable and valid. If the thermometer consistently reads "45," then it is not valid; but, it is still reliable because the measurement is consistent. If the thermometer varied around "32" (31, 33, 34, 30, etc.), then the thermometer may be considered valid but not reliable.

According to Brown and Abeywickrama (2010) and Wright (2010), there are three types of reliability. Brown and Abeywickrama refer to these types of evidence as *student, rater,* and *test administration*. In **student reliability**, reliability is affected by the students themselves, who might experience illness, fatigue, personal problems, or other personal factors. With ELs, student reliability may be affected by time as students are exposed to English and increase their proficiency in the language. However, when ELs leave school for the summer, they might not have sufficient exposure to English during that time, and their scores might be negatively impacted when they return to school in the fall. Wright (2010) defined the consistency of results across differing testing occasions as "stability." In other words, occasions such as eating breakfast, well-being, and family life may cause errors of measurement.

The scoring process affects the consistency of scores in **rater reliability**. For true-false or multiple choice items, rater reliability is not an issue. However, when essays need to be rated, bias could occur due to human error or subjectivity. One way to ensure bias is reduced is to design scoring rubrics that are very detailed and specific and leave no room for subjective interpretation and partiality. **Test administration reliability** is achieved by making sure the conditions under which the assessment is administered are consistent. Wright (2010) refered to this as "alternative forms." Noisy environments, variation in temperature, and lack of familiarity with the testing environment can all potentially have a negative effect on test results. Therefore, test conditions should be the same for all students regarding the time of day or day of the week the instrument is administered. Wright (2010) refered to "internal reliability" when even the most prepared students struggle with poorly written questions on a test. Reliability is consistency, and good test questions are needed to distinguish between those students who are prepared for the test and those who are not. For ELs, testing accommodations should be encouraged on a regular basis to assure their scores are reliable. Familiarity by educators and administrators of permissible accommodations is a key component in ensuring reliability of test scores.

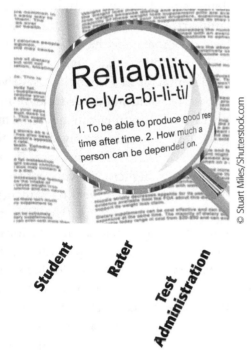

It is important that assessments are both valid and reliable. However, if the test is not practical, it has almost no chance of being implemented. To be **practical**, a test needs to be financially reasonable in terms of administration; should not take a long time to administer and grade; and should have very clear, specific, and time-efficient scoring methods. Díaz-Rico (2014) added the notion of a test being fair. She stated that regardless of how valid, reliable, and practical a test is, if it serves only the teachers' and the institution's goals, then students' language progress may not be promoted. **Testing must be an integral part of every learning environment**. This will encourage students to acquire a second language as a means to fulfill personal and academic goals. One valid way of measuring writing proficiency for ELs is to use **portfolios** containing representative writing samples produced over a semester or an academic year. However, this type of assessment lacks practicality because it requires extensive resources of time and money. Therefore, for assessing ELs' writing competence, portfolios are valid but have limited practicality. There must be a balance between practicality and validity, and promotion of one should not be done at the expense of the other.

Washback is defined as the effect an assessment has on instruction and student learning. Washback can be either positive or negative. Assessment has a great potential to generate positive washback, especially when classroom-based instruments are created with the purpose of positively influencing instruction and student learning. Test results administered in the classroom should be used not just as a way of evaluating student knowledge, but also for assessing the quality of instruction by identifying the gaps in students' knowledge. A returned test should always inform students what they know and what they need to review. **An assessment with a grade and no comment is an example of negative washback; whereas, the same graded assessment accompanied by comments on strengths and weaknesses is a clear example of positive washback.**

Perhaps the most common example of negative washback is teaching to the test. Increasingly, teachers have started to use items taken from standardized tests in their instruction. Exposure to standardized test items is not harmful to students, because they need to familiarize themselves with the format of standardized tests they inevitably have to take several times during their schooling experiences. However, it is very detrimental for ELs when the test drives the instruction instead of using standards to drive instruction that, in turn, drives assessment. In the case of many standardized tests, test designers simply discard test items that do not appropriately discriminate. **Test discrimination** implies that higher achievers get the item correct and that most lower achievers offer incorrect responses. Ideally, an item is able to discriminate between high and low achievers. Items that do not appropriately serve this purpose are withdrawn from the test. For English learners, this can have serious consequences, since core knowledge and background knowledge of a topic are likely to be purposefully ignored by test designers. For example, in social studies norm-referenced tests, items probing the major facts and historical events are unlikely to be selected because these items can probably be answered correctly by a large majority of the test-taking population. However, in the case of ELs, content area teachers need to accurately know if basic knowledge has been mastered before moving to the next level of academic content. Díaz-Rico (2014, 2020) noted that the most effective assessment of what has been learned is that which most closely matches what is taught. **Thus, instruction and assessment should match in order for students to know what to expect and to build on their classroom experiences.**

© Keith Bell/Shutterstock.com

PAUSE AND REFLECT

1. Obtain a test from a teacher and review it for validity, reliability, practicality, and washback.

2. Describe the implications of this testing format for ELs. Is there evidence of cultural or linguistic bias?

TYPES OF ASSESSMENT

There are at least five approaches of categorizing assessment: intention, purpose, format, interpretation, and administration. See **Table 10.1**. In terms of **intention**, assessment can be spontaneous (informal) or systematic (formal). When the purpose is the defining criterion, assessment can be divided into summative assessment, where the focus is on the product of learning, and formative assessment, where the focus is on learning processes. In terms of **format**, assessment can be either traditional, where students select multiple-choice, true-false, and matching responses, or alternative, where, for example, students create portfolios. When it comes to **interpreting results**, assessment can be divided into two categories: **norm-referenced**, where results are compared between students and their peers, and **criterion-referenced**, where the students' performance is compared with a body of knowledge to be mastered. Lastly, in terms of **administration**, there are large-scale assessments as well as classroom-based.

Category	Types
Intention	Informal—Formal
Purpose	Formative—Summative
Format	Traditional—Alternative
Interpretation	Norm-Referenced—Criterion-Referenced
Administration	Large-Scale—Classroom

TABLE 10.1   Categories and Types of Assessment.

TEST ACCOMMODATIONS FOR ELs: DEFINITION AND EXAMPLES

In an effort to support ELs in showing their actual level of academic competency, all states provide accommodations for ELs. An **accommodation** is defined as any support provided to ELs to ensure they can access English content of the assessment; thus, the validity of the assessment is strengthened. Butler and Stevens (1997) identified two categories of accommodations: those that dealt with the modifications of the test itself (access to bilingual translations, glossaries, etc.), and those that dealt with the modifications of the test procedures.

This broad categorization was expanded by Koenig and Bachman (2004) by increasing the number of categories from two to four. The first category they identified refers to EL accommodations that address **presentation**, translating both directions and the test into the native language as examples. The second category was represented by accommodations that were related to **response format**, that is, ELs can respond in their native language or they can use both their native language and English, while the third category of accommodations focused on **scheduling and timing**. Here, ELs are allowed more breaks and extended testing sessions over multiple days. The last category brought together accommodations related to **setting.** Examples of accommodations in this category are small group, separate room, and individual testing administration.

Still, this four-category structure is relatively broad. Therefore, it is beneficial to further separate EL accommodations in order to eliminate any source of ambiguity and confusion. We propose that testing accommodations for ELs be divided into six categories including **modifications to time** (schedule changes, additional time), **testing aids** (dictionaries, computers, etc.), **testing environment** (preferential seating, private setting), **testing directions** (in native language, read aloud), **test response type** (in native language, point to responses in English), and **test presentation** (bilingual version, audio/video recorded).

EFFECTIVENESS OF EL ACCOMMODATIONS

One of the most popular accommodations in Pre-K-12 is giving ELs more time to take standardized state tests. See **Table 10.2**. From a practical standpoint, this accommodation is probably the most practical because it is easy to implement and does not involve huge additional costs. The question is, *is it effective?* To be effective, **an accommodation should ensure that content, and not language proficiency, is assessed in content area tests**. Therefore, for math, science, and social studies, the accommodations should be designed to test academic knowledge and not English language proficiency.

© soliman design/Shutterstock.com

One conclusion that needs to be emphasized is that one accommodation does not fit all ELs. Abedi et al. (2005) indicated that an accommodation that significantly increased EL scores at one grade level did not work as effectively for ELs at a different grade level. **Dictionaries and glossaries seem to be**

State	Accommodations
California	breaks; additional time; English dictionary; bilingual dictionary; English glossary; thesaurus; translated test directions that can be read to the student; translated glossary for construct-irrelevant items; translated test items; text-to-speech; read aloud of test directions and items; read aloud in Spanish of a translated test; separate setting
Texas	extra time; bilingual, standard English, ESL (simplified English) dictionaries; clarification in English of word meaning; reading aloud of text by computer
Florida	flexible setting; flexible scheduling; additional time; assistance in the heritage language for all directions and for specified portions of tests (except reading passages); word-to-word bilingual dictionaries
New York	time extension; separate location; proctors may read the listening passage three times; word-to-words bilingual dictionaries and/or glossaries; written tests in native language; oral direct translations of the English tests; writing responses in the native language (not allowed for English language arts exams)
Illinois	extended time; general administration directions clarified in student's native language by test administrator; general administration directions read aloud and repeated as needed in student's native language; responses dictated in English using scribe or speech-to-text for math assessments; word-to-word bilingual dictionary; separate setting

TABLE 10.2 Accommodations Used in States with Large EL Enrollment.

more effective than test translations. Ariza and Coady (2018) reported, *"One of the greatest dilemmas facing the classroom teacher is the issue of fair and accurate grading of ELs, when the categories on their report cards do not truly reflect the EL's quality of work or academic progress"* (p. 364). Ms. Jones uses a spreadsheet where she aligns ELs' academic performance in science labs, quizzes, and tests to their English proficiency. She provides two scores for every assessment: one for proficiency in English and one for academic knowledge of each science lesson.

PAUSE AND REFLECT

1. What testing accommodations are in place in your school? What are the advantages and limitations of these accommodations?

2. What might you consider in testing ELs who are gifted or who have a learning disability?

3. How will you articulate the testing needs and appropriate accommodations to ELs' families and others in the school community?

ELs AND CLASSROOM-BASED ASSESSMENTS

Assessment of English learners in content areas is often a daunting task for teachers who try to find a balance between English language proficiency and content area knowledge. To address this issue, there are three recommendations for designing and implementing classroom-based assessments that take into consideration the language needs of ELs at all levels of language proficiency. The recommendations can be applied at the design, administration, and grading stages of assessment. See **Figure 10.1**.

DESIGN	ADMINISTRATION	GRADING
Reduce the language barrier.	Use effective state-approved EL accommodations.	Familiarize ELs with grading methods.

FIGURE 10.1   EL Assessment Recommendations for Content Area Teachers.

Creating content area assessments that account for ELs' levels of proficiency is one effective way of reducing language barriers for ELs. *However, how can content area teachers determine the proficiency level of their ELs?* Because of federal legislation, all states now provide a language proficiency test for ELs. For example, ELs may take WIDA ACCESS for ELLs, which measures English proficiency in listening, speaking, reading, and writing. A report indicates the language proficiency level generated for every EL.

Another way to account for ELs' academic proficiency is through the use of visuals and graphic organizers on tests. These should be placed in similar positions as they were in classroom activities. For example, if graphs are placed immediately beside a complex passage to help with comprehension understanding, then that same graph placement should be used on the test.

ELs can also generate visuals to help teachers assess their true level of academic proficiency. In math classes, word problems are especially difficult for ELs because of the linguistic complexity inherent in these types of problems. ELs can "draw" math problems to provide a visual check of their comprehension. By creating their own visuals, math teachers can be sure that ELs understand the problem and are able to apply the right mathematical formula.

In Ms. Jones's science class, ELs are allowed to answer test questions by drawing or matching pictures. At times, she permits them to use their class notes and textbook.

While many content area teachers allow ELs to use bilingual dictionaries on tests, glossaries and customized dictionaries have been shown to be more effective. Bilingual dictionaries are not content or context specific enough to provide all possible translations of a word. For example, the common English word "make" has 50 definitions. However, a glossed text would define "make" within the boundaries of the particular context of that text. For example, in the sentence "*What do you make of his response?*" the word "make" would be glossed at the margin as "think."

How can content area teachers adjust their tests to make them more comprehensible for their ELs? **Table 10.3** provides examples of linguistic modifications that can be incorporated in content area assessments that ease the language burden but still measure content knowledge.

Unmodified Test Item	**Linguistically Modified Test item**
Passive Verbs *A cake is bought by Tom for $25.99. If the sales tax on this item is 9.5 percent, what is the total amount he must pay for the item, including tax?*	**Active Verbs** *Tom buys a cake for $25.99. Tom pays 7.5% sales tax on the cake. What is the total cost of the cake, including tax?*
Conditional Clauses *If Susan is biking at 15 miles per hour, what is her approximate speed in kilometers per hour?*	**Separate Sentences** *Susan is biking at 15 miles per hour. What is her speed in kilometers per hour?*
Relative Clauses *The first heart transplant, which was a success, took place in South Africa.*	**Removed or Modified** *(removed) The first heart transplant took place in South Africa.* *(modified)The first heart transplant was a success. It took place in South Africa.*

TABLE 10.3 Linguistic Modifications.

In many states, ELs are given as much time as they need as long as they complete a particular section or portion of the test within one school day. Classroom teachers are limited by various constraints within the classroom and cannot easily make use of this accommodation. There is a solution, though: instead of giving ELs extra time in class, ELs can be given a test with a reduced number of items that sample the same constructs and objectives found on the full version. Or, they can be given take-home tests.

Translations of test into the native language of students are used in many states and classrooms. However, identical translations are rarely possible. Also, if the language of instruction has been English, it is unlikely that ELs will be familiar with the content in their native language. For example, Mr. Blake plans a lesson on computer skills and literature. If he translates the word 'computer' from English to Spanish to support his ELs, he would use the word 'ordenador'. However, since his ELs have only heard the word 'computer' in the classroom, it is unlikely that they will understand the word 'ordenador' to complete the assignment. **Unless ELs are taught content bilingually, they should not be expected to demonstrate knowledge learned in English in their native language**. Lastly, a closely related difficulty with translation is that **ELs may or may not possess an adequate level of literacy in their native language**. Testing ELs in Chinese is valid if ELs who speak Chinese are able to read and write proficiently at an appropriate level in Chinese. Ms. Whitecage initially provides a list of academic vocabulary to her 3rd graders in their native language and in English. From the surprised looks on their faces, she quickly realizes that some do not read or write in their native language. She adapts quickly and focuses on visuals and other supports so that ELs have a constructive learning experience.

One example of a commonly used grading procedure is represented by evaluation rubrics. For content area teachers, making evaluation rubrics available could significantly improve students' performance on assessments. Evaluation rubrics are an efficient way of measuring how much content ELs have mastered over a set period of time. There are a variety of rubrics content area teachers may select for the assessment of their ELs; for example, there are checklists with identified skills, competencies, and strategies, or more comprehensive rubrics that are either holistic or analytic.

In sum, we presented various modifications and adaptations that benefit ELs and require minimal effort from content area teachers. As seen in the examples throughout the chapter, assessment in content area classes is a complex process that uses language, even in math, which is supposedly a universal language. Consequently, content area teachers need to ensure that English language proficiency (or lack thereof) does not impede an accurate measure of their ELs' academic knowledge. Moreover, all the modifications, adaptations, and accommodations proposed should be included in teaching activities. **Assessment is and should always be an integral part of the learning process, and not an independent activity used for accountability purposes to fulfill a federal or state requirement at the end of a semester or school year.**

 LITERACY STRATEGY: SUM IT UP!

In 20 words, summarize the most important concept of this chapter.

Extended Thinking and Synthesis Questions

1. Imagine that one of your ELs was looking over another student's test. Brainstorm reasons why this EL might have looked at another student's answers. Then, share how you would handle this situation. Keep in mind that "cheating" has cultural connotations.

2. Describe assessment issues that teachers should be aware of in assisting ELs in developing appropriate test-taking skills. Include in your response issues such as cultural and linguistic bias, testing in two languages, sociopolitical and psychological factors, and the differences between language proficiency and standardized tests.

3. Articulate ways for parents of ELs to support their children in preparing them for classroom-based and standardized tests. Include in your response how testing can identify, place, and demonstrate ELs' language growth.

4. Present an overview of your understanding on how to implement district, state, and federal requirements in identifying, reclassifying, and exiting ELs from ESOL programs. Include ways describing how to articulate assessment practices to ELs' families and others in the community.

5. Refer back to the national and state standards listed in the beginning of Part Five, and explain the importance of demonstrating these standards in designing and administering classroom-based and standardized tests for ELs. Go to the ESOL in Higher Ed website for activities and resources in assessing ELs.

REFERENCES

Abedi, J., & Dietal, R. (2005). Challenges in the No Child Left Behind Act for English-language-learners. *Phi Delta Kappan 85*(10).

Ariza, E., & Coady, M. (2018). *Why TESOL? Theories and issues in teaching English to speakers of other languages in K-12 classrooms.* Kendall Hunt Publishing.

Bachman. L. F. (2010). *Fundamental considerations in language testing.* Oxford University Press.

Bachman, L. F., & Palmer, A. S. (2010). *Language assessment and practice: Designing and developing useful language tests.* Oxford University Press.

Boyd-Batstone, P. (2013). *Helping English language learners meet the common core: Assessment and instructional strategies K–12.* Eye on Education.

Brookhart, S. M. (2013). *How to create and use rubrics for formative assessment and grading.* ASCD publication.

Brown, H. D. (2004). *Language assessment: Principles and classroom practices.* Longman Publishers.

Brown, H. D., & Abeywickrama, P. (2010). *Language assessment: Principles and classroom practices* (2nd ed.). Pearson Longman.

Butler, F. A., & Stevens, R. (1997). *Accommodation strategies for English language learners on large-scale assessments: Student characteristics and other considerations.* (CSE Tech Rep No. 448). National Center for Research on Evaluation, Standards, and Student Testing.

Calderon, M. E., Dove, M. G., Staehr-Fenner, D., Gottlieb, M., Honigsfeld, A., Singer, T. W., Slaak, S., Soto, I, & Zaccarian, D. (2020). *Breaking down the wall: Essential shifts for English learners' success.* Corwin Press.

California Department of Education. (2011). *A look at the 3rd grade in California public schools and the common core states standards.* http://www.dmusd.org/cms/lib02/CA01001898/Centricity/Domain/59/3rdgradecurriculum.pdf.

Case, R. E. (2002). The intersection of language, education, and content: Science instruction for ESL students. *The Clearinghouse, 72*(2), 71–74.

Colorado Department of Education Science Academic Standards (2020). https://www.cde.state.co.us/coscience/statestandards.

Díaz-Rico, L. T. (2012). *A course for teaching English learners* (2nd ed.). Pearson Education, Inc.

Díaz-Rico, L. T. (2014). *The crosscultural, language, and academic development handbook: A complete K–12 reference guide* (5th ed.). Pearson Education, Inc.

Díaz-Rico, L. T. (2020). *A course for teaching English learners* (3rd ed.). Pearson Education, Inc.

Egbert, J. L., & Ernst-Slavit, G. (2010). *Access to academics: Planning instruction for K–12 classrooms with ELLs.* Pearson Education, Inc.

Every Student Succeeds Act (ESSA) (2015). Public Law No: 114-95, S.1177.

Figueroa, R. (1990). Assessment of linguistic minority group children. In C. Reynolds and R. Kamphaus (Eds.), *Handbook of psychological and educational assessment of children: Intelligence and achievement* (pp. 671–696). The Guilford Press.

Francis, D. J., Rivera, M., Lesaux, Kiefer, M., & Rivera, H. (2006). *Researched-based recommendations for the use of accommodations in large-scale assessments.* Texas: Center on Instruction.

Gottlieb, M. (2016). *Assessing English language learners: Bridges from language proficiency to academic achievement.* Corwin.

Gottlieb, M., & Ernst-Slavit, G. (2014). *Academic language in diverse classrooms: Definitions and contexts.* Corwin Press.

Gottlieb M., & Honigsfeld A. (2019). Chapter 7: From assessment of learning to assessment for and as learning. *In Breaking down the wall: Essential shifts for English learners success.* Corwin Press.

Herrera, S., Murry, K., & Morales-Cabral, R. (2007). *Assessment accommodations for classroom teachers of culturally and linguistically diverse students.* Pearson.

Herrera, S., Murry, K., & Morales-Cabral, R. (2013) *Assessment accommodations for classroom teachers of culturally and linguistically diverse students* (2nd ed.). Pearson.

Kagan, S. (1994). *Cooperative learning.* Kagan Cooperative Learning.

Koenig, J. A., & Bachman, L. F. (Eds.). (2004). *Keeping score for all: The effects of inclusion and accommodation policies on large-scale assessments.* The National Academies Press.

Lee, F. Y., Silverman, F. L., & Montoya, P. (2002). Assessing the math performance of young ESL students. *Principal 81*(3), 21–31.

Mihai, F. M., & Pappamihiel, N. E. (2014). Accommodations and English learners: Inconsistencies in policies and practice. *The Tapestry Journal: An International Multidisciplinary Journal on English Language Learner Education, 6*(2), 1–9.

No Child Left Behind. (2001). U.S. Department of Education.

O'Malley, J. M. & Pierce, L. V. (1996). *Authentic assessment for English learners: Practical approaches for teachers.* New York: Longman Press.

Pappamihiel, N. E., & Mihai, F. M. (2009). *Accommodations and English language learners: Inconsistencies in policies and practice.* Manuscript submitted for publication.

Rivera, C., & Collum, E. (2006). *State assessment policy and practice for English language learners.* Lawrence Erlbaum Associates.

Rivera, C., & Stansfield, C. (2004). The effects of linguistic simplification of science test items on the performance of limited English proficient and monolingual English speaking students. *Educational Assessment, 9*(3–4), 79–105.

Sato, E., Rabinowitz, S., Gallagher, C., & Huang, C.-W. (2010). *Accommodations for English language learner students: The effect of linguistic modification of math test item sets* (NCEE 2009-4079).

Sireci, S. G., Li, S., & Scarparti, S. (2003). *The effects of test accommodation on test performance: A review of the literature.* Centre for Educational Assessment Research Report No. 485. School of Education, University of Massachusetts.

Staehr-Fenner, D., & Synder, S. (2017). *Unlocking English language learners' potential: Strategies for making content accessible.* Corwin Press.

Whelan-Ariza, E. (2010) *Not for ESOL teachers: What every classroom teacher needs to know about the linguistically, culturally, and ethnically diverse students* (2nd ed.). Pearson Education Inc.

WIDA (2020). https://wida.wisc.edu/.

Wiggins, G. (2014). How good is good enough? *Educational Leadership*, ASCD, *71*(4).

Wright, W. E. (2010). *Foundations for teaching English language learners: Research, theory, policy, and practice.* Caslon Publishers.

10A
Activity!
RUBRICS

In this chapter, you read that Ms. Jones developed a rubric for a 7th grade life science lesson aligned to WIDA proficiency levels. Rubrics are more than an assessment tool. They provide a guide for students to follow as they complete the assignment. Research websites that explain how to develop a rubric. Choose a topic and grade level, and create a rubric that assesses content (e.g., science, math) that takes English proficiency into account. Brainstorm below.

Subject Area: _____
Grade Level: _____
Lesson Topic: _____
Objective(s): _____

Some recommended websites:
- thoughtco.com/how-to-create-a-rubric-4061367
- rubistar.4teachers.org/index.php
- rubric-maker.com

_____
_____

• •

Rubric Ideas

Rubric type?   Analytic   or   Holistic

Brainstorm your criteria here:
(Try to keep this between 4–7 specific & measureable criteria—for example, list 3, describe 4, provide 3, etc.)

Create performance levels:
(Note: Most ratings scales have 3 to 5 levels, such as Novice, Intermediate, Expert, or just 1, 2, 3.)

Write descriptors for each level of performance. (You'll likely need more space for this.)

Use one of the rubric-making sites to generate your rubric. Swap with a friend to give each other feedback. Discuss the challenges and advantages of using rubrics.

10B
Activity!
ASSESSMENT

Math word problems can be especially challenging for ELs who are more likely stumbling over the words than the math concepts. However, all math problems solved in the 'real world' are simply shorthand word problems. *Can she afford it? How many will it serve? How long will it take?* All are real situations using math to tell stories. See if you can find an 'ah-ha!' moment here by reverse-engineering a word problem by first turning a regular math problem into a word problem.

Find the mean, median, and mode for these numbers:

154
288
201
154
243
98
197

> What if you took these numbers and turned them into a story? For instance, these numbers could represent the number of people waiting in various lines at Disney World, or bowling scores. Now, write any math problem, and then provide the 'story' details to bring it to life.

Write your math problem: _ _ _ _ _ _ _ _ _ _ _ _

Now, write the story behind these numbers:

Teachers often forget to read over word problems looking for problem areas. Circle the problem areas below. Discuss why these could present problems for ELs.

Troop 204 was holding a fundraiser ...
Karin wanted to play a game of 8-ball ...
Dave estimated it would take 2 hours to walk ...
Highway 44 is a busy road for tourists ...

Discuss why and how reverse-engineering can help them feel more comfortable with word problems. Discuss how teachers can and should screen word problems for language issues.

10C
Activity!
ASSESS

Preservice teachers often lack sufficient experience in assessment, especially with regard to ELs. Visit this site: http://elllps.squarespace.com/work and click on Elementary, Middle, or High School, depending on what area you plan to teach. Click on a student profile, view the videos, and form your assessments. You will receive feedback to compare your assessments with professional assessments.

Student Name: _____   Age: _____   Grade Level: _____

1. Rate the Oral Language Sample assessment using the SOLOM (provided on the site). After you submit your scores, you will receive a professional score. Provide a brief comparison here:

2. Listen to the Reading Samples 1 and 2 and complete the Running Record Evaluations. After you submit your scores, you will receive a professional score. Provide a brief comparison here:

3. Read both Writing Samples and complete the Writing Evaluations. After you submit your scores, you will receive a professional score. Provide a comparison here:

4. Self-evaluation time! How did you do? In what areas do you need to improve? (Note: You can use this site to practice your assessment development.)

10D
Activity!
SUPPORT

Jot down online resources (e.g., games, language learning sites, translation services) that would be appropriate to support an EL in grade level _____ (fill in the grade level you want to teach).

Website:

_____

_____

_____

_____

_____

_____

_____

_____

_____

_____

Description:

_____

_____

_____

_____

_____

_____

_____

_____

_____

_____

INDEX

A

Academic achievement, 2, 44
Academic language, 132–133
Academic language proficiency, 271
Academic vocabulary, 132
Accelerated Reader (AR), 262
ACCESS for ELLs, 5, 20, 142, 339, 341, 346, 351, 364, 378
    proficiency score, 351
Accommodation for assessment, 375–376, 376–377
Accountability, 5, 11, 107, 110, 165, 233, 363, 370, 379
Achievement gap factors, 44
Acquire
    as opposed to "learn," 157, 346
    as subconscious process, 146
Acquisition, 200, 201
Acquisition/learning process, 201
Acronym, 12–13
Ada, Alma Flor, 45
Additive approach, 65
Additive bilingualism, 243
Adequate Yearly Progress (AYP), 370
Adjective, 160
Administration category of assessment, 375
Advanced fluency stage of second language acquisition, 209
Advanced Placement (AP) reading list, 318
Adventures of Huckleberry Finn, 307, 317, 318
The Adventures of Tom Sawyer, 317
Adverb, 161
Advocacy, 13–15

Affective filter, 201, 346–347
Affective filter hypothesis, 208
Affix, 150
Age-appropriate literacy skills, 96
Allophone, 137
Alternative assessment, 315
Ambiguity, 172–173
Ambiguous phrase, 172
Analysis of language and culture, 52, 53–54
Anchored instruction, 21
Anthropologist, 49
Anxiety, 346, 347
Applied linguistics
    communication through language, 136–178
    language and literacy, 130–134
    theories of second language learning, 198–213
Aptitude, 210, 213
Arabic dialect, 143, 340
Arabic phonemes, 137
Arkansas, WIDA Consortium and, 5
Artecona-Pelaez, Gloria, 17
Articulation, 138
Asher, James, 235
Aspiration, 137, 140
Assessing Comprehension and Communication in English State-to-State (ACCESS), 351. *see also* ACCESS for ELLs
Assessment. *see also* ESOL testing and evaluation
    defined, 369
    of English learners (ELs) with disabilities, 276–277
    gifted students and, 312

Assessment recommendations for content area
teachers, 377
Assessment strategies, 15
Attention Deficit Hyperactive Disorder (ADHD),
132
Attention theory, 235
Attitude, 210, 213
Audiolingual approach, 199
Audiolingual method, 234

B
Balanced bilingual, 243
Behaviorism, 199, 203, 204, 205
Behaviorist model, 199, 207
Benedict, Ruth Fulton, 47
Bilingual, Cross Cultural, Language and Academic
Development (BCLAD), 340
Bilingual education, 262
Bilingual Education Act (BEA), 6, 8, 241
Bilingualism, 237, 240–246
    additive, 243
    balanced, 243
    benefits of, 241–242
    Bilingual Education Act (BEA), 241
    cognitive benefits of, 241, 242
    concepts for teachers, 243–244
    creative thinking and, 242
    dominant, 243
    economic benefits of, 241–242
    history of in U.S., 240–241
    personal benefits of, 241
    from problem to resource, 243
    sequential, 243
    simultaneous, 243
    skill transfer principles, 244
    social benefits of, 241
    students with disabilities and, 242, 262
    subtractive, 243
    teaching for transfer, 245–246
Bilingual special education, 262. *see also* English
Learners (ELs) with disabilities
Bilingual student, 13
Bloom's Taxonomy, 100
Body movement, 49
Book report, 274
Bottom-up process, 271

Bridging proficiency level, 211, 212, 349, 350, 352,
368
Brown v. Board of Education (1954), 8
Bureau of Student Achievement Through Language
Acquisition (SALA), 19, 20
Bush, George W., 5

C
California test accommodations, 376
Canonical order, 158
Case-marked language, 159
Case marker, 159
Case-marking, 159–160
Castañeda v. Pickard (1981), 10
Center for Advanced Research for Language
Acquisition (CARLA), 48
Center for Applied Linguistics (CAL), 341
Charter school, 12
    in Minnesota, 12
Child language socialization, 176
Chisme, 177
Chomsky, Noam, 200, 201
Class expectations, 46
Classroom-based assessments, 377–378
Clayton-Kandor, L., 19
Cloze test, 344
Code-switching, 243
Cognitive Abilities Test (CogAT), Form 6, 312
Cognitive ability, 200, 235
Cognitive benefits of bilingualism, 241, 242
Cognitive development theories, Piaget *vs.* Vygotsky,
202
Cognitive flexibility, 21
Colangelo, Nicholas, 307
Collaboration, 44
Collaborative for Academic, Social, and Emotional
Learning (CASEL), social-emotional learning
competencies, 46
Collectivism, 103–104, 138
Colorado Academic Standard, 367
Colorado Department of Education Office
of Culturally and Linguistically Diverse
Education (CLDE), 340
Comenius, 14, 15
Commodity metaphor, 170
Common Core State Standards (CCSS), 11, 15, 20

Communication, 49
  nonverbal, 49
  verbal, 49
Communication through language, 136–178
  Anticipation Guide, 136
  morphology, 148–156
  phonology, 137–147
  pragmatics, 174–177
  semantics, 164–173
  syntax, 157–163
Communicative language teaching (CLT), 235
Communicative practices, 176
Complex language structure, 236
Comprehensible input, 272, 346
Comprehension, 265
Computer skill, 344
Concept, 170
Conduit metaphor, 170
Connections, establishing, 275
Connotation, 168
Conscious learning process, 147
Consent Decree (META or ESOL Consent Degree),
    15–16, 18, 22. *see also* Florida Consent Decree
    (1990) and Stipulation Modifying the Consent
    Decree (2003)
Consonant, 138
Constructivism, 21
Construct validity, 372
Content-area assessment, 363–379. *see also* ESOL
    testing and evaluation
Content specialist, 97
Content validity, 372
Content words, 149
Context-rich, 236
Contradiction, 171
Contrastive analysis, 199
Contributions approach, 64
Conversational fluency, 271
"Cookie-cutter" approach, 5
Cooperative learning, 107
Copying, 104
Court cases related to ELs, 8
  Brown v. Board of Education (1954), 8
  Castañeda v. Pickard (1981), 10
  Farrignton v. Tokushige (1927), 8

  *Keyes v. School District No. 1, Denver, Colorado
    (1973)*, 9
  Lau v. Nichols (1974), 9
  Meyer v. Nebraska (1923), 7
  Plyler v. Doe (1982), 10
  Ríos v. Reed (1975), 10
  Serna v. Portales Municipal Schools (1972), 9
  United States of America v. State of Texas, et al., 9
Court rulings, 5
Creative thinking, bilingualism and, 242
Criterion validity, 372
Cross cultural, Language and Academic
    Development (CLAD), 340
Cross-linguistic transfer, 244
Cultural and linguistic differences, 44
Cultural assimilation, 62
Cultural background, 49
Cultural gap, 45
Cultural iceberg, 60
Culturally diverse student, 13
Culturally Responsive Teaching (CRT), 44, 106
Cultural pluralism, 58, 62–63
Cultural proficiency, 58–69, 66
Cultural sensitivity, 15
Culture, 48, 50
  characteristics of, 61
  deep, 51, 59–60
  defined, 48
  language and, 49, 52–53
  learning styles and, 62
  surface, 59, 60
Czech language, 160

D

Data analysis and interpretation, 369
DeCapua, Andrea, 91, 130, 138
Decision making, 46
Decoding skills, 265
Decontextualized tasks, 99–103
Deep, or implicit, culture, 51, 59–60
    elements of, 59–60
Deixis, 136, 171, 173
Delaware, WIDA Consortium and, 5
Democratic values, 64
Demographics, 67, 133, 305

Denotation, 168

Derivation, 150

Derivational morphemes, 150

Developing proficiency level, 211, 212, 349, 350, 352, 368

Development errors, 154–166

Dialect, 175

Dictation activities, 344

Dictionary, 166, 168, 376–377

Differentiated instruction, 235

Differentiation, 270

Direct instruction, 275

Direct method, 234

Disabilities, 262

Discrete language skills, 271

Discrete point, 344

Divergent thinking, bilingualism and, 242

Diversity in classroom, 42–55

Dominant bilingual, 243

Double Entry Journal, 56

Dual Language (DL) program, 130

Dual Language school, 12

Dual language student, 13

Due process, 14th Amendment and, 7

E

Early English Language Development (E-ELD) standards, 340

Early-exit program, 130

Early production stage of second language acquisition, 209

Economic benefits of bilingualism, 241–242

Education Commission of the States, EL definition, 12–13

Education for All Handicapped Act, 262

EICM Model. *see* ESOL Integration Curricular Model

Elementary and Secondary Education Act (ESEA), 5

Emergent literate ELs, 95

Emerging proficiency level, 211, 212, 349, 350, 352, 368

Emotionally Challenged (EC), 262

English as a New Language (ENL), 130

English as Second Language (ESL) Standards, 19

English Language Development (ELD) Standards, 20, 340, 348

English language learners (ELLs), 13, 130

English language proficiency (ELP) standards, 5

English learners (ELs), 2, 13, 262

  defined, 12–13

  perceptions and misconceptions about, 305–307

English learners (ELs) with disabilities, 262–277

  academic language proficiency, 271

  action words for, 272

  assessment of, 276–277

  behaviors associated with, 266

  case study, 268–270

  connecting with instruction, 265–266

  conversational fluency, 271

  differentiation and, 270

  discrete language skills, 271

  effective pedagogical approach to, 265

  literacy and, 267

  Piaget's developmental view and, 275

  reading skills strategies for, 270–276

  scaffolding, 272

  Schema theory, 271

  similarities between ELs and behaviors associated with learning disabilities, 266, 269

  Student Biography Card, 266

  teacher reflection, 263–264

English phrase structure, 161

Entailment, 171

Entering proficiency level, 211, 212, 344, 349, 350, 352, 368

Enterprise, 21

Equal Educational Opportunities Act (EEOA) (1974), 18

Equal protection, 14th Amendment and, 7

Equity, 11, 18, 59, 63, 64, 348

Era of Isolationism, 14

ESOL Endorsement, 19

ESOL Integration Curricular Model (EICM), 18, 19, 20–22

ESOL student, 13

ESOL testing and evaluation, 340–341, 344–352, 363–379. *see also* Assessment

  accommodations for ELs, 375–377

  assessment principles, 371–374

  classroom-based assessments and ELs, 377–379

  content-area assessment, 363–370

  proficiency testing, 344–346

  reliability in, 345

  second language acquisition stages, 346–348

types of assessments, 375

validity in, 345

WIDA standards, 348–351

Esquith, Rafe, 318

ESSA Sec. 3102 Purposes, 3

Ethnicity, 66, 66–67

Ethnocentrism, 50

Evaluation rubrics, 379

Every Student Succeeds Act (ESSA), 2, 11, 370

assessment and, 364

gifted students and, 304

purposes for ELs (Sec. 3102), 3

Expanding proficiency level, 211, 212, 349, 350, 352, 368

Eye contact, 50

F

Facial expression, 49

Farrignton v. Tokushige (1927), 8

Federal regulation and policy, 5, 6

"50-State Comparison," 13

Fill-in test, 344

First language (L1), 262

Florida

Consent Decree (1990) and Stipulation Modifying the Consent Decree (2003), 13

ELLs coding, 22

legislation, 15–16

test accommodations, 376

WIDA Consortium, 5

Florida Atlantic University, EICM Model and, 19

Florida Board of Education, 20

Florida Consent Decree (1990) and Stipulation Modifying the Consent Decree (2003), 11, 13, 16

civil rights of ELs and, 18

as framework for compliance with EL education laws, 18

implications of, 18–22

Florida Department of Education (FLDOE), 19

Florida Department of Education's (FLDOE) Course Code Directory, 18–19

Florida Seal of Biliteracy Program, 20

Fluency, 265

Formal academic literacy, 270

Formal education, 97, 100, 102, 103, 104–105

Format, as assessment category, 375

Formative-summative assessment type, 375

Former proficiency assessment, 345

Fossilized, 144

Foundational content knowledge, 97

Four language domains, 348

Fourteenth Amendment, 7

Free morphemes, 148

Fricative, 140, 141

Fries, Charles, 199, 203, 204

Functional category, 157, 158

Future orientation, 104–105

G

Gender, 68

General cognitive theory, 200

Gesture, 50

Gifted English learners, 301–320

characteristics of EL gifted and non-EL gifted, 313

ELs, perceptions and misconceptions about, 308–310

family advocacy and, 312

identification procedures, 311

identifying, 305, 312–314

perceptions and misconceptions about, 305–307

under-representation of ELs in gifted programs, 310–312

serving in mainstream classroom, 315–320

strategies for engagement, 316

teacher training and, 311–312

Glossary, 132, 197, 376–377

Grading procedure, 379

Grammar-translation method, 199–200, 234

Grammatical category, 150

Grant, BEA Act and, 6

Graphics, 378

Group responsibility, 107

Gun metaphor, 170

Gutenberg, Johannes, 14

H

Head, as phrase structure, 161

Herskovits, Melville J., 48

Hidden curriculum, 64

Hindi phonemes, 137

Historical court cases. *see* Court cases related to ELs

The Hobart Shakespeareans, 318

Home Language Survey, 20, 43
Human rights, 64
Humor, 50

I

Identity as learner acquirement, 97
Illinois test accommodations, 376
Illustration drawing, 274
I Love Saturdays and Domingo, 45
Image interpretation, 98
Immediate relevancy, 107
Immigrant, 3, 10, 22, 105, 236, 241, 309–310
    discrimination and, 318
    languages, 240
Indirect request, 171
Individualism, 103–104, 138
Individuals with disabilities Education Act (IDEA),
    262
Indo-European, 210
Inductive approach, 15
Inflectional morpheme, 148
Informal-formal assessment type, 375
Informal ways of learning, 103
Innatism, 203
Innatist, 200, 207
Input, 200, 204, 205, 346
Integrated approach, 344
Intelligence Quotient (IQ), 306, 309, 314
Intention, as assessment category, 375
Interaction, 204, 205
Interactionist, 201
Interconnectedness, 107
Interference or transfer from home language, 146
Intermediate fluency stage of second language
    acquisition, 209
International Baccalaureate (IB) reading list, 318
International Phonetic Alphabet, 137
Interpersonal skills, 15
Interpretation, as assessment category, 375
Interrupted education, 96
Interstate New Teacher Assessment and Support
    Consortium (INTASC) Model Core Teaching
    Standards, 59
Interview, 53–54
Intonation, 146
Invisible meaning, 174

IPA chart, 141
ITBS/ITED, 312

J

Jamaican English, 175
Japanese language, 146, 159
Jim Cummins' Interdependence Hypothesis, 243
Johnson, Lyndon, 5
Journal, 52, 53–54

K

*Keyes v. School District No. 1, Denver, Colorado
    (1973)*, 9
To Kill a Mockingbird, 93, 94
Kluckhohn, Clyde, 47–48
Korean language, 159
Krashen, Stephen, 200, 203, 204, 208, 346
Krashen's theory of second language acquisition,
    346–347

L

Labeling, 101, 102
Lado, Robert, 199, 203, 204
Landmark court rulings on ELs, 5
Language and literacy, 130–134
Language, culture and, 49, 52–53
Language acquisition, 275
Language acquisition device (LAD), 157
Language Arts Through ESOL Guide, 19
Language function, 177
Language-minority student, 13
Language proficiency level, 2
Language proficiency, three dimensions of, 271
Language template, 175
Lantolf, James, 202, 203, 204
Large-scale evaluation, 341, 345, 352, 368–370
    assessment type, 375
Lau v. Nichols (1974), 9, 235
Lawsuit, 5, 9
League of United Latin American Citizens
    (LULAC), 15
*League of United Latin American Citizens (LULAC)
    et al. v. The State Board of Education (SBE) et
    al. Consent Decree (1990)*, 15
Learnability rule, 154–155
Learner identity, 97

Learning, 200

Learning disability, 237, 262–277. *see also* English Learners (ELs) with disabilities

Learning English for Academic Proficiency and Success (LEAPS) Act, 233

Legislation, Florida, 15–16

LeMon, R. E., 19

Lexical category, 157, 158

Lexical morpheme, 148, 149

Lexicon, 173

Limited English proficient student, federal law definition, 12–13

Limited English speaking ability (LESA), 6

Limited formal education, 96

Linguist, 49

Linguistic differences, 44

Linguistic modifications, 378

Listening and speaking, 142–143

Listening proficiency, 378

Literacy, 97–99, 267
   formal education and, 97
   non-literate, 98
   pre-literate, 97–98
   semi-literate, 98

Local education agencies (LEAs), 12

Long, Michael, 203, 204

Lovell, Cindy, 301

Low-literate ELs, 95

Lozanov, Georgi, 235

Lucas, Teresa, 197, 239

LULAC et al. Consent Decree, 15–16

M

Major court cases related to ELs, 7–12. *see also* Court cases related to ELs

Mandarin Chinese, 146, 340

Map labeling, 101, 102

Massachusetts Department of Elementary and Secondary Education, 92

Master of Arts in Teaching (MAT), 340

Mead, Margaret, 47

Meaning, 166

"Me" culture, 103, 138

Mediation, 202

Melting pot, 62, 241

Mendoza, María Beatriz, 197

Mental block, 347

Mental lexicon, 165

META Consent Decree, 16–17. *see also* Florida Consent Decree (1990) and Stipulation Modifying the Consent Decree (2003)

Metaphor, 170

Method, 15

Meyer v. Nebraska (1923), 7

Middle English, 160

Mihai, Florin M., 343, 363

Minimal pair, 136, 142–143

Minnesota, 213
   charter schools and, 12

Modern English, 160

Monitor, 201, 346

Monitor model, 347

Monolingual, 13, 45, 166, 242, 269, 309

Mooncakes, 45

Morphology, 130, 148–156
   derivational morpheme, 150
   developmental errors, 154–156
   English verb, 156
   inflectional morpheme, 152–153
   morpheme classification, 149–150
   roots and stems, 151

Motivation, 210, 213, 346

Multicultural education, 63–65

Multicultural Education, Training, and Advocacy, Inc.(META), 16

Multilingual learner, 348

Multiple choice test questions, 344

Multiple intelligences, 235

Mutually Adaptive Learning Paradigm (MALP®), 106–109, 110
   conditions for learning, 106–107
   instructional model, 109
   new activities for learning, 108
   processes of learning, 107–108
   teacher planning checklist, 110

My Name is Yoon, 45

N

Naglieri Nonverbal Ability Test (NNAT), 312

Name, 177

Nasal, 141

National Association for Gifted Children (NAGC), 310

National Center for Education Statistics (NCES), 12, 67

National Education Association (NEA), 44

National Literacy Panel on Language Minority Children and Youth, 245

Natural approach, 234, 235, 347

Natural order, 200, 346

Navaho culture, 47, 48

Negative transfer, 199

New York State English as a Second Language Achievement Test (NYSESLAT), 131

New York test accommodations, 376

No Child Left Behind (NCLB) Act, 2, 5, 345

Nodding head, 50

Non-lexical morphemes, 148, 149, 150

Non-literate, 98

Nonverbal communication, 49, 50

Nonverbal expression, 49

Nonverbal language, 49

Norm-referenced/criterion-referenced assessment type, 375

Noun, 160, 161

Nuanced (indirect) communication, 176

Null curriculum, 64

NYSESLAT, 131

NYSESLAT proficiency level
commanding, 131
emerging, 131
expanding, 131
transitioning, 131

O

Obama, Barack, 2

Office of Multicultural Students Language Education (OMSLE), 19

Old English, 160

Organs of speech production, 139

P

Paneque, Oneyda, 239

Parent Leadership Council (PLC), 55

Parts of speech, 149

Passive verb, 378

Perkins, Samuel S., 57

Personal benefits of bilingualism, 241

Personality, 213

Phoneme, 137

Phonology, 130, 137–147
English consonants, 138–142
English vowels, 143–144, 145
minimal pairs, 142–143
phonological system, 137–138
suprasegmentals, 146–147

Phrase, 160–161

Piaget, Jean, 200, 202, 275

Pinterest, 197

Pitch, 146

Planning, 15

Platt, Elizabeth, 130, 135, 197

Plyler v. Doe (1982), 10, 47

Poetry, 274

Policy, 6

Portfolio, 373

Practicality, 371, 373

Practical test, 373

Pragmatics, 130, 174–178
child language socialization, 176
dialects and bilingualism, 175
language functions, 177

Pragmatic test, 344

Predicate, 165, 168

Prefix, 150

Pre-literate, 97–98

Preparing Florida Teachers to Work with Limited English Proficient Students guide, 19

Prepositional phrase, 160, 161

Pre-production stage of second language acquisition, 209

Prescriptive *vs.* descriptive rules, 163

Presupposition, 171

Printing press, 14

Professional journal, 52, 53–54

Proficiency, 2, 3

Proficiency level, 367

Proficiency testing, 344–346, 352
goal of, 344

Pronoun, 136, 150, 160

Pronunciation, 139, 140

Pronunciation and spelling of English vowels and diphthongs, 145

Portfolio, 373
Public Law 94-142, 262
Purpose, as assessment category, 375

R
Race, 66
     categories of (2020 U.S. Census), 67
     ethnicity and, 66–67
Rater reliability, 373
Raven's Standard Progressive Matrices, 312
Reaching proficiency level, 344, 352
Reading proficiency, 378
Recorvits, Helen, 45
Referent, 166
Reflection, 44, 52, 53–54
Regular past tense verb forms, 154
Relationship skills, 46
Reliability, 371, 372
     vs. validity, 372–373
Remedial, 97
Renzulli Scales, 313
Research, 44
Response to intervention (RTI), 270
Response type, 375, 376
Responsible decision making, 46
Restructuring, 200
RETELL (Rethinking Equity in the Teaching of
     English Language Learners), 92
Rich academic language, 236
Ríos v. Reed (1975), 10
Rule-governed phonological system, 137
Rodriguez, Diane, 261
Rodriguez, Esmeralda, 261
Roots and stems, 149, 151
Rubric, 45, 368, 379
Rules and routines in classroom, 46
Rules, class expectations and, 46
Russian language, 160, 340

S
Salinger, J. D., 318
Sapir, Edward, 47
Scaffolding, 55, 95, 103, 202, 272
Scale for Rating Behavioral Characteristics of
     Superior Students (SRBCSS), 313
Schedule and time, 375

Schema theory, 271
School-readiness, 44
Second language acquisition (SLA), 130, 198, 347
Second language (L2), 262
Second language (L2) acquisition (SLA), stages, 209
Second language learning theories, 197–213
     acquisition/learning, 200
     acquisition stages, 209
     affective filter, 201
     behaviorist approach, 207
     innatist view, 207
     input, 200
     language development approaches, 199–205
     learner characteristics, 208–209
     monitor, 201
     natural order, 200
     SCT in classroom, 205–206
     SCT perspective, 208
     WIDA performance definitions, 211, 212
Segregation, 8
Self-actualized student, 65
Self-analysis, 53
Self-awareness, 46
Self-confidence, 210, 346
Self-examination, 58, 59
Self-identity, 58
Self-image, 346
Self-management, 46
Self-reflection, 59
Semantics, 130, 164–173
     ambiguity, 172–173
     concepts, 170
     denotation and connotation, 168
     meaning and, 166
     metaphors, 170
     relations, 169, 171
     roles, 169
     semantic roles and relations, 168–170
Semi-literate, 98
Sense of belonging, 46
Sentence, 93, 99, 102
Sentence type, 156
Sequential bilingualism, 243
Serna v. Portales Municipal Schools (1972), 9
Seto, L., 45
Sex, 68

Sexual orientation, 68

Shakespeare, William, 318

Shared context, 174

Sheltered English Immersion (SEI), 92

Sheltered Instruction Observation Protocol (SIOP), 262

Silence, 50

Simultaneous bilingualism, 243

Situated cognition, 21

Skill transfer, 244

Skinner, B. F., 199

Social-action/decision-making approach, 65

Social awareness, 46

Social benefits of bilingualism, 241

Social-emotional needs, 47

Social-emotional skills, 44

Social register, 175

Sociocultural theory (SCT), 202, 203, 204, 205, 205–206, 208, 213

Spanish language, 144, 146, 340

Spanish phonemes, 137

Spatial distance, 49

Speaker meaning, 174

Speaking proficiency, 378

Specifier, 165

Speech acts, 171, 177

Speech community, 175

Speech emergence stage of second language acquisition, 209

Speech parts, 149

Standard #9: Professional Learning and Ethical Practice, 59

Steinbeck, John, 318

Stereotype, 51

Stipulation Modifying the Consent Decree (2003), 16, 18, 19. see also Florida Consent Decree (1990)

Stops, 138, 141

Storymapping, 214

Storytelling, 274

Structurally ambiguous, 172

Student reliability, 373

Students with Limited or Interrupted Formal Education (SLIFE), 92–110, 233

    collectivism and individualism, 103–104

    decontextualized tasks, 99–103

future orientation, 104–105

literacy and, 97–99

Mutually Adaptive Learning Paradigm, 106–109, 110

Subject, 136, 158, 159, 160, 163, 168

Subject/verb/object (SVO), 158

Subtractive bilingualism, 243

Suffix, 150, 151

Suggestopedia, 235

Suprasegmental

    intonation, 146

    length, 146

    pitch, 146

    stress, 146

    tone, 146

Supreme Court. see Court cases related to ELs

Surface, or explicit, culture, 59, 60

    elements of, 59

Swahili sentence explication, 153

Syntax, 130, 157–163

    case-marking, 159–160

    lexical and functional categories, 157, 158

    order of elements in phrases, 160–162

    prescriptive grammar rules, 163

    theoretical issues with, 157

    universals in word ordering, 158

Systemic language, 137

T

TeachersPayTeachers.com, 198

Teamwork approach, 15

Technical Assistance for Teacher Preparation: Meeting the Needs of English Language Learners in Florida, 19, 20

Technological tools, 234, 235, 236

Technology, 133, 235, 236

TESOL ESL Standards, 19, 20

Test, 369–370, 375–376. see also ESOL testing and evaluation

    accommodation, 375, 375–376

    aids, 376

    vs. assessment, 369–370

    defined, 369–370

    directions, 376

    environment, 376

    modifications to time, 376

presentation, 375, 376

response type, 375, 376

scheduling and timing, 375

setting, 375, 376

translations of, 379

Test administration reliability, 373

Test discrimination, 374

Texas test accommodations, 376

Theoretical tenets, 21

Three dimensions of language proficiency
(Cummins), 271

Title VI Civil Rights Act (1964), 8

Title VII of ESEA (1968), 6, 8

Tonal language, 146

Tone, 146

Top-down process, 271

Total Physical Response (TPR), 234, 235

Traditional-alternative assessment type, 375

Transfer, bilingualism and, 245–246

Transformation, 58

Transformation approach, 65

Transformation, in education, 58–59

Transitional Bilingual Education (TBE), 130

Translanguaging, 243

Twain, Mark, 307, 317, 320

Two-dimensional forms, 98

U

Ungrammatical, 157

United States of America v. State of Texas, et al., 9

Universal grammar theory (UGT), 235

Usage of cognates, 272

U.S. Department of Education, 44

V

Validity, 371

Values, 44, 48, 49, 50, 51, 52

Venn Diagram, 100, 101

Verb, 156, 160, 161

Verbal language, 49

Verb phrase, 159

Vietnamese language, 144, 146, 149, 154, 340

Visuals, 378

Vocabulary, 14, 55, 132, 165–166

Voice/voiceless pairs, 140

Voicing, 138, 140, 142

Vowel, 143–144, 145

Vowel system, 143, 144

Vygotsky, Lev, 202

W

"War on Poverty," 5

Washback, 371, 374

WebQuest, 235

"We" culture, 103, 138

WIDA Access for ELLs, 142, 378

WIDA Assessment, 20

WIDA Consortium, 5, 131, 340, 345–346, 348

map link, 5

website, 5, 6

WIDA ELD Standards, 348

WIDA English Language Proficiency Standard, 367

WIDA levels of language proficiency, 346

bridging, 211, 212, 349, 350, 352, 368

developing, 211, 212, 349, 350, 352, 368

emerging, 211, 212, 349, 350, 352, 368

entering, 211, 212, 344, 349, 350, 352, 368

expanding, 211, 212, 349, 350, 352, 368

reaching, 344, 352

WIDA performance definitions, 211, 212, 340, 349,
350, 365, 366

WIDA Standards, 20

WIDA Standards Framework, 351

Wisconsin, WIDA Consortium and, 5

Word-final, 140

Word-initial, 140

Word knowledge types, 165

Word-medial, 140

Word ordering universals, 158

Wordsplash, 232

Writing proficiency, 378

Y

Yarborough, Ralph, 6

Yo-Yo approach, 315

Z

Zone of proximal development (ZPD), 202–203,
235, 272

CPSIA information can be obtained
at www.ICGtesting.com
Printed in the USA
LVHW062020130123
736907LV00002B/4